THE ETERNAL COVENANT
FOR ALL GENERATIONS

THE
TEN
COMMANDMENTS

HRS 7
THE HISTORY OF REDEMPTION SERIES

THE ETERNAL COVENANT FOR ALL GENERATIONS

THE TEN COMMANDMENTS

IN LIGHT OF GOD'S ADMINISTRATION IN THE HISTORY OF REDEMPTION

ABRAHAM PARK

The Ten Commandments: The Eternal Covenant for All Generations

Published by Multi-Language Media

An imprint of CLC Publications

U.S.A.

P.O. Box 1449, Fort Washington, PA 19034

UNITED KINGDOM

Kingsway CLC Trust

Unit 5, Glendale Avenue Sandycroft, Flintshire, CH5 2QP

© 2022 Center for the Movement of Redemptive History

For permission to reprint, please contact us at:

Permissions@clcpublications.com

ISBN (Hardcover): 978-1-61958-348-1

ISBN (E-book): 978-1-61958-349-8

Unless otherwise noted, Scripture quotations are from the New American Standard Bible®, © 1960, 1962, 1963, 1968, 1971, 1972, 1973, 1975, 1977, 1995 by The Lockman Foundation. Used by permission. www.lockman.org

Scripture quotations marked NIV are from the Holy Bible, New International Version, NIV, © 1973, 1978, 1984, 2011 by Biblica, Inc. Used by permission. All rights reserved worldwide.

Scripture quotations marked ESV are from the Holy Bible, English Standard Version, © 2001 by Crossway Bibles, a publishing ministry of Good News Publishers. Used by permission. All rights reserved.

Scripture quotations marked NLT are from the Holy Bible, New Living Translation, © 1996, 2004, 2015 by Tyndale House Foundation. Used by permission of Tyndale House Publishers, Inc., Carol Stream, Illinois 60188. All rights reserved.

Scripture quotations marked RSV are from the Holy Bible, Revised Standard Version. © 1946, 1952 by the Division of Christian Education of the National Council of Churches of Christ in the U.S.A.

Scripture quotations marked NRSV are from the Holy Bible, New Revised Standard Version Bible, copyright © 1989 the Division of Christian Education of the National Council of the Churches of Christ in the United States of America. Used by permission. All rights reserved.

Scripture quotations marked KJV are from the Holy Bible, King James Version, 1611.

Scriptures and additional materials quoted are from the Good News Bible © 1994 published by the British and Foreign Bible Society. Good News Bible © American Bible Society 1966, 1971, 1976, 1992. Used with permission.

Scripture quotations marked KCTB are from the Korean Common Translation of the Holy Bible, copyright © 1977, 1999 by Korean Bible Society. Used by permission. All rights reserved.

Scripture quotations marked HKOT are from the Hebrew-Korean Old Testament, copyright © 2004 by Five Words Bible Society. Used by permission. All rights reserved.

Scripture quotations marked NKSV are from the Holy Bible, New Korean Standard Version, copyright © 1993 by Korean Bible Society. Used by permission. All rights reserved.

Scripture quotations marked WKB are from the Holy Bible, Woorimal Korean Bible, copyright © 2004 by Duranno Publishing. Used by permission. All rights reserved.

Remember the days of old,

consider the years of all generations.

Ask your father, and he will inform you,

your elders, and they will tell you.

Deuteronomy 32:7

CONTENTS

ENDORSEMENT	13
FOREWORD	15
PREFACE	19

PART I. THE COVENANT FOR ALL GENERATIONS — 25

1 Covenants Between Men — 29
- The Purpose of Covenants Between Men
- The Characteristics of Covenants Between Men
- The Consequences of Covenants Between Men

2 God's Everlasting Covenant for All Generations — 35
- "Salvation from Our Enemies"
- "His Holy Covenant"
- "The Oath Which He Swore"

3 The Characteristics of the Sinaitic Covenant — 43
- The Sinaitic Covenant: A Covenant Made with the Nation
- The Covenant that God Spoke Directly to the People
- The First Covenant to Be Set in Writing
- A Covenant to Be Kept and Practiced in the Promised Land

4 THE REDEMPTIVE-HISTORICAL MEANING OF THE SINAITIC COVENANT   57
- A Covenant Made with Blood
- A Covenant with a Mediator
- A Covenant for All Generations to Keep
- A Covenant with a Clear Revelation of Redemption

5 THE SINAITIC COVENANT THAT MUST BE AFFIRMED CONTINUOUSLY   69
- Israel, the Firstborn of Redemptive History
- A Covenant Reaffirmed
- A Covenant that Had to Be Affirmed and Reaffirmed Continuously

PART II. MOSES' EIGHT ASCENTS OF MOUNT SINAI   75

6 DIVINE PROVIDENCE THAT LED THE ISRAELITES TO MOUNT SINAI   79
- Divine Providence for the Israelites to Worship God
- Divine Providence for the Israelites to Sacrifice to God
- Divine Providence for the Israelites to Celebrate with a Feast Before God

7 OVERVIEW OF MOSES' EIGHT ASCENTS OF MOUNT SINAI   85

8 MOSES' EIGHT ASCENTS OF MOUNT SINAI   97
- The First Ascent: Monday, the 2nd Day of the 3rd Month (46 Days after the Exodus)
- The First Descent: Monday, the 2nd Day of the 3rd Month (46 Days after the Exodus)
- The Second Ascent: Tuesday, the 3rd Day of the 3rd Month (47 Days after the Exodus)
- The Second Descent: Tuesday, the 3rd Day of the 3rd Month (47 Days after the Exodus)

- The Third Ascent: Thursday, the 5th Day of the 3rd Month (49 Days after the Exodus)
- The Third Descent: Thursday, the 5th Day of the 3rd Month (49 Days after the Exodus)
- The Fourth Ascent: Friday, the 6th Day of the 3rd Month (50 Days after the Exodus)
- The Fourth Descent: Friday, the 6th Day of the 3rd Month (50 Days after the Exodus)
- Early Next Morning: Saturday, the 7th Day of the 3rd Month (51 Days after the Exodus)
  * *Ratification of the Sinaitic Covenant*
- The Fifth Ascent: Saturday, the 7th Day of the 3rd Month (51 Days after the Exodus)
- The Fifth Descent: Saturday, the 7th Day of the 3rd Month (51 Days after the Exodus)
- The Sixth Ascent: Sunday, the 8th Day of the 3rd Month (52 Days after the Exodus)
- The Sixth Descent: Thursday, the 17th Day of the 4th Month (91 Days after the Exodus)
- The Seventh Ascent: Friday, the 18th Day of the 4th Month (92 Days after the Exodus)
- The Seventh Descent: Tuesday, the 28th Day of the 5th Month (131 Days after the Exodus)
- The Eighth Ascent: Thursday, the 30th Day of the 5th Month (133 Days after the Exodus)
- The Eighth Descent: Monday, the 10th Day of the 7th Month (172 Days after the Exodus)

PART III. THE ESSENCE OF THE SCRIPTURE, THE TEN COMMANDMENTS: THE TEN ESSENTIAL ASPECTS — 147

9 THE TEN COMMANDMENTS AND THE TEN WORDS — 151

10 THE TEN ESSENTIAL ASPECTS OF THE TEN COMMANDMENTS — 155

- *Torah* (תּוֹרָה) — God's Law
- *Eduth* (עֵדוּת), *Edah* (עֵדָה) — God's Testimonies

- *Mishpat* (מִשְׁפָּט) — God's Judgments, God's Ordinances
- *Hoq* (חֹק) — God's Statutes
- *Davar* (דָּבָר) — God's Word
- *Piqqud* (פִּקּוּד) — God's Precepts
- *Mitzwah* (מִצְוָה) — God's Commandments
- *Derekh* (דֶּרֶךְ) — God's Ways (God's Paths)
- *Imrah* (אִמְרָה) — God's Word (God's Promise)
- *Emeth* (אֱמֶת), *Emunah* (אֱמוּנָה) — God's Truth (God's Faithfulness)

11 THE MINOR CONCLUSION OF THE TEN WORDS   193

PART IV. THE CHARACTERISTICS AND PRINCIPLES OF THE TEN COMMANDMENTS, THE COVENANT FOR ALL GENERATIONS   197

12 THE NAMES OF THE TEN COMMANDMENTS: THE PERFECT TEN WORDS   201

13 THE CHARACTERISTICS OF THE TEN COMMANDMENTS   203

- Proclaimed as the Gospel of Freedom, Love, and Grace
- Given in Holiness and Glory
- Spoken by God Himself
- Proclaimed as God's Eternal Covenant
- Written by the Finger of God on Two Tablets of Stone
- Given by God as Testimonies of the Lord
- Summary of All the Revelations of the Old and New Testaments

14 CENTRAL PRINCIPLES FOR UNDERSTANDING THE TEN COMMANDMENTS   213

- Two Major Branches of the Ten Commandments: Our Relationship with God and Our Relationships with Others

- Specific Laws Derived from the Ten Commandments
- The Evangelical Principle of Expanding the Application to the Realm of the Heart
- Various Penalties for Violating Each Commandment (the Fate of the Transgressors)
- Jesus' References to the Ten Commandments

PART V. THE COVENANT FOR ALL GENERATIONS: THE TEN COMMANDMENTS (THE TEN WORDS) — 239

15 THE FIRST COMMANDMENT — 243
- "You shall have no other gods before Me" (Exod 20:3; Deut 5:7)

16 THE SECOND COMMANDMENT — 281
- "You shall not make for yourself an idol, or any likeness of what is in heaven above or on the earth beneath or in the water under the earth. You shall not worship them or serve them" (Exod 20:4-5; Deut 5:8-9)

17 THE THIRD COMMANDMENT — 297
- "You shall not take the name of the LORD your God in vain" (Exod 20:7; Deut 5:11)

18 THE FOURTH COMMANDMENT — 323
- "Remember the sabbath day, to keep it holy" (Exod 20:8-11; Deut 5:12-15)

19 THE FIFTH COMMANDMENT — 355
- "Honor your father and your mother" (Exod 20:12; Deut 5:16)

20 THE SIXTH COMMANDMENT — 377
- "You shall not murder" (Exod 20:13; Deut 5:17)

21 THE SEVENTH COMMANDMENT — 399
- "You shall not commit adultery" (Exod 20:14; Deut 5:18)

22 THE EIGHTH COMMANDMENT   425

- "You shall not steal" (Exod 20:15; Deut 5:19)

23 THE NINTH COMMANDMENT   443

- "You shall not bear false witness against your neighbor" (Exod 20:16; Deut 5:20)

24 THE TENTH COMMANDMENT   461

- "You shall not covet your neighbor's house" (Exod 20:17; Deut 5:21)

Conclusion THE GREAT COMMANDMENTS OF THE TEN COMMANDMENTS   487

NOTES   499

BIBLIOGRAPHY   505

INDEX   509

Endorsement

Dr. Bruce K. Waltke

Book 7 in the History of Redemption Series, *The Ten Commandments: The Eternal Covenant for All Generations* is a comprehensive teaching on the essence of the Ten Commandments, specific laws, principles of worship, fate of those who violated the commandments, and redemptive-historical lessons for New Testament Christians today.

The Holy Spirit graciously used the renowned late Reverend Abraham Park, D. Min., D.D., to give His Church a treasure on this important but misunderstood aspect of the Bible, connecting the Ten Commandments to Jesus Christ who is the Word Himself (John 1:1-14) and the fulfiller of the law. Understanding the spiritual essence of the Ten Commandments is vital to be able to correctly see Jesus in them. The Jewish leaders during Jesus' time misunderstood the Scriptures, and for that reason they did not have the wisdom to recognize Him and stumbled at Jesus' words and actions (Luke 12:24-34; 1 Cor 2:7-10).

To my knowledge, Moses' eight ascents and descents on Mount Sinai have been systematically organized, illustrated and presented in this book for the first time. Furthermore, this entire process of how God ratified the Sinaitic covenant with His people through Moses has been carefully illustrated into a colorful chronological chart so that anybody who reads this book, from the layperson to the theologian, will be blessed and gain great insight into this topic.

Through this book, Christians will discover God's rich mercy and grace given to sinners and will awaken us to the absolute authority and efficacy of God's covenantal Word throughout all generations.

Dr. Waltke is professor emeritus of Regent College in Vancouver, BC, Canada, and distinguished professor emeritus of Knox Theological Seminary in Ft. Lauderdale, FL. He is the award-winning author of *Genesis: A Commentary and An Old Testament Theology*, as well as an authoritative two-volume commentary on Proverbs. Dr. Waltke also was involved in the *New American Standard* and *New International Version* translations of the Bible. He received his Th.D. from Dallas Theological Seminary and his Ph.D. from Harvard University.

Foreword

Dr. Luder G. Whitlock, Jr

Since the publication of the first volume in 2007, the endorsement of the History of Redemption Series books by scholars like Dr. Frank James and Dr. Douglas F. Kelly have attested to the fact that these books authored by Dr. Park reveal the core of God's work of redemptive history. Dr. Bruce Waltke, one of the most outstanding Old Testament scholars, willingly offered praise for The History of Redemption volumes. That is remarkable recognition from the scholarly world. I am unaware of any pastor who has accomplished anything that approximates this series. The fact that one of the finest Old Testament scholars in the world, Dr. Bruce Waltke, warmly endorses this book absolutely attests to the value of this book. Therefore, it gives me great pleasure to offer this foreword to such a valuable collection of scriptural expositions.

It was a great privilege to visit Pyungkang Cheil Church in Seoul, Korea, during the remarkable ministry of Dr. Abraham Park, the author of the History of Redemption Series books. One of the best days of my life was to award the honorary Doctor of Divinity degree in recognition of his global ministry. He is a faithful servant of God whom He used globally to advance the gospel. I was captivated by the global missionary vision of this church and its commitment to reach the world with the gospel. Dr. Abraham Park was a great Christian leader and pastor who developed a large growing ministry that received global recognition. The large Pyungkang Cheil campus also housed an outstanding archaeological museum as well as other museums and ministries. However, the most remarkable dimension of his long ministry was his commitment to teaching the whole counsel of God so that his church members had a full grasp of the message of the Bible and an extraordinary introduction to the structure and flow of the biblical message. Typically, pastors preach portions of Scripture well and some pastors are careful expositors, but his careful exposition of Scripture that clarified the structure and purpose of Scripture was unique. I was able to visit the church prior to Dr. Park's departure to heaven and discovered one of the most spiritually vibrant churches I had ever visited. In addition, there was no doubt about its commitment to global missions coupled with bold missionary outreach.

The Ten Commandments: The Eternal Covenant for All Generations is the title of this seventh volume of the History of Redemption Series. In this volume, Dr. Park begins by describing covenants, then explains the nature of God's everlasting covenant with man as an introduction to his explanation of the redemptive-historical nature of the covenant made at Sinai. He explains why God took His people to Sinai and then describes the ascents to Sinai that usually receive minimal attention. Especially, Dr. Park has systematically organized and presented for the first time in history Moses' eight ascents of Mount Sinai into a beautifully illustrated chart.

Next, the author gives a detailed exposition of the ten essential aspects of the Ten Commandments by using the ten Hebrew words found in Psalm 119. Each of these words gives us a greater understanding of the depth of God's Word. Following this section, the heart of his exposition is found in the Ten Commandments, or Ten Words, that he carefully exposits to uncover the riches of God's plan. For each of the Ten Commandments, Dr. Park gives a very detailed exegesis, the specific laws derived from them, teachings on worship through each, the fate of those who violated each of the commandments, and the redemptive-historical lesson found therein. The Sinaitic Covenant is an eternal covenant for all generations given to God's people. In as such, the author shows how God's redemptive work through this covenant is calling sinners even today to this saving grace of Jesus Christ. In the words of Jesus, He came not to abolish the law but to fulfill it. Therefore, readers will be enlightened through this book as it clearly shows how the Ten Commandments testify to Jesus Christ and His entire ministry of redemption.

I believe this book will awaken Christians to the authority of God's Word and offer deep insight to the core of God's message throughout the Bible. Considering the history of Christianity in Korea, especially periods of great spiritual blessing, it wouldn't be too much to hope that attention to this volume, preferably the whole series, might be used to bring a new period of scriptural understanding and spiritual blessing. More Christians need to read books like this one. I hope this volume touches off a new wave of interest in the Bible and illumines the path for God's people everywhere.

Readers will be enriched and motivated to serve the Lord more faithfully. So, I happily recommend this additional volume to your attention.

Dr. Whitlock is recognized as one of the top five most influential seminary presidents in the latter half of the 20th century, and he served as the executive director of the publication of the *New Geneva Study Bible*. He received his D.Min. from Vanderbilt University.

Preface

Solomon enjoyed the best of what one could possess on this earth—wealth, power, pleasure, honor, and glory. Yet late in life, when he realized the vanity of all those things, he confessed, "Vanity of vanities, … vanity of vanities! All is vanity" (Eccl 1:2). He lamented the tragic existence of human beings who cannot find any hope in this world. Even with wealth and honor, our lives in this world "are just a vapor that appears for a little while and then vanishes away" (Jas 4:14). Job confessed, "My days are swifter than a weaver's shuttle, and come to an end without hope" (Job 7:6). Only Jesus Christ is our hope of glory (Col 1:27) as we live our futile lives that pass swiftly and are gone (Ps 90:10).

As a sojourner passing the twilight years of his life, I feel deeply in my bones the arrow-like speed with which each day flies. Nonetheless, I always embrace hope with gratitude in my heart and lift up praises to God more and more (Ps 71:14) because I long for a better home in heaven (Heb 11:16). Heaven and Earth may pass away, but God's Word is eternal (Matt 24:35), so I have lived my whole life holding onto and relying only on the Word of God as I look forward to the new heaven and the new earth.

It seems like the first volume of the History of Redemption Series, *The Genesis Genealogies*, was published not too long ago, in 2007, but we have already published the sixth volume. In the sixth volume of the History of Redemption Series, *The Eternal High Priest of the*

Covenantal Oath, I worked on themes including the tabernacle, the feasts, and the offerings, and the manuscript became unavoidably voluminous. Thus in the seventh volume I decided to focus on the eternal covenant for all generations: the Ten Commandments. In the eighth volume I will expand on volume 2, *The Covenant of the Torch: A Forgotten Encounter in the History of the Exodus and Wilderness Journey*, with an extended discussion on the fulfillment of the covenant of the torch, along with the ten plagues, the exodus, and Israel's entry into Canaan. The ninth volume will focus on the tabernacle.

The topic of this current volume is the Ten Commandments, in which the sixty-six books of God's Word are summed up. The core message of Scripture pivots around the Ten Commandments. The deeper we understand the Ten Commandments, the clearer we will see who Jesus is and experience in our whole bodies the breadth, length, height, and depth of God's love (Eph 3:18–19). To understand the richness of the redemptive-historical truth embedded in the Ten Commandments, I analyzed the original text verse by verse and phrase by phrase, compared various translations, drew relevant biblical passages as examples, and integrated redemptive-historical exposition. God gave His people the Ten Commandments so that they would "fear the LORD [their] God for [their] good always" (Deut 6:24). The laws in themselves, however, make it clear to us that no human being, not one—since all are corrupt—can keep the laws and avoid God's wrath. God, therefore, made Jesus bear all the wrath and punishment for sinners on the cross and saved all who have believed. Indeed, the cross at Golgotha is the climax and fulfillment of God's love promised in the Ten Commandments.

In the early days of my pastoral ministry, I spent time on Mount Jangan and Mount Jiri wrestling with the Bible and praying. While wandering through mountains of truth to find the Scripture's vein of gold, the powerful illumination of the Holy Spirit opened my eyes little by little to understand the Bible from the redemptive-historical perspective. The Scripture's rich vein of gold is so massive and limitless that I would never be able to discover it in its entirety even with a lifetime of effort. But by God's grace I was able to find a few branches of the vein, which has led to the publishing of the History of Redemption Series. Now the series has been translated into twenty-one different languages, including Modern Hebrew. I have heard that the redemptive-historical interpretations have been refreshing and spiritually awakening for many people. This news humbles me all the more and gives me a greater sense of responsibility.

Since realizing that the Ten Commandments are the essence of the Old and New Testaments, I have spent my fifty-year ministry following the streams of the Ten Commandments from the redemptive-historical perspective in my sermons. Borrowing Luke's words, I sought to become an "eyewitness of the Word" by praying each day ceaselessly, studying the Bible cover to cover, and pouring out all my energy and devotion to do the best I could in all things. Albeit inadequate, with many shortcomings, I prayerfully wish to make even the slightest contribution to the history of Korean Christianity as it nears its 130th anniversary. I can only put my hands together in prayer so that this book could become a gentle guide for all those who love God and want to study the Bible in depth.

I am deeply grateful to my beloved congregation and fellow ministers for their dedicated support, both physical and spiritual, and their tearful prayers. In the name of the Lord, I thank everyone who has devotedly labored to revise and edit my manuscripts. It would have been impossible to publish this book without their effort and dedication.

As Jesus prophesied, lawlessness is increasing, and the love of many is growing cold (Matt 24:12). The pleas of the victims of injustice continue without ceasing. In this pitiful era shrouded by dark clouds of sin, people of all ages thirst for love and yearn to find it. If there exists a special cure that could heal all the cuts and bruises of humanity, if there exists living water that could wash away all impurity, it is the Word of the living God, filled with love. I earnestly hope that God's precious grace be upon all readers that they may experience His love welling up from within their hearts, taste God's kingdom of heaven on this earth, and share the gospel with the world.

Abraham Park

Reverend Abraham Park
An insignificant member of the body of Jesus Christ
on the sojourner's path to heaven
October 3, 2013

THE COVENANT FOR ALL GENERATIONS

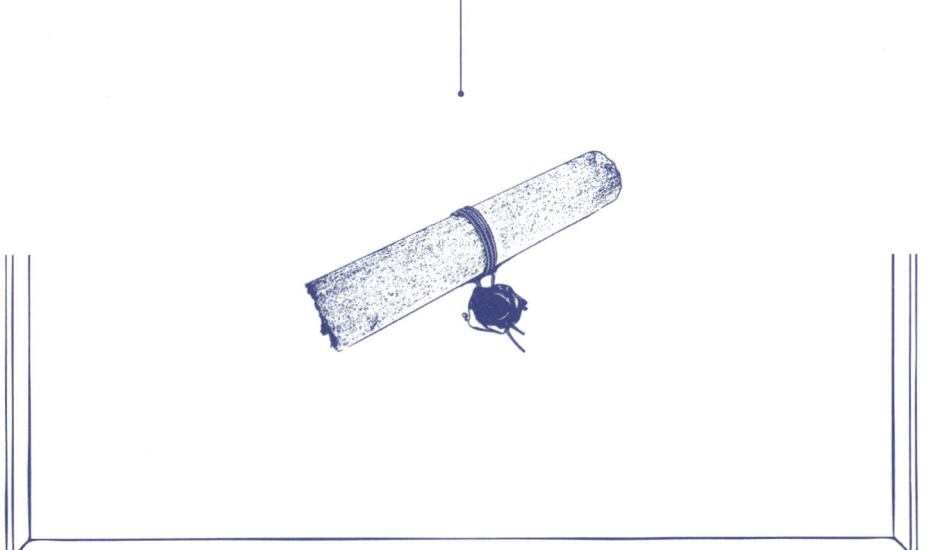

PART I

The history of this world is the history of redemption, centered around the redemptive work of Jesus Christ, which advances without ceasing for the salvation of the chosen people. God's plan for the redemption of fallen mankind was predestined before the foundation of the world (Eph 1:4; 3:11; 2 Thess 2:13). He reaffirmed His will for redemption repeatedly through the covenants He made during various eras throughout history. God's covenants in the Bible are centered upon Jesus Christ and fulfilled in Him. We have received the promise of the eternal covenant through faith in Jesus Christ (Rom 4:16; Eph 1:13; Heb 6:15; 11:9, 33; see also Acts 10:43; 11:17; 13:39; 15:7-9; Rom 3:22-26; Gal 3:22). God's ultimate purpose for the covenant is to give the greatest gift—eternal life—to those who have been redeemed from the bondage of death resulting from sin (1 John 2:25).

The covenants that have been revealed in different ways during different times through the forefathers of faith finally conclude with the new covenant of Jesus Christ. All the covenants point to the atonement of the cross, which is the sole and absolute basis for salvation, and to the eternal kingdom of God to come (Matt 26:27-29; Mark 14:24-25; Luke 22:20; 1 Cor 11:25; see also Heb 9:11-15; 13:20).

CHAPTER 1

Covenants Between Men

Biblical records contain agreements between God and men, between men, and between nations. The central covenant in the Bible is the covenant of salvation that God ratified with mankind by His sovereignty. Besides this, there are other covenants made between men in their daily lives.

I. The Purpose of Covenants Between Men

Covenants made between men have various purposes.

First, people enter into covenants to maintain mutual peace. When Jacob departed from his uncle Laban, he entered into a covenant with him in which they promised not to harm each other (Gen 31:43–55).

Second, people enter into covenants to secure their safety. The Gibeonites from Canaan entered into a covenant with Joshua to secure their safety (Josh 9:3–21), and Israel called it "the oath which we swore" (Josh 9:20).

Third, people enter into covenants as a pledge of mutual friendship. Jonathan entered into a covenant with David, because he loved David as he loved his own soul (1 Sam 18:3; 20:42).

Fourth, people enter into covenants to promote trade between their countries. Hiram, king of Tyre, made a promise to supply Solomon with timbers of cedar and cypress, while Solomon promised twenty thousand kors of wheat and twenty kors of beaten oil in return (1 Kgs 5:7–12).

Fifth, people enter into covenants for military assistance between their countries. When Baasha, king of the northern kingdom of Israel, attacked the southern kingdom of Judah, Asa, Judah's king, asked Ben-hadad, king of Syria, for military assistance on the basis of a covenant. He said, "Let there be a treaty between you and me, as between my father and your father. Behold, I have sent you a present of silver and gold; go, break your treaty with Baasha king of Israel so that he will withdraw from me" (1 Kgs 15:19).

II. The Characteristics of Covenants Between Men

People of this world enter into agreements for mutual benefit and enjoyment. Every agreement presupposes mutual benefit. If the intended benefits become clouded along the way, however, the agreements are broken. Even nonaggression agreements or peace treaties between trusted nations are not permanent—either side may break the agreement in the event that the peaceful conditions between the two nations change. Japan and the Soviet Union once entered into a nonaggression treaty, yet they unsheathed their arms against each other during World War II. The United States and the Soviet Union were also allies during both World War I and World War II, yet they became hostile against one another after the wars and entered into and maintained the Cold War for forty years.

History testifies of the impermanence of covenants between people. Covenants between people are calculated, conditional, and relative. When the original conditions become ineffective, the treaty also becomes ineffective. When the intentions of one party change, the agreement also changes. When the standard of measurement for one party changes, the agreement becomes fragile and is often broken. Many agreements are either made as temporary solutions in moments of crisis or motivated by selfish interests and greed, which cause them to be filled with fraud, deception, and lies.

In agreements made by people, promises seem very sweet at first, as if everything is guaranteed. Yet many agreements fail midway, because they are motivated by self-interest. Your most trusted ally might suddenly turn against you and betray you. Abraham and Abimelech king of Gerar (Gen 20:2) entered into a peace treaty (Gen 21:22–32), but after some time had passed, Isaac, Abraham's son, had to enter into a new peace treaty with Abimelech[1] (Gen 26:26–33). This was because Abimelech's people had broken the peace treaty by seizing Isaac's wells of fresh water (Gen 26:12–22). The agreement between Abraham and Abimelech had not been eternal in its effect.

Agreements between people are easily forgotten. When Joseph interpreted the cupbearer's dream, he made one request, saying, "Only keep me in mind when it goes well with you, and please do me a kindness by mentioning me to Pharaoh and get me out of this house" (Gen 40:14). Although the cupbearer's position was restored to him, according to Joseph's interpretation, the cupbearer remembered neither Joseph nor the promise he had made to him (Gen 40:21–23).

III. The Consequences of Covenants Between Men

When people enter into covenants, they take oaths to confirm their covenants. Abraham and Abimelech became allies after entering into a covenant with an oath (Gen 21:22–32). Genesis 21:31 states that Abraham "called that place Beersheba, because there the two of them took an oath."

Abraham called his oldest servant, who was in charge of all his household possessions, and commanded him to take a wife for his son Isaac; he made his servant swear an oath by putting his hand under Abraham's thigh (Gen 24:2–9, 37–41). Genesis 24:9 states, "The servant placed his hand under the thigh of Abraham his master, and swore to him concerning this matter."

Esau swore to Jacob when he sold his birthright to him. Genesis 25:33 states, "Jacob said, 'First swear to me'; so he swore to him, and sold his birthright to Jacob."

When Jacob and Laban set up a stone pillar and a heap of stones (called *Jegar-sahadutha* in Aramaic and *Galeed* in Hebrew, meaning "heap of witness") to enter into a covenant of reconciliation, Jacob swore by the fear of his father, Isaac (Gen 31:43–53). Thus covenants made between people involved taking an oath to confirm the covenants. Oaths taken by people, however, are always futile in their results. The prophet Hosea pointed out, "They speak mere words, with worthless oaths they make covenants" (Hos 10:4).

A true covenant comes from the everlasting God. Only God is truthful, and only He has the infinite power to take responsibility for His covenant. Putting faith in another human being and entering into a covenant with him is like walking toward tragic end called death. The prophet Isaiah keenly pointed out that the covenant that Israel's leaders had made with Assyria, Egypt, and other forces who had appeared strong in their eyes but whose evil schemes they had not recognized was equivalent to "a covenant with death" and a pact "with Sheol" (Isa 28:15). He reminded the Israelites of their foolishness by saying, "We have made falsehood our refuge and we have concealed ourselves with deception" (Isa 28:15). Furthermore, the prophet Isaiah prophesied concerning the tragic end of those who enter into covenants by faith in men and their power, saying, "Your covenant with death will be canceled, and your pact with Sheol will not stand; when the overwhelming scourge passes through, then you become its trampling place" (Isa 28:18). While those who trust in men and rely on them will face death, those who entrust everything to God in whom is no lie and rely upon Him will be assured of eternal freedom from death.

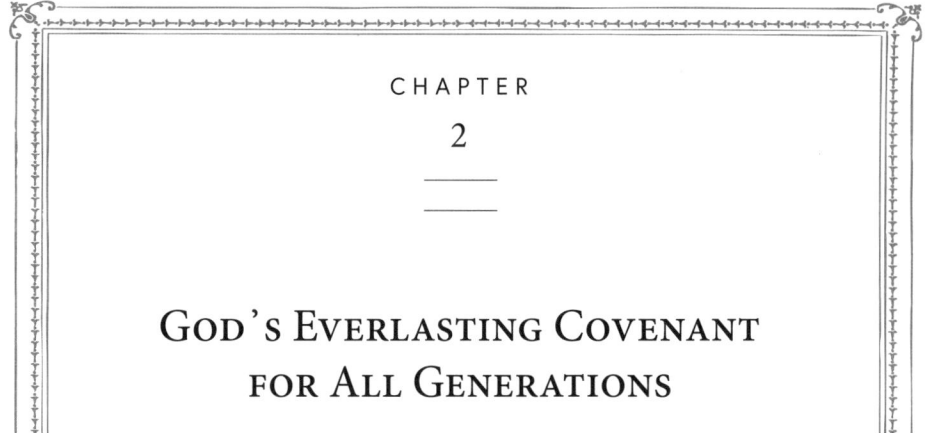

CHAPTER 2

God's Everlasting Covenant for All Generations

Unlike covenants between men, God remembers His covenant with His people forever. It is an eternal covenant for a thousand generations, an everlasting and unchanging promise that will never be broken (Ps 105:8-10). The apostle Paul proclaimed that the "word of God, that is, the mystery which has been hidden from the past ages and generations, ... has now been manifested to His saints" (Col 1:25-26). He proclaimed further that this mystery is "Christ in you, the hope of glory" (Col 1:27; see also Col 2:2).

Here the term "thousand generations" is γενεῶν (*geneōn*) in Greek, which is the genitive feminine plural form of γενεά (*genea*), meaning "generation," and refers to "a number of consecutive generations." The parallel word for "generation" in Hebrew is דֹּרוֹת (*doroth*), the plural form of דּוֹר (*dor*). Thus the term "thousand generations" denotes "consecutive generations from the beginning of the world to the end without a break." The prophet Isaiah recorded, "Who has performed and accomplished it, calling forth the generations from the beginning? 'I, the LORD, am the first, and with the last. I am He'"

(Isa 41:4). Indeed, God is the sovereign ruler over all history, not only over past generations but also over the generations to come. God's covenant is truly a covenant for a thousand generations, the eternal covenant (see Ps 90:1-2), because He fulfills His covenants through the thousand generations—all generations.

Luke 1:68-79 records the first prophetic poem from the New Testament era. It contains the hymn of Zechariah the priest that he sang after realizing God's profound and mysterious providence embedded in God's everlasting covenant. Zechariah was childless until his old age, but then he received a son, John the Baptist, according to God's promise. Zechariah became unable to speak for ten months, however, because of his unbelief when the angel Gabriel brought the word of God (Luke 1:20). Yet when God opened his mouth and loosened his tongue, he was filled with the Holy Spirit and made an articulate confession (Luke 1:64, 67). His statement contained no traces of human joy or emotion regarding the son gifted to him in his old age. He expressed only overflowing thanksgiving, great joy, and praises before God who had fulfilled His promise without fail.

The content of the hymn can be summarized as follows:

1. Thanksgiving for sending the Messiah (Luke 1:68-71)
2. Praises for the fulfillment of the covenant of salvation (Luke 1:72-75)
3. A song regarding the mission of John the Baptist (Luke 1:76-77)
4. Praises regarding the salvation of the Messiah (Luke 1:78-79)

The greatness of the covenant that the Spirit-filled Zechariah articulated is summarized in Luke 1:71-73 in the following three points.

I. "Salvation from Our Enemies"

Luke 1:71 speaks of "salvation from our enemies, and from the hand of all who hate us." Here the word "salvation" is σωτηρία (*sōtēria*) in Greek, and it clarifies that the purpose of the coming of the Messiah is our salvation. The salvation of Jesus Christ is so powerful, so complete, and so certain that nothing in this world can change it (Rom 8:38-39). This is the covenant of salvation that saves sinners from sin and death—salvation through the forgiveness of sins (Luke 1:77). This is the spiritual exodus through Jesus Christ.[2]

Luke 1:71 describes our tormentors as "our enemies" and "all who hate us." The enemies that human power cannot overcome are sin and death (1 Cor 15:55-56). God gives us the victory, however, through Jesus Christ (1 Cor 15:57). Jesus paid the price for sin on the cross and saved His people from sin and death (Matt 1:21). Psalm 106:10 states, "He saved them from the hand of the one who hated them, and redeemed them from the hand of the enemy."

Indeed, Jesus Christ is the "horn of salvation" for sinners (Luke 1:69). A horn symbolizes absolute power, strength, and competence. So the term "horn of salvation" denotes the strength, competence, and absoluteness of salvation (1 Sam 2:10; Ps 18:2; Rev 5:6). Those who have been saved from sin through Jesus Christ must serve the Lord without fear, in holiness and righteousness before Him all the days of their lives (see Luke 1:75). While they were once slaves of sin and death, now they have become children of God whose sins have been forgiven through Jesus Christ (Rom 8:15).

II. "His Holy Covenant"

Zechariah's hymn summarizes the mood of the times: "in darkness and the shadow of death" (Luke 1:79). The marvelous coming of Jesus Christ to His land during such gloomy times was the fruit of God's remembrance of His holy covenant. Luke 1:72 states that God visited Israel "to show mercy toward [their] fathers, and to remember His holy covenant" (see Exod 2:23–25; Pss 105:8, 42; 106:45). If human beings, the other party in the covenant, had been sinless and pure, holiness would not have needed to be mentioned. However, God's holiness is always the first of His divine attributes mentioned, because human beings are sinful. Concerning the divine covenant with human beings, the Scripture states that "God has spoken in His holiness" (Ps 60:6) and that "the Lord GOD has sworn by His holiness" (Amos 4:2). God also said, "Once I have sworn by My holiness" (Ps 89:35). God always enters into a covenant by His own holiness.

The "holy covenant" that Zechariah praised comes from the Greek term διαθήκης ἁγίας (*diathēkēs hagias*). The word ἅγιος (*hagios*), the nominative form for "holy," denotes things strictly set apart from the common and secular. Thus "holy covenant" refers to a covenant that has been set apart for a specific purpose. It implies that no matter how long it takes and how extreme situations may become, God will uphold His covenant until its purpose is accomplished. The first biblical record of the phrase "holy covenant" is found in the prophet Daniel's prophecy regarding future events. He mentioned the holy covenant (בְּרִית קֹדֶשׁ, *berith qodesh*) three times while prophesying about the tragic fall of Jerusalem and her temple at the hands of Antiochus IV (Dan 11:28, 30). He upheld that God's holy covenant would be preserved pure and the day of its fulfillment would surely come even as the power of worldly evil (impurity) would rise violently to attack and destroy God's temple.

Spiritual darkness was at its climax when Jesus Christ came to His own land (John 1:5). Yet by God's absolute, sovereign providence, the holy covenant was fulfilled and Jesus Christ came to this world. When Zechariah's mouth was opened, he made a heartfelt confession, saying, "Blessed be the Lord God of Israel, for He has visited us and accomplished redemption for His people" (Luke 1:68). The phrase "He has visited" is ἐπισκέπτομαι (*episkeptomai*) in Greek, meaning "to look after," and it means "God has come to help his people" (Luke 7:16, NIV). As a result, the rising sun comes upon us from above and chases away completely the shadow of darkness and death, and our feet are guided into the path of peace (Luke 1:78-79).

III. "The Oath Which He Swore"

Luke 1:73 refers to "the oath which He swore to Abraham our father." The phrase "the oath that He swore" is ὅρκον ὃν ὤμοσεν (*horkon hon ōmosen*) in Greek. The Greek word *horkon*, translated as "oath," is from *horkos* (ὅρκος), which is used when guaranteeing something with an oath (Heb 6:17). The Greek word *ōmosen*, translated as "he swore," is from ὀμνύω (*omnyō*), which generally means "to swear" (Acts 2:30; Heb 6:13, 16). While an oath itself affirms that a promise will be kept, the redundant expression "the oath that He swore" strongly emphasizes the faithfulness and certainty of the fulfillment of God's covenant. God's oath, once sworn, stands firm. Psalm 110:4 states, "The LORD has sworn and will not change His mind" (see also Ps 102:26-27).

The characteristics of God's oath can be summarized as follows.

An Oath that God Swore by Himself

Since there is no one greater than God Himself, God swears by Himself when He enters into a covenant. He repeatedly said, "By Myself I have sworn" (Gen 22:16), "I ... swear, as I live forever" (Deut 32:40, ESV), "I have sworn by My holiness" (Ps 89:35), and, "I have sworn by My great name" (Jer 44:26). These expressions indicate that the basis of God's promise is God Himself. He is greater than all (John 10:29); He is the "great God" (Ezra 5:8; Neh 4:14; Ps 95:3; Dan 2:45; Titus 2:13). All nations are as nothing before God; He considers them "as less than nothing and meaningless" (Isa 40:17). God accomplishes all His desire, will, thought, plan, Word, and administration without fail (Job 42:2; Pss 115:3; 135:6; Isa 14:24–27; 46:9–11; 55:11). Nothing is impossible with God (Gen 18:14; Jer 32:17; Mark 9:23; Luke 1:37). Once God swears, no one dares stop Him (Job 34:29) and no one questions Him regarding His work (Dan 4:35). Human experience and intellect are as nothing before the omnipotent God (see 1 Cor 1:25).

An Oath with a Guarantee

Hebrews 6:17 states, "In the same way God, desiring even more to show to the heirs of the promise the unchangeableness of His purpose, interposed with an oath." God not only made a promise, but He guaranteed (μεσιτεύω, *mesiteuō*) it with an oath (ὅρκος, *horkos*). God will take full responsibility for His oath until His promise of salvation is fulfilled.

The guarantee of this oath is Jesus Christ the mediator. In taking an oath, the oath taker accepts the curse that will befall him if he does not speak the truth. Thus God's guarantee with an oath foretells the death of Jesus Christ as the mediator for sinners, the other party in the oath.[3] Jesus Christ accepted the priesthood as the mediator for sinners with an oath (Heb 7:20–21) and became "the guarantee of a better covenant" (Heb 7:22). By offering His own life as a sacrifice, Jesus became the guarantee of God's covenant and demonstrated God's love. Romans 5:8 states, "God demonstrates His own love toward us, in that while we were yet sinners, Christ died for us."

An Oath Based on Love

God is a faithful (πιστός, *pistos*, "trustworthy") God whose words surely bear fruit without fail (Isa 55:11), in whose mouth are no lies (Heb 6:17–18), and whose promise is fulfilled with certainty (1 Cor 1:9; 10:13; 2 Cor 1:18; 1 Thess 5:24; 2 Tim 2:13; Heb 10:23; 11:11; 1 Pet 4:19; 1 John 1:9). No matter what He speaks, He is not like a man that He should lie (Num 23:19). He is the Almighty God who possesses perfect authority and does not oppose His own holiness, nor does He do anything contradictory. In truth, the absolute God does not need an oath to prove the trustworthiness of His words. Yet God frequently swore with an oath to emphasize His firm will.[4] He did this to express His great love for all mankind. This is *agape* love (ἀγάπη, "love"), God's infinite love that used oaths to prove the certainty of His covenant. God delivered the Israelites from the house of slavery in Egypt to fulfill the covenant that He had sworn to their ancestors, and He did it all out of His zealous love for the Israelites. Deuteronomy 7:8 states, "Because the LORD loved you and kept the oath which He swore to your forefathers, the LORD brought you out by a mighty hand and redeemed you from the house of slavery, from the hand of Pharaoh king of Egypt."

A Faithful Oath

Psalm 132:2 and 132:11 both contain the word "swear." Verse 2 contains David's oath to God, while verse 11 contains God's oath to David. The word "truth" in verse 11 refers to God's oath, but there are no words that describe David's oath in verse 2. Although we may not fulfill our oaths to God faithfully, God faithfully keeps His oath to us. People may change, but God is the same yesterday, today, and forever (Heb 13:8). God's covenant, made with His truth and His oath, is an eternally immutable promise that cannot be abrogated in any circumstance.

Agreements in this world are prone to distortions, changes, and reversals over time. Often mutual trust collapses and honesty disappears, resulting in broken promises. We live in an evil age in which brothers become enemies and do not hesitate to kill one another.

God's promise, however, is an immutable, eternal covenant for *all generations* that will surely be fulfilled (Gen 9:16; 17:7, 13, 19; Exod 31:16; Lev 24:8; 2 Sam 23:5; 1 Chr 16:17; Isa 24:5; 55:3; Ezek 16:60; 37:26; Heb 13:20). Just as God spoke by the mouths of various prophets (Luke 1:70; Heb 1:1–2), so He also visited His people in the fullness of the time by sending His Son (Luke 1:76–77; Gal 4:4). By the tender mercy of God, the Sunrise from on high shone great light upon the people walking in darkness (Luke 1:78; see Isa 9:2). This covenant is the *covenant for all generations*, which has been fulfilled continually through God's passionate love and mercy. This covenant will neither break nor change in its course.

Among the covenant for all generations, this book's specific focus will be the Sinaitic covenant and the Ten Commandments.

CHAPTER

3

THE CHARACTERISTICS OF THE SINAITIC COVENANT

God ratified the Sinaitic covenant with the Israelites through Moses the mediator. He gave them the Ten Commandments and all the ordinances after the exodus, while the Israelites were encamped in the wilderness of Sinai (Exod 24:1–8). The covenant was ratified at Mount Sinai, "the mountain of God" (Exod 3:1; 4:27), through Moses "the man of God" (Deut 33:1; 1 Chr 23:14; Ezra 3:2; see also John 1:17; 7:19). It was a covenant ratified under God's plan and His sanctified redemptive-historical providence. Moses built an altar at the foot of Mount Sinai and sprinkled half the blood of the sacrifice on the altar before reading "the book of the covenant," the written Word of God given to the Israelites on Mount Sinai (Exod 24:4–7). In response the Israelites swore, "All that the LORD has spoken we will do, and we will be obedient!" (Exod 24:7). Moses sprinkled the blood on the people and proclaimed the ratification of the Sinaitic covenant, saying, "Behold the blood of the covenant, which the LORD has made with you in accordance with all these words" (Exod 24:8).

The Sinaitic covenant was made with the first generation of Israelites during the wilderness journey, right after the exodus. At the end of the wilderness journey, it was reaffirmed with the second generation at the forty-first campsite on the plains of Moab (Deut 29; known as the covenant on the plains of Moab). The Sinaitic covenant was a significant covenant from the redemptive-historical perspective because it officially elevated the Israelites into the *covenant people*.

The Israelites arrived at the wilderness of Sinai on the forty-fifth day after the exodus (Exod 19:1).[5] God ratified the covenant with the Israelites on Mount Sinai with Moses as the mediator. This covenant ratification was a redemptive-historical event that marked the renewal of the Israelites' relationship with God that had continued since the covenant of the torch had been ratified with Abraham. In ratifying this covenant, God publicly declared that the Israelites were His covenant people.

I. The Sinaitic Covenant: A Covenant Made with the Nation

After the Israelites encamped in the wilderness of Sinai, God called Moses to Mount Sinai for the first time and commanded him to "tell the sons of Israel" (Exod 19:3). This implies that the other party in the covenant was made up of the entire people of Israel. While God had previously ratified covenants with individuals, such as Adam, Noah, Abraham, Isaac, and Jacob, He was now covenanting with the entire nation of Israel (Exod 24:3-8). God's redemptive work had begun focused on one person and proceeded through one family; now the focus expanded to include one whole nation. The twelve pillars symbolizing the twelve tribes, which were set up while ratifying the covenant, also indicated that the whole nation of Israel was entering into the covenant with God (Exod 24:4).

The Israelites Were Redeemed Out of the House of Slavery in the Land of Egypt

The Ten Commandments, which contain the essence of the Sinaitic covenant, begin with the words "I am the LORD your God, who brought you out of the land of Egypt, out of the house of slavery" (Exod 20:2). Before ratifying the covenant, God emphasized how He had saved Israel from Egypt and reminded them of their tragic past as slaves. The oppression and toil had created intolerable suffering for the Israelites, so the Bible describes the experience as "the iron furnace, from Egypt" (Deut 4:20), "from Egypt, from the midst of the iron furnace" (1 Kgs 8:51), and "the land of Egypt, from the iron furnace" (Jer 11:4). The Israelites had been weak and powerless slaves who had not had the strength to overcome their suffering in Egypt and establish themselves as an independent nation. In this respect the exodus was a miraculous event entirely fashioned by God's "mighty hand" and "outstretched arm" (Deut 5:15; 11:2; Ps 136:12), by "the signs and the wonders and the mighty hand and the outstretched arm" (Deut 7:19; 26:8), and "with signs and with wonders, and with a strong hand and with an outstretched arm and with great terror" (Jer 32:21).

"The sons of Israel were fruitful and increased greatly, and multiplied, and became exceedingly mighty, so that the land was filled with them" (Exod 1:7). Then a new king who did not know Joseph sat on the throne and afflicted them with hard labor. Yet "the more they [the Egyptians] afflicted them, the more they [Israel] multiplied and the more they spread out, so that they [the Egyptians] were in dread of the sons of Israel" (Exod 1:12). Troubled by the Israelites, the Egyptians oppressed them even more with rigorous labor. Furthermore, to restrict the multiplication and growth of the Israelites, the Egyptian king ordered the Hebrew midwives, saying, "When you are helping the Hebrew women to give birth and see them upon the birthstool, if it is a son, then you shall put him to death" (Exod 1:16). God protected the Israelites, however, from the dangers of genocide by placing the fear of Him above the fear of the king of Egypt in the midwives' hearts (Exod 1:17). This showed a vivid contrast between Israel's crisis and humiliation and God's grace and power. God broke the Israelites' pride and displayed for all the nations to see that the exodus was entirely the work of God's grace with no human effort or initiative involved.

When God entered into the Sinaitic covenant with the Israelites, they had not accomplished any works deserving of the covenant, nor did they possess righteousness worthy of it (see Deut 7:7; 9:4–6). Before God laid His merciful eyes upon Israel, they were like a fragile baby abandoned by the wayside. For an insignificant nation like Israel, the exodus was indeed the work of God's boundless mercy and grace (see Ezek 16:1–14).

Likewise, we too were under the authority of sin and death and hurtling toward eternal death. It was only through Jesus Christ, the only Son of God, that we received eternal life (1 John 2:25) and the Spirit of adoption to call God "Abba! Father!" (Rom 8:15; Gal 4:6). This is God's profound and infinite care for us, His perfect love bestowed by grace, and His unconditional love granted without considering our status (Eph 2:4–8).

Israel Was Established as a Great Nation in Fulfillment of God's Covenant with Abraham

The Sinaitic covenant was initiated by God's remembrance, as recorded in Exodus 2:24: "God heard their groaning; and God remembered His covenant with Abraham, Isaac, and Jacob." In Exodus 6:5, God also said, "I have heard the groaning of the sons of Israel, because the Egyptians are holding them in bondage, and I have remembered My covenant." The exodus was neither coincidental nor the result of Israel's efforts; it was the fulfillment of God's covenant with Abraham, Isaac, and Jacob (Deut 9:5). From the outset it was possible only through God's faithfulness to His covenant.

In number the Israelites were now a "great nation," just as God had promised Abraham (Gen 12:2). Exodus 1:7 states, "The sons of Israel were fruitful and increased greatly, and multiplied, and became exceedingly mighty, so that the land was filled with them." They were not only great in number but also exceedingly mighty. Just as Pharaoh exclaimed, "Behold, the people of the sons of Israel are more and mightier than we" (Exod 1:9), so the Israelites had become "a great and mighty nation" (Gen 18:18) in accordance with God's covenant. They were no longer a weak nation of slaves desperate to escape oppression in Egypt. They had grown into a confident, conquering nation of people who held onto God's covenant and marched out of Egypt in martial array as God's army (Exod 12:41; 13:18; Num 33:1).

II. The Covenant that God Spoke Directly to the People

God proclaimed the Sinaitic covenant directly to the whole nation from the midst of fire (Exod 20:1–19; Deut 5:4, 23–24). This type of covenant was the first of its kind in the history of mankind. Deuteronomy 4:32–33 questions three times, "Has anything been done like this great thing, or has anything been heard like it? Has any people heard the voice of God speaking from the midst of the fire, as you have heard it, and survived?" What is the answer? In terms of time, there had been no such event "since the day that God created man on the earth"; in terms of space, there had been no such thing "from one end of the heavens to the other" (Deut 4:32). Even today no nation but Israel has ever heard the voice of God directly; equally, no people but Israel has survived after hearing the voice of God (see also Exod 20:19; Deut 5:25; 18:16; Heb 12:18–20).

Truly the Sinaitic covenant was the first covenant in which God had spoken to the entire nation of Israel. Thus Deuteronomy 4:8 declares, "What great nation is there that has statutes and judgments as righteous as this whole law which I am setting before you today?" In Psalm 147:19-20, the psalmist sang, "He declares His words to Jacob, His statutes and His ordinances to Israel. He has not dealt thus with any nation; and as for His ordinances, they have not known them. Praise the LORD!"

III. The First Covenant to Be Set in Writing

A notable characteristic of the Sinaitic covenant was that it was the first covenant to be concretized into writing. The Ten Commandments were engraved on two stone tablets (Exod 31:18). God Himself made the stone tablets and engraved the word. Exodus 32:16 confirms, "The tablets were God's work, and the writing was God's writing engraved on the tablets." Deuteronomy 9:10 also attests, "The LORD gave me the two tablets of stone written by the finger of God." The expression "written by the finger of God" testifies to the extent to which God cherished the Sinaitic covenant.

Moses received the precious tablets of the testimony from God after forty days and nights of fasting and prayer on Mount Sinai. The Israelites at the foot of the mountain, however, seeing that Moses delayed in coming down, made a golden calf and worshiped before it (Exod 32:1-6). As soon as Moses arrived and saw this scene, he threw the tablets at the foot of the mountain in great anger (Exod 32:19). Then "[h]e took the calf which they had made and burned it with fire, and ground it to powder, and scattered it over the surface of the water and made the sons of Israel drink it" (Exod 32:20). When he said "Whoever is for the LORD, come to me!" (Exod 32:26), the tribe of Levi stood on God's side, put their swords upon their thighs, and went back and forth from gate to gate in the camp and killed about three thousand men (Exod 32:25-28). The next day Moses went up again to Mount Sinai to make atonement for the Israelites' sin and spent another forty days offering up intercessory prayer. He then came down from the mountain, pitched a tent outside the camp, and prayed again for the sinners. After all this Moses himself cut "two stone tablets like the former ones" (Exod 34:1) and went up to Mount Sinai. God wrote the Ten Commandments (ten words; Exod 34:1, 28) on the tablets with His finger "on both sides ... on one side and the other" (Exod 32:15).

God also gave many ordinances (Exod 20:22–23:33). Exodus 24:4 states, "Moses wrote down all the words of the LORD," and Exodus 24:7 states that Moses "took the book of the covenant and read it in the hearing of the people." God's covenant was not only recorded in the book of the covenant but also quite extensive in its content, reflecting the unprecedented immensity of God's grace (see Hos 8:12).

The engravement of God's covenant on the stone tablets and its recording in the book of the covenant indicate that the covenant was to be preserved eternally for all generations. Later, when King Hezekiah forsook God's covenant and formed an alliance with Egypt to fight against Assyria, God warned that there would be judgment for it (Isa 30:1–7). God commanded that this warning be written down on a tablet and inscribed in a book to be preserved for later generations in Isaiah 30:8: "Now go, write it on a tablet before them and inscribe it on a scroll, that it may serve in the time to come as a witness forever." The New Living Translation renders this verse as, "Now go and write down these words. Write them in a book. They will stand until the end of time as a witness." If what is inscribed on a (wooden) tablet can be preserved for future generations as a witness forever, the words engraved on stone tablets will be preserved forever and evermore.

IV. A Covenant to Be Kept and Practiced in the Promised Land

From Mount Sinai, the Israelites headed to Canaan. The concretization of the promise regarding the land that God had made clear in the Sinaitic covenant foretold the Israelites' impending entry into Canaan. Geographically "Canaan" referred to the entire land west of the Jordan River; the Bible describes it as "from Dan to Beersheba" (Judg 20:1; 1 Sam 3:20). Geopolitically it was a region where three continents—Asia, Europe, and Africa—met. The history of the Middle and Near East shows that two great powers, Mesopotamia from the north and Egypt from the south, frequently fought on this land.

Ezekiel 38:12 calls the land of Canaan the "center of the world." The word "center" is טַבּוּר (*tabbur*) in Hebrew and means "middle" or "navel." Just as the navel is located at the center of the human body, so the land of Canaan—situated in the intersection of the three continents of Asia, Europe, and Africa—was the center of the known world at the time.

The Promised Land

The land of Canaan was promised to Israel through the Abrahamic covenant (Gen 12:7; 13:14–17; 15:7, 18–21; 17:8). God commanded Abraham to lift up his eyes and look in every direction and then said, "All the land which you see, I will give it to you and to your descendants forever" (Gen 13:15). The fact that God gave Canaan to Israel's forefathers in His covenant with them repeatedly appears in each era of the Old and New Testaments.[6] There are many designations for the land of Canaan:

- "The land which the LORD your God is giving you" (Deut 4:40; 9:23; 15:5, 7; 16:20; 17:14; 18:9; 19:10, 14; 21:1; 25:15; 26:2; 27:2–3; 28:8, 52)
- "The land of Canaan, which I give you for a possession [or inheritance or heritage]" (Lev 14:34; Deut 4:21; 9:6; 12:10; 19:2–3; 21:23; 24:4; 1 Kgs 8:36; 2 Chr 6:27; Ps 136:21; Ezek 33:24)
- "The land of the LORD" (Isa 14:2; Ezek 36:20; Hos 9:3)
- "Exceedingly good land" (Num 14:7)
- "Fertile land" (Neh 9:25, 35; Jer 2:7)
- "A land flowing with milk and honey" (Exod 3:8, 17; 13:5; 33:3; Lev 20:24; Num 13:27; 14:8; 16:13–14; Deut 6:3; 11:9; 26:9, 15; 27:3; 31:20; Josh 5:6; Jer 11:5; 32:22; Ezek 20:6, 15)
- "Pleasant land" (Ps 106:24; Jer 3:19; 12:10; Zech 7:14)
- "Rich and plenteous" (Isa 30:23; Ezek 36:29–30)
- "Without scarcity" (Deut 8:9)
- "Good land" (Deut 1:35; 3:25; 4:21–22; 6:18–19; 8:7, 10; 9:6; 11:17; Josh 23:13, 15–16; 1 Chr 28:8)
- "A land for which the LORD your God cares" (Deut 11:12)

This promise of the land of Canaan to the forefathers began to concretize with the ratification of the Sinaitic covenant. This covenant, ratified before Israel's entry into Canaan, was filled with details regarding the land. Exodus 23:10–33 records the contents of the Sinaitic covenant, including the laws regarding the Sabbath and the Sabbatical Year (23:10–13), the three great feasts (23:14–19), and regulations regarding the conquest of the land (23:20–33).

The book of Deuteronomy repeatedly emphasizes that all God's Ten Commandments as well as His specific commands, regulations, and laws given through the Sinaitic covenant were to be kept and practiced by the Israelites in the land of Canaan (Deut 4:1, 5, 13–14; 5:31; 6:1). God promised Israel that if they loved and trusted Him and obeyed His promises while they lived in the blessed promised land, He would bless them with abundance and prosperity in all things.

First, He would bless their livelihoods:
He will give the rain for your land in its season, the early and late rain, that you may gather in your grain and your new wine and your oil. He will give grass in your fields for your cattle, and you will eat and be satisfied. (Deut 11:14–15; see also Deut 7:12–14; 11:10–11; 28:12)

Second, He would bless them to multiply greatly:
O Israel, you should listen and be careful to do it, that it may be well with you and that you may multiply greatly, just as the LORD, the God of your fathers, has promised you, in a land flowing with milk and honey. (Deut 6:3; see also Deut 8:1)

Third, He would bless them with longevity:
That your days and the days of your sons may be multiplied on the land which the LORD swore to your fathers to give them, as long as the heavens remain above the earth. (Deut 11:21; see also Deut 4:40; 5:33; 6:2; 11:9)

Fourth, He would bless them to dispossess great nations:
The LORD will drive out all these nations from before you, and you will dispossess nations greater and mightier than you. (Deut 11:23; see also Deut 9:1)

Fifth, He would bless them with victory so that no one could stand against them:
No man will be able to stand before you; the LORD your God will lay the dread of you and the fear of you on all the land on which you set foot, as He has spoken to you. (Deut 11:25; see also Deut 6:18–19)

The disobedient, however, could not enjoy the blessing of abundance in the promised land. The promised land would spew the Israelites out if they forgot their covenant with God, disobeyed His Word, married Gentiles, or fell into idolatry (Lev 18:24–28; 20:22).

Conquest of the Land Through Hornets (God's Sovereign Work)

Simply put, the promised land was a land of God's presence. Thus Canaan without God would have been meaningless to the Israelites (see Exod 33:1–3, 14–16). The tabernacle, which was the center of life for the Israelites in the wilderness and the promised land, was an external sign that God was among the people (Exod 25:22; 29:42–43). In Exodus 29:45–46, God said, "I will dwell among the sons of Israel and will be their God. They shall know that I am the LORD their God who brought them out of the land of Egypt, that I might dwell among them; I am the LORD their God." Indeed, it was the merciful and compassionate promise of the Almighty God to dwell among them—to sit down with them, lie down with them, and live among them—and pour His grace upon them. In 1 Chronicles 17:5, God said, "I have not dwelt in a house since the day that I brought up Israel to this day, but I have gone from tent to tent and from one dwelling place to another" (see also 2 Sam 7:6). This is testimony that God always dwelt among the Israelites, whether they were journeying through the wilderness with the tabernacle at its center or were settled in the promised land.

If the Israelites would believe in God's promise and keep them, then God would conquer the land for them (Exod 34:11; Lev 25:18; Deut 7:1; 8:1). In Kadesh-barnea God strongly commanded the Israelites through Moses to boldly conquer the land, saying, "Do not fear them, for the LORD your God is the one fighting for you" (Deut 3:22; see also Deut 1:21; 2:31; 3:18; 9:23). The Israelites did not trust God's word to them, however. They implored that spies be sent into the land, and God reluctantly allowed them to choose twelve representatives from each of the tribes to explore the land for forty days (Deut 1:19–23;

see also Num 13:1–25). Yet after spying out the land, ten of the twelve spies brought out a bad report and died immediately by a plague before the Lord (Num 14:36–37). Only two spies, Joshua and Caleb, who brought out a good report regarding the land, received permission to enter into the land of Canaan (Num 14:30, 38). The Israelites who grumbled against God due to the bad report were sentenced to forty years of wandering in the wilderness, one year for each day the spies had explored the land (Num 14:27, 34).

The land of Canaan was not conquered by swords and bows but by God's sovereign work through hornets, in accordance with His promise in the Sinaitic covenant: "I will send hornets ahead of you so that they will drive out the Hivites, the Canaanites, and the Hittites before you" (Exod 23:28; see also Deut 7:20; Josh 24:12).

God promised to send hornets especially to destroy the three nations with the strongest military forces (the Hivites, Canaanites, and Hittites). Hornets are the largest of the stinging insects. These fearsome creatures travel in swarms and have stingers with venom so toxic that even one sting can be fatal. Deuteronomy 7:20 states, "The LORD your God will send the hornet against them, until those who are left and hide themselves from you perish." The hornets would kill every enemy, and even the ones hiding would be found and destroyed; even those hiding behind locked doors would be found (Deut 7:21–24). The book of Deuteronomy frequently refers to how Sihon, king of the Amorites, and Og, king of Bashan, were killed by these hornets (Deut 1:4; 2:26–35; 4:46–47; 29:7; 31:4; see also Josh 24:12).

The Israelites had not yet entered the promised land when the Sinaitic covenant was ratified; the land was still to be entered. Before the ratification of the covenant (Exod 24), God said, "[I will] bring you into the place which I have prepared" (Exod 23:20), and added in Exodus 23:30, "until you become fruitful and take possession of the land." This was an assured promise that God would surely give them the land of Canaan. Through the Sinaitic covenant, God made the Israelites look forward to the promised land of Canaan.

God mobilized methods unimaginable to human beings and fulfilled the work of salvation for Israel by His sovereignty. The God who promises is faithful and always fulfills His word. Second Corinthians 1:18–20 states, "God is faithful, ... for as many as are the promises of God, in Him they are yes." Hebrews 10:23 states, "Let us hold fast the confession of our hope without wavering, for He who promised is faithful" (see also Heb 11:11). Faithfulness is trustworthiness without any fabrication or deceit (Deut 7:9; Isa 49:7), which is one of God's attributes. First Thessalonians 5:24 states, "Faithful is He who calls you, and He also will bring it to pass." If we confess our sins to the faithful God, He will forgive our sins (1 John 1:9) and protect us and take responsibility for us until the end (2 Thess 3:3). Although we may lack faithfulness, He is always faithful (2 Tim 2:13). God's faithfulness cannot be nullified (Rom 3:3). His faithfulness is our true hope.

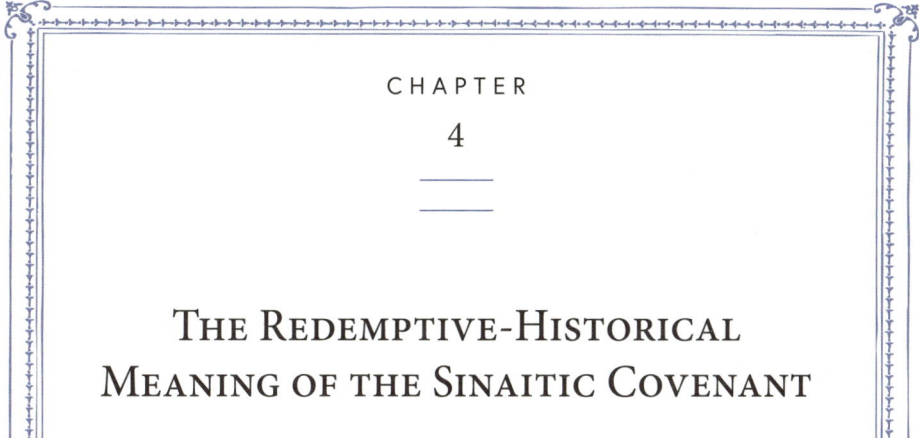

The Redemptive-Historical Meaning of the Sinaitic Covenant

The Sinaitic covenant was made with blood through a mediator. This reminds us of our redemption in Jesus Christ, who shed His blood on the cross as our mediator. For this reason the Sinaitic covenant is for all generations; it must be kept from generation to generation.

I. A Covenant Made with Blood

Moses ratified the covenant with the Israelites with the word he had received from God on his fourth ascent of Mount Sinai. Moses took the blood of the sacrifice from burnt offerings and peace offerings, put half of it in basins, and sprinkled the other half on the altar (Exod 24:5–6). Then he read the book of the covenant before the Israelites, and after they responded, he took the blood and sprinkled it on the people (Exod 24:7–8). Moses proclaimed, "Behold the blood of the covenant, which the LORD has made with you in accordance with all these words" (Exod 24:8). Thus the Sinaitic covenant was a covenant ratified with blood. The proof of the covenant was the blood, and its written certificate was called "the book of the covenant" (Exod 24:7).

What is the significance of the Sinaitic covenant being ratified with blood?

Sprinkling Blood on the Altar Before God Meant that Israel Became United as One Community with God

Sprinkling the blood on the altar meant that the people had received forgiveness of sins through the blood of the sacrifice and that the path to God had been opened so that God and sinful human beings were spiritually unified. People who have been defiled by sin cannot enter into a covenant with the holy God on equal footing. Thus this blood of atonement signified the blood of grace that allowed them to participate in the covenant. Hence the Sinaitic covenant was ratified entirely by God's sovereign grace.

The Blood Signified Moses' Firm Promise to Keep the Covenant

The sprinkling of blood was an act of ratifying the covenant. The blood symbolizes life (Gen 9:4–5; Lev 17:11, 14; Deut 12:23). Moses' sprinkling of the blood as he vowed to abide by the laws meant that he vowed with his life to keep them. It was a pledge that he would give up his life if he broke this covenant.

The book of Hebrews records one event that is not in Exodus: the blood was also sprinkled on the book of the covenant (Heb 9:19–20). Moses brought the book of the covenant and read it before the people and then sprinkled the blood on both the book and the people (Exod 24:6–8). The blood that was sprinkled on the book of the covenant was a sign that God was the guarantor of the book. In line with this principle, we can say that the sixty-six books of the Old and New Testaments of the Bible are the gospel sprinkled with the everlasting blood of Jesus Christ.

The Blood Foreshadowed the Covenant of the Blood by Jesus

During the Last Supper Jesus said, "This cup which is poured out for you is the new covenant in My blood" (Luke 22:20; see also Matt 26:27-28; Mark 14:23-24; 1 Cor 11:25). The blood of the sacrifice sprinkled by Moses pointed to Jesus Christ, who would shed His blood on the cross as the sacrifice for all mankind (Heb 9:12, 14; 10:12-14; 12:24). The laws given to the Israelites through the Sinaitic covenant were their guidelines for living as God's people until the coming of Jesus Christ, the true essence of the covenant of blood. Indeed, these laws were the foundation that prepared God's people for Jesus' coming (John 5:39, 45-47; Gal 3:24).

II. A Covenant with a Mediator

Moses became a mediator of the covenant between God and Israel by ascending and descending Mount Sinai a total of eight times until the Sinaitic covenant was finally ratified (Exod 19:9; 20:18-21; Deut 5:5, 23-27, 31). Regarding the process through which Moses received the laws, the apostle Paul explained that the law had "been ordained through angels by the agency of a mediator, until the seed would come to whom the promise had been made" (Gal 3:19; see also Acts 7:38, 53; Heb 2:2). The apostle John also narrated, "The Law was given through Moses; grace and truth were realized through Jesus Christ" (John 1:17). While Moses was a mediator of the old covenant, Jesus Christ is the mediator of the new covenant (Heb 9:15; 12:24; see also

1 Tim 2:5). A mediator is a person who reconciles people who have grown distant from each other (1 Sam 2:25; Job 33:23) or aims to bring peace and unite two sides that are hostile toward each other or arguing about right and wrong (Isa 38:14). In other words, a mediator is a reconciler or a peacemaker appointed to solve a matter before the divided parties go to court.

Today all our prayers are offered to God through the mediation of Jesus Christ (John 15:16; 16:23-24). Regarding the ministry of Jesus Christ as the mediator of the new covenant, Hebrews 8:6 testifies, "He has obtained a more excellent ministry, by as much as He is also the mediator of a better covenant, which has been enacted on better promises." Here the word "better" is a translation of the Greek word κρείττων (*kreittōn*), which means "stronger" or "superior." In this context it highlights the superiority of the new covenant over the old covenant. Thus Jesus Christ is the guarantor of a better covenant (Heb 7:22) and the only true mediator. First Timothy 2:5 also states, "There is one God, and one mediator also between God and men, the man Christ Jesus."

III. A Covenant for All Generations to Keep

The Sinaitic covenant between God and the people of Israel was ratified when the people arrived at the wilderness of Sinai, the eleventh campsite. The covenant was reaffirmed forty years later, on the plains of Moab, the forty-first campsite, just before Israel's entry into Canaan. For this reason it is called the covenant on the plains of Moab. God's reaffirmation of the Sinaitic covenant through Moses testifies to its importance and emphasizes that Israel was to remember the covenant before entering Canaan.

What did Moses especially emphasize as he reiterated the Sinaitic covenant on the plains of Moab (in the book of Deuteronomy)?

The Human Party in the Sinaitic Covenant: "All Those of Us Alive Here Today"

Deuteronomy 5:2 states, "The LORD our God made a covenant with us at Horeb." Deuteronomy 5:3 then emphasizes that the other party in the covenant, besides the Lord, was the nation of Israel—every one of the people there that day: "us, with all those of us alive here today" (פֹּה הַיּוֹם כֻּלָּנוּ חַיִּים, *foh hayyom kullanu hayyim*). Deuteronomy 5:3 may be read with the following emphasis: "The LORD did not make this covenant with our fathers, but with us, that is, with all of us alive here today." The phrase "with us," which is the first-person plural pronoun (אִתָּנוּ אֲנַחְנוּ, *ittanu anahnu*), is repeated twice. The words "our" and "us" occur a total of five times in 5:2–3. This emphasizes that the party involved in God's covenant was not the forefathers but the nation of Israel—all those who were standing on the plains of Moab.

This emphasizes the presentness of the covenant. The Sinaitic covenant was not an old covenant made with the forefathers in the past but a covenant made with those who were living and standing before God right then. The timing of God's covenant is always present, that is, today (הַיּוֹם, *hayyom*).

The place of the covenant was also not limited to Mount Sinai, where the Ten Commandments were given. It also included "here" (פֹּה, *poh*), the land of Moab to the east of the Jordan where the second generation of Israelites were dwelling (Deut 1:5).

God's covenant is made with those of us living here and now. The forefathers who had experienced God's presence and entered into the covenant at Mount Sinai about forty years before had all been killed due to their disobedience and grumbling. Those who had been killed because of disobedience, therefore, were no longer parties in the covenant. The second generation of Israelites was faithful and obedient to the covenant and thus safely journeyed through the wilderness. This second generation—those who had reached "here" at the plains of Moab in that day—was the party with whom God made the covenant.

Extension of the Human Party in the Sinaitic Covenant: "Those Who Are Not with Us Here Today" (Deut 29:14-15)

The first generation of Israelites had already died by the time this message was proclaimed (Num 14:28-35; 26:63-65; Deut 2:14-15). Thus the phrase "those who stand here with us today" in Deuteronomy 29:15 refers to the second generation who were listening to Moses' sermon on the plains of Moab. Moreover, the phrase "those who are not with us here today" (29:15) signifies a limitless extension of the party involved in the covenant transcending both time and space. This includes those who are Jews not only outwardly but also inwardly through the circumcision of the heart (Rom 2:28-29), that is, all believers who have become spiritual Israelites. We who have become spiritual descendants of Abraham by the righteousness of faith (Rom 4:11-16; Gal 3:7-9, 29) are also participants in this everlasting covenant.

The reaffirmation of the Sinaitic covenant on the plains of Moab and the extension of its meaning to future generations reminds us of the infinite power of life in God's Word. The Bible is meaningful not only to past generations but also to us here, as it is the Word of life and a living covenant. Covenants between human beings become invalid when one of the parties dies (Rom 7:1-3), but God is the Alpha and the Omega, the beginning and the end (Rev 1:8, 17; 2:8; 21:6; 22:13). He is the living One who is the same yesterday, today, and tomorrow (Heb 1:12; 13:8). His covenant, therefore, is everlasting. He is the God of believers who live today with faith that is alive; He is the God of the living (Matt 22:32; Mark 12:26-27; Luke 20:38). We must remember that we are the central figures of this everlasting covenant because this covenant is for us who are alive today.

Once God enters into a covenant, He keeps it faithfully at all times, yesterday, today, and tomorrow, without altering it. God is faithful to His covenant with steadfast love and sincerity (Ps 89:33-35). Indeed, He is not a man that He should change or annul His own promise (Num 23:19; 1 Sam 15:29). The earth may change and the mountains may shake, but the covenant that God Himself established shall stand firm and not be shaken (Isa 54:10).

In Psalm 105:8–10, the psalmist sang that God's covenant with Abraham was for a thousand generations and an everlasting covenant for the Israelites. He praised the faithfulness and eternity of God's covenant (1 Chr 16:15–18). The book of Deuteronomy specifically emphasizes the eternal efficacy of the Sinaitic covenant, as the covenant is valid not only for those on Mount Sinai but also for all generations to come. This covenant, therefore, is called the covenant for all generations. God's covenant is not a dead covenant bound to the past but a living one that gives life to God's people in the present. That is to say, the tense of the covenant is the present; the place of the covenant is here; the party involved in the covenant with God are those of us who are living today.

IV. A Covenant with a Clear Revelation of Redemption

God's covenant in His redemptive administration has never been broken; it has always progressed precisely and been fulfilled with perfection. God first covenanted with Adam and Noah and continued to enter into covenants with Abraham, Isaac, and Jacob. The Sinaitic covenant was not independent from these other covenants. It lay within the progressive development of the previous covenants. The proclamation of the law on Mount Sinai did not stop or nullify the previous covenants; rather, it developed them even more. The law that came 430 years after God's original covenant could not nullify or invalidate His original promise:

> What I am saying is this: the Law, which came four hundred and thirty years later, does not invalidate a covenant previously ratified by God, so as to nullify the promise. (Gal 3:17)

All covenants in God's redemptive history aim to save sinful mankind. In particular, the Sinaitic covenant was ratified with an even greater focus on sin and demonstrated its solution for this problem most explicitly. Thus the Sinaitic covenant reveals that the purpose of God's covenant was to redeem His chosen people. The apostle Paul explained that the law, the essence of the Sinaitic covenant, manifests the following redemptive revelations.

The Law Humbles Us by Making Us Thoroughly Aware of the Nature of Sin

Keeping the law does not lead to salvation for mankind (Rom 5:13–20; Gal 2:16–21; 3:19–22; Heb 7:19–28). Thus the apostle Paul posed the question, "Why the Law then?" and answered by saying, "It was added because of transgressions" (Gal 3:19). This answer means that because people broke God's laws and their transgression increased, God gave the laws so that people could understand the multitude of their sins (Rom 4:15; 5:20). This is comparable to what is written in Romans 7:7–8. The law does not possess the power to save mankind from sin (Acts 13:39; Gal 3:11). It leads us only to a keen awareness of sin (Rom 7:7; 1 Tim 1:9–10), makes sin come alive (Rom 7:9), exposes sin as utterly sinful (Rom 7:13), and eventually causes transgression to increase (Rom 5:20). Therefore Paul said, "By the works of the Law no flesh will be justified in His sight; for through the Law comes the knowledge of sin" (Rom 3:20).

Ultimately, the law is like a prison for sinners. It oppresses, imprisons, and guards everyone who does not abide by it. The law has shut up all humanity under the authority of sin, the curse of the law, and God's judgment (Rom 3:19; Gal 3:10, 22–23; see also Gal 4:3–5). The apostle Paul thus made an honest and desperate confession that our flesh is utterly weak and powerless to keep the law or reject the powers of sin (Rom 7:14–25).

The Jews, however, did not understand this purpose of the law. They considered themselves righteous and were filled with a sense of entitlement as a covenant people and thus treated the lawless Gentiles as unclean sinners (Gal 2:15). In reality, they were already utterly condemned sinners (see Matt 3:7–10). Moreover, their ignorance of God's original purpose to lead His people to Christ through the law (Rom 3:21; Gal 3:24) resulted in their slavery to the law and a fatal outcome: the total rejection of Jesus Christ (Acts 13:26–27). Hence the apostle Paul made a sharp criticism that the Jews dwelling in "the present Jerusalem," that is, the earthly Jerusalem, were "in slavery with her children" because they misunderstood the fundamental purpose of the law. They could have become "the Jerusalem above" (Gal 4:26) had they understood God's providence for salvation (Gal 4:25–31).

The Law Leads to Great Anticipation of Jesus Christ

Only through the law that exposes sin can human beings realize that they are destined to perish and so entrust themselves to Christ. The law brutally exposes the sinfulness of mankind and leads them to long after redemption in Jesus Christ. In Galatians 3:19, Paul asked, "Why the Law then? … until the seed would come to whom the promise had been made." He continued, "The Scripture has shut up everyone under sin, so that the promise by faith in Jesus Christ might be given to those who believe" (Gal 3:22). The law leads us to a realization of sin and the anticipation of Jesus Christ, the promised seed, and acts as a tutor that leads us to Christ (Gal 3:24–29).

Jesus Christ was hung on a cross and became a curse for us and "redeemed us from the curse of the Law" (Gal 3:13). At the fullness of the time, Jesus was born under the law "that He might redeem those who were under the Law, that we might receive the adoption as sons" (Gal 4:4–5). Hebrews 2:14–15 testifies that Jesus came in the flesh to this earth so that He "might free those who through fear of death were subject to slavery all their lives."

Jesus did not come to abolish the law but to fulfill the law (Matt 5:17–20; Rom 10:4). The law is still the means to righteousness (Rom 2:13), and faith does not abolish the law but establishes it (Rom 3:31). Thus Jesus shed new light on the understanding of the law as He repeated six times, "You have heard that … but I say to you," in the Sermon on the Mount, and He fulfilled the law Himself (Matt 5:21–22, 27–28, 31–32, 33–34, 38–39, 43–44).

The purpose of Jesus' coming to the earth was to deliver us from sin and give us true freedom (John 8:32). All have sinned; no one is without sin (Rom 3:10, 23; 5:12). Even the smallest sins, once committed, viciously trap and enslave those who have committed them.

When Jesus was teaching in the temple, the scribes and the Pharisees brought a woman caught in adultery and set her in the midst of the people. They asked Jesus, "Now in the Law Moses commanded us to stone such women; what then do You say?" (John 8:5). Meanwhile, Jesus bent down and wrote with His finger on the ground, but they persisted in asking the question (John 8:6–7). Then Jesus stood up and said, "He who is without sin among you, let him be the first to throw a stone at her" and stooped down again and wrote on the ground (John 8:7–8). The crowd was pricked in their consciences, and they left one by one, from the older to the younger, until only Jesus and the woman were left (John 8:9). Then Jesus said to her, "I do not condemn you, either. Go. From now on sin no more" (John 8:11). Jesus proclaimed this woman's liberation from the sins that had bound her. Indeed, sin results in terrifying condemnation and oppression, extreme humiliation, and the curse of being stoned to death (John 8:3–5). Yet Jesus proclaimed true freedom through His Word to this woman standing at the threshold of death (John 8:11). Jesus said to her, "You will know the truth, and the truth will make you free" (John 8:32). He continued, "Truly, truly, I say to you, everyone who commits sin is the slave of sin. The slave does not remain in the house forever; the son does remain forever. So if the Son makes you free, you will be free indeed" (John 8:34–36).

We must hold firmly to the truth and stand at the center of freedom. The mind set on the flesh is death, but the mind set on the Spirit is life and peace (Rom 8:6). Without the spirit of Christ, we do not belong to Him (Rom 8:9). Our bodies do not belong to us; they are the temples of the Holy Spirit purchased with the blood of Christ (1 Cor 6:19–20). Therefore, whether we eat or drink, or whatever we do, we must do it for the glory of God (1 Cor 10:31) and present our bodies and entire lives as living sacrifices, holy and pleasing to God (Rom 12:1).

CHAPTER

5

THE SINAITIC COVENANT THAT MUST BE AFFIRMED CONTINUOUSLY

I. Israel, the Firstborn of Redemptive History

The Israelites in Egypt were in the same wretched state as an abandoned child. Ezekiel 16:4 states, "As for your birth, on the day you were born your navel cord was not cut, nor were you washed with water for cleansing; you were not rubbed with salt or even wrapped in cloths." Ezekiel 16:6 further states, "When I passed by you and saw you squirming in your blood, I said to you while you were in your blood, 'Live!' Yes, I said to you while you were in your blood, 'Live!'" More fragile than a bruised reed and more feeble than dimming candlelight, such a child barely holds on to each breath. If no one takes care of the child, its life will soon fade away. Ezekiel 16:5 states, "You were thrown out into the open field, for you were abhorred on the day you were born."

The word "abhorred" is גֹּעַל (*goal*) in Hebrew and means "to loathe" or "to disdain." This expression describes the misery of Israel in slavery in Egypt, left abandoned and helpless. God took this new-born that had been abandoned mercilessly by the wayside into His bosom and brought it out in the exodus.

God then proclaimed that Israel was His "firstborn." He commanded Moses to declare before Pharaoh, "Israel is My son, My firstborn … Let My son go that he may serve Me" (Exod 4:22-23). The Israelites were mere slaves to Pharaoh, but God proclaimed that they were His son, His firstborn. This is similar to the ancient Near Eastern practice in which a master chooses a particular slave and adopts him as his son. From the exodus until their arrival at Mount Sinai, the Israelites' wilderness journey can be described as a guided journey on God's spread wings. Just as an eagle stretches its wings to carry its young, so God carried Israel, His young firstborn, on His back for forty years. In Exodus 19:4, God proclaimed, "You yourselves have seen what I did to the Egyptians, and how I bore you on eagles' wings, and brought you to Myself."

The Sinaitic covenant was a legal agreement officially made between God and His adopted son, Israel. God was the Father of Israel, and Israel was His son called by His name (see Num 6:27; Deut 28:10; 2 Chr 7:14; Isa 43:7; 63:19; Jer 14:9; 15:16; Dan 9:19). After the Sinaitic covenant, the Israelites who had become God's son were numbered as an army (Num 1:1-3) and grew into a nameworthy redemptive-historical firstborn who could build the kingdom of God.

II. A Covenant Reaffirmed

The Sinaitic covenant was made with the first generation of Israelites at the beginning of the exodus era. When this covenant was later reaffirmed on the plains of Moab, where the Israelites were in their forty-first encampment just before entering into Canaan, it was called the covenant on the plains of Moab. In the fortieth year of the exodus, on the first day of the eleventh month, God made the covenant in Moab with the second generation of Israelites who were about to enter into the land of Canaan (Deut 1:3; 29:1–29).

By this time everyone belonging to the older generation, except for Joshua and Caleb, had already died before the Israelites crossed the brook Zered (Num 14:26–35; 26:64–65; Deut 2:13–15). The older generation of people who had entered into the Sinaitic covenant had been God's firstborn—those over the age of twenty years who could go out to war. They had totaled 603,550 soldiers (Num 1:46). Among these, 603,548 men had died, except for Joshua and Caleb. Those who had died had not believed in God's Word and had not obeyed it; instead, they had grumbled against the Lord. This was in fulfillment of the prophecy in Numbers 14:29–30: "Your corpses will fall in this wilderness, even all your numbered men, according to your complete number from twenty years old and upward, who have grumbled against Me. Surely you shall not come into the land in which I swore to settle you, except Caleb the son of Jephunneh and Joshua the son of Nun."

Through the renewal of His covenant, God now established the second generation as His firstborn and retold them His Word to use them as leaders in the new work of redemption. They were to enter the land of Canaan as central figures in building the kingdom of God on this earth.

As previously examined in chapter 4, "The Redemptive-Historical Meaning of the Sinaitic Covenant," Moses renewed the covenant with the second generation, emphasizing that the other party besides God in the Sinaitic covenant was not made up of the forefathers who died in the wilderness but of the Israelites who were currently receiving the Word. In Deuteronomy 5:2–3, Moses said, "The LORD our God made a covenant with us at Horeb. The LORD did not make this covenant with our fathers, but with us, with all those of us alive here today." Here Moses emphasized that the covenant of Mount Sinai (Mount Horeb) was no longer for the first generation who had died in the wilderness. Moses declared that the Sinaitic covenant was now with the second generation standing before God at that moment in time, even though they had not participated in the covenant ratification.

The renewal was to remind the second generation about all the grace that God poured upon them in the past. This generation had neither known the arduous life of slavery in Egypt nor experienced firsthand God's work of salvation that had parted the Red Sea. Yet because they were the new covenant people who would enter the land of Canaan as God's firstborn and build His kingdom, God called upon them to possess a strong sense of responsibility and live in absolute obedience to the Word. Hence Deuteronomy 4:1 presses, "O Israel, listen to the statutes and the judgments which I am teaching you to perform, so that you may live and go in and take possession of the land which the LORD, the God of your fathers, is giving you."

III. A Covenant that Had to Be Affirmed and Reaffirmed Continuously

The Sinaitic covenant was ratified in the third month of 1446 BC and reaffirmed in the eleventh month of 1407 BC. The Sinaitic covenant, however, is ultimately a covenant that must be reaffirmed continuously. This is because Deuteronomy 29:14–15 states, "Not with you alone am I making this covenant and this oath, but both with those who stand here with us today in the presence of the LORD our God and with those who are not with us here today." The verse clarifies that the efficacy of the covenant extends even to "those who are not with us here today." To whom do these people refer? They refer to the descendants of the Israelites who would be born in the future. Additionally, they include spiritual Israelites who would emerge in the gospel of Christ (Rom 2:28–29; 4:11, 16; Gal 3:7–9, 29). The covenant renewal resulted in expanding the recipients of the covenant. This foreshadowed the eventual renewal of the essence of the Sinaitic covenant—the new covenant—which would ultimately grow into a universal covenant. We who exist today also did not directly participate in the original ratification of the covenant. Nevertheless, the continual reaffirmation of the Sinaitic covenant leads us to see this "new covenant" that is fulfilled in Jesus Christ. We who are here today, therefore, transcend time and space to inherit the Sinaitic covenant by faith and reaffirm it as the eternal covenant in our lives.

The Ten Commandments are the essence of the Sinaitic covenant that we will inherit. God gave the Ten Commandments (Exod 20:1-17) prior to the specific laws (Exod 20:22-23:33). Thus the Ten Commandments are the head of all the laws, and all the laws depend on them. Jesus also summarized the Ten Commandments as the two commandments "Love the Lord your God" and "Love your neighbor as yourself" and explained that "on these two commandments depend the whole Law and the Prophets" (Matt 22:36-40). The verb "depend" is κρεμάννυμι (*kremannymi*) in Greek and means "hang." Accordingly, Jesus proclaimed that all the laws hang on the Ten Commandments, as they are the head, the core, and the essence of all the laws.

Starting in the next chapter, we will closely examine the Ten Commandments—the essence of the Sinaitic covenant—beginning with Moses' eight ascents of Mount Sinai. As we understand God's intent for the Ten Commandments and keep the commandments in a way that is pleasing to Him, the Sinaitic covenant will continue to be reaffirmed in our era, and the kingdom of God will expand increasingly upon this earth.

PART II

MOSES' EIGHT ASCENTS OF MOUNT SINAI

PART II

God called one man, Abraham, and entered into a covenant with him. He then founded Israel through him and devised a plan to save all humanity through this nation. During its 430 years in Egypt, Israel grew into a great nation of nearly two million people (Exod 12:37–38, 40–41; Num 1:45–46; Acts 7:17; see also Gen 15:13–14). After calling Moses at the burning bush and establishing him as their leader, God finally brought the Israelites out of Egypt on the fifteenth day of the first month in 1446 BC (the first year of the exodus; Num 33:3). That year the Israelites arrived at the wilderness of Sinai on the first day of the third month (Exod 19:1) and entered into the Sinaitic covenant with God (Exod 19:1–24:11). The Israelites settled there for eleven months and twenty days until they set forth to the wilderness of Paran on the twentieth day of the second month in the second year after the exodus (Num 10:11–12).

The year spent in the wilderness of Sinai brought about the dawning of a new nation: the Hebrew people went from being slaves in Egypt to becoming the nation of Israel, filled with hope and passion. This was a founding era for the nation as well as a preparatory period for Israel's conquest of Canaan. As soon as Israel arrived at the wilderness of Sinai, Moses ascended and descended Mount Sinai a total of eight times. This was a critical time during which Moses mediated between God and Israel for the ratification of the Sinaitic covenant (Exod 24:1–11). He also received the Ten Commandments (Exod 20:1–17), the specific laws (Exod 20:22–23:33), and the blueprint for the tabernacle (Exod 25:1–31:11) and then delivered them to the people.

CHAPTER

6

———
———

Divine Providence that Led the Israelites to Mount Sinai

God promised Abraham on multiple occasions that He would give the land of Canaan to his descendants (Gen 12:1-3, 7; 13:14-17; 15:13-21; 17:7-8). God later saved the people of Israel from their suffering in Egypt and led them into Canaan according to His covenant in the past. While only seventy persons had migrated to Egypt (Gen 46:26-27), they had multiplied and grown into a mighty nation of about two million people during their 430 years in Egypt so that even the Egyptian Pharaoh felt threatened (Exod 1:7-22). At last, on the day when Israel's 430-year-long sojourn in Egypt was completed (Exod 12:40-41), God, by His great power and mighty hand (Exod 32:11), rescued nearly two million men and women of Israel and even their livestock from the cruel hand of the Egyptians (Exod 12:37-41).

On that day, in fulfillment of the covenant of the torch ratified during Abraham's time, the Israelites came out of Egypt with great wealth (Gen 15:14; see also Exod 3:22; 11:2-3; 12:36; Ps 105:37-38). By God's sovereign and mysterious providence, lowly slaves became exceedingly wealthy overnight.

The following three Hebrew verbs concisely depict God's providence by which He freed Israel from Egypt and led them to Mount Sinai:

- The Hebrew עָבַד (*avad*), which means "to serve"
- The Hebrew זָבַח (*zavah*), which means "to offer a sacrifice"
- The Hebrew חָגַג (*hagag*), which means "to keep festival"

I. Divine Providence for the Israelites to Worship God

God said, "Certainly I will be with you [Moses], and this shall be the sign to you that it is I who have sent you: when you have brought the people out of Egypt, you shall worship God at this mountain" (Exod 3:12).

This verse testifies that the Israelites' worship of God on "this mountain" (Mount Sinai) would be the sign that God had sent Moses. The word "worship" is עָבַד (*avad*), which means "to work, perform acts of worship, or serve" (Gen 14:4; 15:13; 27:29; 29:18, 20; 30:29; Ps 100:2). In general, it refers to the whole aspect of a person's faith in God (Deut 6:13; 10:12, 20; 11:13; Josh 24:14-15; Mal 3:14). As the ten plagues smote the land of Egypt, Moses held onto this word from his first calling and proclaimed before the stubborn Pharaoh several times, "The Lord, the God of the Hebrews, sent me to you, saying, 'Let My people go, that they may serve Me in the wilderness'" (Exod 4:23; 7:16; 8:1, 20; 9:1, 13; 10:3; see also Exod 10:24-26). With the authority of God's Word given to him, Moses made his proclamations with boldness, like a commander declaring his decision to his staff.

The actual purpose of the exodus was for the Israelites to serve God, which was the rightful duty of God's firstborn (Exod 4:22-23). For this reason God told Moses at the time of his calling that the Israelites' worship of God at Mount Sinai would be the sign to him that it was God who had sent him (Exod 3:12).

Even the purpose of the ten plagues that God sent upon Egypt was to release Israel, His firstborn, so that the people could worship Him (Exod 10:1–3). When the eighth plague of locusts was forewarned (Exod 10:4–6), Pharaoh's servants pleaded with Pharaoh, "Let the men go, that they may serve the LORD their God. Do you not realize that Egypt is destroyed?" (Exod 10:7). Momentarily shaken, Pharaoh said to Moses and Aaron, "Go, serve the LORD your God! Who are the ones that are going?" (Exod 10:8). Moses and Aaron answered that they would go with their young and old, their sons and daughters, and their flocks and herds (Exod 10:9). Instantly Pharaoh changed his words, saying, "Go now, the men among you, and serve the LORD" (Exod 10:11). He continued to be stubborn and would not release Israel.

II. Divine Providence for the Israelites to Sacrifice to God

God commanded Moses to go, along with the elders of Israel, and tell Pharaoh, "Please, let us go a three days' journey into the wilderness, that we may sacrifice to the LORD our God" (Exod 3:18; see Exod 3:16–18; 5:3). Here the verb "sacrifice" comes from the Hebrew word זָבַח (*zavah*), which means "to slaughter for a sacrifice." When this verb occurs with the preposition "to" (לְ, *le*), the phrase means "to sacrifice to someone" (see also 1 Sam 1:3). When Moses and Aaron proclaimed these words to Pharaoh, the tyrant persecuted the Israelites all the more (Exod 5:6–23). Only after the plague of flies, the fourth of the ten plagues, did he tell Moses and Aaron to sacrifice to God but to do so in Egypt (Exod 8:25). When Moses responded that the Israelites should go to the wilderness since the Egyptians despised slaughtering animals for sacrifice (Exod 8:26–27), Pharaoh allowed them to leave under certain conditions: "You shall not go very far away. Make supplication for me" (Exod 8:28). As soon as the swarms of flies left

Egypt, however, Pharaoh hardened his heart even more and did not allow the Israelites to leave (Exod 8:31–32).

From this time on, the plagues' intensity increased and went beyond tormenting people to causing direct financial loss. The fifth plague caused damage to the Egyptian livestock (Exod 9:1–7), and the sixth plague caused a skin disease, namely boils, on the bodies of every Egyptian and animal (Exod 9:8–12). Even the magicians were struck with boils and could not stand before Moses from that time on (Exod 9:11).

God spared not only the Israelites but also their livestock, as the animals were necessary for the sacrifice. Israel's livestock was set apart from that of the Egyptians, and none were killed (Exod 9:4, 6). During the seventh plague of hail, Goshen, the land where the Israelites dwelt, was also set apart (Exod 9:26). Among Pharaoh's servants, those "who feared the word of the LORD" brought their servants and livestock into their houses to avoid the plague (Exod 9:19–20). Yet those who "paid no regard to the word of the LORD" left their servants and livestock in the field (Exod 9:21) and incurred great losses (Exod 9:22–25).

During the ninth plague of darkness, Pharaoh said, "Go, serve the LORD; only let your flocks and your herds be detained. Even your little ones may go with you" (Exod 10:24). Moses, however, replied, "Our livestock too shall go with us; not a hoof shall be left behind, for we shall take some of them to serve the LORD our God. And until we arrive there, we ourselves do not know with what we shall serve the LORD" (Exod 10:26). Moses boldly declared before Pharaoh that every person and all their belongings must go with them to serve God with nothing left behind.

Pharaoh finally surrendered before God's sovereign work. In the final plague, that of the death of the firstborn, God struck down all the Egyptians' eldest sons, from the firstborn of Pharaoh to the firstborn of the captive in a dungeon to the firstborn of the slave girl behind the handmill and even to the firstborn of the livestock (Exod

11:5; 12:29). Only then did Pharaoh submit and say, "Take both your flocks and your herds, as you have said, and go, and bless me also" (Exod 12:32).

By God's sovereign work, all the Israelites' livestock was set apart as holy to serve God (see Exod 3:12, 18; 4:23; 5:3; 7:16; 8:1, 20, 25, 27–28; 9:1, 13; 10:3, 8, 11, 24–26; 12:31–32). The Israelites brought out all their livestock (flocks and herds) to sacrifice to God and left nothing behind. A very large number of livestock of flocks and herds came out of Egypt during the exodus along with the Israelites (Exod 12:38).

III. Divine Providence for the Israelites to Celebrate with a Feast Before God

Moses and Aaron stood before Pharaoh by the authority of God's Word. They boldly proclaimed, "Thus says the LORD, the God of Israel, 'Let My people go that they may celebrate a feast [חַג, hag] to Me in the wilderness'" (Exod 5:1).

Exodus 10:9 also testifies, "Moses said, 'We shall go with our young and our old; with our sons and our daughters, with our flocks and our herds we shall go, for we must hold a feast to the LORD.'" The Hebrew word for "feast" (חַג, hag), originated from the word חָגַג (hagag), which means "to celebrate, dance, keep a feast, circle, or cycle." This is because feasts come around at the same time each year and are festive by nature.

Just before the exodus, God gave the Israelites the standard to determine the date of the feast by saying, "This month shall be the beginning of months for you; it is to be the first month of the year to you" (Exod 12:2). He also spoke of the Passover, saying, "This day will be a memorial to you, and you shall celebrate it as a feast [חַג, hag] to the LORD; throughout your generations you are to celebrate it as a permanent ordinance" (Exod 12:14; see also Exod 12:17–18).

So we see that even before the exodus, God had plainly instructed the Israelites as to what they were to do once they arrived at Mount Sinai. Ultimately, God's three purposes for Israel—that they worship Him, sacrifice to Him, and celebrate with a feast before Him—were preparation for Him to enter into a covenant with them when Moses ascended and descended Mount Sinai as many as eight times to receive the Ten Commandments and ratify the covenant. This was a crucial turning point in redemptive history, a transition from the focus on Abraham the individual to the grander focus on the entire nation of Israel.

CHAPTER

7

Overview of Moses' Eight Ascents of Mount Sinai

While entering into the Sinaitic covenant, Moses ascended Mount Sinai (7,497 feet or 2,285 meters in altitude) a total of eight times. Moses' eight ascents of Mount Sinai are recorded in detail in Exodus 19:1–25; 20:1–21; 24:1–18; 32:7–35; 33:1–6; 34:1–35; Deut 4:10–40; 5:1–33; 9:9–29; and 10:1–11. The timeline of his eight ascents of Mount Sinai bears great redemptive-historical significance and provides important background information for the Ten Commandments, the tabernacle, and the feasts.

Moses ascended Mount Sinai breathlessly, climbing to "the top of the mountain" (רֹאשׁ הָהָר, *rosh hahar*), not to its foot or side (Exod 19:20; 34:2). Moreover, he prepared early in the morning and ascended the mountain, faithfully fulfilling his role as mediator for the ratification of the covenant (Exod 24:4; 34:2, 4).[7]

After Israel's arrival in the wilderness of Sinai on Sunday, the first day of the third month (Exod 19:1), Moses began his ascent of Mount Sinai on the next day, Monday, the second day of the third month. The eight ascents of Mount Sinai ended with his last descent on Monday, the tenth day of the seventh month, spanning 127 days in total.

The following is a brief summary of Moses' eight ascents and descents.

*The years for the exodus and Moses' ascents of Mount Sinai are dated in Tishri years.

Order		Content
First	Ascent, second day of the third month (Mon)	**God proposed the Sinaitic covenant** (Exod 19:1–6) • After the sons of Israel arrived in the wilderness of Sinai and camped in front of Mount Sinai, Moses ascended Mount Sinai (Exod 19:1–3). • God proclaimed for the first time that Israel's exodus had been by His absolute power and sovereign grace (Exod 19:4). • God promised that if the chosen people of Israel would obey His Word and keep His covenant, they would be His "own possession among all the peoples, … a kingdom of priests and a holy nation" (Exod 19:5–6; see also Deut 4:6).
	Descent	**Moses conveyed to the people God's proposal for the Sinaitic covenant** (Exod 19:7–8) • Moses called the elders of the people and told them all that the Lord had said to him (Exod 19:7). • "All the people answered together and said, 'All that the LORD has spoken we will do!'" (Exod 19:8).

Second	Ascent, third day of the third month (Tues)	**God commanded Israel to consecrate themselves for three days** (Exod 19:8-13; Deut 4:10) • Moses reported Israel's words to God (Exod 19:8-9). • God came down in a thick cloud (Exod 19:9). • God commanded, "Go to the people and consecrate them today and tomorrow, and let them wash their garments; and let them be ready for the third day" (Exod 19:10-11). • God commanded the people to set bounds all around the mountain and prohibited them from going to the mountain or even touching its border (Exod 19:12). Anyone who violated the border was to be stoned or shot through to death (Exod 19:13).
	Descent	**Moses conveyed God's command for consecration, and the Israelites obeyed** (Exod 19:14-15) • Moses consecrated the Israelites, and they washed their garments (Exod 19:14). • Moses gave the instruction, "Be ready for the third day; do not go near a woman" (Exod 19:15).
Third	Ascent, fifth day of the third month (Thurs)	**The Lord came down upon Mount Sinai on the morning of the third day** (Thursday, the fifth day of the third month) (Exod 19:16-19) • On the morning of the third day, thunder, lightning, and a thick cloud were upon the mountain, and a very loud trumpet sounded, so all the people in the camp trembled (Exod 19:16).

- Moses brought the people out from the camp to meet with God at the foot of the mountain. The Lord descended amid the fire; Mount Sinai was filled with smoke that rose as from a furnace, and the entire mountain quaked violently (Exod 19:17–18).
- As the trumpet sound grew louder, Moses spoke, and God answered by voice (Exod 19:19).

God strictly prohibited the people from approaching Mount Sinai (Exod 19:20–24)
- The Lord called Moses to the top of Mount Sinai, and Moses ascended (Exod 19:20).
- The Lord earnestly commanded Moses to forbid the people to approach Mount Sinai, saying, "Go down, warn the people" (Exod 19:21).
- The Lord commanded the priests to consecrate themselves lest He break out against them (Exod 19:22).
- Instead of immediately obeying the Lord, Moses assured the Lord that the people would not approach Mount Sinai. The Lord rebuked him, saying, "Go down and ... do not let the priests and the people break through to come up to the LORD" (Exod 19:23–24).

Descent	**Moses immediately obeyed in response to God's rebuke (Exod 19:25)**
	- Moses immediately went down to the people and warned them (Exod 19:25).

Fourth	Ascent, sixth day of the third month (Fri)	**God bestowed the Ten Commandments and the law** (Exod 20:1–23:33; Deut 5:1–6:9), **and the people assembled** (Deut 5:22; 9:10; 10:4; 18:16) • God spoke the Ten Commandments (Exod 20:1–17) before all Israel in His voice (Exod 20:22; Deut 4:12, 33; 5:22, 24). • After hearing the Ten Commandments spoken in God's voice and witnessing His majesty, the people were terrified and pleaded to receive His Word through Moses the mediator. The laws (Exod 20:22–23:33) were given indirectly to Israel through Moses the mediator (see Exod 20:18–21; Deut 5:22– 33). • God commanded Moses to come near Him as a representative of the entire people (Exod 24:1–2; Deut 5:28–33).
	Descent	**Moses conveyed all God's Word to the people and recorded it** (Exod 24:3–4) • Moses came down from the mountain and conveyed all the Lord's Word and His ordinances. All the Israelites responded with one voice that they would keep all the Lord's words (Exod 24:3). • Moses stayed up all night and recorded all the words of the Lord (Exod 24:4). It was "the book of the covenant" (Exod 24:7). **The ratification ceremony for the Sinaitic covenant was held early the next morning (Saturday, the seventh day of the third month) (Exod 24:4–8)** • Early in the morning Moses built an altar at

		• the foot of the mountain and set up twelve pillars for the twelve tribes. He sent young men of Israel to offer burnt offerings and peace offerings (Exod 24:4–5). • Moses took the blood from the sacrificial offering and poured half of it in basins and sprinkled the other half on the altar (Exod 24:6). • Moses read the book of the covenant to the people, and they responded, "All that the LORD has spoken we will do!" (Exod 24:7). • Moses took the blood and sprinkled it upon the people and said, "Behold the blood of the covenant, which the LORD has made with you in accordance with all these words" (Exod 24:8).
Fifth	Ascent, seventh day of the third month (Sat)	**The covenant meal was shared on Mount Sinai (Exod 24:9–11)** • After the covenant ratification, Moses, Aaron, Nadab, Abihu, and seventy elders of Israel went up Mount Sinai (Exod 24:9). • When they saw the God of Israel, "under His feet there appeared to be a pavement of sapphire, as clear as the sky itself" (Exod 24:10). • They were called "the nobles of the sons of Israel." They saw God but did not die; they beheld God, ate, and drank (Exod 24:11).
	Descent	**No clear record of the descent is recorded** • Since Moses asked Aaron, Hur, and the elders to take care of the people just before his

		sixth ascent, Moses must have come down after the fifth ascent (Exod 24:12–14).
Sixth	Ascent, eighth day of the third month (Sun)	**Moses fasted and prayed for forty days for the first time; God gave the two stone tablets of the Ten Commandments written with His finger; Moses received the revelation of the pattern of the tabernacle** (Exod 24:12–31:18; 32:15–16; Deut 9:9–11) • The Lord said to Moses, "Come up to Me on the mountain and remain there," indicating that Moses might stay on the mountain for a long time (Exod 24:12). • The Lord said, "I will give you the stone tablets with the law and the commandment which I have written for their instruction" (Exod 24:12). • Moses went up to the mountain of God with Joshua, his servant (Exod 24:13). • As soon as Moses reached the top of the mountain, the cloud covered the mountain and the glory of the Lord rested on Mount Sinai (Exod 24:15–16). The cloud covered the mountain for six days, and on the seventh day (Saturday, the fourteenth day of the third month), the Lord called to Moses from the midst of the cloud (Exod 24:16). • Moses remained on the mountain for forty days and forty nights without eating bread or drinking water (Exod 24:18; Deut 9:9). • Moses received the revelation on the pattern of the tabernacle (Exod 25:1–31:11).

- God gave Moses the two stone tablets of the covenant (tablets of the testimony) written with His finger (Exod 24:12; 31:18; 32:15–16; Deut 9:9–11).

Descent, seventeenth day of the fourth month (Thurs)	**Israel worshiped the golden calf, and Moses destroyed the two stone tablets** (Exod 32:1–29; Deut 9:15–17, 21)

- When the Israelites saw that Moses was delayed in coming down from the mountain, they doubted the Word of the covenant and disobeyed the Lord and asked for a god to guide them. Under Aaron's leadership, all the people took off gold rings from their ears and made an idol in the form of a golden calf and worshiped it (Exod 32:1–8).
- Before Moses' descent God told Moses that He would wipe out the Israelites because they had quickly turned aside from God's Word and corrupted themselves. Moses pleaded with God in intercessory prayer (Exod 32:7–14; Deut 9:12–14; see also Deut 4:16, 25; 31:29).
- Moses came near to the camp and was angry at the sight of the people dancing before the golden calf. He threw the tablets at the foot of the mountain and shattered them (Exod 32:15–19, 25; Deut 9:15–17).
- On that day each Levite put his sword on his thigh and went back and forth from gate to gate in the camp and killed three thousand men among their brothers, friends, and neighbors (Exod 32:26–28).

Overview of Moses' Eight Ascents of Mount Sinai 93

		• After this slaughter of the golden-calf worshipers, Moses praised and blessed the Levites, saying, "Today you have been ordained for the service of the LORD, each one at the cost of his son and of his brother" (Exod 32:29, ESV).
Seventh	Ascent, eighteenth day of the fourth month (Fri)	**Moses interceded in prayer for forty days** (Exod 32:30–35; Deut 9:25–29; 10:10–11) • Moses went up Mount Sinai after saying, "I am going up to the LORD, perhaps I can make atonement for your sin" (Exod 32:30–31). • Moses put his life on the line and prayed for the forgiveness of the people's sin (Exod 32:31–32). • God struck the Israelites with a deadly plague after saying that He would punish them for their sin (Exod 32:33–35). • Deuteronomy 9:25 records, "I fell down before the LORD the forty days and nights," summarizing Moses' intercessory prayer regarding the people's worshiping of the golden calf (Deut 9:25–29; 10:10–11).
	Descent, twenty-eighth day of the fifth month (Tues)	**Israel removed their ornaments after Moses' forty-day intercessory prayer** (Exod 33:1–6); **a temporary tent of meeting for intercessory prayer was set up on Wednesday, the twenty-ninth day of the fifth month** (132 days after the exodus) (Exod 33:7–23) • All the Israelites removed their ornaments and repented after hearing the tragic message

		• that God would not go with them to the land flowing with milk and honey (Exod 33:1–6).
• Moses pitched a temporary tent of meeting outside the camp (Wednesday, the twenty-ninth day of the fifth month) and went out to it (Exod 33:7–8).
• When Moses entered the tent, God was present in the pillar of cloud and spoke with Moses just as a man talks with his friend (Exod 33:9–11).
• As a result of Moses' intercessory prayer, God promised that He would be with the Israelites and guide them to Canaan (Exod 33:12–17).
• God showed Moses His back when Moses asked God to reveal His glory to confirm His promise (Exod 33:18–23).
Eighth	Ascent, thirtieth day of the fifth month (Thurs)	**Moses fasted and prayed for forty days a second time; God bestowed the two stone tablets of the Ten Commandments written by the finger of God** (Exod 34:1–28; Deut 9:18, 10:1–4)
• According to God's command, Moses cut out two stone tablets just like the first ones and went up Mount Sinai early in the morning (Exod 34:4; Deut 10:1–3).
• God reestablished His covenant with the Israelites and sternly proclaimed the ordinance prohibiting idolatry to prevent further cases like the golden-calf incident (Exod 34:10–17).

	- God commanded Israel to observe the three feasts and the Sabbath (Exod 34:18–26). - Moses recorded the Word of God (Exod 34:10–26) and proclaimed that God had made a covenant with Israel (Exod 34:27). - Moses was with God on Mount Sinai and fasted for forty days and nights. God inscribed the words of the covenant, the Ten Commandments, on the tablets just as He had done the first time (Exod 34:28; Deut 9:18; 10:2, 4).
Descent, tenth day of the seventh month (Mon)	**Moses brought down the second set of stone tablets, and his face radiated** (Exod 34:29–35; Deut 10:5) - When Moses came down from the mountain with the two stone tablets of the testimony, the skin of his face was shining because he had spoken with the Lord (Exod 34:29). - Moses allowed the people of Israel, who were trembling in fear, to come near to him, and he delivered the words that the Lord had spoken to him on Mount Sinai (Exod 34:30–32). - After he had finished speaking, Moses covered his face with a veil. He took the veil off when he went before the Lord (Exod 34:33–34). - Moses covered his face again with a veil because the Israelites saw the radiance of his face (Exod 34:35).

CHAPTER

8

Moses' Eight Ascents of Mount Sinai

Mount Sinai is 7,497 feet (2,285 meters) high and sits on the barren wilderness of Sinai. It is a dangerous mountain, as most of it is covered with large rocks. *Sinai* (סִינַי) as in Mount Sinai means "a place with thorn bushes or shrubs," and is sometimes called *Horeb* (חֹרֵב, "a dry place"; Exod 3:1; 17:6; 33:6; Deut 1:2, 6, 19; 4:10, 15; 5:2; 9:8; 18:16; 29:1).

Mount Sinai was the place of the glorious presence of God, who created all things and governs life and death and the blessings and the curse. Mount Sinai, therefore, is not the mountain of Moses (*Jebel Musa*), as the Arabians call it, but "the mountain of God" (Exod 3:1; 4:27; 24:13; see also Exod 18:5; Num 10:33).

Far from the wilderness where the people had pitched their tents, Moses went up the high mountain to meet with God and came back down to deliver God's message. He did this eight times. We must not be ignorant of Moses' eight arduous ascents and descents by overlooking them as unnecessary labor or strange occurrences. Moses did not go up and down the mountain of his own volition; he moved according to God's command. He devotedly and faithfully fulfilled his crucial role as mediator between God and the Israelites in the momentous event of covenant ratification. Moses went down and conveyed God's holy will to the people so that the people would trust and follow God's promise. Then Moses went back up to God and delivered the Israelites' various thoughts and intentions (Exod 19:7–8; 20:18–21; 24:1–3, 12).

In each of the first through the fifth ascents, Moses ascended and descended on the same day, but in the sixth, seventh, and eighth ascents, he remained on the mountain to pray for forty days each time. During the sixth and eighth ascents, Moses offered up fasting prayers, while during the seventh ascent, he offered up intercessory prayers. In total Moses offered up three forty-day prayers:

- First forty-day fasting prayer (eighth day of the third month through seventeenth day of fourth month) (Exod 24:12–18; Deut 9:9–14)
- Second forty-day intercessory prayer (eighteenth day of the fourth month through twenty-eighth day of fifth month) (Exod 32:30–33:6; Deut 9:25–29; 10:10–11)
- Third forty-day fasting prayer (thirtieth day of the fifth month throughtenth day of seventh month) (Exod 34:1–28; Deut 9:18; 10:1–5)

The entire process—from the Israelites' exodus to their arrival at the wilderness of Sinai with eight ascents of Mount Sinai and the ratification of the Sinaitic covenant—was fulfilled mysteriously within God's profound providence. This process also revealed the future fulfillment of God's redemptive administration through His sovereign intervention. When we accurately understand the sequence and events during Moses' every ascent and closely examine the background, process, and timing behind the Sinaitic covenant ratification, we will gain deep and rich insight into God's redemptive providence therein.

I. The First Ascent: God Proposed the Sinaitic Covenant
(Exod 19:1-6)

> Monday, the second day of the third month
> (forty-six days after the exodus)

The Israelites arrived at the wilderness of Sinai on the third month of the first year of the exodus (1446 BC) and camped before "the mountain" (Mount Sinai; Exod 19:1-2). Upon their arrival at the wilderness of Sinai, Moses went up "to God" (Exod 19:3). Moses went up Mount Sinai without any instruction from God because he had been told before the exodus that an important event would occur on this mountain. In Exodus 3:12, God called Moses and said, "This shall be the sign to you that it is I who have sent you: when you have brought the people out of Egypt, you shall worship God at this mountain [Mount Sinai]."

When Moses went up the mountain, God called him and said, "You shall say to the house of Jacob and tell the sons of Israel" (Exod 19:3), and instructed him to prepare for the covenant ratification. Here God called the people with whom He would enter into the covenant the "house of Jacob" and the "sons of Israel." This is reminiscent of Jacob's history. Even though Jacob had fled from his brother, Esau, to Paddan-aram empty-handed (Gen 27:41-28:22), because God was with him he eventually returned to his homeland of Canaan with great possessions and a large family (Gen 31:1-18; 33:1-20). Similarly, the Israelites—the descendants of Jacob—were still in a pitiful state, for they had just left their lives of slavery. But they were about to experience great works, for God was going to ratify a covenant with them and be with them. Furthermore, just as God had promised Jacob (Gen 28:14; 35:11), the people of Israel had multiplied and become great in number (Exod 12:37-38; Num 1:45-46). Indeed, God had demonstrated His faithfulness in fulfilling His promise to their forefathers.

What message did Moses receive from God to deliver to the Israelites on his first ascent of Mount Sinai?

God's Sovereign Grace Delivered the Israelites from Egypt and Led Them to Where They Were

You yourselves have seen what I did to the Egyptians, and how I bore you on eagles' wings, and brought you to Myself. (Exod 19:4)

While God punished the Egyptians with His amazing power to save the Israelites who had been suffering in slavery, the Israelites were kept under God's complete protection as if on the outstretched wings of an eagle soaring through the sky. Just as an eagle carries its young on its wings, so God delivered Israel, His firstborn, from evil oppression (Deut 32:11; see also Isa 40:31).

God's deliverance began when He saved Israel from the ten plagues that He had sent upon Egypt and Pharaoh. The ten plagues were as follows: first, the plague of water turning into blood for seven days (Exod 7:14–25); second, the plague of frogs (Exod 8:1–15); third, the plague of the dust of the earth turning into gnats on men and beasts (Exod 8:16–19); fourth, the plague of flies (Exod 8:20–32); fifth, the plague of pestilence on the livestock (Exod 9:1–7); sixth, the plague of boils on men and beasts (Exod 9:8–12); seventh, the plague of hail and fire flashing in the midst of hail (Exod 9:18–35); eighth, the plague of locusts (Exod 10:1–20); ninth, the plague of darkness for three days (Exod 10:21–29); and tenth, the plague of the death of all the firstborn (Exod 11:4–10; 12:29–36). In the final plague against the firstborn, every firstborn in Egypt—from that of Pharaoh who sat on the throne to the firstborn of the slave girl who was behind the handmill and even the firstborn of the captive in the dungeon—was dead; even every firstborn of the livestock was dead (Exod 11:5; 12:29–30).

After the final plague, Pharaoh again changed his mind about allowing Israel to leave Egypt. When he began chasing Israel, God moved the angel of the Lord and the pillar of cloud that had been advancing before Israel so that they now stood behind the people. Then He sent darkness to the Egyptian camp but gave light to Israel's camp. He divided the Red Sea by sending a strong east wind (Exod 14:21) and allowed all Israel to cross on dry land amid the sea (Exod 14:1-22, 31). Indeed, Israel crossed the Red Sea on eagles' wings, upon God's back. Moreover, Israel experienced God the healer at Marah in the wilderness of Shur (Exod 15:22-26), the God who provided manna and quail in the wilderness of Sin (Exod 16:1-36), the God who gave water from the rock in Rephidim (Exod 17:1-7), and the God who gave the victory of Yahweh Nissi (Exod 17:8-16) during the battle against the Amalekites.

All Israel without exception arrived safely in the wilderness of Sinai, where Mount Sinai, the mountain of God, was located. This was by the guidance of God's absolute sovereignty, which no other power could hinder or oppose.

God Promised that If the Chosen People of Israel Would Obey His Voice and Keep His Covenant, They Would Be His Own Possession, a Kingdom of Priests, and a Holy Nation

> *"If you will indeed obey My voice and keep My covenant, then you shall be My own possession among all the peoples, for all the earth is Mine; and you shall be to Me a kingdom of priests and a holy nation." These are the words that you shall speak to the sons of Israel. (Exod 19:5-6)*

Israel was God's possession. The nation of Israel was feeble in comparison to the nations of the world. Because of God's election, however, Israel was certainly above all nations. In Exodus 33:16, Moses spoke to God about how the Israelites were "distinguished from all the other people who are upon the face of the earth." As long as they obeyed God's Word and kept His covenant, they would be God's possession, distinguished from all others on the earth.

God is the Creator of all creation and the Lord over all creatures. Thus Moses said, "Behold, to the LORD your God belong heaven and the highest heavens, the earth and all that is in it" (Deut 10:14). He went on, saying, "Yet on your fathers did the LORD set His affection to love them, and He chose their descendants after them, even you above all peoples, as it is this day" (Deut 10:15).

The word "possession" in Exodus 19:5 is סְגֻלָּה (*segullah*) in Hebrew and means "special treasure, a hidden treasure." It refers to a most valuable possession, especially protected from the outside world (see also 1 Chr 29:3; Eccl 2:8). Deuteronomy 7:6 refers to Israel as "a people for His own possession," and Deuteronomy 26:18 calls the people "a treasured possession." Psalm 135:4 also states, "The LORD has chosen Jacob for Himself, Israel for His own possession" (see also Isa 43:1-4; Mal 3:17). Furthermore, the people of Israel were called the "precious sons of Zion, weighed against fine gold" (Lam 4:2). This expression speaks of the precious firstfruit, the firstborn among many children. God protected Israel, His treasured possession, so that no one could covet her even for a single moment.

The saints on this earth are also majestic in God's eyes (Ps 16:3), and God protects them until the end. Psalm 34:7 states, "The angel of the LORD encamps around those who fear Him, and rescues them" while Psalm 125:2 states, "As the mountains surround Jerusalem, so the LORD surrounds His people from this time forth and forever." Jesus also confirmed, "My Father, who has given them to Me, is greater than all; and no one is able to snatch them out of the Father's hand" (John 10:29).

Israel was a kingdom of priests. The expression "a kingdom of priests" in Exodus 19:6 is מַמְלֶכֶת כֹּהֲנִים (*mamlekheth kohanim*) in Hebrew and is used only one time in the Old Testament. Variations of this term include "a kingdom that is set apart like a priest," "priests who have become kings," "kings who are like priests," or "priests who are like kings."[8] In the Bible the word מַמְלֶכֶת (*mamlekheth*) means both "royal authority and dignity" and "kingdom" (2 Chr 13:5; Jer 27:1; 28:1). The term "a kingdom of priests" in Exodus 19:6 can also be interpreted as royal authority.[9]

The Septuagint (LXX), the Greek translation of the Old Testament, uses the wording βασίλειον ἱεράτευμα (*basileion hierateuma*) for this term. The basic form of the noun *basileia* (βασιλεία) means "royal authority," "royal reign," and "kingdom," while *hierateuma* (ἱεράτευμα) means "priesthood." Thus the combination of the two words clearly shows that Israel was God's kingdom of royal priests. Accordingly, 1 Peter in the New Testament also uses the term "a royal priesthood" (1 Pet 2:9).

Just as priests dedicated their entire lives to serving God, so Israel was a nation that served only God perpetually. Just as a priest mediated between God and His people, Israel was the mediating nation that would bring the rest of the world before God. Israel was a powerful nation superior to all other nations, as it possessed royal authority. This absolute right and blessing were enjoyed exclusively by Israel, the elect (Deut 26:18–19).

Israel was a holy nation. The phrase "a holy nation" in Exodus 19:6 is גּוֹי קָדוֹשׁ (*goy qadosh*) in Hebrew. The word קָדוֹשׁ (*qadosh*) appears in the Old Testament about one hundred times with emphasis on "being separated, set apart." Thus as the party in the covenant with God the Creator and master of the universe, Israel was a "holy nation" set apart to be used only for God's work. These people who entered into a covenant with God were called "a holy people to the LORD" and God's "own possession" (Deut 7:6; 14:2; 26:19; 28:9; Dan 7:27).

God granted such incredible status to the Israelites not because they were qualified in any way but because they were His covenant people. He had promised His covenant people that if they obeyed

Him and kept His covenant, they would earn praise and fame, as people would say of them, "Surely this great nation is a wise and understanding people" (Deut 4:6; see also Deut 4:8).

Today we too must receive the Word of God with hearts of fear and strive to keep it. "The fear of the LORD is the beginning of knowledge" (Prov 1:7), the beginning of "wisdom" (Job 28:28; Ps 111:10; Prov 9:10; 15:33), and "this applies to every person" (Eccl 12:13). The fear of the Lord enables us to escape from the snares of death and reach the fountain of life (Prov 14:27). The eyes of God are on those who fear Him (Ps 33:18), and God remembers His promise to them forever (Pss 25:14; 111:5).

II. The First Descent: Moses Delivered God's Proposal to Make a Covenant with Israel (Exod 19:7-8)

Monday, the second day of the third month
(forty-six days after the exodus)

Moses came down from the mountain and delivered all God's words to the Israelites. Exodus 19:7 states, "Moses came and called the elders of the people, and set before them all these words which the LORD had commanded him." The word "set" (שׂוּם, *sum*) means "to put" or "to place." Here it is used in the waw-consecutive and means "so he placed," indicating that Moses presented God's Word before the elders of the people immediately and exactly as he had received it. Moses did not add his personal thoughts or emotions to God's Word. The elders and the people of Israel answered in one voice, "All that the LORD has spoken we will do!" (Exod 19:8). It was an answer overflowing with confidence and the willingness to do whatever God required.

III. The Second Ascent: God Commanded a Three-Day Consecration (Exod 19:8–13; Deut 4:10)

Tuesday, the third day of the third month
(forty-seven days after the exodus)

Moses ascended Mount Sinai the second time and reported immediately to God Israel's firm willingness to obey. Exodus 19:8 states, "Moses brought back the words of the people to the LORD." The phrase "brought back" is expressed by the Hebrew verb שׁוּב (*shuv*) in the waw-consecutive stem and means "to turn back" or "to return." This shows that Moses went straight back to Mount Sinai on the following day, immediately after receiving the people's answer. Moses, the mediator, reported the people's thoughts to God without delay.

Upon Moses' return God said to him, "Behold, I will come to you in a thick cloud, so that the people may hear when I speak with you and may also believe in you forever" (Exod 19:9). The phrase "in a thick cloud" (בְּעַב הֶעָנָן, *beav heanan*) refers to "a cloud amid a mass of dark clouds" that looks as if it will bring rain any minute. God then gave a solemn command for Israel's consecration, saying, "Go to the people and consecrate them today and tomorrow, and let them wash their garments; and let them be ready for the third day, for on the third day the LORD will come down on Mount Sinai in the sight of all the people" (Exod 19:10–11).

Before proclaiming His holy words, God commanded His people to consecrate themselves "today and tomorrow," for two days, and wash their garments to prepare for the third day. The Hebrew verb for "consecrate" is קָדַשׁ (*qadash*) meaning "to be holy, to set apart." God loves holiness more than anything else (Zech 14:20; Mal 2:11; Heb 12:14; see also Exod 28:36; Jas 3:17; 4:8). This is why Job offered burnt offerings (worship services) every day for the consecration of all his family members (Job 1:5).

IV. The Second Descent: Moses Delivered God's Command for Consecration, and the Israelites Complied
(Exod 19:14–15)

> Tuesday, the third day of the third month
> (forty-seven days after the exodus)

As soon as Moses returned from the mountain, he delivered God's command, and the Israelites obeyed and consecrated themselves. The description "they washed their garments" in Exodus 19:14 was not a simple reference to washing clothes but to a ritual for inward consecration.

Furthermore, in Exodus 19:15 Moses commanded, "Be ready for the third day; do not go near a woman." The expression "go near" in the command "do not go near a woman" (אַל־תִּגְּשׁוּ אֶל־אִשָּׁה, *al-tiggeshu el-ishah*) uses the Hebrew Qal imperfect verb נָגַשׁ (*nagash*), which means "to draw near, to approach." This word describes the act of approaching someone or something closely to touch (Gen 27:21), eat (Gen 27:25), kiss (Gen 27:27), or hug (Gen 48:10). A "woman" (אִשָּׁה, *ishah*) refers to a married woman or wives. According to the law, anyone who had sexual relations, even with one's own spouse, was considered unclean until the next evening. Since a man's semen caused both the man and the woman to become unclean, they needed a consecrating ceremony to wash their whole bodies in water and to wash their garments (Lev 15:16–18; see also Deut 23:10–11).

God required consecration before every significant redemptive-historical event. God commanded consecration before the Israelites crossed the Jordan River to enter the land of Canaan (Josh 3:5). Before giving the holy bread to David, Ahimelech the priest confirmed that David and his young men were sexually consecrated (1 Sam 21:4). David assured him, saying, "Surely women have been kept from us as previously" (1 Sam 21:5), and he received the holy bread (1 Sam 21:6). The apostle Paul also taught married couples to stay apart for some time to remain consecrated before devoting themselves to fasting prayer (1 Cor 7:5).

Now the Israelites were about to receive God's Word and enter into the historic covenant for the whole nation. Thus God commanded a strict three-day consecration, even restricting sexual relations for married couples, so that they would be clean and pure both in body and soul. Sinful human beings cannot draw near to God without consecration (see Heb 12:14). Thus in Leviticus 11:44–45, God said, "Consecrate yourselves therefore, and be holy, for I am holy. … You shall be holy, for I am holy." God's consecrated people must be able to meet with Him and confess, "I shall behold Your face in righteousness; I will be satisfied with Your likeness when I awake" (Ps 17:15). Those consecrated in Jesus Christ will behold God's face in heaven (Matt 5:8; Rev 22:3–4).

Today the saints are consecrated through the sprinkling of the blood of Jesus Christ, which allows them to realize their evil consciences and wash their bodies with clean water. Through this they can draw near to God with a sincere heart and pure faith (Heb 10:22; Jas 4:8). In the end times, anyone who has not washed their garments white in the blood of the Lamb will not be able to stand before God (Rev 7:14; 22:14). Furthermore, those who are consecrated will have salvation and rewards, but those who are not consecrated will not escape the final judgment (Mal 2:11–12; 3:2; see also 2 Cor 7:1).

V. The Third Ascent: The Lord Came upon Mount Sinai on the Morning of the Third Day and Strictly Forbade the People to Approach Mount Sinai (Exod 19:16–24)

Thursday, the fifth day of the third month
(forty-nine days after the exodus)

On the morning of the third day, when the Israelites had finished consecrating themselves according to God's command (Exod 19:16), Moses brought them out of the camp to the foot of the mountain to meet with God (Exod 19:17).

The Scene of God's Descent upon Mount Sinai

The scene of God coming upon Mount Sinai was so terrifying that all the people shook in fear:

> *It came about on the third day, when it was morning, that there were thunder and lightning flashes and a thick cloud upon the mountain and a very loud trumpet sound, so that all the people who were in the camp trembled. And Moses brought the people out of the camp to meet God, and they stood at the foot of the mountain.*
> *Now Mount Sinai was all in smoke because the Lord descended upon it in fire; and its smoke ascended like the smoke of a furnace, and the whole mountain quaked violently. When the sound of the trumpet grew louder and louder, Moses spoke and God answered him with thunder. The LORD came down on Mount Sinai, to the top of the mountain; and the LORD called Moses to the top of the mountain, and Moses went up. (Exod 19:16–20)*

There were thunder, lightning flashes, and a thick cloud upon the mountain (Exod 19:16). Thunder and lightning are fascinating meteorological phenomena. These powerful sounds and bright lights can be quite terrifying. Thunder is often likened to God's voice. The Old and New Testaments contain frequent occurrences of God speaking in the midst of thunder and lightning (2 Sam 22:14; Job 37:2–5; Pss 18:13; 29:3; Jer 10:13; John 12:27–30; see also Isa 42:13; Jer 25:30; Hos 11:10; Joel 3:16; Amos 3:8). In the book of Revelation, thunder and lightning repeatedly appear in the context of God's judgment. Some examples include, "Out from the throne come flashes of lightning and sounds and peals of thunder" (Rev 4:5), "There followed peals of thunder and sounds and flashes of lightning and an earthquake" (Rev 8:5), "He [a strong angel] cried out with a loud voice, as when a lion roars; and when he had cried out, the seven peals of thunder uttered their voices" (Rev 10:3), "The ark of His covenant appeared in His temple, and there were flashes of lightning and sounds and peals of thunder and an earthquake and a great hailstorm" (Rev 11:19), and, "There were flashes of lightning and sounds and peals of thunder; and there was a great earthquake, such as there had not been since man came to be upon the earth, so great an earthquake was it, and so mighty" (Rev 16:18).

Furthermore, God secretly appeared among the thick clouds to hide Himself. Psalm 18:11 states, "He made darkness His hiding place, His canopy around Him, darkness of waters, thick clouds of the skies." In the Bible clouds represent God's glorious theophany. When the ark of the covenant was brought into Solomon's temple, God's glorious cloud was so thick that the priests could not stand to minister (1 Kgs 8:10–11; 2 Chr 5:13–14). During the second coming, Jesus will come with the clouds (Dan 7:13; Acts 1:9–11; 1 Thess 4:16–17; Rev 1:7) in great power and glory (Matt 24:30; Mark 13:26; Luke 21:27).

Why did God come in thick clouds? According to Exodus 19:9, it was so the people would believe that Moses was God's representative and mediator:

> *The LORD said to Moses, "Behold, I will come to you in a thick cloud, so that the people may hear when I speak with you and may also believe in you forever." Then Moses told the words of the people to the LORD.*

God wanted the Israelites to believe in Moses so that all the laws and statutes, which were to be given to the Israelites through Moses, would possess authority as God's commands. Furthermore, God wanted the Israelites to have full confidence that the laws and statutes were not Moses' own creations but from God Himself. God ensured that the people would trust Moses completely in order to secure to them the authority and trustworthiness of His Word that they would receive through Moses the messenger. If the messenger of God's Word did not have the people's trust, the Word would be to them as only noise in the wind and the sound of clanging cymbals. When those who have God's Word live pure and holy lives and show themselves as knowing and seeking the truth, the authority of God's Word will be heightened, and His Word will continue to spread and prevail (Acts 6:7).

There was a very loud trumpet sound (Exod 19:16–19). The trumpet sound increased as God appeared amid thunder, lightning, thick clouds, smoke, and fire. Just as God had instructed, saying, "When the ram's horn sounds a long blast, they shall come up to the mountain" (Exod 19:13), all the Israelites went out from their camp, trembling, to meet with God as the sound of the trumpet grew very loud (Exod 19:16–17). As the trumpet sound grew louder and louder, Moses spoke, and God answered with His voice (Exod 19:19). The Bible makes four references to the trumpet during the theophany on Mount Sinai (Exod 19:13, 16, 19; 20:18). Since the Israelites could estimate the time of God's appearance by the growing sound of the trumpet, the trumpet sound was the warning signal for God's coming.

The trumpet sound on Mount Sinai was not the natural sound made by a man blowing into a trumpet. Neither Moses nor any of the Israelites blew the trumpet.¹⁰ The trumpet sound was from God's miraculous trumpet used to declare God's work (1 Thess 4:16). The loud sound of the miraculous trumpet announced the presence of God, and the people assembled in response to the sound. The trumpet sound was a signal to listen to God's Word. Revelation 8:6 states that the angels prepared themselves to sound the trumpets.

In the Old Testament, the Israelites blew the trumpet (שׁוֹפָר, *shofar*) to announce numerous events: the Year of Jubilee, the Day of Atonement (Lev 25:9–10), the new moon (Ps 81:3), a fast or an assembly (Joel 2:15), the making of an oath to the Lord (2 Chr 15:14), and the bringing of the ark of the Lord from the house of Obed-edom to the city of David (2 Sam 6:15; 1 Chr 15:28). The Old Testament prophesied that the trumpet sound would be used to announce the great works on the "day of the LORD" (Isa 27:13; Joel 2:1; Zeph 1:16; Zech 9:14). In the Bible the trumpet sound generally refers to the voice of God and of Jesus Christ (Rev 1:10; 4:1).¹¹ This trumpet sound is to announce God's judgment (Joel 2:1–2; Zeph 1:14–16; Rev 8:2–9:21; 11:15–19), the resurrection of the dead (1 Cor 15:52; 1 Thess 4:16), and also to gather God's chosen people from the ends of the earth (Isa 27:13; Matt 24:31).¹²

Just as the people trembled at the loud sound of the trumpet that resounded for the first time on Mount Sinai (Exod 19:16), the whole world will shake when the sound of the last trumpet resonates at the second coming of Jesus Christ. Together with the "great trumpet," God will gather His elect from the four winds, from one end of the sky to the other (Matt 24:31). "At the last trumpet" God will perform His work of salvation, and the dead will be raised imperishable, and the living will all be changed (1 Cor 15:51–52). The apostle Paul called this the work of "the trumpet of God" (1 Thess 4:16–17). Furthermore, Revelation 10:7 states, "In the days of the voice of the seventh angel, when he is about to sound, then the mystery of God is finished, as He preached to His servants the prophets." Revelation 11:15 also states, "Then the seventh angel sounded; and there were loud voices in heaven, saying, 'The kingdom of the world has become the kingdom of our Lord and of His Christ; and He will reign forever and ever.'"

Mount Sinai was covered with smoke, and the smoke went up like the smoke of a furnace (Exod 19:18). In the phrase "all in smoke" (כֻּלּוֹ עָשַׁן, *ashan kullo*), "all" (כֻּלּוֹ, *kullo*) consists of the word כֹּל (*kol*, "all") and the suffix וֹ (*oh*), referring to the mountain. Thus the phrase emphasizes how the entire Mount Sinai was wrapped in smoke.

Furthermore, the verse describes the dynamic scene of God's descent with the expression "the smoke went up like the smoke of a furnace." A "furnace" (כִּבְשָׁן, *kivshan*) refers to a furnace used to refine metals; some Bible versions (e.g., RSV, ESV) translate the word as "kiln" (Exod 9:8, 10). Such dense and fierce smoke results from burning materials; in the Bible it signifies God's wrath and judgment (Rev 9:18). In Psalm 74:1, the psalmist asked, "Why does Your anger smoke?" and Isaiah 30:27 states, "Burning is His anger and dense is His smoke." Abraham realized the judgment upon Sodom and Gomorrah when he saw how "the smoke of the land ascended like the smoke of a furnace" (Gen 19:27–28; see also Ps 18:8). Similarly, Revelation 9:2 states, "He opened the bottomless pit, and smoke went up out of the pit, like the smoke of a great furnace; and the sun and the air were darkened by the smoke of the pit."

The smoke dynamically depicts the powerful presence of God, who judges the whole world, and vividly announces His coming. Revelation 15:8 states, "The temple was filled with smoke from the glory of God and from His power." Thus God's presence upon Mount Sinai amid full smoke powerfully revealed His glory and majesty as the judge and ruler of the whole world.

God descended in fire (Exod 19:18). Fire (אֵשׁ, *esh*) in general represents judgment because it burns and destroys materials. God's descent on Mount Sinai in fire reveals God as the judge, the "consuming fire" who burns and destroys all unrighteousness and sin (Deut 4:11–12, 24, 33; 5:4, 24; 10:4; Heb 12:29). God consumes sin and unrighteousness in the fire to purify His people holy. The God who descended on Mount Sinai in fire sought to consume all the sin and unrighteousness of the Israelites so that they would be reborn as a covenant people as pure as gold (see Job 23:10). This is why the law given on Mount Sinai was called "a fiery law" (Deut 33:2, KJV). This description is that of "the voice of God speaking from the midst of the fire" (Deut 4:33) or the law that functions as fire (see Rom 3:19-20).

God also provides bright light through fire. The law and the Ten Commandments gave bright light to the souls of the Israelites who had been spiritually ignorant and without understanding (Ps 119:130). Likewise, Jesus Christ came to this world as the true light and shed His light upon our ignorance and spiritual darkness through the atonement of the cross (John 1:4-9; 8:12; 9:5; Acts 26:18).

The whole mountain quaked violently (Exod 19:18; see Heb 12:26). The description "the whole mountain quaked violently" does not refer to light shaking due to thunder but to seismic tremors accompanied by earthquakes that shook the whole mountain. All the creatures and plant life on the mountain, along with the entire people of Israel at the foot of the mountain, shook in fear before God's presence. The Hebrew word for quake is חָרַד (*harad*), which also often means "to tremble, to tremor, to shock."

Thus a quake (as in an earthquake or strong ground shaking) is a major indication of God's presence (Judg 5:4-5; Pss 29:8; 60:2; Isa 2:21). The great tremor on the ground due to God's presence reflected the authority and power of God's Word. This scene reminds us of the psalmist's praise, "The voice of the LORD shakes the wilderness" (Ps 29:8), and Isaiah's prophecy, "At the sound of the tumult peoples flee; at the lifting up of Yourself nations disperse" (Isa 33:3). Such a quake occurs with God's presence, as the psalmist stated: "O God, when You went forth before Your people, when You marched through the wilderness, Selah. The earth quaked; the heavens also dropped rain at the presence of God; Sinai itself quaked at the presence of God, the God of Israel" (Ps 68:7-8). The prophet Isaiah also described, "He arises to make the earth tremble" (Isa 2:19, 21). Haggai prophesied, "Once more in a little while, I am going to shake the heavens and the earth, the sea also and the dry land" (Hag 2:6). This quake will grow and eventually "shake all the nations" (Hag 2:7). "All nations" (הַגּוֹיִם־כָּל, *kal-haggoyim*) refers to all the nations on the earth.

Notably, the author of the book of Hebrews, while speaking of the Sinaitic covenant in Exodus 19 and the Ten Commandments in Exodus 20, stated that the earth shook because of "His voice" (Heb 12:26). "His voice" refers to God's voice spoken on Mount Sinai. Moses also recorded the events involving the Sinaitic covenant in Deuteronomy, saying, "Behold, the LORD our God has shown us His glory and His greatness, and we have heard His voice from the midst of the fire" (Deut 5:24).

Indeed, the clouds and smoke that represented God's presence and majesty engulfed Mount Sinai, and His glory radiated across the entire mountain like a fiercely flaming fire (Deut 4:11; Heb 12:18–19; see also Ps 97:2–3; Isa 4:5). The people fell on their faces in fear, overwhelmed by God's majesty.

At that time, the Israelites heard the Ten Commandments being spoken directly by God (Exod 20:1–17, 18–20; Deut 5:4–5, 22–29), which had been engraved on the two stone tablets that Moses had received (Deut 5:22) as ordinances to be passed down and kept throughout the generations forever.

The Command Forbidding the People and the Priests to Ascend Mount Sinai

The Lord descended to the top of Mount Sinai and called to Moses, who had ascended the Mount for the third time (Exod 19:20). At this time God strictly forbade the Israelites to ascend Mount Sinai. The Lord pressed Moses to warn the Israelites so that the people and the priests would not climb the mountain; He also commanded the priests to consecrate themselves (Exod 19:21–24). Here the word "warn" (עוּד, *ud*) means "to repeat, to do again, to return." The usage of this word implies that it was an important command of which the people were to be fully informed and warned repeatedly; otherwise the Lord might break out against the people (Exod 19:22, 24). The Hebrew word for "break out" (פָּרַץ, *parats*) occurs in the imperfect tense and refers to continuous destruction through a sudden attack as in a military maneuver (2 Sam 6:8; 1 Chr 13:11; 15:13). When God instructed Moses to warn the people not to ascend the mountain (Exod 19:12, 21), Moses answered, "The people cannot come up to Mount Sinai, for You warned us, saying, 'Set bounds about the mountain and consecrate it'" (Exod 19:23). Moses was confident that the people would not enter the mountain because he had already set boundaries all around as God had commanded (Exod 19:12) and warned the people that any person or animal that crossed over would be stoned to death or shot through (Exod 19:13).

God, however, sternly instructed Moses once again, "Go down and come up again, you and Aaron with you; but do not let the priests and the people break through to come up to the LORD, or He will break forth upon them" (Exod 19:24). By this God strictly forbade the people of Israel from ascending Mount Sinai except for Moses and Aaron (Exod 19:24).

VI. The Third Descent: Moses Immediately Obeyed in Response to God's Rebuke (Exod 19:25)

Thursday, the fifth day of the third month
(forty-nine days after the exodus)

Exodus 19:25 states, "Moses went down to the people and told them." The phrase "went down ... and told them" (וַיֵּרֶד ... וַיֹּאמֶר, *wayyered ... wayyomer*) repeatedly occurs in the waw-consecutive stem, indicating that Moses descended the mountain without delay and delivered God's warning to the people immediately. Moses, who had been sternly rebuked by God for taking His solemn Word lightly by prioritizing his own thoughts that the people would not come up to the mountain, did his best to deliver God's message to the people (Exod 19:21–25).

God's warning prohibiting the people and the priests from entering the mountain seemed strict and even frightening. This, however, was a display of God's profound thoughts and incredible care and love as He sought to prevent even one person from being killed for sinning. Human thoughts are shortsighted and shallow and therefore often erroneous and foolish, but God's loving-kindness is ever so boundless and perfect (Pss 36:5; 103:11). Those who fear God and are quick to obey His commands, therefore, will receive the fruits of the fulfillment of His covenant (Pss 25:14; 111:5; Jer 32:40; Mal 2:5). They will not meet calamity or be put to shame, wherever they go or whatever they do (Pss 22:5; 25:3, 20; 69:6; 71:1; Isa 54:4).

VII. The Fourth Ascent: God Gave the Ten Commandments and the Law on the "Day of the Assembly"
(Exod 20:1–24:2; Deut 5:1–6:9; 9:10; 10:4; 18:16; see also Deut 5:22; Acts 7:38)

> Friday, the sixth day of the third month
> (fifty days after the exodus)

After Moses came down from his third ascent of Mount Sinai, he solemnly warned the Israelites not to approach the mountain. The next day God descended on Mount Sinai and assembled the Israelites at its base and gave them the Ten Commandments (Exod 20:1–19; Deut 5:22, 23–27). When Moses ascended Mount Sinai for the fourth time, God gave the law to the Israelites through Moses (Exod 20:21–23:33; Deut 5:28–6:9). God spoke the Ten Commandments directly to all the Israelites (Exod 20:1–17) while He gave the law through Moses the mediator (Exod 20:22–23:33).

When God gave the Ten Commandments, not only Moses but all the Israelites heard it together. Exodus 20:22 states, "The LORD said to Moses, 'Thus you shall say to the sons of Israel, "You yourselves have seen that I have spoken to you from heaven."'"

In Deuteronomy 5:22, Moses affirmed, "These words the LORD spoke to all your assembly." Deuteronomy 5:23 also states, "You heard the voice from the midst of the darkness," and Deuteronomy 5:24 confirms, "We have heard His voice from the midst of the fire."

The Ten Commandments that the Israelites heard were in the form of an absolute proclamation. These commandments were proclaimed again to the second generation of the Israelites during Moses' farewell sermon at the plains of Moab (Deut 5:7–21).

The Ten Commandments are listed as follows.

1st Commandment	Exod 20:3; Deut 5:7	"You shall have no other gods before Me."	לֹא יִהְיֶה־לְךָ אֱלֹהִים אֲחֵרִים עַל־פָּנָי
2nd Commandment	Exod 20:4–6; Deut 5:8–10	"You shall not make for yourself an idol, or any likeness of what is in heaven above or on the earth beneath or in the water under the earth. You shall not worship them or serve them."	לֹא תַעֲשֶׂה־לְךָ פֶסֶל וְכָל־תְּמוּנָה אֲשֶׁר בַּשָּׁמַיִם מִמַּעַל וַאֲשֶׁר בָּאָרֶץ מִתָּחַת וַאֲשֶׁר בַּמַּיִם מִתַּחַת לָאָרֶץ לֹא־תִשְׁתַּחֲוֶה לָהֶם וְלֹא תָעָבְדֵם
3rd Commandment	Exod 20:7; see also Deut 5:11	"You shall not take the name of the LORD your God in vain."	לֹא תִשָּׂא אֶת־שֵׁם־יְהוָה אֱלֹהֶיךָ לַשָּׁוְא
4th Commandment	Exod 20:8–11; Deut 5:12–15	"Remember the sabbath day, to keep it holy."	זָכוֹר אֶת־יוֹם הַשַּׁבָּת לְקַדְּשׁוֹ
5th Commandment	Exod 20:12; Deut 5:16	"Honor your father and your mother."	כַּבֵּד אֶת־אָבִיךָ וְאֶת־אִמֶּךָ
6th Commandment	Exod 20:13; Deut 5:17	"You shall not murder."	לֹא תִּרְצָח
7th Commandment	Exod 20:14; Deut 5:18	"You shall not commit adultery."	לֹא תִּנְאָף
8th Commandment	Exod 20:15; Deut 5:19	"You shall not steal."	לֹא תִּגְנֹב
9th Commandment	Exod 20:16; Deut 5:20	"You shall not bear false witness against your neighbor."	לֹא־תַעֲנֶה בְרֵעֲךָ עֵד שָׁקֶר
10th Commandment	Exod 20:17; see also Deut 5:21	"You shall not covet your neighbor's house."	לֹא תַחְמֹד בֵּית רֵעֶךָ

While listening to God speaking the Ten Commandments to them one by one, the Israelites were seized with fear by His majesty and grew faint. Deuteronomy 5:23 states that they "heard the voice from the midst of the darkness," and Exodus 20:18 states, "All the people perceived the thunder and the lightning flashes and the sound of the trumpet and the mountain smoking; and when the people saw it, they trembled and stood at a distance." The entire mountain was full of God's glory and majesty; Mount Sinai was "the mountain of God" indeed (Exod 3:1; 4:27; 18:5; 24:13).

The people were frightened and seized with the fear of death after experiencing the resounding thunders and trumpet sounds, the thick smoke and darkness that hindered visibility, the mountain burning in the fire, and God's voice in the midst of it. In Deuteronomy 5:25, the chiefs and elders of Israel said, "Now then why should we die? For this great fire will consume us; if we hear the voice of the LORD our God any longer, then we will die." Indeed, it was a dire confession based on the vivid realization that a sinful man who encounters God will surely die. Thus they unanimously pleaded with Moses, "Speak to us yourself and we will listen; but let not God speak to us, or we will die" (Exod 20:19; see also Deut 5:27). The people begged Moses so that they would not have to listen to God's voice directly. God heard their request, and it was acceptable to Him; from that time on He spoke through Moses the mediator (Deut 5:28, 30–31). Moses then comforted the people who were trembling in fear, saying, "Do not be afraid; for God has come in order to test you, and in order that the fear of Him may remain with you, so that you may not sin" (Exod 20:20).

After this the Israelites went away to their camps at the mountain base, and Moses drew even closer to God, who was in the thick darkness (Exod 20:21). There Moses received the laws and ordinances from God (Exod 20:22–23:33). God appeared in the thick darkness in order to hide Himself from His people (Exod 20:21; Deut 5:22; Ps 18:11; Isa 45:15). This demonstrates that sinful human beings are utterly incapable of standing before God's glory and holiness. God hid Himself in the thick darkness before the sinners out of mercy and compassion because He knew all too well human weaknesses.

Henceforth, Moses was the sole mediator in ratifying the Sinaitic covenant. Moses alone was to "come near" (וְנִגַּשׁ, *weniggash*), while the representatives of Israel—Aaron, his two sons, and seventy elders—could not draw near to God's presence on Mount Sinai but were to worship "at a distance" (מֵרָחֹק, *merahoq*; Exod 24:1–2). Moreover, the Israelites were prohibited from going near the mountain (Exod 24:2). Only Moses could ascend the mountain of God's presence, on behalf of the entire people.

VIII. The Fourth Descent: Moses Recounted God's Word in Its Entirety to the Israelites and Wrote It Down (Exod 24:3–4)

Friday, the sixth day of the third month
(fifty days after the exodus)

After receiving the laws from God, Moses descended from the mountain and recounted all God's words and ordinances to the people (Exod 24:3). These words included everything recorded in Exodus 20:22–23:33 except for the Ten Commandments (Exod 20:1–17). Then Moses "wrote down all the words of the LORD" (Exod 24:4), which became the book of the covenant (Exod 24:7). While the Ten Commandments were spoken by God directly to the entire nation of Israel (Exod 20:18–20; Deut 5:23–26), only Moses heard all the words and ordinances, so he recounted them faithfully to the people (Exod 20:22–23:33).

These ordinances included detailed civil laws. Exodus 20:22–23:19 contains about seventy specific clauses essential for the practical application of the Ten Commandments. Moses established these clauses following God's instructions. In Exodus 21:1, the Lord said, "Now these are the ordinances which you are to set before them." The term "ordinances" (מִשְׁפָּט, *mishpat*) means "judgment, a decision." It refers to civil laws that deal with social morals and present norms for judgments in court. The Ten Commandments were God's absolute commands, whereas the ordinances were given in the form of cases, which included hypothetical court scenarios and their verdicts. God also called them "the ordinances which you are to set before them." The word "set" (שׂוּמ, *sum*) means "to put, appoint, established." This means that the ordinances God has set in place will certainly be enforced without change.

About three thousand five hundred years ago, God gave these ordinances according to His holy, righteous, and good nature so that His people who believed in Him could enjoy freedom, economic equality, and peace in a society with high moral standards.

The following is a summary of the detailed ordinances.

Exodus 20:22–26	Prohibition of idolatry and ordinances for the altar
Exodus 21:1–11	Ordinances for slaves 1. For male slaves (21:1–6) 2. For female slaves (21:7–11)
Exodus 21:12–17	Cases leading to the death penalty 1. Ordinances for murderers (21:12–14) 2. Punishment for unfilial children (21:15, 17) 3. Ordinances for human trafficking (21:16)
Exodus 21:18–27	Cases involving physical harm
Exodus 21:28–32	Cases in which an ox gores a person to death

Exodus 21:33–36	Cases involving harm to another's animal
Exodus 22:1–4	Theft of a neighbor's property
Exodus 22:5–15	Cases involving damage of a neighbor's property 1. Restitution for damages caused by improper care of an animal or by fire (22:5–6) 2. Damage of goods entrusted to another (22:7–15)
Exodus 22:16–17	Ordinances for violating a virgin
Exodus 22:18–20	Those sentenced to death due to a religious offense 1. A sorceress (22:18) 2. Anyone who lies with an animal (22:19) 3. An idolater (22:20)
Exodus 22:21–27	Social protection for the weak 1. A sojourner must not be oppressed (22:21) 2. A widow or a fatherless child must not be afflicted (22:22–24) 3. The poor shall not be charged with interest (22:25) 4. Ordinance regarding taking the cloak of the poor as a pledge (22:26–27)
Exodus 22:28–31	Basic ordinances for order in religious life 1. Prohibition on reviling a judge or the rulers of the people (22:28) 2. Ordinance on offering God the first of the harvest, the firstborn, and the firstborn of the animals (22:29–30) 3. Forbiddance to eat the meat of animals torn by wild beasts of the field (22:31)
Exodus 23:1–9	Ordinances on lawsuits for justice and well-being 1. Forbiddance to bear false report (23:1–3) 2. Protection for even an enemy's property (23:4–5) 3. Prohibition of bribes and ordinances on fair judgment (23:6–8) 4. Prohibition of oppressing a sojourner (23:9)

Exodus 23:10–19	Ordinances on the feasts 1. Observance of the Sabbatical Year and the Sabbath day (23:10–12) 2. Observance of the three annual feasts of Israel (23:14–19)
Exodus 23:20–33	The conclusion of the book of the covenant The proper way for Israel to live in the land of Canaan

The Israelites who received these words answered with "one voice" (קוֹל אֶחָד, *kolehad*), "All the words which the LORD has spoken we will do!" (Exod 24:3).

IX. Early Next Morning: Moses Ratified the Sinaitic Covenant (Exod 24:4–8)

> Saturday, the seventh day of the third month
> (fifty-one days after the exodus)

Moses spent all night writing down the Word of God and then woke up early in the morning and built an altar at the foot of the mountain (Exod 24:4). The altar was a place of God's presence. Moses set up twelve pillars for the twelve tribes and sent young men of Israel to offer burnt offerings and sacrifice young bulls as peace offerings (Exod 24:4–5). Building stone piles or setting up pillars was a common practice during ancient times to commemorate alliances between nations that entered into agreements (Gen 31:44–46; Josh 4:3–9, 20; 24:26–27).

Then Moses took the blood from the sacrificial offering and placed half of it in basins and sprinkled the other half on the altar (Exod 24:6). Sprinkling half the blood on the new altar signified the strong bond created between God and His people through the covenant. The sprinkling of the blood represented the covenanted parties' commitment to the promise, since they were willing to take responsibility by death should they breach the covenant. Moses read the book of the covenant for the people. Just as they had done previously, the people responded, "All that the LORD has spoken we will do!" (Exod 24:7).

Moses wrote down God's holy Word, word by word (Exod 24:4). He then read them before all the people, and the people confessed that they were "all that the LORD has spoken" (Exod 24:7). Likewise, Scripture clearly attests that it is itself the Word of God (see Rom 3:2; Eph 6:17; Heb 4:12). The divine authority of Scripture comes from Scripture itself. Scripture is *self-authenticating* (αὐτοπιστία, *autopistia*), meaning Scripture proves itself to be true. The Word of God is perfect, certain, truthful, and pure (Ps 19:7–10). Scripture does not contain human thoughts but is the Word of the living God (2 Tim 3:16; 1 Pet 1:23; 2 Pet 1:21). The mouth of God has commanded it, and His Spirit has gathered it; there is nothing missing in it or without a pair (Isa 34:16). A proper interpretation of Scripture, therefore, comes from Scripture alone.

After sprinkling half the sacrificial blood on the altar (Exod 24:6), Moses sprinkled the other half of the blood that he had placed in various basins on the people. As he sprinkled the blood, he declared, "Behold the blood of the covenant, which the LORD has made with you in accordance with all these words" (Exod 24:8). With this the covenant between God and the Israelites was completely ratified. An important ritual of this ceremony was the sprinkling of the blood—half upon the altar, which represented God's presence, and the other half upon the people. On the one hand, this act was a solemn oath agreeing that the one who broke this promise would pay for it with blood, that is, his life. On the other hand, it showed Israel's union with God through the covenant He had initiated. In Exodus 24:8, Moses proclaimed that the blood was "the blood of the covenant" that had been made with the Israelites "in accordance with all these words" (עַל, *al*, "in"). This shows that the Word God had proclaimed to Moses on Mount Sinai thus far was the foundation and essence of the covenant that was then made with blood on Mount Sinai. Thus the book of Hebrews records that the blood was sprinkled also on the book of the covenant, which was not recorded in the book of Exodus:

> *When every commandment had been spoken by Moses to all the people according to the Law, he took the blood of the calves and the goats, with water and scarlet wool and hyssop, and sprinkled both the book itself and all the people, saying, "This is the blood of the covenant which God commanded you."* (Heb 9:19–20)

Just as Moses had sprinkled the blood during the covenant ceremony on Mount Sinai, so the precious blood of Jesus Christ, the holy Son of God, was sprinkled upon all mankind on the cross. Anyone who participates in the covenant of the cross, that is, has been redeemed by the blood, can become God's child and draw near to Him (see Col 1:20). The foundation of this covenant is the Word that God has given us.

X. The Fifth Ascent: Moses, Aaron, Nadab, Abihu, and Seventy Elders Shared a Covenant Meal on Mount Sinai (Exod 24:9–11)

Saturday, the seventh day of the third month
(fifty-one days after the exodus)

The Bible describes Moses' fifth ascent by saying, "Then Moses went up with Aaron, Nadab and Abihu, and seventy of the elders of Israel" (Exod 24:9). In celebration of the covenant ratification, Moses, Aaron, Nadab, Abihu, and the seventy elders of Israel participated in a special meal during which they beheld God as they ate and drank together (Exod 24:10–11). At the final confirmation of the covenant following the solemn ratification ceremony, they tasted joy and peace as they gave thanks and celebrated their covenantal relationship. Before the covenant ratification, extreme tension and fear had seized the people as God had forbidden them to even approach Mount Sinai (Exod 19:12–24). After the ratification of the covenant, however, a festivity of great joy and reconciliation ensued.

On this day Moses, Aaron, Nadab, Abihu, and the seventy elders of Israel were called "the nobles of the sons of Israel" (Exod 24:11). The seventy elders—seventy-two including Nadab and Abihu—were a group of six leaders selected from each of the twelve tribes see (Exod 3:16; Deut 31:28).[13] The word "nobles" (אָצִיל, *atsil*) means "a chief, a leader."

The Bible emphasizes twice that the nobles saw God on this day (Exod 24:10–11).

First, Exodus 24:10 testifies, "They saw the God of Israel." The statement "they saw" is written in the Qal imperfect stem of the Hebrew verb רָאָה (*raah*), meaning that they had had a vivid encounter and were able to discern the One they had seen. They had seen God's feet, the lower part of God's glorious throne. Exodus 24:10 states, "Under His feet there appeared to be a pavement of sapphire, as clear as the sky itself." Below His feet was a pavement of sapphire, pure and crystal clear and shining brightly. Indeed, the glorious throne was so unapproachably holy that no spoken or written words could express its beauty.

Second, Exodus 24:11 also testifies that "they saw God." The Hebrew word for "saw" is different from the word רָאָה (*raah*) in verse 10 as it is the Qal imperfect stem of the Hebrew verb חָזָה (*hazah*), which was used in reference to a spiritual epiphany or special cases in which a person saw something through a revelation (Num 24:4; Job 36:25; Pss 17:15; 63:2). Until that day the nobles of Israel had known God as the God of their forefathers (Exod 3:6, 13, 15; 4:5); now they realized clearly that He had become their God.

Furthermore, they not only beheld God but also "ate and drank" with Him (Exod 24:11). The Hebrew verb for "ate" is אָכַל (*akhal*), meaning "to eat, to taste," but it also means "to feast." Similarly, the Hebrew verb שָׁתָה (*shathah*) for "drink" means "to drink, to absorb," but it also means "feasted." The nobles did not merely eat and drink with God, but they also had a feast of great joy and gladness with Him (see Esth 7:1; Job 1:4; 21:25; Eccl 6:2).

Although anyone who saw God was not to escape death (see Gen 32:30; Exod 33:20; Judg 6:22-23; 13:22), on this day God "did not stretch out His hand against the nobles" (Exod 24:11). This verse emphasizes that they saw God but did not die. This was a special grace bestowed upon the leaders of the covenant people. It was proof that God had acknowledged them as true nobles, as a covenant community made holy and blessed through the blood of the covenant.

The theological term for the celebration meal shared by two parties in a covenant is "covenant meal."[14] The act of two parties having a meal together implies respect and love for one another. Jesus befriended lowly sinners (disciples, tax collectors, and prostitutes) and shared meals with them to embrace, love, and respect them (Matt 9:10-13; 11:19; Mark 2:15-17; Luke 5:29-32; 15:1-2; 19:5-10). God acknowledged the covenant people as the most honorable people on this earth. He covered their weaknesses and bestowed grace upon them in place of judgment.

Blessed are those whose weaknesses are covered on this earth. In Psalm 32:1–2, the psalmist sang, "How blessed is he whose transgression is forgiven, whose sin is covered! How blessed is the man to whom the LORD does not impute iniquity, and in whose spirit there is no deceit!" (see Rom 4:7–8). Jesus also said, "Blessed are the pure in heart, for they shall see God" (Matt 5:8). Likewise, even those destined to die because of sin will receive forgiveness if they enter into a covenant by faith in Jesus Christ. Then they will be able to overcome death and enjoy the spiritual fellowship of eating and drinking before God.

After God ratified the covenant and confirmed it, God and Israel were now officially in a covenantal relationship.

XI. The Fifth Descent: No Explicit Record of the Descent
(Exod 24:12–14)

Saturday, the seventh day of the third month
(fifty-one days after the exodus)

Moses, Aaron, Nadab, Abihu, and the seventy elders probably came down late at night from Mount Sinai after eating and drinking and enjoying a joyful feast with God. While there is no record that they came back down from the fifth ascent, the fact that Moses entrusted the care of the people of Israel into the hands of Aaron, Hur, and the elders of Israel before his sixth ascent implies that they had all come down from the mount (Exod 24:12–14).

XII. The Sixth Ascent: Moses First Fasted and Prayed for Forty Days; God Gave the Two Stone Tablets of the Ten Commandments Written with His Finger (Exod 24:12; 31:18; 32:15–16; Deut 9:9–11); Moses Received the Revelation Regarding the Pattern for the Tabernacle (Exod 25:1–31:11)

Sunday, the eighth day of the third month
(fifty-two days after the exodus)

After the covenant meal during the fifth ascent of Mount Sinai, Moses descended with Aaron, his two sons, and the seventy elders. He ascended again when God called him for the sixth time, saying, "Come up to Me on the mountain and remain there, and I will give you the stone tablets with the law and the commandment which I have written for their instruction" (Exod 24:12).

Although Moses had just descended, he did not delay in ascending the mountain of God again with his servant Joshua as soon as God commanded it (Exod 24:13). Predicting that he might be away for a long time, Moses made a special request to the elders, saying, "Wait here for us until we return to you. And behold, Aaron and Hur are with you; whoever has a legal matter, let him approach them" (Exod 24:14).

As soon as Moses ascended the mountain, clouds covered the mountain, and the glory of the Lord was upon Mount Sinai (Exod 24:15–16). The cloud of God's glory covered the mountain for six days. On the seventh day, the Lord called Moses from the midst of the cloud (Exod 24:16). So Moses spent six days amid God's glory and the cloud covering the mountain, and then on the seventh day, he finally heard God's voice clearly through the clouds. The Bible explains that God's glory, which filled the mountaintop, looked "like a consuming fire" to the Israelites at the foot of the mountain (Exod 24:17). The expression "consuming" (אָכַל, akhal) means "to eat, to devour." To the people below the mountain, God's glory on top of the mountain was so terrifying and intense that it looked as if it would devour the whole mountain.

Moses went into the cloud and was on the top of the mountain (Exod 24:18). He remained on the mountain for forty days and forty nights without eating bread or drinking water (Exod 24:18; Deut 9:9). He fasted from the eighth day of the third month until the seventeenth day of the fourth month. During this time God gave Moses His Word regarding the tabernacle (Exod 25:1–31:11) and the Sabbath (Exod 31:12–17). Later Moses constructed the tabernacle (Exod 40:19, 21, 23, 25, 27, 29, 32) exactly according to the pattern that God had shown him (Exod 25:9, 40; 26:30; 27:8; Num 8:4; Heb 8:5). On the first day of the first month in the second year after the exodus, the tabernacle that God had shown Moses was built perfectly on the earth (Exod 40:2, 17).

Forty days and forty nights after Moses' ascent, God gave Moses the two stone tablets of the covenant (Exod 31:18; Deut 9:9–11). God Himself had prepared the tablets and written on them with His own finger (Exod 24:12; 31:18; Deut 9:10–11). Exodus 32:16 testifies, "The tablets were God's work, and the writing was God's writing engraved on the tablets."

XIII. The Sixth Descent: Israel Worshiped the Golden Calf, and Moses Shattered the Two Stone Tablets of the Ten Commandments (Exod 32:1–29; Deut 9:15–17, 21)

Thursday, the seventeenth day of the fourth month
(ninety-one days after the exodus)

Unlike the other times, when Moses had ascended the mountain for the sixth time, he had anticipated that he would be away for an extended period (Exod 24:12). He had told the elders, "Wait here for us until we return to you," and continued, "Aaron and Hur are with you; whoever has a legal matter, let him approach them" (Exod 24:14). Soon after this incident, Exodus 32 narrates how quickly the Israelites corrupted themselves (Exod 32:7–8; Deut 9:12, 16).

Their leader, Moses, had gone up Mount Sinai at God's command soon after the covenant had been ratified with the sprinkling of the blood. Yet about forty days after this event, the Israelites began to worship the golden calf. The words that came out of the people's mouths reveal clearly how evil their hidden intentions were:

> *When the people saw that Moses delayed to come down from the mountain, the people assembled about Aaron and said to him, "Come, make us a god who will go before us; as for this Moses, the man who brought us up from the land of Egypt, we do not know what has become of him." (Exod 32:1)*

The Israelites "saw that Moses delayed to come down from the mountain" (Exod 32:1). The phrase "saw that ... delayed" is בֹּשֵׁשׁ ... וַיַּרְא *(wayyar ... voshesh)* in Hebrew. The word "delayed" is *voshesh*, the intensive form of its root verb בּוֹשׁ *(bosh)*, which means "to be ashamed, to be disappointed." This word is used to describe unbearable shame or embarrassment due to failure (Job 6:20; Ps 25:2–3; Jer 14:3). Instead of being concerned about Moses' delay, the faithless and rebellious people decided that it was useless and foolish to wait for Moses any longer.

The Israelites "assembled about Aaron and said to him, 'Come'" (Exod 32:1). The word "assembled" (וַיִּקָּהֵל, *wayyiqqahel*) is the Niphal (passive) stem of קָהַל *(qahal)*, which means "to gather, to convene." The usage of this word hints at the kind of force that compelled them to assemble. When they saw that Moses had delayed for almost forty days, they were seized with disappointment and anxiety, and they gathered under the influence of mob mentality. In general, when the Niphal stem of *qahal* is used with the preposition *al* (עַל, "unto"), the preposition means "against." This is the case with the usage of the word "against" in Numbers 16:3, 42; 20:2. The Israelites threatened Aaron and said, "Come, make us a god who will go before us" (Exod 32:1). The imperative form "come" (קוּם, *qum*) shows that they had threatened and intimidated Aaron.

The Israelites said, "Make us a god who will go before us" (Exod 32:1). Their complaint at this time was not a lack of food or water or the desire for meat. The request "make us a god who will go before us" reveals their inherent evil. It shows their intent to set aside Moses, whom they had followed until this time. Aaron, who assisted Moses, was weak-willed and passive, so he submitted himself to them, saying, "Tear off the gold rings which are in the ears of your wives, your sons, and your daughters, and bring them to me" (Exod 32:2). When all the people had taken off the gold rings from their ears and brought them to Aaron, he fashioned the gold with an engraving tool and made a golden calf (Exod 32:3-4). Not all the gold jewelry was collected; only the gold rings in the wives' and children's ears were accepted (Exod 32:2).

Of all the images that Aaron could have made, he chose a calf, which was the Egyptian god Apis. This shows that he had not completely broken free from Egyptian influence. Then Aaron proclaimed, "Tomorrow shall be a feast to the LORD" (Exod 32:5). It was a false proclamation, however, as God had not called for a feast on that day. Yet by Aaron's proclamation, the Israelites woke up early the next morning and offered burnt offerings and peace offerings before the golden calf. They sat down to eat and drink; they got up to dance and play (Exod 32:6, 19).

The Israelites were no longer God's people, for they had turned themselves back into slaves from Egypt. If only Aaron had stood on God's side along with Moses and armed himself with the mind of a martyr, he and the entire people of Israel would have walked the proper path and enjoyed great blessings and glory.

The Israelites said, "As for this Moses, the man who brought us up from the land of Egypt, we do not know what has become of him" (Exod 32:1). The term "this Moses" was a derogatory expression showing that they despised their leader who had faithfully led them thus far. Moreover, the phrase "the man who brought us up from the land of Egypt"[15] can be interpreted literally as "the man who caused us to ascend from the land of Egypt." Moses was the only mediator whom God had appointed to lead the Israelites from Egypt to Canaan, the promised land. In Exodus 19:9, the Lord said to Moses, "Behold, I will come to you in a thick cloud, so that the people may hear when I speak with you and may also believe in you forever." Yet the people who now gathered around Aaron had no concern for whether Moses was alive or dead. They mocked the great work of salvation that God had fulfilled through Moses and deceitfully instigated a mob to oust Moses. Highlighting their disparaging tone, the Woorimal Korean Bible translates, "Who cares about this fellow Moses who brought us from Egypt?" (Exod 32:1).

In his sermon, Stephen the deacon exposed the two actual motives behind the Israelites' request for a god. In Acts 7:39–40, Stephen explained, "Our fathers were unwilling to be obedient to him, but repudiated him and in their hearts turned back to Egypt, saying to Aaron, 'Make for us gods who will go before us; for this Moses who led us out of the land of Egypt—we do not know what happened to him.'" First, they had in their hearts the desire to disobey Moses and reject him. Second, their hearts turned back to Egypt.

With his words, the deacon Stephen keenly pointed out Israel's treacherous hearts. He continued in Acts 7:41, "At that time they made a calf and brought a sacrifice to the idol, and were rejoicing in the works of their hands." Exodus 32:6 also states, "The people sat down to eat and to drink, and rose up to play." When they had entered into a covenant with God on Mount Sinai, some of them had seen God and shared a meal with Him (Exod 24:11). Now the people chose to "play" before an idol. The word "play" in Hebrew is צָחַק

(*tsahaq*). When this word occurs in the Qal (root) stem, it means "to laugh" (Gen 17:17; 18:12-13; 21:6). When it occurs in the Piel (intensive) stem, however, it means "jesting" (Gen 19:14) or "mocking" (Gen 39:14, 17). Notably, this word is also used for "caressing" between a man and woman (Gen 26:8). Based on these occurrences, the word "play" in Exodus 32:6 implies sexual activity between the men and women (Gen 39:14-17). They engaged in lewd and indecent sexual activity as they worshiped idols. Of this God said, "Moses saw that the people were out of control—for Aaron had let them get out of control to be a derision among their enemies" (Exod 32:25). The phrase "out of control" also means "uncovered" in the original Hebrew language, meaning that while they worshiped idols, they followed the pagan practice of uncovering themselves in wild raves.

These were the same people who had not long ago ratified the covenant, confessing, "All that the LORD has spoken we will do!" (Exod 19:8), "All the words which the LORD has spoken we will do!" (Exod 24:3), and "All that the LORD has spoken we will do, and we will be obedient!" (Exod 24:7).

The idolatry of a people who had covenanted with God through the sprinkling of blood was no ordinary sin. They unlawfully broke their glorious covenant with God and entered into a new covenant with idols. This was an unprecedented and exceedingly wicked sin. In Psalm 106:19-20, the psalmist recalled, "They made a calf in Horeb and worshiped a molten image. Thus they exchanged their glory for the image of an ox that eats grass." Indeed, they had "exchanged the glory of the incorruptible God for an image in the form of corruptible man and of birds and four-footed animals and crawling creatures" (Rom 1:23).

God told Moses that the Israelites had corrupted themselves (Deut 9:12; see also Deut 4:16, 25; 31:29) and turned quickly away from His Word and made for themselves an idol at the foot of the mountain. God said that He would destroy the nation ("blot out their name from under heaven"; Deut 9:14) and build a great and mighty nation through one man, Moses (Exod 32:7-10; Deut 9:12-14).

Moses was probably greatly distressed from the moment he heard of God's plan to destroy Israel for turning quickly away from His Word. Yet because he was a thoughtful and meek man (Num 12:3), he approached God in prayer. Moses' earnest prayer (Exod 32:11-13) turned God from His wrath, and God changed His mind about the destruction that He had said He would bring upon Israel and did not judge them (Exod 32:14).

As Moses approached the camp and saw the people dancing before the calf, he became greatly angered and threw the two stone tablets to the bottom of the mountain and shattered them in their sight (Exod 32:15-19; Deut 9:15-17). The verb "shatter" in Exodus 32:19 is in the Piel (intensive) stem of the Hebrew word שָׁבַר (shavar), which means "to break in pieces" (Gen 19:9; Jer 2:20). This verb in the Piel stem refers to shattering something so that it becomes irrecoverable. Moses did not destroy the tablets because he could not control his emotions. Rather, he expressed holy wrath based on God's righteousness. He broke the tablets to prevent the destruction of the people of Israel. In the ancient Near East, when the tablets of a covenant were broken, their contents became invalid.[16] If God had judged Israel according to the commandments written on the tablets, Israel would not have been able to avoid imminent catastrophe.

Moses threw the tablets "at the foot of the mountain" (Exod 32:19). The expressions "the nether part of the mount" (Exod 19:17, KJV) and "under the hill" (Exod 24:4, KJV) come from the same Hebrew word as in Exodus 32:19, meaning that Moses threw the tablets in the place where the Israelites had made the covenant with God. The word "at" (תַּחַת, tahath) means "beneath" or "lower parts" (Isa 44:23). "At the foot of the mountain" refers to an area beneath the mountain where the slope begins. This was the place where God had ratified the covenant with Israel (Exod 24:4). When Moses had stood before God at Mount Horeb, God had said to him, "Assemble the people to Me," and the people had come near and stood at this place "at the foot of the mountain" (Deut 4:10–11).

Moses now burned the calf the people had made, ground it into a fine powder, scattered it onto the water, and made the people of Israel drink it (Exod 32:20). In Deuteronomy 9:21, Moses said, "I took your sinful thing, the calf which you had made, and burned it with fire and crushed it, grinding it very small until it was as fine as dust; and I threw its dust into the brook that came down from the mountain." Just as a woman charged with adultery had to drink the "water of bitterness that brings a curse" (Num 5:24), so God made the Israelites drink water scattered with the powder from the burnt idol so that they could realize that idolatry results in a great curse, suffering, and destruction.

Even today the Israelites penitently observe the seventeenth day of the fourth month (Tammuz) as the day on which the tablets of the Ten Commandments were shattered.

God's wrath against the sin of Israel did not stop there. When Moses said, "Whoever is for the LORD, come to me!" the sons of the Levites volunteered (Exod 32:26). Moses commanded them to take their swords upon their thighs and go back and forth from gate to gate in the camp and kill their brothers, friends, and neighbors (Exod 32:27). The word "kill" refers to slaughtering without mercy. The sons of Levi did as Moses commanded, and on that day (בַּיּוֹם הַהוּא, *bayom hahu*, "that day") about three thousand idol worshipers who had betrayed God bled to death (Exod 32:28).

The Levites obeyed and acted immediately without hesitation as soon as God's will became clear. As a result, Moses honored and praised them, saying, "Dedicate yourselves today to the LORD—for every man has been against his son and against his brother" (Exod 32:29). They received the great blessing of the priesthood—the blessing of teaching Israel the laws and ordinances and of offering sacrifices to God (Exod 32:29; Deut 33:9–11).

Although most of the Israelites at the foot of Mount Sinai had taken off their gold rings to worship idols (Exod 32:3), God did not wipe out all Israel (see Exod 32:10, 14). He listened to Moses' intercessory prayer and, because of the dedication of the sons of Levi, allowed only about three thousand people to fall (Exod 32:26-29). It is likely that these three thousand people had either actively seduced the people of Israel or refused to repent and challenged Moses even after he rebuked them.

The severe punishment of the sinners through cruel fratricide was to purge the seed of sin that had corrupted the people. Furthermore, just as foreshadowed by the ritual of sprinkling the blood, it made the people utterly realize that breaching the covenant would result in death (Exod 24:6-8). God taught His people that they must pay for their sins and that breaking the covenant to worship idols was a great abomination that would bring dreadful consequences.

XIV. The Seventh Ascent: Moses Interceded in Prayer for Forty Days (Exod 32:30-35; Deut 9:25-29; 10:10-11)

> Friday, the eighteenth day of the fourth month
> (ninety-two days after the exodus)

The day after the sons of Levi slaughtered about three thousand of their own people and purged the sin from Israel, Moses ascended Mount Sinai for the seventh time, saying to Israel, "Now I am going up to the LORD, perhaps I can make atonement for your sin" (Exod 32:30). Moses ascended the mountain in order to plead with God for forgiveness by putting his own life on the line:

> *Then Moses returned to the LORD, and said, "Alas, this people has committed a great sin, and they have made a god of gold for themselves. But now, if You will, forgive their sin—and if not, please blot me out from Your book which You have written!" (Exod 32:31-32)*

After Moses' prayer, God responded, saying, "The LORD said to Moses, 'Whoever has sinned against Me, I will blot him out of My book. But go now, lead the people where I told you. Behold, My angel shall go before you; nevertheless in the day when I punish, I will punish them for their sin'" (Exod 32:33–34). The phrase "in the day when I punish, I will punish" is וּבְיוֹם פָּקְדִי וּפָקַדְתִּי (*uveyom paqdi ufaqadti*) in Hebrew and repeats twice the verb פָּקַד (*paqad*) meaning "to visit, to search, to number." The phrase emphasizes that God Himself will visit, investigate, and punish people based on His examination of them. The Korean Common Translation Bible carefully articulates the meaning of *paqad* in its translation of this verse: "The day of my visitation for them must come, on which day I will punish their sin."

God's wrath did not stop there. Exodus 32:35 testifies, "The LORD smote the people, because of what they did with the calf which Aaron had made." The word "smote" (נָגַף, *nagaf*) means "to plague, to strike." This implies that God sent a fatal plague immediately upon the Israelites.

Then as God spoke to Moses, He referred to Israel as "the people whom you have brought up from the land of Egypt" (Exod 33:1). He continued and said, "I will not go up in your midst, because you are an obstinate people, and I might destroy you on the way" (Exod 33:3). The description "obstinate" was usually used for beasts such as oxen or horses that would not listen to their owners. Thus this term refers to disobedience in stubborn people who refuse to listen to any advice, as they are full of self-centered thoughts. These people justify their behavior and claim to be righteous and do not submit to God. They slander God without a thought of repentance.

The book of Deuteronomy reiterates Moses' intercessory prayer in connection with Israel's idolatry with the golden calf. Particularly, it records that Moses fell down before God for forty days and nights in repentance, which is not recorded in the book of Exodus (Deut 9:25–29; 10:10–11):

> *I fell down before the LORD the forty days and nights, which I did because the LORD had said He would destroy you. (Deut 9:25)*

וָאֶתְנַפַּל לִפְנֵי יְהוָה אֵת אַרְבָּעִים הַיּוֹם וְאֶת־אַרְבָּעִים
הַלַּיְלָה אֲשֶׁר הִתְנַפָּלְתִּי כִּי־אָמַר יְהוָה לְהַשְׁמִיד אֶתְכֶם

waethnappal lifne yehwah (Adonai) eth arbaim hayyom weeth-arbaim hallaylah asher hithnappalti ki-amar yehwah (Adonai) lehashmid ethkhem

The verse literally says, "I fell before the Lord forty days and forty nights in which I fell down, because [כִּי, *ki*] the Lord said that He would destroy you." The forty days here refer to the period of Moses' intercession for the forgiveness of Israel's sin of idolatry, not to the period Moses spent receiving the first or second set of stone tablets with the Ten Commandments.[17] This period of intercessory prayer was from the eighteenth day of the fourth month to the twenty-eighth day of the fifth month. Including his two occasions of forty-day fasting prayers (on the sixth and eighth ascents) and this one of intercessory prayer, Moses offered up to God three forty-day prayers on Mount Sinai.[18]

The word "fell" in Deuteronomy 9:25 is used in the Hithpael (intensive reflexive) stem of נָפַל (*nafal*), which means "to fall, to throw." The verb *nafal* is repeated two times in one sentence (וָאֶתְנַפַּל, ... הִתְנַפָּלְתִּי, *waethnappal ... hithnappalti*). Furthermore, the usage of the word "fell" (וָאֶתְנַפַּל, *waethnappal*) implies that Moses prayed continuously for forty days and nights, pouring out his heart and soul.

Indeed, Moses' prayer was earnest and sacrificial (Deut 9:25–29). He pleaded with God in tears to save the sinful Israelites. "I prayed to the LORD and said, 'O Lord GOD, do not destroy Your people, even Your inheritance, whom You have redeemed through Your greatness, whom You have brought out of Egypt with a mighty hand'" (Deut 9:26). Moses confessed the sinful nature of Israel—"stubbornness," "wickedness," and "sin" (Deut 9:27). Moses found the strength to make this last plea to God by looking to the forefathers of the covenant. Deuteronomy 9:27 states, "Remember Your servants, Abraham, Isaac, and Jacob; do not look at the stubbornness of this people or at their wickedness or their sin."

Moses' forty-day intercessory prayer demonstrates how frightening and perilous was the sin of breaking the covenant by turning away from God and despising His Word. It brings us to the painful realization that while it may be easy to sin, receiving forgiveness is difficult and painful. Yet although God thoroughly punishes sin, He is also the God of love and the God of the covenant who surely saves His covenant people (see Exod 34:6–7). He is love itself (1 John 4:7–10, 16, 19). His love is boundless, unchanging, and remains the same perpetually (Heb 1:12; 13:8).

XV. The Seventh Descent: The Israelites Removed Their Ornaments After the Forty-Day Intercessory Prayer (Exod 33:1–6); Moses Built the Temporary Tent of Meeting and Offered Intercessory Prayer (Exod 33:7–23)

> Tuesday, the twenty-eighth day of the fifth month
> (one hundred thirty-one days after the exodus),
> and Wednesday, the twenty-ninth day of the fifth month
> (one hundred thirty-two days after the exodus)

After Moses came down from his forty-day intercessory prayer, the Israelites heard that God had said, "I will not go up in your midst" (Exod 33:3). They were saddened by this grievous message and took off their ornaments as God had commanded (Exod 33:4–6). After the people removed their ornaments, Moses pitched a temporary tent of meeting outside the camp as a place to meet with God.

Exodus 33:7 narrates, "Now Moses used to take the tent and pitch it outside the camp." This phrase "used to take" occurs in the imperfect tense of the verb לָקַח (*laqah*), which implies that Moses, after he had first set up the temporary tent of meeting following the forty-day intercessory prayer, continued to pitch the tent. All the people stood at the doors of their tents when Moses approached the tent of meeting (Exod 33:8). When Moses entered the tent, the pillar of cloud came down to stand at the door of the tent of the meeting. When the Lord spoke with Moses and all the people saw the pillar of cloud standing at the entrance of the tent, the people rose up and worshiped at the doors of their tents (Exod 33:9–10). The word "worship" occurs in the Hithpael (intensive reflexive) stem of שָׁחָה (*shahah*), meaning "to bow down, prostrate." This describes Israel's voluntary and passionate repentance before God.

Not only did the entire nation of Israel repent, but Moses also implored God, saying, "I pray You, if I have found favor in Your sight, let me know Your ways that I may know You, so that I may find favor in Your sight. Consider too, that this nation is Your people" (Exod 33:13).

As a result, God turned away from His plan and declared, "My presence shall go with you" (Exod 33:14). God then placed Moses in the cleft of a rock and showed Moses His back (Exod 33:21–23). The psalmist recalled this event and confessed, "He said that He would destroy them, had not Moses His chosen one stood in the breach before Him, to turn away His wrath from destroying them" (Ps 106:23).

Indeed, the repentance of all Israel and Moses' life-risking intercessory prayer triggered God's bestowal of His boundless mercy, compassion, and forgiveness. Without Moses' intercession, Israel would have perished at Mount Sinai.

On that day, by showing His back to Moses who had entreated Him to show His glory, God declared the restoration of His relationship with His people (Exod 33:18–23).

XVI. The Eighth Ascent: Moses Fasted and Prayed for Forty Days a Second Time and Received the Two Stone Tablets of the Ten Commandments Written by the Finger of God (Exod 34:1–28; Deut 9:18, 10:1–4)

Thursday, the thirtieth day of the fifth month
(one hundred thirty-three days after the exodus)

God commanded Moses, "Cut out for yourself two stone tablets like the former ones, and I will write on the tablets the words that were on the former tablets which you shattered" (Exod 34:1; Deut 10:2). God instructed Moses to cut stone tablets "like the former ones" (Deut 10:1). Moses was the only person who had seen the first set of tablets that God had prepared. Moses cut new stone tablets exactly like the ones God had first made. In an era without a machine that cuts rocks, the cutting process probably required arduous labor and a long time. According to God's instruction, Moses then woke up early in the morning and went up Mount Sinai with the two stone tablets in his hand (Exod 34:2, 4).

While Moses was with God on Mount Sinai, he ate no bread and drank no water for forty days and nights, just as he had done on the sixth ascent (Exod 34:28; Deut 9:18). This second forty-day period of fasting and prayer lasted from the thirtieth day of the fifth month to the tenth day of the seventh month. Then God inscribed the Word of the covenant, the Ten Commandments, on the two stone tablets (Exod 34:28; Deut 10:4).

XVII. The Eighth Descent: Moses Brought the Second Pair of Stone Tablets, and His Face Radiated (Exod 34:29–35; Deut 10:5)

> Monday, the tenth day of the seventh month
> (one hundred seventy-two days after the exodus)

When Moses was descending from the mountain with the two stone tablets of the testimony, the skin of his face was shining, because he had spoken with the Lord (Exod 34:29). At first, he did not know that his face was shining. When Aaron and all the Israelites saw his face and did not want to draw near to him out of fear, Moses called Aaron and all the rulers in the congregation to himself and spoke to them. Then all Israel came near to him (Exod 34:30–32). Moses spoke to them all the words that the Lord had commanded him on Mount Sinai; when he was finished speaking, Moses covered his face with a veil (Exod 34:32–33). After this time Moses took off the veil whenever he spoke with God. He covered his face again when he spoke to the Israelites about all that God had commanded them and kept it covered until he went again before God (Exod 34:34–35).

The radiance coming from Moses' face was the reflection of God's glory, not the radiance of visible sunlight. Since the Israelites "saw" (רָאָה, *raah*, "gave attention" or "examined"; Exod 34:30, 35) the radiance of Moses' face, he put the veil on his face so that they would not look intently at his face (Exod 34:33, 35; see also 2 Cor 3:13).

The apostle Paul spoke of the radiance of Moses' face as the glory of the law, which was a glory that would fade away (2 Cor 3:7, 11, 13). Moreover, he pointed out the Jews' unawareness of the temporary nature of the Mosaic law and their inability to recognize the gospel of greater glory because of their hardened hearts. He likened this condition to a veil covering their hearts (2 Cor 3:13–15). This veil was to be taken away in Christ (2 Cor 3:14, 16), but the Jews could not accept Jesus Christ, because the veil had covered their hearts.

The apostle Paul also taught that if Moses' face had shone with glory after receiving the commandments engraved in stones, an even greater glory existed for the stewards of the new covenant (2 Cor 3:6–9). The glory of the old covenant, which faded away after a short period, cannot compare to the glory of the new covenant. Once we return to the Lord, we will see God's glory continuously, as one who looks into a mirror with an unveiled face. As a result, we will be transformed into the image of the Son of God from glory to glory through the Spirit of the Lord (2 Cor 3:18).

At first, God gave Moses the stone tablets that He Himself had prepared (Exod 31:18; 32:16). After those tablets were broken, however, God commanded Moses to cut and prepare two stone tablets, and He inscribed His Word upon them (Exod 34:1, 4, 28; Deut 10:1–4). Moses brought down from the mountain the two stone tablets upon which God had inscribed the Word of the covenant with His finger and placed them inside the ark of the covenant (Exod 25:16, 21; 40:20; Deut 10:5; 1 Kgs 8:9). Later, on the plains of Moab, Moses finished writing the words of the law in a book and entrusted the book of the law to the priests, the sons of Levi, who carried the ark of the covenant, and to all the elders of Israel. He commanded them to place the book of the law by the side of the ark of the covenant so that it would be a witness for them (Deut 31:9, 24–26).

PART III

THE ESSENCE OF THE SCRIPTURE, THE TEN COMMANDMENTS:
THE TEN ESSENTIAL ASPECTS

PART III

The overarching theme of the Old and New Testaments is God's salvation. The history of the Bible is redemptive history that shows salvation in Jesus Christ to all mankind, who have been sentenced to death because of their sin.

God's redemptive history flows continuously through the covenants. These covenants are not dead covenants tied to the past. They are living covenants that give life to God's chosen people in the past, present, and future for a thousand generations. Jesus Christ stands at the center of all the covenants and redemptive history (John 5:39; 1 Cor 1:30), and the cross is the crux of redemptive history. The New Testament church was born through Jesus Christ's evangelical movement of the gospel of the kingdom, and redemptive history will be consummated through the second coming of Jesus Christ in the last days.

The essence of the gospel is condensed in the Ten Commandments that God gave through Moses. The Ten Commandments are the ten words, and their essence is summarized in Psalm 119. In Psalm 119, the psalmist explains God's Word using ten Hebrew words, which, like the Ten Commandments, can be considered the ten words. Psalm 119 is immensely helpful in understanding the essence of the Ten Commandments.

CHAPTER

9

THE TEN COMMANDMENTS AND THE TEN WORDS

Jesus reinterpreted the Ten Commandments in His Sermon on the Mount. He summarized the Ten Commandments into two commands to love God and to love one's neighbors. Matthew 22:38–40 states, "On these two commandments depend the whole Law and the Prophets." Here Jesus used the word "depend" (κρεμάννυμι, *kremannymi*), which means "to hang on, to be tied together by, only have meaning because of," implying that the Ten Commandments are the essence of the entire Bible.

Psalm 119:160 states, "The sum [ראש, *rosh*, "head"] of Your word is truth." This verse expresses that all God's Word—and the ten words, or the Ten Commandments, which reiterate all those words—are the unchanging truth from the beginning. God's people must therefore depend on these words and keep them in their daily lives.

Psalm 119 is of great significance because, of all passages in the Bible, it most clearly captures the ten essences of the Ten Commandments. Moreover, Psalm 119 is at the center of the Old and New Testaments, and its 176 verses all praise a single theme: God's Word.

This psalm has no heading, so it is unclear who composed it, when the author wrote it, and the circumstances under which it was written. While Psalm 119 is quite long, with 176 verses, its compositions are orderly from beginning to end in a unique form called an acrostic poem (a poem in which the first letter in each line spells out a word or phrase). The first letters of each line or stanza throughout Psalm 119 spell out the Hebrew alphabet in order. Among the nine acrostic poems in the book of Psalms (Pss 9, 10, 25, 34, 37, 111, 112, 119, 145), Psalm 119 is most beautifully perfect and thus considered the quintessential acrostic poem.

Psalm 119 consists of twenty-two stanzas, each consisting of eight lines. Each stanza begins with a letter of the Hebrew alphabet in order from the first letter א (*aleph*) to the last letter ת (*taw*)—twenty-two letters in total. This demonstrates that the Word of God is the *alpha* ("beginning") and the *omega* ("last") in the lives of His saints (Isa 41:4). Moreover, all eight lines of each stanza begin with the same letter of the Hebrew alphabet.

None of the psalm's 176 verses is repeated meaninglessly or tediously merely for format's sake. Each verse is filled with complete and accurate lessons infused with dynamic expression. Together they embody the joy, sorrow, grief, and happiness the psalmist experienced in his walk with the Word of God.

- The Word of God that the psalmist experienced was upright (Pss 19:8; 119:137).
- The Word of God that the psalmist experienced was righteous (Pss 19:9; 119:62, 106, 123, 142, 160, 164, 172; see also Ezra 9:15; Neh 9:8; Pss 7:9; 89:16; 116:5; 145:17).
- The Word of God that the psalmist experienced was perfect (Pss 19:7; 119:96).
- The Word of God that the psalmist experienced was holy and pure (Pss 12:6; 19:8–9; 77:13; 93:5; 105:42; see also Rom 7:12; 2 Pet 2:21).
- The Word of God that the psalmist experienced was everlasting

(Pss 119:160).

- The Word of God that the psalmist experienced was a wellspring of life that revived him (Pss 119:25, 37, 40, 50, 93, 107, 116, 144, 149, 154, 156, 159).
- The Word of God that the psalmist experienced was tried and pure (Pss 18:30; 119:140). The word "tried" is צָרַף (*tsaraf*) in Hebrew, which means "to refine, to prove, to examine." God's Word is a lamp that always provides bright guidance and proper instruction (Ps 119:105). Things that we easily overlook God examines carefully with justice and fiery discernment and comes to an accurate judgment regarding them. We address, hurriedly, only large issues that are apparent to us. But God addresses all issues, whether significant or seemingly insignificant, even invisible psychological issues, to bring abundant peace and reconciliation among neighbors. Thus anyone, without exception—weak or strong, poor or rich—can find infinite comfort and love in the Word of God.

The author of Psalm 119 sang solely about God's Word. He sang of the Lord's law, the Lord's testimonies, the Lord's ordinances, the Lord's statutes, the Lord's Word, the Lord's precepts, the Lord's commandments, the Lord's ways, the Lord's promise, and the Lord's truth. All these characteristics of the Word are, in fact, attributes of God. They reveal the weighty truth that the Word is God Himself (John 1:1), so it is impossible to know God without knowing His Word.

Psalm 119 sums up the Word of God and summarizes the whole Bible using ten Hebrew words. Simply put, Psalm 119 reveals the essence of God's Word. God's Word is such that its intrinsic attributes always result in action. Hence the Ten Commandments are specific codes of conduct for those who receive the Word. In this respect the ten words in Psalm 119 are the essence of the Ten Commandments and precise guidelines for our deeds concerning each commandment.

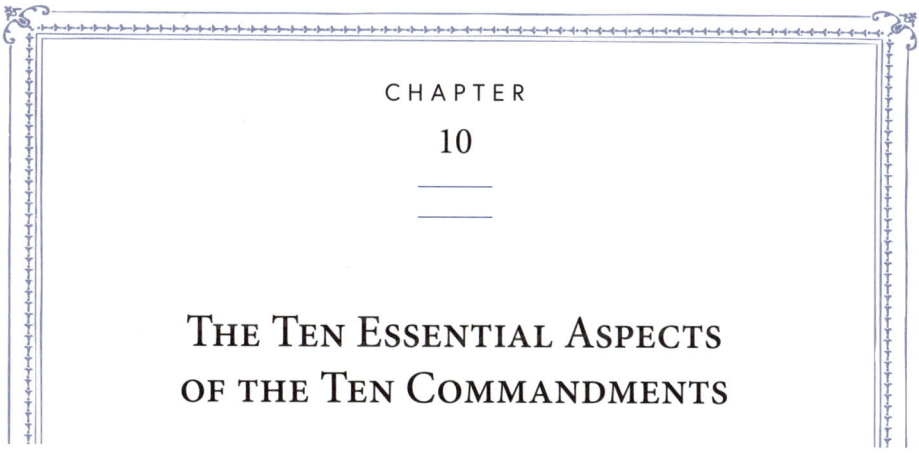

The Ten Essential Aspects of the Ten Commandments

The Ten Commandments embody the essence of the Old and New Testaments. Psalm 119 vividly praises this aspect of the Ten Commandments through ten Hebrew words that express the attributes of the Word of God. Psalm 119 contains detailed guidelines on how to observe each of the ten words of the Ten Commandments.

1. *Torah*	תּוֹרָה	"law"
2. *Eduth, edah*	עֵדָה, עֵדוּת	"testimony"
3. *Mishpat*	מִשְׁפָּט	"judgment" ("ordinance")
4. *Hoq*	חֹק	"statute"
5. *Davar*	דָּבָר	"word"
6. *Piqqud*	פִּקּוּד	"precept"

7. Mitswah	מִצְוָה	"commandment"
8. Derekh	דֶּרֶךְ	"way" ("path")
9. Imrah	אִמְרָה	"word" ("promise")
10. Emeth, emunah	אֱמוּנָה, אֱמֶת	"truth" ("faithfulness")

Each of these ten Hebrew words reflects a characteristic of God's Word and helps us clearly understand the Word of God with a broader perspective. Of its 176 verses, every verse in Psalm 119 except verse 122 includes at least one of these ten words and expresses its precise meaning. In Psalm 119, God's laws are by no means expressed as restrictions that act as fetters to bind people. Rather, God's laws reveal the fundamental faith deeply rooted in believers' lives: trust, love, dependency, and absolute obedience to God. While Psalm 119 was composed during a time when various rituals and sacrifice laws were strictly kept in the temple, it does not include any language on rituals, sacrifices, or Pharisaic observances of the laws. It expresses only how the psalmist deeply loves and enjoys the law. He considers it a treasure more precious than life and cherishes it deep in his heart. When we meditate upon these words, we will discover spiritual treasures that will captivate our hearts and gift us with overflowing joy, delight, and great hope throughout each day. Hallelujah!

Henceforth in our study of the ten Hebrew words that refer to God's Word in Psalm 119, we will examine each word's etymology, translation, usage, lessons, exemplary attitude toward the Word, and redemptive-historical meanings concerning Jesus Christ. Please note that this book has selected only the verses in Psalm 119 in which the ten words refer specifically to God's Word.

I. *Torah* (תּוֹרָה)—God's Law

Bible Verses

Psalm 119:1, 18, 29, 34, 44, 51, 53, 55, 61, 70, 72, 77, 85, 92, 97, 109, 113, 126, 136, 142, 150, 153, 163, 165, 174 (twenty-five times)

Etymology and Meaning

The word *torah* originates from the verb יָרָה (*yarah*) and means "to throw, to shoot an arrow." When this verb occurs in the Hiphil (active) stem, it means "to stretch a hand, to point with a finger."[19] It refers to the act of stretching out one's arm to point to a path, but the meaning was expanded to mean "to teach, to instruct," which later became "teachings, lessons, the law" (Job 22:22; Ps 78:1; Isa 1:10). The word *torah* occurs most frequently in reference to the law. This shows that only the Word of God teaches and guides people to the right path.

Usage

The word *torah* appears for the first time in Genesis 26:5: "Abraham obeyed Me and kept My charge, My commandments, My statutes and My laws [*torah*]." Before arriving at Mount Sinai, Moses set the foundation for the administrative order and application of the law (*torah*) that would rule Israel by effectively distributing the power of leadership among able Hebrew men according to the advice of his father-in-law, Jethro (Exod 18:16–20).

Lesson

The Word (*torah*) that God instructed was actually God's law and revelation. To the psalmist it was much more precious than thousands of pieces of gold and silver (Ps 119:72) and an object of love and delight (Ps 119:70, 77, 92, 97, 113, 163, 165, 174). He confessed that he would keep the Word (*torah*) with all his heart forever (Ps 119:2, 34, 44, 55, 136). Those who forsake *torah*, he wrote, are the wicked (Ps 119:53), the arrogant who persecute the righteous (Ps 119:51, 85), the double-minded (Ps 119:113), and the deceitful (Ps 119:29, 163). There is great peace, however, for those who love the *torah*: "Those who love Your law have great peace, and nothing causes them to stumble" (Ps 119:165).

Exemplary Attitude

In Psalm 119:97, the psalmist confessed, "O how I love Your law! It is my meditation all the day." Here the word "meditation" is שִׂיחָתִי (*sihathi*), from the noun שִׂיחָה (*sihah*), meaning "meditation"; it is used with the first-person pronominal suffix. It literally means, "Your law is my meditation all the day" (see Ps 1:2). The psalmist meditated on the Word and conducted himself according to it all day long. Never wanting to deviate from the standard of the Word, he considered the Word's meaning and kept it in his heart before he spoke or performed any deed (Neh 8:3). Those who sincerely love the Word do not sway away from it even for a moment. They are always led in the path of righteousness, even in darkness.

Redemptive-Historical Meaning

Jesus and the law are inseparable. By the time of our Lord's incarnation, the law's ordinances had completely saturated Israel's entire society. No one understood God's purpose in giving the law, however. The relationship between Jesus and the law is as follows:

The law bears witness to Jesus. In Luke 24:44, Jesus said, "All things which are written about Me in the Law of Moses and the Prophets and the Psalms must be fulfilled." In John 1:45, Philip spoke of Jesus as "Him of whom Moses in the Law and also the Prophets wrote." In Romans 3:21, Paul wrote of Jesus as "being witnessed by the Law and the Prophets" (see also John 5:39, 45–47). Since the law bears witness to Jesus, those who truly love the law (*torah*) will certainly come to Jesus (Gal 3:24).

Jesus is the end of the law and the fulfiller of the law. In Romans 10:4, Paul said, "Christ is the end of the law for righteousness to everyone who believes." In Matthew 5:17 Jesus said, "Do not think that I came to abolish the Law or the Prophets; I did not come to abolish but to fulfill." Thus no matter how much people love the law and keep it, if they do not come to Jesus, their love for the law is incomplete. Through the law we must come to Jesus.

Ultimately, through the law we come to fully acknowledge ourselves as sinners (Rom 3:20; 7:7–9, 13). However, through faith in Jesus, we are freed from sin and become righteous. In Galatians 2:16, Paul wrote, "Knowing that a man is not justified by the works of the Law but through faith in Christ Jesus, even we have believed in Christ Jesus, so that we may be justified by faith in Christ and not by the works of the Law; since by the works of the Law no flesh will be justified" (see also Rom 3:28; Gal 3:11).

II. *Eduth* (עֵדוּת), *Edah* (עֵדָה)—God's Testimonies

Bible Verses

Psalm 119:2, 14, 22, 24, 31, 36, 46, 59, 79, 88, 95, 99, 111, 119, 125, 129, 138, 144, 146, 152, 157, 167, 168 (twenty-three times)

Etymology and Meaning

The word *eduth* originates from עוּד (*ud*), which primarily means "to encircle." In the Hiphil (active) stem, however, it means "to warn, to assure, to call a witness" (Exod 19:23). In Deuteronomy 4:26, 30:19, and 31:28, Moses said, "I call heaven and earth to witness." In Genesis 21:30 and 31:52, the word is used to mean "a witness." *Edah* or *eduth* could refer to a witness in court or an object that acts as a witness (Job 16:8). In the headings of Psalms 60 and 80, *eduth* particularly means "revelatory poem."[20]

Usage

Deuteronomy 6:17 states, "You should diligently keep the commandments of the LORD your God, and His testimonies [*eduth*] and His statutes which He has commanded you." This shows that God's testimonies must be kept just as His commandments and statutes are to be kept (Deut 4:44–45). Also, *eduth* is translated in Nehemiah 9:34 as God's "admonitions" (*eduth*, עֵדְוֹת). In other cases the word is used to mean "the law of the LORD" (Ps 19:7) or "covenant" (Ps 25:10).

Lesson

The faith of the saints grows firm and unwavering, preparing them for any situation, when they become rich with the testimonies (*eduth*) of God. Testimonies of unfailing faith come only from God's Word; our faith grows stronger and fully assured when we listen to God's Word (Rom 10:17). Psalm 19:7 states, "The testimony of the LORD is sure, making wise the simple" (see also Ps 93:5).

The word "simple" describes a person who is easily tempted or swayed. We say that we believe in God, but how often do we feel tempted and allow our faith to grow dull? When our faces darken and frustration and foolishness fill our hearts, there is only one bright solution: the Word of the living God, the perfect solution and the perfect wisdom. When we return to the Word, grace will come upon us to help us untangle all our problems at once. We will be filled with wisdom, discernment, and understanding, and the eyes of our hearts will be opened.

Exemplary Attitude

In Psalm 119:31, the psalmist sang, "I cling to Your testimonies [עֵדוּת, *eduth*]; O LORD, do not put me to shame!" The word "cling" (דָּבַק, *davaq*) means "to cleave to, to hold fast, to pursue closely." The same word occurs in Genesis 2:24: "A man shall leave his father and his mother, and be joined to his wife; and they shall become one flesh." The psalmist clung to the Word every day, as if he had become one body with God's testimonies. God will not forsake those people who have become one body with the Word but will certainly protect them to the end.

Redemptive-Historical Meaning

Jesus is the essence of all the testimonies in His Word. His testimony is "greater than the testimony of John" (John 5:36). All the Scriptures testify of Jesus (John 5:39), and His works themselves bear witness to Him (John 5:36; 10:25). Jesus fulfilled every stroke to the letter of the testimonies about Him in the Old Testament, and every deed He performed was according to the Word (Matt 5:17–20). Jesus is the testimony of God Himself, more than any testimony in the world. Why?

Jesus bore witness to what He directly saw and heard. Even in this world, the most credible witness is one who has actually seen and heard something firsthand. Because Jesus bore witness to what He had directly seen and heard from the Father, His testimony is the surest and strongest. John 3:32 states, "What He has seen and heard, of that He testifies." Yet from the Pharisees' perspective, Jesus' testimony was false, since Jesus was all alone in testifying about Himself (John 8:13). Jesus boldly answered them with conviction, however, saying, "Even if I testify about Myself, My testimony is true, for I know where I came from and where I am going; but you do not know where I come from or where I am going" (John 8:14). Jesus testified to what the Father had shown Him or spoken to Him and all that He saw the Father doing (John 5:19–20; 8:38; 12:49–50). Jesus' testimonies, therefore, are always true and sure.

God the Father and God the Holy Spirit bear witness to Jesus. The law states that the testimony of two men is true (Deut 17:6; 19:15; John 8:17). Jesus said in John 8:18, "I am He who testifies about Myself, and the Father who sent Me testifies about Me." The Pharisees and the Israelites did not understand the meaning of Jesus' declaration, "The Father who sent Me, He has testified of Me." However, because God the Father indeed bore witness to Jesus (John 5:37; 1 John 5:9), Jesus could make this declaration, and His testimony could only be true. Moreover, God the Holy Spirit also bears witness to Jesus. In John 15:26, Jesus said, "When the Helper comes, whom I will send to you from the Father, that is the Spirit of truth who proceeds from the Father, He will testify about Me" (see also 1 John 5:7–8).

Fallen mankind must believe and obey only the most certain and truthful testimony, that is, the testimony of Jesus. The testimony of Jesus Christ must be confirmed more and more in our hearts each day (1 Cor 1:6). Only those who possess the testimony of Jesus can be part of the remnant amid the severe tribulation that will come in the last days (Rev 12:17).

III. *Mishpat* (מִשְׁפָּט)—God's Judgments, God's Ordinances

Bible Verses

Psalm 119:7, 13, 20, 30, 39, 43, 52, 62, 75, 84, 91, 102, 106, 108, 120, 121 ("righteousness"), 132 ("after your manner"), 137, 149, 156, 160, 164, 175 (twenty-three times)

Etymology and Meaning

The word *mishpat* is derived from the verb שָׁפַט (*shaphat*), meaning "to judge, govern," and it means "judgment, decision, sentence." *Mishpat* occasionally occurs in parallel with חֹק (*hoq*, "statute"; Exod 15:25) and תּוֹרָה (*torah*, "law"; Isa 42:4). The ordinances of the Pentateuch are *mishpat* (Lev 5:10; 9:16, etc.), and, in fact, each stipulation of the Mosaic law is *mishpat* (Deut 33:10, 21).

Usage

In Marah, the fourth campsite in the wilderness journey, when the Israelites had not yet arrived at Mount Sinai, God established for Israel a statute (חֹק, *hoq*) and an ordinance (מִשְׁפָּט, *mishpat*) to train them (Exod 15:25–26). Also, in Exodus 21:1, God introduced the articles of the law in the book of the covenant (Exod 21–23), saying, "Now these are the ordinances which you are to set before them." Later the contents of the book of the covenant governed civil cases in Israel, and this precedence created codes of conduct and ordinances for the Israelites.[21] God commanded the people to observe even the feast of Passover "according to all its ordinances" (Num 9:3). Moreover, Numbers 27:5 states, "Moses brought their case [that of the daughters of Zelophehad] before the LORD." It was here that the word *mishpat* was first translated as "case." From then on *mishpat* became "a statutory ordinance [*mishpat*] to the sons of Israel" (Num 27:11).

Lesson

The author of Psalm 119 consoled himself by remembering the Lord's ordinances (*mishpat*) "of old" (Ps 119:52). He confessed that the heavens and the earth stood "this day" according to the Lord's ordinances (*mishpat*; Ps 119:91) and that all the Lord's righteous ordinances (*mishpat*) were "everlasting" (Ps 119:160). God's judgment searches people's innermost heart, so it is always truthful and righteous (Jer 11:20; 17:10; 20:12; 1 Pet 1:17). Thus those who believe in God's judgment (*mishpat*) and follow it will never fail and will bear fruits of righteousness and goodness (Ps 119:7, 39, 62, 75, 106, 137, 160). Conversely, sinful human beings are neither qualified nor competent to judge themselves. Human judgment can be inaccurate or easily distorted; in many cases it can lead to unrighteous judgments or futile falsehoods that will not guarantee anything (Job 11:11; Rom 3:4). Hence we must live in humble obedience to

God's correct and righteous judgment (Ps 62:12; Prov 24:12; Eccl 12:14; 2 Cor 5:10). God blesses those who follow and keep His statutes (*mishpat*), saying that they "may live" if they do them (Lev 18:4–5).

God's judgment is accurate and always righteous. For this reason God's judgment (*mishpat*) can bring a harsh rebuke or fearful punishment to our daily lives. In this world court judgments are firm and show no mercy. A close examination of God's judgment, however, reveals His limitless love, mercy, patience, and grace that do not count our former sins (Rom 3:25). In Psalm 119:132, the psalmist prayed, "Turn to me and be gracious to me, after Your manner [*mishpat*] with those who love Your name." It is a sincere prayer asking God to bestow grace upon those who love His name, just as He has always done.

Not many people embrace rebuke. No matter how valid and beneficial a rebuke may be, people feel hurt and offended the moment they receive it. Yet David confessed that rather than receiving sweet compliments from the wicked, he would prefer to receive bitter reproof from the righteous and accept it as oil on his head. In Psalm 141:5, he said, "Let the righteous smite me; it shall be a kindness: and let him reprove me; it shall be an excellent oil, which shall not break my head: for yet my prayer also shall be in their calamities" (KJV). Here David confessed that he would pray sincerely for the righteous who had rebuked him, even when they faced calamity. His confession demonstrates amazingly mature faith.

Truly if we listen to God's reproofs (*mishpat*) and obey them, we will become priceless people in this world. Just as beautiful ornaments suit beautiful people, so Proverbs 25:12 confirms, "Like an earring of gold and an ornament of fine gold is a wise reprover to a listening ear." Those who willingly accept and obey God's rebuke will ultimately experience His steadfast love and the light of life therein (Prov 6:23; Eph 5:13).

Exemplary Attitude

The psalmist's heart was moved to praise God each time he considered God's righteous works that unfolded according to His judgment (*mishpat*). He confessed, "Seven times a day I praise You, because of Your righteous ordinances [*mishpat*]" (Ps 119:164). Here the number "seven" symbolizes completeness. It implies that the psalmist did not cease singing praises all day long because he had experienced firsthand that God's judgment (*mishpat*) was most righteous and always accurate.

We too must have praise on our lips all day long. When we experience God's Word working in our lives and are deeply touched by His boundless love and mercy, joyful praise will automatically flow from our hearts. This is the sacrifice of praise to God and the fruit of our lips (Isa 57:19; Col 3:16; Heb 13:15). The souls of God's saints are filled and satisfied with the fruit of their lips (Prov 18:20).

Redemptive-Historical Meaning

In the Septuagint (LXX) *mishpat* is mainly translated as κρίμα (*krima*), which means "dispute, judgment, decision, evaluation." Although the law's decisions and judgments were correct, Jesus' decisions and judgments are far better.

Jesus' judgments are true. In John 8:16, Jesus said, "Even if I do judge, My judgment is true; for I am not alone in it, but I and the Father who sent Me." A judgment that is in tune with God the Father is always true. People of this world judge according to what they see and hear. Jesus, however, knows what is in the human heart and does not judge based on what He sees and hears (Isa 11:3; John 2:24–25; 7:24; 8:15). Because Jesus judges with integrity (Ps 9:7–8; Isa 11:4), His judgment is always true.

Jesus possesses the authority to judge. Jesus revealed, "For judgment [κρίμα, *krima*] I came into this world" (John 9:39). Jesus attested to

His divine authority and the righteousness of His judgment, saying, "Not even the Father judges anyone, but He has given all judgment to the Son" (John 5:22, 29–30). The apostles also testified that Jesus was "the One who [had] been appointed by God as Judge of the living and the dead" (Acts 10:42). Jesus' judgments are most righteous (Ps 96:13; John 5:30).

Mishpat guides people to look toward Jesus Christ, the righteous judge who will come to judge the world. All mankind, without exception, will stand before the judgment of Christ (2 Cor 5:10; Heb 9:27). In order to pass from death to life at that time, we must believe in the Word of Jesus and in Him who sent Jesus (John 5:24). In John 12:48, Jesus said, "He who rejects Me and does not receive My sayings, has one who judges him; the word I spoke is what will judge him at the last day."

IV. *Hoq* (חֹק)—God's Statutes

Bible Verses

Psalm 119:5, 8, 12, 16[22], 23, 26, 33, 48, 54, 64, 68, 71, 80, 83, 112, 117, 118, 124, 135, 145, 155, 171 (twenty-two times)

Etymology and Meaning

The word *hoq* means "something prescribed, owed" or "what is appointed." It comes from the root word חָקַק (*haqaq*), which means "to inscribe, cut in, mark, decree" (see Isa 22:16; Ezek 4:1). It also means "boundaries" (Job 38:10; Jer 5:22) or a "required amount" of labor (Exod 5:14; Prov 31:15). The word *hoq* highlights the binding force and perpetuity of the Scripture and the law of God. In the ancient Near East, it was understood as a royal order or decree, because in those days laws were inscribed on stone monuments or tablets and set in public places. Thus Isaiah 30:8 records, "Go, write it on a tablet before them and inscribe [*haqaq*] it on a scroll, that it may serve in the time to come as a witness forever."

Usage

After the exodus the Israelites camped for the fourth time at Marah. There God gave them a statute (*hoq*) and an ordinance and tested their obedience (Exod 15:25–26). In Isaiah 10:1, which states, "Woe to those who enact evil statutes," the word "enact" is *haqaq*. In Psalm 2:7, God stated, "I will surely tell of the decree," and the noun "decree" is *hoq* in Hebrew. When the noun חֻקָּה (*huqqah*), which is derived from *hoq*, is used with עוֹלָם (*olam*), the phrase is translated as a "statute forever" (Exod 12:14, 17; Lev 3:17; 6:22; 10:9; 16:29, 31, 34, 17:7; 23:14, 21, 31, 41; 24:3, 9; Num 10:8).

Lesson

The author of Psalm 119 repeatedly entreated, "Teach me Your statutes [*hoq*]" (Ps 119:12, 26, 33, 64, 68, 124, 135, 171). Furthermore, as a sojourner wandering through a foreign land without a moment of peace, he confessed, "Your statutes [*hoq*] are my songs in the house of my pilgrimage" (Ps 119:54). Likewise, as sojourners and wayfarers living on this earth temporarily (1 Chr 29:15; 1 Pet 2:11), we must humbly seek wisdom from God's Word and inscribe it in our hearts. We must seek wisdom to know how to navigate our uncharted life journeys and where we are to seek our eternal home (1 Pet 1:17).

Exemplary Attitude

In Psalm 119:83, the psalmist said, "Though I have become like a wineskin in the smoke, I do not forget Your statutes [*hoq*]." Here the word "wineskin" is נֹאד (*nod*) in Hebrew and refers to a leather bag made from animal skins to store wine or milk (Josh 9:4, 13; Judg 4:19). These wineskins became unsightly as they slowly dried and darkened from the smoke of a fireplace in the tent. Thus the expression "wineskin in the smoke" describes the psalmist's physical, mental, and spiritual torment after enduring various tribulations and sufferings. The word "forget" is שָׁכַח (*shakhah*) in Hebrew and does not refer merely to forgetting something cognitively but to the act of ignoring God's Word and departing from God (Deut 8:11, 19). In this respect the psalmist did not give up his faith in God's statutes (*hoq*), even in times of despair when it was difficult to obey God's Word. He inclined his heart to perform God's statutes forever, even to the end (Ps 119:112).

Redemptive-Historical Meaning

Jesus is the aim of the statutes (*hoq*) of the Old Testament. A statute is a regulation that has binding power and must be obeyed. Of all statutes, only God's possess everlasting binding power. God's statutes are deeply connected to Jesus Christ.

Jesus delivered the statute (the Word). In Psalm 2:7, the Scripture testifies, "I will surely tell of the decree [*hoq*] of the LORD: He said to Me, 'You are My Son, today I have begotten You.'" The first-person pronoun "I" refers to a king established by God, ultimately, Jesus the Son of God. While some consider "my Son" to be Solomon, it does not ultimately refer to Solomon. This is because this king is to possess the very ends of the earth, and Solomon did not. Jesus' possessions, however, indeed reach to the ends of the earth (Ps 2:8).

Jesus is the preacher of God's decree. Thus His Word alone possesses everlasting binding power.

Jesus delivered God's statute (Word) just as God had spoken it. The expression "tell of" in Psalm 2:7, "I will surely tell of the decree," is written in the Piel stem of סָפַר (*safar*). This indicates that Jesus would recount God's Word just as God had spoken it, without any change. Jesus indeed delivered the decree just as God had spoken it. In John 12:49–50, Jesus said, "I did not speak on My own initiative, but the Father Himself who sent Me has given Me a commandment as to what to say and what to speak. I know that His commandment is eternal life; therefore the things I speak, I speak just as the Father has told Me." Likewise, Jesus preached solely what God had spoken (John 5:19–20; 14:24; 17:8, 14).

The saints are to preserve and preach the Word just as Jesus spoke it, without adding or taking anything away. Revelation 22:18–19 warns us, "I testify to everyone who hears the words of the prophecy of this book: if anyone adds to them, God will add to him the plagues which are written in this book; and if anyone takes away from the words of the book of this prophecy, God will take away his part from the tree of life and from the holy city, which are written in this book" (see also Deut 4:2; 12:32; Prov 30:6; Eccl 3:14).

V. *Davar* (דָּבָר)—God's Word

Bible Verses

Psalm 119:9, 16, 17, 25, 28, 42, 43, 49, 57, 65, 74, 81, 89, 101, 105, 107, 114, 130, 139, 147, 160, 161, 169 (twenty-three times)

Etymology and Meaning

The Hebrew word *davar* originates from the verb דָּבַר (*davar*) meaning "to speak," and it means "word" or "command." When the prophets delivered God's Word, they explicitly used the term "the word of the LORD" countless times. They had the conviction that they were delivering God's Word rather than their own thoughts (Jer 22:1–2; Ezek 22:1; Hos 1:1; Joel 1:1; Jonah 1:1; Mic 1:1; Zeph 1:1; Hag 1:1; Zech 1:1; Mal 1:1).

The word *davar* is translated as "all the words of this law" (Deut 17:19; 27:3, 8; 28:58; 29:29; 31:12; 32:46; Josh 8:34), "the words of this law" (Deut 27:26; 31:24; 2 Kgs 23:24; 2 Chr 34:19; Neh 8:9, 13), "the word which I am commanding you" (Deut 4:2; 6:6; 32:46), "all these words which the LORD had commanded" (Exod 19:7), a "royal edict" or "command" (Esth 1:19; Jer 35:14). In addition, *davar* also refers to the Ten Commandments (Exod 34:28; Deut 4:13; 10:4).

Usage

In the Old Testament, *davar* occurs in its verb form 1,140 times and in its noun form 1,455 times, mostly to mean the "word." The expression *devar yehwah* (Adonai) (דְּבַר־יְהוָה), that is, the "word of the LORD," appears 259 times.

The Bible typically uses the words *davar* (דָּבַר) and *amar* (אָמַר) for the verb "to speak." Besides referring to the "word," the noun *davar* could also mean "acts" (1 Kgs 14:19, 29; 15:23; 16:20; 2 Chr 9:29; 13:22).

In the Old Testament, the verb *davar*, meaning "to speak," occurs for the first time in Genesis 8:15. *Davar* is translated as "spoke" in the sentence, "Then God spoke to Noah, saying ..." Here *davar* occurs in its Piel stem; this implies that God spoke to Noah emphatically that he should come out from the ark. The word "saying" in Genesis 8:15 is *amar* (אָמַר) in Hebrew. While *amar* usually occurs in reference to God's speech, *amar* and *davar* begin to appear together after Noah came out of the ark.

Lesson

The Word (*davar*) is light (Ps 119:105, 130), the truth without deceit (Ps 119:43, 160), eternally unchanging (Ps 119:89), a mystical, life-giving power (Ps 119:25, 107), an enlightening power for the simple (Ps 119:130), and a hiding place and a strong shield during times of extreme suffering (Ps 119:114). The Word (*davar*), therefore, is the only hope for which all mankind must yearn (Ps 119:49, 81, 147). We must fear God and trust His Word with all our lives (Ps 119:42, 57, 74, 161). The Word (*davar*) is a ray of light that cuts through pitch darkness to reveal the walkway. It is the decisive step toward a solution as one is drowning in a sea of continuous problems.

Jesus Himself is the Word from the beginning who came to this earth in the flesh (John 1:1, 14). He is the true light of life that drives out the darkness of the world (John 1:4–5, 9; 8:12; 11:9–11; 2 Cor 4:6). Jesus said in John 9:5, "While I am in the world, I am the Light of the world." He continued, "For a little while longer the Light is among you. Walk while you have the Light, so that darkness will not overtake you; he who walks in the darkness does not know where he goes. While you have the Light, believe in the Light, so that you may become sons of Light" (John 12:35–36). Jesus is the true light and the source of light that allows each person to live a life of hope and happiness.

While human words are often empty, God's Word (*davar*) possesses the power to fulfill His will. God's Word surely bears fruit (Isa 55:11), and those who receive the Word will surely bear fruit of fulfillment as they live according to it. In Psalm 119:9, the psalmist affirmed, "How can a young person stay on the path of purity? By living according to your word [דָּבָר, *davar*]" (NIV). Thus we can fulfill the Word in our lives by keeping the Lord's Word (*davar*).

Exemplary Attitude

In Psalm 119:28, the psalmist prayed, "My soul weeps because of grief; strengthen me according to Your word [*davar*]." The word "grief" (תּוּגָה, *tugah*) means "anguish, sorrow." The psalmist suffered such great sorrow that his soul felt as if it were melting away. In Psalm 119:107, he revealed, "I am exceedingly afflicted," and again in 119:25, "My soul cleaves to the dust." During hardship in which he could barely hold himself up, the psalmist looked toward the Word (*davar*) of the Lord and cried out, "Strengthen me according to Your word" (119:28). Here, "strengthen" (קוּם, *qum*) describes the state of standing firm. Only God's Word (*davar*) establishes us firm, even during times of extreme sorrow.

Redemptive-Historical Meaning

More than any other, the word "Word" (*davar*) clearly represents Jesus who was to come. The "Word" (*davar*) is another name for Jesus; it reveals His essence.

At His first coming, Jesus was the "Word" incarnate. The Greek equivalent of *davar* is λόγος (*logos*). John 1:1 narrates, "In the beginning was the Word [*logos*], and the Word was with God, and the Word was God." Everything came into being through the Word, and nothing came into being without the Word (John 1:3, 10; Heb 11:3). Yet this Word became flesh and dwelt among us, and He was Jesus (John 1:14). While on the earth, Jesus taught the Word without rest until His ascension (Matt 5:1–7:29; Mark 1:21–22; Luke 24:25–27, 44–49). Jesus' Word is not dead knowledge but a living and active Word that exercises actual power (Heb 4:12). The Word embodies spirit and life (John 6:63), so when Jesus spoke the Word, the dead were raised (John 5:25; 11:43–44), and the Spirit came upon those who heard the Word (Acts 10:44).

At His second coming, the "Word" is the name of the Lord. In Revelation 19:11, the apostle John saw "a white horse, and He who sat on it." His name is "Faithful and True," and He judges and wages war in righteousness. In Revelation 19:13, John continues, "He is clothed with a robe dipped in blood, and His name is called The Word [*logos*] of God." The apostle John had earlier referred to Jesus as "the Word [*logos*] of Life" who was "from the beginning" (1 John 1:1).

Jesus is the Word (*logos*). Thus the saints cannot live apart from the Word. Jesus said in John 15:5, "he who abides in Me and I in him," and in John 15:7, He said, "If you abide in Me, and My words abide in you ..." In saying this He made Himself equal with His Word. When we receive His Word in faith, we are accepting Jesus in faith (John 1:12).

VI. *Piqqud* (פִּקּוּד)—God's Precepts

Bible Verses

Psalm 119:4, 15, 27, 40, 45, 56, 63, 69, 78, 87, 93, 94, 100, 104, 110, 128, 134, 141, 159, 168, 173 (twenty-one times)

Etymology and Meaning

Piqqud comes from the verb פָּקַד (*paqad*), which means "to visit, to attend, to bring punishment." The noun *piqqud* generally means "commandment, precept, statute." It is generally used in the plural form and refers to all the articles of the law. Scholars have said that no other word in the Old Testament is as hard to translate as *paqad*, which occurs about three hundred times.[23] *Paqad* was used frequently in reference to entrusting a task to a manager or supervisor so that it could be carried out to the best of one's abilities. Thus the word פִּקּוּד

(*piqqud*), derived from *paqad*, refers to a precept or responsibility that must be kept.

Usage

The Hiphil stem of *paqad* was used as "appoint" when the Levites were put over the tabernacle in Numbers 1:50 and Joshua was put over the congregation in Numbers 27:16, as "committed" when King Rehoboam gave the shields of bronze into the care of the commanders in 1 Kings 14:27, as "commit" in committing one's spirit to God in Psalm 31:5, and as "attended to" regarding the leaders of Israel's responsibility to shepherd God's flock in Jeremiah 23:2. Managers and supervisors meticulously examine all tasks from small to great in order to complete everything that has been entrusted to them. They make sacrifices and do not rest until their work is done. Likewise, those who are entrusted with God's Word keep it "diligently" (Ps 119:4), from very little things to many great things (Luke 16:10; see also Matt 25:21, 23; Luke 19:17).

Lesson

The author of Psalm 119 made a great confession that he would continuously observe the Lord's precepts with all his heart (pour his heart into, devote himself to, give his best efforts to; Ps 119:69) even when the arrogant forged lies against him (Ps 119:69), when the proud subverted him with lies (Ps 119:78), when the wicked almost destroyed him (Ps 119:87), when the wicked laid a snare for him (Ps 119:110), when he was oppressed (Ps 119:134), and when he was despised (Ps 119:141).

During extreme ordeals, the psalmist placed the Word (*piqqud*) at the center of his heart and so liberated himself from his enemies (Ps 119:45). He received understanding by departing from evil and keeping God's precepts (*piqqud*) (Ps 119:100, 104; see also Job 28:28). He was revived (Ps 119:93, 159) through the Word (*piqqud*) and experienced the Lord's hand, which was always ready to help him (Ps 119:173).

Exemplary Attitude

Psalm 119:87 states, "They almost destroyed me on earth, but as for me, I did not forsake Your precepts [*piqqud*]." The word "destroyed" is the Piel stem of כָּלָה (*kalah*), which means "to finish, annihilate, fail." The psalmist was at the brink of destruction. He was like a feeble candle flame about to be blown out by the storm. Although he was not at fault, arrogant evildoers had persecuted him for no reason (Ps 119:78, 85–86). Yet he confessed, "As for me, I did not forsake Your precepts [*piqqud*]" (Ps 119:87). The word "forsake" (עָזַב, *azav*) also means "to abandon" (Deut 12:19; 14:27). True faith means not abandoning God's precepts (*piqqud*) but keeping them until the end, even if the world utterly forsakes one or threatens his life (Rev 14:12).

Redemptive-Historical Meaning

Piqqud refers to the duty and responsibility entrusted to a manager or supervisor. The Old Testament prophesied that Jesus would come as a shepherd (Isa 40:11; Ezek 37:24). As a shepherd who oversaw His flock, Jesus completed the redemption of His elect by keeping God's precepts (*piqqud*) with His whole body.

Jesus fulfilled His responsibility to shepherd His flock. Jesus was the "good shepherd" (John 10:11, 14), "a Ruler who [would] shepherd [His] people Israel" (Matt 2:6), "the great Shepherd of the sheep" (Heb 13:20), "the Shepherd and Guardian of [our] souls" (1 Pet 2:25), and "the Chief Shepherd" (1 Pet 5:4). Jesus called His own sheep by name and led them out (John 10:3). Jesus also led other sheep that were not of the fold of Israel (John 10:16). This reveals how Jesus saved not only the Jews but also the Gentiles of all nations in the world. He gave life to the sheep He led so that they would have it abundantly. Jesus fully carried out His responsibility as the shepherd (John 10:10).

Jesus was a shepherd who laid down His life to fulfill His responsibility. A hired shepherd does not want to take responsibility for the sheep. When in danger, he abandons the sheep to save himself, as he has no love for the sheep (John 10:12-13). A true shepherd, however, lays down his life to save the sheep. As the true shepherd, Jesus laid down His life on the cross and fulfilled His responsibility. Jesus said in John 10:11, "I am the good shepherd; the good shepherd lays down His life for the sheep." In John 10:15, He continued, "Even as the Father knows Me and I know the Father; and I lay down My life for the sheep." This is the life of *piqqud*.

Just like Jesus, His saints must faithfully dedicate their lives to completing their tasks from God. In Acts 20:24, the apostle Paul confessed, "I do not consider my life of any account as dear to myself, so that I may finish my course and the ministry which I received from the Lord Jesus, to testify solemnly of the gospel of the grace of God" (see also 2 Tim 4:7).

VII. *Mitzwah* (מִצְוָה)—God's Commandments

Bible Verses

Psalm 119:6, 10, 19, 21, 32, 35, 47, 48, 60, 66, 73, 86, 96, 98, 115, 127, 131, 143, 151, 166, 172, 176 (twenty-two times)

Etymology and Meaning

The noun *mitzwah* is derived from the verb צָוָה (*tsawah*), which means "to lay charge (upon), to appoint, to order." *Mitzwah* refers to the commandment of God's Word that must be kept, since it has been proclaimed with the highest authority. The verb *tsawah*, from which *mitzwah* derives, appeared in Scripture for the first time when God commanded Adam not to eat the fruit of the tree of the knowledge of good and evil (Gen 2:16). Later it was used when God commanded Noah (Gen 6:22; 7:5) and Abraham (Gen 18:19) according to the covenant. Psalm 105:8 calls the covenant given to Abraham, Isaac, and Jacob "the word which He commanded [צִוָּה, *tsawah*] to a thousand generations." Moreover, when Moses received and obeyed the instructions regarding the construction of the tabernacle, the Scripture testifies that the people had done "just as the LORD had commanded [*tsawah*] Moses" (Exod 39:1, 5, 7, 21, 26, 29, 31, 32, 42, 43; 40:16, 19, 21, 23, 25, 27, 29, 32). Likewise, Lamentations 3:37 states, "Who is there who speaks and it comes to pass, unless the Lord has commanded [*tsawah*] it?"

Usage

The noun *mitzwah* occurs about 180 times in the Old Testament; it parallels the various meanings of *torah* and was used interchangeably with *torah* at times (Gen 26:5; Exod 16:28; 24:12; Num 36:13; Deut 30:10, 16).[24] *Mitzwah* can refer to the Ten Commandments, as in Exodus 24:12: "I will give you the stone tablets with the law and the commandment [*mitzwah*]." *Mitzwah* can also refer to a covenant and its details (2 Kgs 23:3). According to Deuteronomy 30:16, keeping *mitzwah* (the commandment) is the way for God's people to live, multiply, and be blessed by God.

God added a legal order for His people to place a tassel of blue cord on each corner of their garments so that they would not fail to understand and forget the Word (*mitzwah*) of the highest authority—authority higher than the heavens (Num 15:37-40). The tassels at the corners of their garments emphasized the authority of God's Word that was to be kept at every moment. The authority of the Word is, in other words, the authority of God who commanded the Word.[25]

Lesson

The author of Psalm 119 struggled to keep all the Lord's commandments without exception (Ps 119:6, 10, 32, 60, 115, 166). Thus he confessed, "I have seen a limit to all perfection; Your commandment is exceedingly broad" (Ps 119:96). Although nothing in this world is perfect, as even the seemingly perfect soon reveals its limits, God's Word is absolutely perfect, without blemish or flaw. Those who believe wholeheartedly in this perfect Word, therefore, will live without blemish before God each and every day by His grace (1 Cor 1:8; 2 Cor 7:1; 1 Thess 3:13; 5:23; 2 Pet 3:14).

Exemplary Attitude

The psalmist concluded in the last verse of Psalm 119, "I have gone astray like a lost sheep; seek Your servant, for I do not forget Your commandments [*mitzwah*]" (Ps 119:176). The psalmist likened his desperate run from his enemies to a lost sheep going astray. Yet he confessed that, even in his dire situation, he did not forget God's commandments (*mitzwah*). He also confessed, "Trouble and anguish have come upon me, yet Your commandments are my delight" (Ps 119:143). Indeed, those who inscribe every detail of the Lord's commandments (*mitzwah*) on their hearts will never be ashamed.

Redemptive-Historical Meaning

Mitzwah refers to God's command or commandments. The whole Bible can be rightly called God's command and commandments. Jesus lived out absolute obedience to God's command. Jesus is a model of how the saints must keep God's command as He lived a life of absolute obedience.

Jesus accepted God's command as eternal life and kept it. In John 12:50, Jesus said, "I know that His commandment is eternal life; therefore the things I speak, I speak just as the Father has told Me." The Word of God the Father is eternal life. Thus eternal life is guaranteed to those who obey His Word but not so to the disobedient.

Jesus kept God's commandments completely. Jesus abided in God's love by keeping His commandments. Jesus said in John 15:10, "If you keep My commandments, you will abide in My love; just as I have kept My Father's commandments and abide in His love," and in John 8:55, "[I] keep His word." Philippians 2:8 also states regarding Jesus, "He humbled Himself by becoming obedient to the point of death, even death on a cross."

Just as Jesus was obedient to the commandments of God the Father, the saint must be obedient to Jesus' commands. The miracle of the water turning into wine during the wedding feast at Cana was possible because the people obeyed Jesus' Word (John 2:7-9). At the time Mary said to the servants, "Whatever He says to you, do it" (John 2:5). Those who do not keep Jesus' commandments do not love Him (John 14:15, 21, 23-24). They are liars and do not have the truth in them (1 John 2:4). Even at the end of the world, only those who keep God's commandments will endure tribulation and be victorious (Rev 12:17; 14:12).

VIII. *Derekh* (דֶּרֶךְ)—God's Ways (God's Paths)

Bible Verses

Psalm 119:3, 14, 27, 30, 32, 33, 37 (seven times)

Etymology and Meaning

The noun *derekh*, meaning "way, manner, journey," is derived from the verb *darakh* (דָּרַךְ), which means "to tread, to march forth." *Derekh* is most often used in reference to our life journeys. We can discover the right course and direction of our life journeys only through a proper relationship with the God of the covenant.

Usage

All people, without exception, are sojourners in this world. When Jacob stood before the Egyptian king, Pharaoh, he confessed how difficult his 130-year sojourn on this earth had been (Gen 47:9; see also Lev 25:23; Ps 39:12; 1 Pet 2:11). David also reflected, "We are sojourners before You, and tenants, as all our fathers were" (1 Chr 29:15). Sojourners face many hardships in untraveled foreign lands. Meeting an accurate and kind guide, therefore, is like encountering an oasis in the desert.

Lesson

The author of Psalm 119 sang that דֶּרֶךְ (*derekh*) was "the way of [God's] testimonies" (Ps 119:14), "the way of [God's] precepts" (Ps 119:27), "the faithful way" (Ps 119:30), "the way of [God's] commandments" (Ps

119:32), and "the way of [God's] statutes" (Ps 119:33). God leads each person to the proper path. In Isaiah 48:17, God reminded His people, "I am the LORD your God, who teaches you to profit, who leads you in the way you should go." Thus God's Word itself is the true path for all people. Exodus 18:20 also says, "Teach them the statutes and the laws, and make known to them the way [*derekh*] in which they are to walk and the work they are to do."

Jesus Christ alone is a kind companion for sojourners; He is the true way for those on the direct path to heaven (John 14:6). Those who abandon this path to take the way of this world will sin; they will be deprived of peace and find themselves in misery. The wicked enemy will come upon them and take away both life and blessings (Ps 7:3–5; Jer 6:16–19).

Exemplary Attitude

In Psalm 119:37, the psalmist prayed, "Turn away my eyes from looking at vanity, and revive me in Your ways." Here the word "vanity" (שָׁוְא, *shawe*) means "vain, emptiness, falsehood, worthless." Having fully realized the emptiness of not only worldly idols but also wealth, honor, pleasure, and lust, the psalmist earnestly prayed that God would turn his eyes from worthless things. In the previous verse, he had prayed, "Incline my heart to Your testimonies and not to dishonest gain" (Ps 119:36).

Jesus taught the importance of what we see with our eyes, saying, "If your eye causes you to stumble, pluck it out and throw it from you. It is better for you to enter life with one eye, than to have two eyes and be cast into the fiery hell" (Matt 18:9). We must set our eyes on God's Word alone rather than on worthless things (Job 31:1; Ps 119:18, 82, 123, 147–148; Prov 23:5). We will receive life when our eyes focus on God's way (*derekh*) and we walk in it. The English Standard Version renders Psalm 119:37 as, "Turn my eyes from looking at worthless things; and give me life in your ways."

Redemptive-Historical Meaning

There are various paths in this world. Some paths lead us quickly and directly to our intended destination, while others take time but eventually lead us to it. Some even lead us nowhere near the destination. Jesus alone is the true way (*derekh*).

Jesus is the true way to the Father. John 14:6 states, "Jesus said to him [Thomas], 'I am the way, and the truth, and the life; no one comes to the Father but through Me.'" The word "way" is ἡ ὁδός (*hē hodos*) in Greek and means "the way." This meaning implies that Jesus is not just one of many ways in the world but the only way in the world. The phrase "I am," which is εἰμί (*eimi*) in Greek, is in the present tense, which emphasizes that Jesus being the only way to the Father is a constant and unchanging truth.

Jesus is the true way to eternal life. Jesus explained two types of paths in Matthew 7:13–14: "Enter through the narrow gate; for the gate is wide and the way is broad that leads to destruction, and there are many who enter through it. For the gate is small and the way is narrow that leads to life, and there are few who find it." The way to eternal life is found in Jesus, and it is also Jesus who enables people to enter into this way. Through the Word of the cross, Jesus leads us to this eternal life. Thus "the word of the cross is folly to those who are perishing, but to us who are being saved it is the power of God" (1 Cor 1:18).

We who are following in Jesus' footsteps must take up our own crosses and follow Him (Matt 16:24; Mark 8:34; Luke 9:23; 1 Pet 2:21). The path of the cross, however, is neither broad nor level. It co be a road of suffering and solitude and even be life-thre road, however, is the way that leads to eternal li

IX. *Imrah* (אִמְרָה)—God's Word (God's Promise)

Bible Verses

Psalm 119:11, 38, 41, 50, 58, 67, 76, 82, 103, 116, 123, 133, 140, 148, 154, 158, 162, 170, 172 (nineteen times)

Etymology and Meaning

Imrah means "word" or "speech" and occurs thirty-seven times in the Old Testament. It appears nineteen times in Psalm 119 alone and seven times in other psalms (Pss 12:6 [2x]; 17:6; 18:30; 105:19; 138:2; 147:15). *Imrah* originated from the verb אָמַר (*amar*). The word *amar* occurs more than five thousand three hundred times in the Old Testament. It is similar in meaning to the English verb "to say." This expands the meaning of the word to include "to utter," "to think," "to command," and "to promise."

Usage

Deuteronomy 33:9 testifies that observing the "word" of the Lord is equivalent to keeping His "covenant." Psalm 147:15 describes God sending forth His "command [*imrah*]." The Revised Standard Version mostly translates *imrah* as "promise" (Ps 119:38, 41, 50, 58, 76, 82, 116, 123, 133, 140, 148, 154). On six occasions it translates it as "word" and one as "commands" (Ps 119:158). *Amar*, the verb form of *imrah*, used in relation to God, connotes God's creation, command,

occurs in the context of God's ministry of creation. The times in the context of creation in Genesis 1 (Gen 26, 28, 29). The word "spoke" in Psalm 33:9 is *amar* in Hebrew: "He spoke, and it was done."

The word occurs in the context of God's command. Amar was used when God warned Adam in Genesis 2:16–17, "The LORD God commanded the man, saying [*amar*], 'From any tree of the garden you may eat freely; but from the tree of the knowledge of good and evil you shall not eat, for in the day that you eat from it you will surely die.'" It was also used when God commanded Abraham in Genesis 12:1: "The LORD said [*amar*] to Abram, 'Go forth from your country, and from your relatives and from your father's house, to the land which I will show you.'"

The word was used in the context of God's promise. Amar was used when God promised to give David and his offspring a lamp always (2 Kgs 8:19) and also when God promised to give Israel the land of Canaan (Neh 9:15, 23).

Lesson

Every verse of Psalm 119 contains vivid accounts of the psalmist's experience with the Word. He kept the Word (*imrah*) in his heart and experienced how it helped him from sinning (Ps 119:11). He found comfort from the Word in his affliction (Ps 119:50). He tasted the Lord's Word and found it to be sweeter than honey (Ps 119:103). He longed for God's Word until he reached a state of exhaustion (Ps 119:82, 123). Having discovered the joy of understanding God's Word (*imrah*), he described it as the joy of reaping great spoils after a victory in battle (Ps 119:162).

It is worth noting that the verbs used together with *imrah* in Psalm 119 are in the Hiphil (causative) stem, showing causative action by God. Psalm 119:38 states, "Establish [Hiphil stem of קוּם, *qum*] Your word to Your servant, as that which produces reverence for You." Psalm 119:133 states, "Establish [Hiphil stem of כּוּן, *kun*] my footsteps in Your word." Psalm 119:170 states, "Deliver [Hiphil stem of נָצַל, *natsal*] me according to Your word." These verses show that the ministry of the Word depends completely upon God's sovereign work rather than our own strength.

Exemplary Attitude

Psalm 119:148 reads, "My eyes anticipate the night watches, that I may meditate on Your word [*imrah*]." The psalmist not only turned his eyes away from worthless things but also set his eyes on the Word (*imrah*) of the Lord. Here, the expression "night watches" comes from the Hebrew word אַשְׁמוּרָה (*ashmurah*), which denotes a "night guard." The expression "before dawn" occurs in the previous verse (Ps 119:147), and the word "dawn" is נֶשֶׁף (*neshef*), meaning "twilight." Through these expressions we learn that the psalmist rose during the darkest and coldest hours before sunrise and meditated on God's Word like a night watchman standing guard. He confessed, "My eyes fail with longing for Your salvation and for Your righteous word [*imrah*]" (Ps 119:123); the author was so focused on his meditation of the Word that he even lost track of time.

Redemptive-Historical Meaning

Imrah most frequently occurs with the proclamation of God's Word. Jesus is the "Word" from "the beginning" (John 1:1), and all His ministry is based on the Word. Jesus' ministry in relation to *imrah* is as follows.

Jesus is the agent of creation. In 1 Corinthians 8:6, Paul said, "There is but one God, the Father, from whom are all things and we exist for Him; and one Lord, Jesus Christ, by whom are all things, and we exist through Him" (see also John 1:3, 10). This statement implies that all creatures were created through God the Son. This creation was performed through *imrah*, the Word. *Imrah* comes from the verb אָמַר (*amar*), which is usually translated as "to say." *Amar* occurs eleven times in the creation account in Genesis 1, ten times as "God said" (Gen 1:3, 6, 9, 11, 14, 20, 24, 26, 28, 29) and one time as "saying" (Gen 1:22). The world was created through the Word (Heb 11:3).

Jesus proclaimed imrah, the Word. Just as the phrase "then God said" (וַיֹּאמֶר אֱלֹהִים) occurs frequently in the Old Testament (Gen 6:13; 9:8, 12, 17; 17:9, 15, 19), so the phrase "Jesus said" (Ἰησοῦς λέγει) occurs frequently in the New Testament (Matt 8:22; 21:16; Mark 2:17; 10:23, 27, 42; 11:22, 33).

For the most part, Jesus' ministry was the proclamation of the Word. Jesus was the true teacher (or rabbi) of the Word from heaven (John 3:2). Jesus was a teacher of the Word at birth. In His earliest days he was a teacher of the Word to His parents and to the teachers He met in the temple of Jerusalem (Luke 2:46–51). He was a teacher of the Word in the synagogue at Capernaum, on the mountains, and by the seashore (Matt 4:23; 5:1–2; Mark 1:21; Luke 4:31; John 6:59). He was also a teacher in the temple of Jerusalem (Matt 21:12–13). He was a servant teacher (John 13:13–15). The people listened to His teachings, and "the crowds were amazed at His teaching; for He was teaching them as one having authority, and not as their scribes" (Matt 7:28–29; see also Mark 1:22).

After Jesus completed the ministry of atonement on the cross, rose again, and ascended to heaven, the early church began to record Jesus' teachings in writing. These writings became the four Gospels and then the New Testament. The apostle John revealed the purpose of writing the Scripture: "These have been written so that you may believe that Jesus is the Christ, the Son of God; and that believing you may have life in His name" (John 20:31). The Word spoken by Jesus and written in the Scripture gives us hope (Rom 15:4). We have the hope of promise called the Word (*imrah*), and this glorious hope is none other than Jesus Christ Himself (Col 1:27).

X. *Emeth* (אֱמֶת), *Emunah* (אֱמוּנָה)—God's Truth (God's Faithfulness)

Bible Verses

Psalm 119:30, 43, 75, 86, 90, 138, 142, 151, 160 (nine times)

Etymology and Meaning

Emeth originates from the Hebrew verb אָמַן (*aman*), which means "to establish, to trust, to confirm." The word "amen," which we frequently confess during worship, is derived from this word *aman*. "Amen" is a response to prayers during worship services (Neh 8:6; Ps 106:48; Rev 5:14; 7:12) and generally means that we agree with what has been spoken (Gal 6:18; Eph 3:21; Phil 4:20; 1 Tim 6:16; 2 Tim 4:18; Heb 13:21; 1 Pet 4:11). Jesus, however, used this word at the *beginning* of important messages, often saying "truly" ("amen"). This expression occurs twenty-eight times in Matthew, thirteen times in Mark, and six times in Luke.[26] In the Gospel of John, Jesus began His messages with the words "truly, truly" twenty-five times.[27] This expression emphasizes that Jesus' words are the eternally unchangeable Word of God and that they have authority, since God Himself has agreed with them (2 Cor 1:20).

Usage

The word *emeth* is translated differently in different contexts. It is translated as "truth" in Isaiah 39:8, "faithfulness" in Psalm 71:22 (NIV), "truly" in Genesis 47:29 (KJV), and "true" in Psalm 19:9. In Psalm 119, what is true (*emeth*) is the law of the Lord (Ps 119:142), all the Lord's commandments (Ps 119:151), and the sum of the Lord's Word (Ps 119:160). Also, the word "faithfulness" in Psalm 119:90 is אֱמוּנָה (*emunah*) in Hebrew and originates from the same word as *emeth*.

Before his death David called his son Solomon and said to him, "Keep the charge of the LORD your God, to walk in His ways, to keep His statutes, His commandments, His ordinances, and His testimonies, according to what is written in the Law of Moses, that you may succeed in all that you do and wherever you turn" (1 Kgs 2:3). Then David summed up his final will by telling Solomon to walk before God in "truth" (*emeth*; 1 Kgs 2:4). The words "statutes," "commandments," "ordinances," and "testimonies" are all used synonymously for *emeth*.

Lesson

The psalmist confessed in Psalm 119:160, "The sum of Your word is truth [*emeth*]," and in 119:151, "You are near, O LORD, and all Your commandments are truth [*emeth*]." He stated further in 119:90, "Your faithfulness [*emunah*] continues throughout all generations," and in 119:138, "You have commanded Your testimonies in righteousness and exceeding faithfulness [*emunah*]." He praised God's Word as the apex of "truth" and "faithfulness." When praising God's law as *emeth*, he did not merely testify that God's Word is the truth and not a lie. Instead, he asserted that God's law and Word are ever so trustworthy, certain, and steadfast that people can lean on them with all their lives.

The word "faithfulness" represents God's steadfastness. God is faithful. Faithfulness means being "trustworthy, true to one's word, and without deceit" (Deut 7:9; Ps 119:86). In Hebrew faithfulness is אָמַן (*aman*), which means "to put trust" or "to be faithful." Just as Paul testified in 2 Corinthians 1:19, "The Son of God, Christ Jesus, … was not yes and no, but is yes in Him," God is never vague, and He does not contradict Himself in His speech.

God is unchanging and does not cast shifting shadows (Jas 1:17). People change, but God does not (Mal 3:6); He is the same yesterday, today, and forever (Heb 1:12; 13:8). Ultimately, God's faithfulness is the great driving force that propels the covenant's fulfillment in redemptive history.

Exemplary Attitude

Psalm 119:43 states, "Do not take the word of truth [*emeth*] utterly out of my mouth, for I wait for Your ordinances." In the previous verse, the psalmist had said that he would have "an answer" for the man who reproached him if God bestowed upon him kindness and salvation according to His Word (Ps 119:42). In this context Psalm 119:43 is a sincere prayer asking God to fill the psalmist's mouth with the Word of truth so that he can continue to proclaim His Word. A person cannot proclaim anything unless he is filled with the Word of God. We must longingly seek after the Word until it fills the depths of our hearts. In Psalm 119:43, the psalmist confessed, "I wait for Your ordinances." Here the verb "wait" occurs in the Piel stem of יָחַל (*yahal*), which means "to wait expectantly, to trust, to hope." Thus it expresses an intense longing for God's Word. Those who yearn for God's Word will be filled with His Word even in the depths of their hearts so that they can fearlessly proclaim the Word wherever they go.

Redemptive-Historical Meaning

Jesus is the truth (*emeth*). In John 14:6, Jesus said, "I am the way, and the truth, and the life; no one comes to the Father but through Me." Here the word "truth" is ἡ ἀλήθεια (*hē alētheia*) in Greek, which means "the truth"—the single truth that is not of this world.

Jesus is the Amen. Emeth and "amen" come from the same word. The Bible introduces Jesus as the Amen. In Revelation 3:14, Jesus is referred to as "the Amen." Jesus is the fulfiller of all the prophecies in the Bible and the Amen who completes every Word. He did not come to abolish the law or the prophets but to fulfill them; that is the ministry of the Amen (Matt 5:17). Jesus came to fulfill all the "Law of Moses and the Prophets and the Psalms" (Luke 24:44) that had been written about Him. He ultimately fulfilled all of them on the earth and became "the Amen."

Jesus is true. No deceit can be found in Jesus (see Heb 6:19; Titus 1:2). *Emeth* is truth and what is true. The prophet Isaiah spoke of the end times, "He who is blessed in the earth will be blessed by the God of truth" (Isa 65:16). "The God of truth" refers to God who is true. Likewise, Jesus is called "the faithful and true Witness" (Rev 3:14) and "Faithful and True" (Rev 19:11).

Thus everything that Jesus does is trustworthy, and we can entrust our lives to His will without any doubting. Jesus alone is our Amen and the truth. He alone will take full responsibility for our entire lives. Therefore, like the apostle John, let us yearn for His quick coming and join in John's confession, "Amen. Come, Lord Jesus" (Rev 22:20).

CHAPTER 11

The Minor Conclusion of the Ten Words

The Ten Commandments are the essence of all God's laws and the main standard by which God's chosen people of Israel were to live. A standard is a model or law that people are to rightly follow, and the Ten Commandments were the fundamental model that the people of the covenant were to follow. This model, however, was not reserved for the Israelites alone. It presents the standard of living for everyone in the world.

Nothing else has been more influential to human life in history than the Ten Commandments. Martin Luther, the flag bearer of the religious Reformation, while publishing a shorter catechism with three hundred questions in 1529, made a testamentary request, stating that preachers should not change the wording of the Ten Commandments (along with the Lord's Prayer and the Apostles' Creed) but should always use the same wording and Bible passages so that readers could memorize and recite them. The Ten Commandments were the foundation for the Reformation and for its ongoing driving force.

While ethical codes for society differ slightly depending on countries, people, and societies, they are based on the same standard: the Ten Commandments that were spoken directly by God and written by His own finger (Deut 6-7; 12-26). The Ten Commandments stand above all the ancient laws, and nothing has exerted a greater influence on religions, ethics, morals, and life in general.

The Ten Commandments were not given as a temporary measure. They are the everlasting Word for all generations of all mankind. In other words, the Ten Commandments are the ultimate foundation for human ethics. Anyone seeking to reform corrupted ethics or initiate a movement to reinforce morals must return to the Ten Commandments, the Word of God, upon which they are rooted.

Thus the Ten Commandments and all God's laws are God's commands, God's judgments, God's teachings, God's testimonies, God's statutes, God's Word, God's promises, God's precepts, God's commandments, God's way, and God's truth. Through the Ten Commandments and all the laws, the people of God learn rules of truth about how to obey God's will as well as the order and laws of life that God desires.

These ten words that appear in Psalm 119 provide a driving force, vitality, substance, and guide that enable God's people to keep the Ten Commandments by grace. As we learned in Psalm 119, God's people must fill themselves completely from head to toe with the essence of these ten words. When we embody God's Word in our lives, we will be able to keep the Ten Commandments voluntarily and actively. I pray that the hearts and lives of all God's people will be filled up with the ten words in Psalm 119.

PART

IV

The Characteristics and Principles of the Ten Commandments, THE COVENANT FOR ALL GENERATIONS

PART IV

The Bible calls Israel, the chosen nation of God's covenant, the center of the world (Ezek 38:12; see also 5:5, 7, 14–15). At the center of Israel was Jerusalem (Pss 48:2; 125:2; Isa 2:2–3; Jer 51:50). At the center of Jerusalem was the temple. At the center of the temple was the most holy place, and at the heart of the most holy place was the ark of the covenant (Exod 25:21–22; 26:33). The ark of the covenant went ahead of the Israelites when they crossed the Jordan to enter the land of Canaan (Josh 3:1–17; 4:1–18) during the conquest of the city of Jericho (Josh 6:1–27) and also whenever they faced an obstacle as a nation. At the heart of the ark were the two stone tablets (Exod 25:16) upon which God had written the Ten Commandments with His own finger (Exod 24:12; 31:18; 32:15–16; 34:28; Deut 4:13; 9:9–11; 10:2–4). Hence the Ten Commandments were the center of the temple, of Israel, and of the world. The Ten Commandments should likewise be the center of our lives.

The Ten Commandments are the essence of the Sinaitic covenant that God made with the people of Israel. They are recorded in two places—Exodus 20:3–17 and Deuteronomy 5:7–21. Exodus 20 is a record of God's direct speech to the first generation of Israelites in the wilderness after the exodus; the record in Deuteronomy 5 is Moses' reiteration of the Ten Commandments to the second generation in the wilderness just before the people's entry into Canaan.

CHAPTER

12

The Names of the Ten Commandments: The Perfect Ten Words

The Ten Commandments were the words (commands) directly spoken by God in a loud voice to Moses and the Israelites on the sixth day of the third month in the year of the exodus (1446 BC, fifty days after the exodus), just before Moses' fourth ascent of the mountain (Deut 5:22). The expression "Ten Commandments" occurs in three places in Scripture (Exod 34:28; Deut 4:13; 10:4). In Hebrew the term is עֲשֶׂרֶת הַדְּבָרִים (asereth haddevarim), which means "the ten words." Exodus 34:28 states, "He [the Lord] wrote on the tablets the words of the covenant, the Ten Commandments." Here, the expression "the words of the covenant, the Ten Commandments" is translated from the Hebrew דִּבְרֵי הַבְּרִית עֲשֶׂרֶת הַדְּבָרִים (divre habberith asereth haddevarim). The phrase literally means "the words of the covenant, the ten words." Note that דָּבָר (davar), which means "word," occurs twice.

The Septuagint (LXX), the Greek translation of the Old Testament, translates the phrase as δέκα λόγους (deka logous). Logous is the plural form of logos, which means "word" (see John 1:1). Thus it is called the Ten Commandments, or the Decalogue—the scholarly term that comes from the combination of the Greek words δέκα (*deka*) and λόγους (*logous*).

"Ten" is a complete number and represents a state of fullness—having as much as is needed and being without lack. It represents the end of the first ten basic numbers as well as a return to the beginning.

Before Israel's exodus the ten plagues struck the land of Egypt (Exod 7:14–12:36). In Solomon's temple the two cherubim of olive wood on top of the ark were ten cubits high with five cubit-long wings on each side; the total width, from the tip of one wing to the other end, was ten cubits (1 Kgs 6:23–27). Offering one tenth of our income to God is an expression of faith in which we, the saints, confess that we are offering everything we have to God. Daniel's wisdom and understanding were ten times better than that of all the magicians and conjurers of the kingdom (Dan 1:20); his wisdom and understanding were extraordinary and complete (see Dan 6:3–4). During Job's suffering he said to his friends who harassed him, "These ten times you have insulted me; you are not ashamed to wrong me" (Job 19:3). In Revelation 2:10, Jesus said, "You will have tribulation for ten days. Be faithful until death." The number "ten" represents the period of tribulation that God's people must overcome (Dan 1:12–16; see also Dan 7:20, 24; Rev 12:3; 13:1; 17:3, 7, 12, 16).

The fact that there are ten clauses in the Ten Commandments conveys that the commandments, both in order and in content, contain the entirety of God's will without anything missing; they are the absolutely superior laws.

CHAPTER

13

THE CHARACTERISTICS OF THE TEN COMMANDMENTS

The Scripture introduces the Ten Commandments with the preface, "God spoke all these words, saying, 'I am the LORD your God, who brought you out of the land of Egypt, out of the house of slavery'" (Exod 20:1-2). The preface to any law is very important. The preface to the Ten Commandments begins with "God spoke all these words" (Exod 20:1), proclaiming that God Himself is both the author and giver of the law.

The Ten Commandments begin with God's grace and love. Their bestowal process was divine and glorious; it was powerfully proclaimed and executed with God's authority. The stone tablets with the Ten Commandments written on them were later specially kept in the ark of the covenant in the most holy place (Exod 25:16, 21-22; 40:20; Deut 10:1-5; 1 Kgs 8:9; Heb 9:4). All these confirm the superiority of the Ten Commandments over all other laws.[28]

The Ten Commandments, therefore, are perpetual and unchangeable, and their efficacy is everlasting. They are fundamental laws for daily living proclaimed not only to the Israelites but also to everyone in the world; they are unabolishable and eternal commandments for all generations (Matt 5:17-19). The following are discussions on the superior characteristics of the Ten Commandments over other laws.

I. Proclaimed as the Gospel of Freedom, Love, and Grace

In the preface to the Ten Commandments, God proclaimed that the commandments contained His burning love by saying, "I am the LORD your God, who brought you out of the land of Egypt, out of the house of slavery" (Exod 20:2). The people had been liberated first from the land of Egypt and second from the house of slavery.

"The land of Egypt" represents the sinful land of idolatry (Exod 12:12; Num 33:4; Rev 11:8). Saving the idolatrous Israelites from such a land was an expression of God's great mercy and compassion (Lev 17:7; Josh 24:14; Ezek 20:5-9).

"The house of slavery" represents the Israelites' distress, persecution, and misery under the tyrant Pharaoh of Egypt. God liberated the Israelites by rescuing them from "the house of slavery" by His sovereign power and absolute grace. The exodus that followed the ten plagues, especially the last plague that killed all the firstborn of Egypt, is frequently referenced as a significant event not only in the Old Testament but also in the New Testament (Acts 7:36; 13:17; Heb 3:16; 8:9; 11:28-29).

After the exodus God guided the people through the pillar of cloud and the pillar of fire from Etham (Exod 13:20-22). He divided the Red Sea, and the people walked across on dry land (Exod 14:15-25). He guided them to the cool shades at Elim, where there were twelve springs of water and seventy palm trees (Exod 15:27). When the people ran out of food in the wilderness of Sin, God sent them manna from heaven (Exod 16). In Rephidim He allowed them to taste living waters flowing like a river from the rock (Exod 17:1-7; see also Pss

78:16; 105:41). He gave them great victory over the Amalekites, their enemies (Exod 17:8–16).

The Ten Commandments, therefore, are not fearful and dreadful commandments. We must remember that they are God's gospel of love and grace that gifted slaves with true freedom. Moses poetically described the majestic scene of the Israelites receiving the Ten Commandments at the foot of Mount Sinai: "Indeed, He loves the people; all Your holy ones are in Your hand, and they followed in Your steps; everyone receives of Your words" (Deut 33:3).

While we were living in the world, far away from God, serving the gods of this world (John 12:31; 14:30; 16:11; 2 Cor 4:4), and while we were living miserable lives of slavery under the oppression of the heinous Satan, Jesus redeemed us by the blood of His cross (Rom 3:24; 1 Cor 1:30; Eph 1:7; Col 1:13–14; 1 Pet 1:18–19). True freedom is liberation from the bondage of sin (Rom 8:21). Galatians 5:1 states, "It was for freedom that Christ set us free; therefore keep standing firm and do not be subject again to a yoke of slavery." Luke 4:18 also speaks of proclaiming "release to the captives." Second Corinthians 3:17 states, "Now the Lord is the Spirit, and where the Spirit of the Lord is, there is liberty." John 8:32 states, "You will know the truth, and the truth will make you free." Thus we taste true liberation and salvation only in Jesus, who is the truth (John 14:6).

II. Given in Holiness and Glory

The scene of God's bestowal of the Ten Commandments to His people was divine, majestic, and glorious even from its preparation.

First, in preparation for receiving the Ten Commandments, the Israelites consecrated themselves by washing their garments and not going near women for three days (Exod 19:10–11, 14–15).

Second, God set limits all around the mountain for the people and warned them, saying, "Beware that you do not go up on the mountain or touch the border of it; whoever touches the mountain shall surely be put to death" (Exod 19:12–13). Again, He solemnly commanded Moses, saying, "Go down, warn the people, so that they do not break through to the Lord to gaze, and many of them perish" (Exod 19:21).

Third, when God gave the Ten Commandments, the Israelites trembled at the scene of thunder, lightning, and a thick cloud on top of the mountain as well as at the loud trumpet blast. The Lord descended amidst the fire, and Mount Sinai was covered with smoke, which ascended like the smoke of a furnace; the whole mountain quaked violently (Exod 19:16–18; 20:18). The Israelites listened to God's voice amid the fire (Deut 4:33; 5:24–26). They were so captivated by their fear that they set their eyes, ears, and hearts entirely on God's Word and stood in awe of Him (Exod 20:18–21; Deut 5:23–27).

Fourth, the Israelites received through Moses the fiery law from the right hand of the Lord, who was in the midst of the heavenly hosts (Deut 33:2; see also Acts 7:53; Gal 3:19).

Fifth, God wrote all the Ten Commandments with His own finger (Exod 31:18; 32:15–16; 34:1, 28; Deut 4:13; 5:22; 9:10; 10:2–4).

Sixth, God instructed Moses to keep the two stone tablets of the Ten Commandments in the ark of wood, which had been made according to the measurements and materials specified by God (Deut 10:1–5).

III. Spoken by God Himself

The Ten Commandments were the first words that God gave directly to the entire people of Israel at Mount Sinai. It was unprecedented for a nation that had had no sovereignty for 430 years and had just come out of slavery fewer than two months before (Exod 19:1–2; Num 33:3) to build itself up as an independent country and become a holy nation (Deut 4:32–33). This amazing historical event was possible only because God directly spoke the Ten Commandments to the people (Exod 20:1–17; Deut 5:22). After this there is no biblical record of God speaking directly to the entire nation of Israel the way He did when He gave them the Ten Commandments. Regarding Israel's receipt of the Ten Commandments at Mount Sinai, Kalisch said that the delivery of the Decalogue on Sinai "formed a decisive epoch in the history of the human race" and was even perhaps "the greatest and most important event in human history" up to the time of its occurrence.[29]

The Ten Commandments are not merely God's Word from the past but also the living and active Word of God in the present (Heb 4:12). Before the commandments were given, the preface began with this truth: "God spoke all these words, saying …" (Exod 20:1–2). Here "all these words" (כָּל־הַדְּבָרִים הָאֵלֶּה, *kal-haddevarim haelleh*) refers to the ten words that were about to be proclaimed, namely, the Ten Commandments.

The preface also confirms that "God" (אֱלֹהִים, *Elohim*) instituted all these Words. The eternal God who had created heaven and earth by His providence (Gen 1:1) spoke these commandments; therefore these words must be kept. God's power works mightily wherever His Word goes (Acts 6:7; 19:20; Heb 4:12). Those who concentrate on God's Word by remembering, pondering, meditating, and believing in them wholeheartedly will receive the strength to observe these commandments from the Almighty God (1 Thess 2:13).

IV. Proclaimed as God's Eternal Covenant

Before God gave the Ten Commandments, He made a clear distinction between the author of the Word ("I") and the receiver of the Word ("you") and clarified that the Ten Commandments bound Him and Israel together in a covenantal relationship. In Exodus 20:2, God said, "I am the LORD your God, who brought you out of the land of Egypt, out of the house of slavery." Here, "I" (אָנֹכִי, *anokhi*) is *Yahweh*, the Lord of the covenant, and "you" represents the other party in the covenant, a people who had lived as humble slaves in the land of Egypt, in the house of slavery, for 430 years (Exod 12:40–41). In the Hebrew Bible, the second-person singular pronoun "you" is used in each of the commandments, underlining the fact that the covenant is made with each individual as well as the entire community. God emphasized that the God who had brought Israel out of slavery in Egypt had now become "[their] God" (אֱלֹהֶיךָ, *eloheykha*). By repeating the phrase "the LORD your God" (יְהוָה אֱלֹהֶיךָ, *yhwh [adonai] eloheykha;* Exod 20:2, 5, 7, 10, 12; Deut 5:6, 9, 11–12, 14–15 [3x], 16 [2x]), God highlighted the unbreakable covenantal relationship between Israel and Himself.

The Ten Commandments were given as a covenant (בְּרִית, *berith*; Exod 34:27). Deuteronomy 4:13 confirms this: "He declared to you His covenant [בְּרִית, *berith*] which He commanded you to perform, that is, the Ten Commandments; and He wrote them on two tablets of stone." When God gave the two stone tablets of the Ten Commandments a second time through Moses (Exod 34:1–7; Deut 10:1–5), He renewed the covenant, saying, "Behold, I am going to make a covenant" (Exod 34:10). Exodus 34:28 narrates, "He wrote on the tablets the words of the covenant [בְּרִית, *berith*], the Ten Commandments." In Deuteronomy 29:9, Moses said, "Keep the words of this covenant [בְּרִית, *berith*] to do them." Moreover, the two stone tablets of the Ten Commandments were called "the tablets of the covenant" (Deut 9:9, 11), "the two tablets of the covenant" (Deut 9:15), and "the tables of the covenant" (Heb 9:4).

If God's covenant is everlasting (Gen 17:7; 1 Chr 16:17; Ps 105:10), then the Ten Commandments are also an eternal covenant for all generations. Thus the Ten Commandments were not only for the Israelites three thousand five hundred years ago; they continue to be applied as the absolute standard for godly living for each and every saint who is a part of God's people. In the progressive development of redemptive history, the Ten Commandments were fulfilled through

Jesus Christ during the New Testament era. Furthermore, they became the standard for the judgment of those who refuse to repent until the end. Indeed, the Ten Commandments are an eternal covenant that can never be abolished.

V. Written by the Finger of God on Two Tablets of Stone

All Scripture is "inspired by God" (2 Tim 3:16), and no prophecy was "ever made by an act of human will, but men moved by the Holy Spirit spoke from God" (2 Pet 1:21). Of all God's statements to man, the Ten Commandments was the only one spoken directly by God to the entire nation of Israel (Deut 5:4, 22-24) and written directly by God's own finger. In Deuteronomy 9:10, Moses wrote, "The LORD gave me the two tablets of stone written by the finger of God." The expression "written by the finger" is כְּתֻבִים בְּאֶצְבַּע (*kethuvim beetsba*) in Hebrew, that is, "something that is written by a finger." Similarly, in Deuteronomy 4:13, Moses says of the Ten Commandments that God "wrote them on two tablets of stone."

God inscribed the Ten Commandments with His finger not on paper or on wood but on stone tablets. Unlike paper or wooden material, stone preserves what is inscribed on it permanently. Except for the fact that the words were written on both sides of the stone tablets—on the front and on the back (Exod 32:15)—it is not known exactly how each of the Ten Commandments was organized on the tablets. The total number of Hebrew consonants in the Ten Commandments as per Exodus 20 is 579 letters, while the total in Deuteronomy 5 is eighty-eight more, that is, 667 letters. The amount of writing dedicated to each commandment is not equal. The fourth commandment is much longer (more than one third of the entire Decalogue) than the others. The second commandment comes next in length (more than one fourth), and then the fifth and tenth commandments, then the third, then the first, then the ninth, and then the sixth, seventh, and eighth commandments. Indeed, the Ten Commandments are God's precious Word that He wrote, letter by letter, for His own people of the covenant.

When Moses ascended Mount Sinai for the eighth time, he offered up to God a fasting prayer for forty days and nights (Exod 34:28; Deut 9:18). Then God inscribed the Ten Commandments the second time, just as He had done the first time, on the two stone tablets that He had commanded Moses to prepare (Exod 34:1, 28; Deut 10:1–5). God Himself inscribed the Ten Commandments on the two stone tablets, ascribing eternal efficacy to them.

VI. Given by God as Testimonies of the Lord

Scripture refers to the stone tablets of the Ten Commandments as the "tablets of the testimony." Exodus 16:34; 25:16, 21; and 40:20 use the term "the testimony," while Exodus 31:18 and 32:15 say "the two tablets of the testimony." Thus the Ten Commandments are God's testimony. The Hebrew word עֵדוּת (*eduth*), meaning "testimony," is derived from עֵד (*ed*), which means "witness" or "evidence." The Word of the Ten Commandments is God's living witness to us and transforms us to become His witnesses.

Psalm 119 introduces the entirety of God's Word as "testimonies" (*eduth or edah*), not just the Ten Commandments, and they are "the Lord's testimonies" (Ps 119:2, 14, 22, 24, 31, 36, 46, 59, 79, 88, 95, 99, 111, 119, 125, 129, 138, 144, 146, 152, 157, 167–168).

We must not, therefore, abandon the Ten Commandments or turn aside from God's Word. We must meditate upon the Lord's testimonies (Ps 119:99), incline our hearts to them (Ps 119:36), cling to them (Ps 119:31), understand them (Ps 119:144), keep them (Ps 119:88, 129), rejoice in them (Ps 119:14), and speak of them (Ps 119:46) each day. The laws and all the testimonies of the prophets in the Old Testament bear witness of Jesus Christ (Rom 3:21).

We must embody the words of the Ten Commandments and inscribe them on the tablets of our hearts. Then, as people of the covenant, we will become God's witnesses and will be letters on behalf of Jesus Christ that proclaim to the whole world the infinite love of the eternal God (Matt 5:16; 2 Cor 3:2–3).

VII. Summary of All the Revelations of the Old and New Testaments

Jesus summarized the Ten Commandments in two succinct commands that are recorded in Matthew 22:37 and 22:39. The first commandment is, "You shall love the Lord your God with all your heart, and with all your soul, and with all your mind" (Deut 6:5). The second is, "You shall love your neighbor as yourself" (Lev 19:18). Jesus explained in Matthew 22:40, "On these two commandments depend the whole Law and the Prophets." Here the word "depend" is κρεμάννυμι (kremannymi) in Greek, which means "to hang, to hang on." This means that all the Word and the law hang on these two succinct commandments that summarize all the Ten Commandments. Indeed, the Ten Commandments are both the head and the summary of all the Word. The Ten Commandments, which consist of the "ten words," are perfectly summarized revelations of God's will toward not only Israel but also all humanity. Hence, they sum up all sixty-six books of the Bible.[30]

The sentences for each of the "ten words" are concise and simple. In Hebrew the sixth, seventh, and eighth commandments consist of two words each. Their messages, however, are clear, and each contains profound meaning. Just as the heart pumps and supplies blood throughout the body and revives it, so the Ten Commandments are the origin of the Word of God that revives the dead. The Old and New Testaments were written based on the two streams of life that surge from the Ten Commandments. All specific articles of the law stem from these "ten words." Exodus 20:22–23:33 and Deuteronomy 6–26, especially, were written either based on the Ten Commandments or according to their order. The prophet Hosea wrote that "ten thousand precepts" were recorded (Hos 8:12), and the Orthodox Judaism asserts that the Pentateuch contains 613 laws.[31]

We cannot understand the Christian gospel's essence without knowing the Ten Commandments, which are the summation of the entire Scripture. Furthermore, without understanding the Ten Commandments, we cannot fully understand Jesus Christ, who is the essence of eternal life and the mystery of God's kingdom (Col 1:27; 2:2).

Today, the living waters flowing through the Ten Commandments continue to resonate in the ears of every Christian and revive His people without ceasing. Thus I hope that by meditating on the Ten Commandments from the perspective of God's administration in redemptive history, we can fully understand Jesus Christ so that each of us, without exception, can receive the gift of eternal life.

CHAPTER

14

Central Principles for Understanding the Ten Commandments

I. Two Major Branches of the Ten Commandments: Our Relationship with God and Our Relationships with Others

Human beings live in relationship with the invisible God as well as with many people in their lives. At times they sin against God and at other times against other people. In Matthew 22:40, Jesus spoke about the two main branches of the Ten Commandments. The first four of the Ten Commandments are associated with the command to love God (Deut 6:5), while the remaining six are commands to love our neighbors (Lev 19:18). It is impossible for people to guard their hearts against feelings of jealousy, envy, hatred, and greed toward their neighbors. Thus the Ten Commandments cannot be kept without love, and only with love its perfect interpretation becomes possible.

Every sin, without fail, goes against the principle of love. People who love God do not serve other gods, make an image of an idol, or take God's name in vain. People who love their neighbors never murder, steal, deceive, condemn, or covet what their neighbors have. People who love their neighbors do not commit evil acts against them (Rom 13:10; 1 Cor 13:5). Love for God and for one's neighbors, therefore, is the primary source of power that enables people to keep the law.

Of the Ten Commandments, the first through the fourth commandments pertain to the relationship between the Israelites and God. The fifth through the tenth commandments pertain to the mutual relationships among the covenant people of Israel. In the first through the fourth commandments, the expression "the Lord your God" appears repeatedly. Relationship with God comes before relationship with other people, because we cannot have healthy relationships with people unless our relationship with God is right. Thus 1 John 4:21 says, "This commandment we have from Him, that the one who loves God should love his brother also."

The first through the fourth commandments can also be understood from the perspective of worship. The first commandment clarifies *whom* we must worship; the second *how* we must worship; the third *the proper mindset* of our worship; and the fourth *when* we must worship.

The fifth through the tenth commandments can be understood from the perspective of dignity. Dignity refers to an inviolable nobility or elevation of a person or status. Hence the fifth commandment teaches the dignity of honoring one's parents and their authority; the sixth, the dignity of life; the seventh, the dignity of family and purity; the eighth, the dignity of another person's possessions; the ninth, the dignity of truth; and the tenth, the dignity of self-sufficiency and contentment.

II. Specific Laws Derived from the Ten Commandments

Exodus 21–23

Exodus 20:1–17 records the Ten Commandments, after which Exodus 21–23 records the specific laws. This means that God did not give the Ten Commandments and the specific laws separately; after laying out the covenant's basic principles through the Ten Commandments, God expanded the covenant through the specific laws and elaborated on their daily life application.[32] In other words, the specific laws are an extension of the Ten Commandments and provide their interpretation.

While the specific laws in Exodus do not follow the order of the Ten Commandments, we can categorize them as the following.

Exposition of the commandment	First	Forbiddance to have other gods (Exod 22:18, 20, 29–31; 23:13–19, 24–33)
	Second	Forbiddance to make idols (Exod 20:22–26)
	Third	Honoring God's name (Exod 20:24; 23:20–23)
	Fourth	Observing the Sabbath (Exod 21:1–11; 23:10–12)
	Fifth	Honoring parents (Exod 21:15, 17; 22:28)
	Sixth	Forbiddance to murder (Exod 21:12–27; 23:4–5)
	Seventh	Forbiddance to commit adultery (Exod 22:16–17, 19)
	Eighth	Forbiddance to steal (Exod 21:16; 22:1–15)

	Ninth	Forbiddance to bear false witness (Exod 22:21–27; 23:1–3, 6–9)
	Tenth	Forbiddance to covet a neighbor's wife or possessions (Exod 22:7–15)

Deuteronomy 6–26 (Deut 6–7 and 12–26)

The Ten Commandments given through the Sinaitic covenant (Exod 20:1–17) were later proclaimed on the plains of Moab to the second generation of Israel in the wilderness almost in their original form (Deut 5:7–21). Just as God had given the specific laws after giving the Ten Commandments in the Sinaitic covenant (Exod 21–23), so Deuteronomy 5–26 records the Ten Commandments followed by a lengthy discussion on the specific laws associated with them. Deuteronomy 6–7 contains the specific laws regarding the Ten Commandments' first two commandments. Deuteronomy 8–11 contains Moses' sermon exhorting the people, and Deuteronomy 12–26 contains the specific laws regarding each of the Ten Commandments.

Deuteronomy consists of Moses' three sermons (Deut 1:1–4:43; 4:44–26:19; 27:1–30:20) and the conclusion of the entire Pentateuch in its final chapters (Deut 31–34). Moses' second sermon in Deuteronomy 4:44–26:19 is the heart of Deuteronomy. It is a reiteration of the laws (statutes and ordinances) that are centered on the Ten Commandments:

- Deuteronomy 4:44–5:6: proclamation of the covenant (introduction to the statutes and ordinances)
- Deuteronomy 5:7–21: the Ten Commandments
- Deuteronomy 5:22–33: the people's request for Moses' mediation after the proclamation of the Ten Commandments

- Deuteronomy 6–11: the specific laws from the first two commandments and Moses' exhortative sermon
- Deuteronomy 12–26: the specific laws from each of the commandments

The Ten Commandments are the core of the book of Deuteronomy,[33] and the order of the specific laws in Deuteronomy 12–26 generally follows the order of the Ten Commandments (Deut 5:7–21).[34] The specific laws in their entirety are systematically structured around the Ten Commandments.

Although it is difficult to categorize all the specific laws (Deut 6:10–7:26; 12–26) according to the Ten Commandments, since they are all interrelated, we can organize them generally according to the order of the Ten Commandments as follows.

Exposition of the commandment	First	Forbiddance to have other gods (Deut 6:14–15; 12:2–13:18; 17:1–7; 18:9–14)
	Second	Forbiddance to make idols (Deut 6:10–7:26; 16:21–22)
	Third	Honoring God's name (Deut 14:1–22)
	Fourth	Observing the Sabbath (Deut 15:1–16:17)
	Fifth	Honoring parents (Deut 16:18; 18:1–8, 15–22; 21:18–21)
	Sixth	Forbiddance to murder (Deut 19:1–22:8)
	Seventh	Forbiddance to commit adultery (Deut 22:9–23:18)
	Eighth	Forbiddance to steal (Deut 23:19–24:7)

Ninth	Forbiddance to bear false witness (Deut 24:8–25:4)
Tenth	Forbiddance to covet a neighbor's wife or possessions (Deut 25:5–26:15)

The specific laws that God gave after the Ten Commandments were detailed expansions of the original commandments. They provide essential principles for the application and practice of the Ten Commandments in our daily lives.

As we read through the specific laws, however, they may begin to seem like a mere list of restrictions and we may feel skeptical of or bored by them and skip through them carelessly. Nevertheless, they are filled with brilliant spiritual gems more beautiful than pearls. God's purpose in giving the laws to the Israelites was not to bind them. Instead, it was to protect life and establish impartiality, justice, and order in their daily lives (see Deut 4:40; 6:24–25; 10:13–15). If a society was void of God's laws and its people were selfish in their thoughts and deeds, chaos and dispute between neighbors would become the norm in everyday life. In this respect we are deeply inspired as we discover God's mercy toward humanity in His bestowal of the specific laws.

III. The Evangelical Principle of Expanding the Application to the Realm of the Heart

The Ten Commandments do not command or forbid only apparent behaviors; they apply also to the implicit matters of the heart. For example, the commandment that forbids murder must include an understanding of the root of murder—anger, hatred, jealousy, and covetousness (see Col 3:5; 1 John 3:15). This is the same principle upon which Jesus reinterpreted the Ten Commandments and the laws (see Matt 5:17–48). In Matthew 15:19, Jesus spoke about seven types of sin that stem from the heart (evil thoughts, murder, adultery, sexual immorality, theft, false witness, and slander). In Mark 7:21–23, Jesus spoke about thirteen types of sins (evil thoughts, sexual immorality, theft, murder, adultery, coveting, wickedness, deceit, sensuality, envy, slander, pride, and foolishness). These thirteen sins from the heart are all directly related to the Ten Commandments.

Thus all sins forbidden in the Ten Commandments are joined by the root. James 2:10 states, "Whoever keeps the whole law and yet stumbles in one point, he has become guilty of all." First Timothy 6:10 states that "the love of money is a root of all sorts of evil," revealing that greed for money is the cause of all evil. Setting the mind "on the flesh" is the beginning of ten thousand sins (Rom 8:6–8), and greed in the heart gives birth to sin (Jas 1:15).

We may be able to hide fleeting thoughts from other people, but we cannot hide them from God, who searches our minds and hearts (1 Sam 16:7; 1 Kgs 8:39; Pss 7:9; 11:5; 139:1–4; Prov 16:2; 21:2; Jer 11:20; 17:10; 20:12). All our days are open and laid bare (John 2:24–25; Heb 4:13) before God's seven eyes that are like flames of fire (Zech 3:9; 4:10; Rev 1:14; 2:18; 5:6; 19:12; see also Ezek 1:18; Dan 10:6). God's scale that weighs our hearts and deeds is accurate and does not add or subtract anything to our deeds (1 Sam 2:3; Prov 24:12; Dan 5:27); He repays us exactly according to the weight of our faith (Ps 62:12; Eccl 12:14; Matt 16:27; Rom 2:6; 2 Cor 5:10).

IV. Various Penalties for Violating Each Commandment
(the Fate of the Transgressors)

According to the specific laws as well as the entire Scripture, there are various punishments for breaking each of the Ten Commandments, depending on the degree of violation.

Penalties for violating the first commandment

Death without forgiveness (by stoning).

> He who sacrifices to any god, other than to the LORD alone, shall be **utterly destroyed.** *(Exod 22:20)*

> If... [anyone] entice you secretly, saying, "Let us go and serve other gods,"... you shall not yield to him or listen to him ... But you shall surely kill him ... You shall **stone him to death.** *(Deut 13:6–10)*

Death by stone or sword.

> You shall surely **strike** the inhabitants of that city **with the edge of the sword, utterly destroying** it and all that is in it and its cattle **with the edge of the sword.** *(Deut 13:15; see Deut 13:12–16)*

> [If a man or woman] has gone and served other gods and worshiped them, or the sun or the moon or any of the heavenly host, which I have not commanded, ... then you shall bring out that man or that woman who has done this evil deed to your gates, that is, the man or the woman, and you shall **stone them to death.** On the evidence of two witnesses or three witnesses, he who is to die shall be **put to death;** he shall not be put to death on the evidence of one witness. *(Deut 17:3–6)*

Death for false prophet or sorceress.

> That prophet or that dreamer of dreams shall be **put to death.** *(Deut 13:5)*

> You shall **not allow** a sorceress **to live.** *(Exod 22:18; see also Lev 20:6, 27)* *(Reference: Deut 6:14–15 ; 7:4 ; 8:19 ; 11:16–17, 28; 30:17–18)*

Penalties for violating the second commandment

Utter destruction.

> When you ... make an idol in the form of anything, and do that which is evil in the sight of the LORD your God so as to provoke Him to anger, I call heaven and earth to witness against you today, that you will **surely perish quickly** from the land where you are going over the Jordan to possess it. You shall **not live long** on it, but will be **utterly destroyed**. *(Deut 4:25–26)*

Banishment.

> The graven images of their gods you are to **burn with fire** ... You shall not bring an abomination into your house, and like it come **under the ban;** you shall utterly detest it and you shall utterly abhor it, for it is something **banned**. *(Deut 7:25–26)*

Being cursed.

> [The Levites shall then answer,] "**Cursed** is the man who makes an idol or a molten image, an abomination to the LORD, the work of the hands of the craftsman, and sets it up in secret." And all the people shall answer and say, "Amen." *(Deut 27:15)*
> (Reference: 2 Kgs 11:18; Pss 115:4–8; 135:15–18; Isa 44:9–11)

Penalties for violating the third commandment

Death (by stoning).

> The son of the Israelite woman blasphemed the Name and cursed. So they brought him to Moses ... Then the LORD spoke to Moses,

> saying, "Bring the one who has cursed outside the camp, and let all who heard him lay their hands on his head; then **let all the congregation stone him.** You shall speak to the sons of Israel, saying, 'If anyone curses his God, then he will bear his sin. Moreover, the one who blasphemes the name of the LORD shall **surely be put to death;** all the congregation shall certainly stone him. The alien as well as the native, when he blasphemes the Name, **shall be put to death.**'" *(Lev 24:11–16)*

Death for a prophet who speaks in the name of other gods.

> It shall come about that whoever will not listen to My words which he shall speak in My name, I Myself will **require it of him.** But the prophet who speaks a word presumptuously in My name which I have not commanded him to speak, or which he speaks in the name of other gods, that prophet **shall die.** *(Deut 18:19–20)*
> *(Reference: Deut 28:58–61; Jer 14:14–16; Zech 13:3)*

Penalties for violating the fourth commandment

Death.

> You shall surely observe My sabbaths ... Everyone who profanes it shall **surely be put to death;** for whoever does any work on it, that person shall be **cut off from among his people** ... Whoever does any work on the sabbath day shall **surely be put to death.** *(Exod 31:13–15)*

> For six days work may be done, but on the seventh day you shall have a holy day, a sabbath of complete rest to the LORD; whoever does any work on it shall be **put to death.** *(Exod 35:2)*
> *(Reference: Num 15:32–36; Neh 13:17–18; Ezek 20:12–13)*

Penalties for violating the fifth commandment (honoring parents)

Death.

> *He who strikes his father or his mother shall **surely be put to death**. (Exod 21:15; see also Exod 21:17)*

> *If any man has a stubborn and rebellious son who will not obey his father or his mother, and when they chastise him, he will not even listen to them, … then all the men of his city shall **stone him to death**. (Deut 21:18–21)*
> *(Reference: Prov 30:17; Matt 15:4; Mark 7:10; Rom 1:30–32)*

Penalties for violating the sixth commandment (murder)

Death.

> *He who strikes a man so that he dies shall **surely be put to death**. But if he did not lie in wait for him, but God let him fall into his hand, then I will appoint you a place to which he may flee. If, however, a man acts presumptuously toward his neighbor, so as to kill him craftily, you are to take him even from My altar, that **he may die**. (Exod 21:12–14)*

Repayment of loss caused to others.

> *If men have a quarrel and one strikes the other with a stone or with his fist, and he does not die but remains in bed, if he gets up and walks around outside on his staff, then he who struck him shall go unpunished; he **shall only pay for his loss of time, and shall take care of him until he is completely healed**. (Exod 21:18–19)*

Punishment.

> *If a man strikes his male or female slave with a rod and he dies at his hand,* **he shall be punished.** *If, however, he survives a day or two, no vengeance shall be taken; for he is his property. (Exod 21:20) (Reference: Exod 21:22-36; Ps 55:23)*

Penalties for violating the seventh commandment (adultery)

Death (by stoning).

> *If there is a man who commits adultery with another man's wife, one who commits adultery with his friend's wife, the adulterer and the adulteress shall* **surely be put to death.** *(Lev 20:10)*

> *[Those who commit incest, homosexuality, bestiality]* **shall surely be put to death.** *(Lev 20:11-21; Exod 22:19)*

> *If a man is found lying with a married woman,* **then both of them shall die,** *the man who lay with the woman, and the woman; thus you* **shall purge** *the evil from Israel. (Deut 22:22)*

> *If there is a girl who is a virgin engaged to a man, and another man finds her in the city and lies with her, then you shall bring them both out to the gate of that city and you shall stone them to death. (Deut 22:23-24)*

Being burned with fire.

> *If there is a man who marries a woman and her mother, it is immorality; both he and they* **shall be burned with fire.** *(Lev 20:14)*

The daughter of any priest, if she profanes herself by harlotry, she profanes her father; she **shall be burned with fire.** *(Lev 21:9)*

Paying a dowry.

If a man seduces a virgin who is not engaged, and lies with her, he **must pay a dowry for her to be his wife.** *If her father absolutely refuses to give her to him, he* **shall pay money equal to the dowry for virgins.** *(Exod 22:16–17)*
(Reference: Lev 18:6–30; Deut 22:28–29; Heb 13:4)

Penalties for violating the eighth commandment (stealing)

Death for kidnappers.

He who kidnaps a man, whether he sells him or he is found in his possession, shall **surely be put to death.** *(Exod 21:16; Deut 24:7)*

Making restitution and bringing a guilt offering.

If a man steals an ox or a sheep and slaughters it or sells it, he **shall pay** *five oxen for the ox and four sheep for the sheep. If the thief is caught while breaking in and is struck so that he dies, there will be no bloodguiltiness on his account. But if the sun has risen on him, there will be bloodguiltiness on his account. He* **shall surely make restitution;** *if he owns nothing, then he shall be sold for his theft. If what he stole is actually found alive in his possession, whether an ox or a donkey or a sheep, he* **shall pay double.** *(Exod 22:1-15)*

When a person sins and acts unfaithfully against the LORD, and deceives his companion in regard to a **deposit** *or a* **security** *entrusted to him, or through* **robbery,** *or if he has* **extorted** *from*

> his companion, or has found what was lost and lied about it and sworn falsely, so that he sins in regard to any one of the things a man may do; then it shall be, when he sins and becomes guilty, that he shall restore what he took by robbery or what he got by extortion, or the deposit which was entrusted to him or the lost thing which he found, or anything about which he swore falsely; he shall make restitution for it in full and add to it one-fifth more. He shall give it to the one to whom it belongs on the day he presents his **guilt offering.** Then he shall bring to the priest his guilt offering to the LORD, a ram without defect from the flock, according to your valuation, for a **guilt offering.** (Lev 6:2–6)

Penalties for violating the ninth commandment (lying)

Retributive justice, restitution, and bringing a guilt offering.

> If a malicious witness rises up against a man to accuse him of wrongdoing, … the judges shall investigate thoroughly, and if the witness is a false witness and he has accused his brother falsely, then you **shall do to him just as he had intended to do to his brother.** Thus you shall purge the evil from among you. The rest will hear and be afraid, and will never again do such an evil thing among you. Thus you shall not show pity: **life for life, eye for eye, tooth for tooth, hand for hand, foot for foot.** (Deut 19:16–21)

Restitution and bringing a guilt offering.

> When a person sins and acts unfaithfully against the LORD, and deceives his companion in regard to a deposit or a security entrusted to him, or through robbery, or if he has extorted from his companion, or has found what was lost and lied about it and sworn falsely, so that he sins in regard to any one of the things a man

may do; then it shall be, when he sins and becomes guilty, that he shall restore what he took by robbery or what he got by extortion, or the deposit which was entrusted to him or the lost thing which he found, or anything about which he swore falsely; he **shall make restitution for it in full and add to it one-fifth more. He shall give it to the one to whom it belongs on the day he presents his guilt offering.** *Then he shall bring to the priest his* **guilt offering to the LORD**, *a ram without defect from the flock,* **according to your valuation, for a guilt offering.** *(Lev 6:2–6)*
(Reference: Pss 12:2–3; 59:12; Prov 18:21; 19:5, 9; 21:28; Jer 6:12–13; Hos 7:16)

Penalties for violating the tenth commandment (covetousness)

Death (indirectly).

The rabble who were among them [the Israelites] had greedy desires ... So the name of that place was called Kibroth-hattaavah, because there they **buried the people who had been greedy.** *(Num 11:4–34)*

When I [Achan] saw among the spoil a beautiful mantle from Shinar and two hundred shekels of silver and a bar of gold fifty shekels in weight, then **I coveted them and took them;** *... Joshua said, "Why have you troubled us? The LORD will trouble you this day." And all Israel* **stoned them with stones;** *and they* **burned them with fire** *after they had stoned them with stones. They raised over him a great heap of stones that stands to this day, and the LORD turned from the fierceness of His anger. Therefore the name of that place has been called the valley of Achor to this day. (Josh 7:21–26)*

Shortened lifespan.

> So are the ways of everyone who gains by violence; **it takes away the life of its possessors.** *(Prov 1:19)*

> A leader who is a great oppressor lacks understanding, but he who **hates unjust gain will prolong his days**. *(Prov 28:16)*

The wrath of God.

> Consider the members of your earthly body as dead to immorality, impurity, passion, evil desire, and **greed**, which amounts to idolatry. For it is because of these things that the **wrath of God** will come upon the sons of disobedience. *(Col 3:5-6)*
> (Reference: Luke 12:15; Eph 5:5)

The death penalty was a common punishment for those who violated the commandments. This implies that the observance of the commandments is directly related to life. After God Himself gave the Ten Commandments during the ratification of the Sinaitic covenant and the specific laws through Moses, many people ignored and disobeyed these basic principles of faith and sinned, bringing upon themselves God's stringent judgment. The Ten Commandments were the legal basis that preserved the covenantal relationship between God and Israel. Thus God sternly punished or disciplined those who broke the covenant.

Historically, every single one of those who violated the Ten Commandments met a miserable end. Although every biblical account cannot be listed, a few examples demonstrate the absolute authority of the Ten Commandments, that is, God's Word. The ten words of the Ten Commandments transcend time and remain even to this day as God's living Word proclaimed by His absolute authority. The tragic fate of those who violate the Ten Commandments will serve as examples and warnings that will cut to the heart of all believers living in the end times (1 Cor 10:11).

V. Jesus' References to the Ten Commandments

The Ten Commandments are truly the wondrous Word that overarches both the Old and the New Testaments. God commanded Adam and Eve not to eat the fruit of the tree of the knowledge of good and evil. Yet they disobeyed and sinned by stretching their arms out to take the fruit and eat it, leading them to be expelled from the garden. Because each of God's commandments is closely connected to the others, the violation of one commandment leads to the violation of all the commandments (see Mark 10:21–22; Jas 2:10–11). In essence, Adam and Eve violated the entire Ten Commandments the moment they ate the fruit.[35]

Through the Ten Commandments, God unraveled Adam's sin into ten violations and expounded on each violation one by one. Thus the Ten Commandments contain God's great redemptive plan and purpose to restore the fallen world to its original form.

Jesus, who came to restore the fallen world, reinterpreted the Ten Commandments and expanded their meaning to add to them richness and depth. Jesus did not come to abolish the law but to fulfill it (Matt 5:17). He said, "Truly I say to you, until heaven and earth pass away, not the smallest letter or stroke shall pass from the Law until all is accomplished" (Matt 5:18). He continued, "Whoever then annuls one of the least of these commandments, and teaches others to do the same, shall be called least in the kingdom of heaven; but whoever keeps and teaches them, he shall be called great in the kingdom of heaven" (Matt 5:19). Not even the most minor part of the law can be altered; future reward in the kingdom of heaven will depend on whether or not a person ignored or kept laws that appeared the most trivial and unimportant. Furthermore, Jesus said that people cannot enter the kingdom of heaven unless their righteousness surpasses that of the scribes and Pharisees (Matt 5:20).

Jesus clearly demonstrated that the laws are being fulfilled in Him within God's redemptive-historical administration from the Old to the New Testament eras, even until the end, when the kingdom of God will be established. Jesus is the only person in history who ultimately satisfied the demand for righteousness that all the laws require from sinners (John 19:30; Rom 8:3–4; Gal 3:13). Jesus Christ is the end of the law for righteousness to everyone who believes (Rom 10:4). We, therefore, can enter the kingdom of heaven when we have the perfect righteousness that surpasses that of the scribes and the Pharisees (Rom 3:21–24) by receiving it in faith from Jesus (Rom 3:28).

By clearly interpreting the meaning of the laws from their very foundation, Jesus magnified them into perfect moral laws. The following are representative Scripture verses in which Jesus directly quoted from the Ten Commandments.

Matthew 5:21–48 (Luke 6:27–36)

Jesus' Sermon on the Mount is one of the keys to understanding the true meaning and redemptive-historical interpretation of the Ten Commandments. In the Sermon on the Mount, Jesus reinterpreted the sixth commandment, "You shall not murder" (Matt 5:21–26), and the seventh commandment, "You shall not commit adultery" (Matt 5:27–32). Jesus said, "You have heard that the ancients were told, 'You shall not commit murder' and 'Whoever commits murder shall be liable to the court.' But I say to you that everyone who is angry with his brother shall be guilty before the court; and whoever says to his brother, 'You good-for-nothing,' shall be guilty before the supreme court; and whoever says, 'You fool,' shall be guilty enough to go into the fiery hell" (Matt 5:21–22). He continued to teach, "Everyone who looks at a woman with lust for her has already committed adultery with her in his heart" (Matt 5:28). Jesus then reinterpreted the sum of the Ten Commandments, "You shall love your neighbor" (Lev19:18), by expanding it to "Love your enemies and pray for those who persecute you" (Matt 5:44, see Matt 5:38–48) and "Do good to those who hate you ... Love your enemies, and do good, and lend, expecting nothing in return" (Luke 6:27–35).

Matthew 15:1–20 (Mark 7:1–23)

When the scribes and Pharisees found fault with Jesus' disciples, who had eaten bread without washing their hands, Jesus reproached them for breaking God's commandment for the sake of the traditions of the elders. Then Jesus spoke about the fifth commandment, "Honor your father and mother" (Matt 15:1–6; Mark 7:1–13). The word "tradition" generally refers to teachings, practices, or customs passed down from ancestors to their descendants in various forms (Matt 15:2–3). The New Testament mentions positive traditions that should be maintained and passed down as well as negative ones that must not be passed down.

The apostles passed down blessed traditions in the form of epistles that explained the Gospels. During the early church days, the apostles used epistles to teach God's Word and guide the congregations' lives with advice for the church. Paul referred to these epistles as "traditions which you were taught, whether by word of mouth or by letter from us" (2 Thess 2:15; see also 1 Cor 11:23). The apostle Paul even exhorted the people, saying, "Keep away from every brother who leads an unruly life and not according to the tradition which you received from us" (2 Thess 3:6).

The elders (leaders) of the Jews, however, interpreted God's laws as they saw fit depending on the circumstances and passed down evil oral laws. The New Testament referred to these as "the tradition of the elders" (Matt 15:2; Mark 7:3, 5), "ancestral traditions" (Gal 1:14), and "the tradition of men" (Mark 7:8; Col 2:8). These traditions were a greater priority to the Jews at the time than God's Word, so Jesus rebuked them, saying, "Neglecting the commandment of God, you hold to the tradition of men" (Mark 7:8; see Gal 1:14). Similarly, the apostle Peter used a provocative expression when he referred to the tradition of unbelief as "your futile way of life inherited from your forefathers" (1 Pet 1:18). The word "futile" (μάταιος, *mataios*) means "vain, useless, fruitless." Anyone following such traditions will find only unending despair and death. God's saints must abandon the traditions of unbelief. Instead, they must give thanks for their redemption through the precious blood of Jesus Christ, the unblemished and spotless Lamb, and follow the Word of God in order to bear fruit to eternal life (1 Pet 1:18–19).

As such, Jesus sharply reproached the corrupt religious leaders who were accustomed to their hypocritical beliefs, saying, "In vain do they worship Me, teaching as doctrines the precepts of men" and "neglecting the commandment of God" (Mark 7:6-9; see also Matt 15:5–9). He explained that what defiles a person is not eating with unwashed hands but "evil intentions" (Mark 7:21, NRSV) from within, that come from the heart of man. He then listed one by one examples of sins that broke the Ten Commandments: "fornications, thefts, murders, adulteries, deeds of coveting and wickedness, as well as deceit, sensuality, envy, slander, pride and foolishness" (Mark 7:18-23) and "murders, adulteries, fornications, thefts, false witness, slanders" (Matt 15:17-20).

Matthew 19:1–12 (Mark 10:1-12; Luke 16:18)

When Jesus departed from Galilee and reached the region of Judea beyond the Jordan, Pharisees who were well versed in the law came and tested Him, saying, "Is it lawful for a man to divorce his wife for any reason at all?" (Matt 19:3). They were asking if a husband was permitted to abandon his wife for any reason he desired. Jesus answered them with the original principle of marriage at creation, saying, "He who created them from the beginning made them male and female … What therefore God has joined together, let no man separate" (Matt 19:4–6).

The Pharisees rebutted Jesus, referencing Deuteronomy 24:1–3: "Why then did Moses command to give her a certificate of divorce and send her away?" (Matt 19:7). Jesus pointed out that Moses had done so because of the hardness of their hearts, but "from the beginning it [had] not been this way" (Matt 19:8). The word "beginning" in verses 4 and 8 is ἀπ' ἀρχῆς (*ap' archēs*) in Greek and means "from the beginning, originally, from creation." The parallel passage in Mark 10:6 uses the expression "from the beginning of creation." There was no such thing as divorce at the beginning of the world. Thus Jesus said, "Whoever divorces his wife, except for immorality, and marries another woman commits adultery" (Matt 19:9).

Because the Pharisees were ignorant of the world as it was in the "beginning," which Jesus often spoke of, they contended with Jesus by taking what had not been so in the beginning and changed it as if it had always been that way from the beginning. Hence Jesus corrected the Pharisees' distortion of the seventh commandment. When Jesus expounded the Ten Commandments, He did not create something new or revise the original content; He clarified the original meaning of the Word "from the beginning."

Matthew 19:16–30 (Mark 10:17–31; Luke 18:18–30)

A rich young man came and kneeled before Jesus and asked, "Teacher, what good thing shall I do that I may obtain eternal life?" (Matt 19:16). Jesus answered, "If you wish to enter into life, keep the commandments" (Matt 19:17). When the young man asked Him which commandments to keep, Jesus answered with some of the Ten Commandments. Without mentioning the first through the fourth commandments (concerning our relationship with God), Jesus listed the fifth through the tenth commandments (concerning our relationships with others): "You shall not commit murder; you shall not commit adultery; you shall not steal; you shall not bear false witness; honor your father and mother; and you shall love your neighbor as yourself" (Matt 19:18–19; Mark 10:19; Luke 18:20). Full of confidence, the young man said, "All these things I have kept; what am I still lacking?" (Matt 19:20; Mark 10:20; Luke 18:21). Jesus answered him, "If you wish to be complete, go and sell your possessions and give to the poor, and you will have treasure in heaven; and come, follow Me" (Matt 19:21; Mark 10:21; Luke 18:22). When the young man heard Jesus' answer, he went away grieving, because he had great possessions (Matt 19:22; Mark 10:22; Luke 18:23). After the man went away, Jesus warned His disciples about greed, saying, "It is hard for a rich man to enter the kingdom of heaven … It is easier for a camel to go through the eye of a needle, than for a rich man to enter the kingdom of God" (Matt 19:23–24; Mark 10:23–25; Luke 18:24–25).

The young man proudly proclaimed that he had kept the commandments from his youth (Matt 19:20; Mark 10:20; Luke 18:21). Yet as Jesus pointed out, he lacked one thing (Mark 10:21; Luke 18:22): the young man had failed to love his neighbors, which is the core of the commandments concerning relationships among people (the fifth through the tenth commandments). That is why Jesus, seeing through this man's heart, did not even mention to him the commandments about loving God or having a personal relationship with Him (the first through the fourth commandments). In the end, although the young man had met the Lord of eternal life, he went away grieving because of his great possessions (Matt 19:22; Mark 10:22; Luke 18:23) and never returned to Him.

Matthew 22:34–40 (Mark 12:28–34)

When a lawyer came to Jesus and asked what the greatest commandment was, Jesus' answer to him revealed the two major branches of the Ten Commandments. The first and greatest commandment, He said, was, "You shall love the Lord your God with all your heart, and with all your soul, and with all your mind" (Matt 22:37; Mark 12:30). The second commandment was, "You shall love your neighbor as yourself" (Matt 22:39; Mark 12:31). Then Jesus declared, "On these two commandments depend the whole Law and the Prophets" (Matt 22:40).

Luke 10:25–37

A lawyer came to Jesus asking the same question about eternal life as the young rich man had. Jesus answered him with a question: "What is written in the Law? How does it read to you?" (Luke 10:26). Then the lawyer answered, "You shall love the Lord your God with all your heart, and with all your soul, and with all your strength, and with all your mind; and your neighbor as yourself" (Luke 10:27). Jesus responded, "You have answered correctly; do this and you will live" (Luke 10:28). When the man asked captiously who his neighbor was, Jesus gave a moving answer about a true neighbor using a parable about a Samaritan who showed mercy (Luke 10:29–37).

Luke 12:13–21

A man who coveted the inheritance of wealth approached Jesus, and Jesus spoke to the man the tenth commandment (Luke 12:13–15). He said, "Beware, and be on your guard against every form of greed; for not even when one has an abundance does his life consist of his possessions" (Luke 12:15). Moreover, using the parable of the foolish rich man, Jesus taught the reality of covetousness and its futile consequences (Luke 12:16–21).

It is truly meaningful that Jesus, the Word incarnate, frequently referenced the Ten Commandments. Accordingly, the most frequently cited scriptures in the New Testament from the Old Testament come from the book of Deuteronomy (more than eighty), which is centered around the Ten Commandments.

Studying the redemptive-historical lessons of the Ten Commandments reinterpreted by Jesus, therefore, will lead us to the most accurate, comprehensive, and profound understanding of them.

Just as God spoke and recorded truth through various prophets in various forms from of old (Luke 1:70; John 1:45; Rom 3:21), so He sent His Son in the fullness of the time (Gal 4:4) and spoke to us "in these last days":

> *God, after He spoke long ago to the fathers in the prophets in many portions and in many ways, in these last days has spoken to us in His Son, whom He appointed heir of all things, through whom also He made the world. (Heb 1:1–2)*

Scripture reveals the essence of the Ten Commandments through Jesus Christ, who was the Word from the beginning but became flesh to come to us. After a long period of distortion and perversion at the hands of mankind, the original meaning of the Ten Commandments came to life when Jesus Christ reinterpreted them, making them more powerful and clear through the living Word of God. Truly, in Jesus Christ the Ten Commandments were proven in perfection to be the eternal covenant for all generations.

In the next section, we will study each commandment in greater detail and the redemptive-historical lessons therein.

PART V

THE COVENANT FOR ALL GENERATIONS:
THE TEN COMMANDMENTS
(THE TEN WORDS)

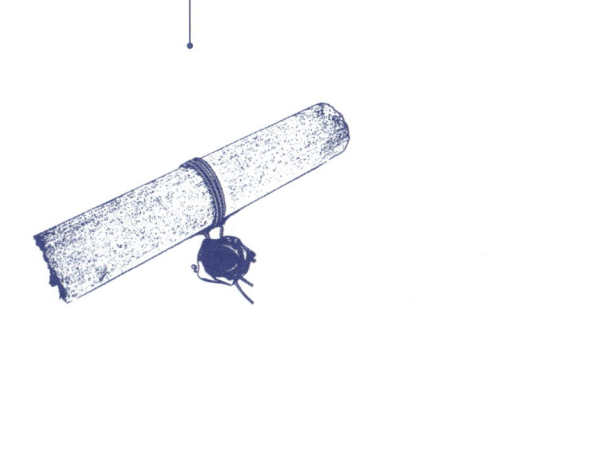

PART V

The Ten Commandments, or the ten words, are recorded in two places in the Old Testament, Exodus 20:3–17 and Deuteronomy 5:7–21, with almost identical content. Although the Ten Commandments amount to a mere ten lines, their meaning's broadness, profundity, depth, and gravity are beyond what anyone can express in words.

As we study the Ten Commandments according to the exegetical principles found in the Scriptures, we will begin to fathom their gravity and depth as well as their overarching presence throughout the Old and New Testaments. As a result, even the simple will receive spiritual wisdom to understand God's Word (Ps 119:130) and taste the essence of the Word that is sweeter than drippings from the honeycomb (Pss 19:9–10; 119:103; Prov 16:24; 24:13–14).

In the following pages, we will interpret each of the Ten Commandments based on their Hebrew texts and examine their specific laws. Then, we will study the lessons and the fate of the violators of each commandment and conclude with the amazing redemptive-historical lessons in each one. As we delve into the commandments, let us pray earnestly for wisdom to understand the true meaning of each one.

CHAPTER

15

The First Commandment

You shall have no other gods before Me.

Exodus 20:3; Deuteronomy 5:7

Both Exodus 20:3 and Deuteronomy 5:7 state, "You shall have no other gods before Me." The original Hebrew text also shows no difference between Exodus 20:3 and Deuteronomy 5:7. The first commandment strongly asserts that the One whom we must worship is the one and only God.

THE FIRST COMMANDMENT

You shall have no other gods before Me.

לֹא יִהְיֶה־לְךָ אֱלֹהִים אֲחֵרִים עַל־פָּנָי

Exodus 20:3; Deuteronomy 5:7

I. Exegesis of the First Commandment

"You" (לְךָ)

The Hebrew word לְךָ (*lekha*) in Exodus 20:3 and Deuteronomy 5:7 is translated as "you" in English. "You" refers to everyone who was brought out of the land of Egypt, the house of slavery. God delivered the Israelites from the oppression of Egypt (Exod 20:2; Deut 5:6). This "you" refers to the person who was delivered from Egypt as well as the person who has been saved from this world that is like Egypt. Notably, "you" here occurs in the second-person singular, emphasizing that the recipient of God's covenant and the one who has the duty to keep His commandments is not the nation, the society, or the family but each individual who has been saved.

"Shall Have No" (לֹא יִהְיֶה)

"No" is the Hebrew word לֹא (*lo*). It is the primary Hebrew term for absolute negation, which is further emphasized since it occurs at the beginning of the Hebrew text. It is a solemn warning against things that should never be done. Eight commandments out of ten, except the fourth and fifth, begin with לֹא (*lo*; Exod 20:3, 4, 7, 13, 14, 15, 16, 17; Deut 5:7–8, 11, 17–21).

The word "have" is the imperfect stem of the Hebrew verb הָיָה (*hayah*) and means "to be" or "to exist." Thus the first commandment, "You shall have no other gods before Me" (Exod 20:3), can be literally translated as "There should be no other gods to you before My face." Since both הָיָה (*hayah*) and לֹא (*lo*) mainly appear together when God is making a formal agreement between Himself and Israel (Gen 9:11, 15), this means that violating the first commandment is equivalent to violating an agreement with God.

The ultimate purpose for the Israelites was to glorify God (Isa 42:8; 43:7). Therefore, they were not to have any other gods in their lives (Isa 43:10–12; 44:6, 8; 45:14, 18, 21–22; 46:9). In other words, the allowance of other gods in the lives of the Israelites would have defeated the very purpose of their existence.

"Other Gods" (אֱלֹהִים אֲחֵרִים)

The Israelites forgot about God and became rebellious when they lived in Egypt. They defiled themselves with Egyptian idols and indulged themselves in idolatry:

> *They shall no longer sacrifice their sacrifices to the goat demons with which they play the harlot. This shall be a permanent statute to them throughout their generations. (Lev 17:7)*

> *Fear the LORD and serve Him in sincerity and truth; and put away the gods which your fathers served beyond the River and in Egypt, and serve the LORD. (Josh 24:14)*

> *I said to them, "Cast away, each of you, the detestable things of his eyes, and do not defile yourselves with the idols of Egypt; I am the Lord your God." But they rebelled against Me and were not willing to listen to Me; they did not cast away the detestable things of their eyes, nor did they forsake the idols of Egypt. Then I resolved to pour out My wrath on them, to accomplish My anger against them in the midst of the land of Egypt. But I acted for the sake of My name, that it should not be profaned in the sight of the nations among whom they lived, in whose sight I made Myself known to them by bringing them out of the land of Egypt. (Ezek 20:7–9)*

Truly, the 430 years in Egypt were a period of idolatry, and the Israelites forgot their covenant with God. The ten plagues that fell upon Egypt were judgment upon the Egyptian gods that the people relied on (Exod 12:12; Num 33:4).[36] The exodus was God's great blessing of delivering the Israelites from idolatry. Thus He commanded them, "You shall have no other gods before Me," so that they would never worship idols again (Exod 20:3).

The words "other gods" are אֱלֹהִים אֲחֵרִים (*elohim aherim*) in Hebrew. The word אֱלֹהִים (*Elohim*) is a name for God and also the first name for God introduced in the Bible (Gen 1:1). *Elohim* occurs about 2,570 times in the Old Testament; of these, 2,310 occurrences refer to the true God.[37] At times *elohim* in its plural form was used for "judges" (Exod 21:6, KJV; see Exod 22:8) or "angels" (Ps 8:5, KJV; "heavenly beings," ESV) or pagan gods (Exod 18:11; 22:20; 1 Kgs 14:9; Ps 97:7). In these cases *elohim* referred to multiple judges, angels, or pagan gods. When used together with the Hebrew word *aherim*, the plural form of *aher*, meaning "other," it referred to false gods or pagan gods (Exod 23:13; Deut 6:14; 8:19).

For this reason, in the first of the Ten Commandments, God taught that there are no other *elohim* (gods) except for Him and that He alone is the true *Elohim*. As it is written in Deuteronomy 10:17, "God is the God of gods [אֱלֹהֵי הָאֱלֹהִים, *elohe haelohim*] and the Lord of lords [אֲדֹנֵי הָאֲדֹנִים, *adone ha-adonim*]." God cannot be compared to any of these numerous pagan gods, as He alone is the true God (Isa 37:16; Mark 12:29; John 5:44; 17:3).

Even during the early church period, many gods were known among the people, but none were true gods (1 Cor 8:5–6). Because the Lord God alone is the true God, the Creator, and the Savior, God warned His people not to serve or worship other gods except Him (Isa 45:14). The Lord God is a personal and living God (Acts 14:15; 1 Tim 3:15). Gods made by human hands, however, are all false and futile objects (Deut 32:21; 2 Chr 13:9; Jer 10:14; 18:15).

Besides idols made by human hands, anything that sits in God's place is an idol. In Matthew 6:24, Jesus says, "No one can serve two masters; for either he will hate the one and love the other, or he will be devoted to one and despise the other. You cannot serve God and wealth." This passage shows people's inclination to make money their god (1 Tim 6:10, 17; 2 Tim 3:2).

When Jesus told the rich young man, "Sell your possessions and give to the poor ... and come, follow me," the young man went away grieving and did not come back (Matt 19:21-22; see Mark 10:21-22; Luke 18:22-23). There was only one reason the young man did not return: he was rich and owned much property (Matt 19:22; Mark 10:22; Luke 18:23). Although he sought eternal life, he abandoned Christ because he could not give up his idols of wealth and self (1 Tim 6:10, 17).

Additionally, if power (Jer 5:31), honor (John 12:43), pleasure (2 Tim 3:4), people (Isa 2:22; Jer 17:5), or success is prioritized over God, they are indeed "other gods." Greed is also idolatry (Col 3:5; see also Eph 5:5). When people fill their hearts with greed, they do not see fit to acknowledge God any longer (Rom 1:28; see also Rom 1:24, 26).

Furthermore, many people love and idolize themselves (John 12:25; 2 Tim 3:2). They are engrossed with themselves and focus only on serving themselves with all their wealth (Luke 12:13-21). Such people also have violated the first commandment and are serving other gods.

"Before Me" (עַל־פָּנָי)

The phrase "before Me" is עַל־פָּנָי (*al-Panaya*) in Hebrew, which combines *al* and *panim*. *Al* means "upon," and *panim* means "face," and therefore the phrase means "before Me" or "before My face."

There are many religions in the world, but there is only one true God:

> *Even if there are so-called gods whether in heaven or on earth, as indeed there are many gods and many lords, yet for us there is but one God, the Father, from whom are all things and we exist for Him; and one Lord, Jesus Christ, by whom are all things, and we exist through Him. (1 Cor 8:5–6)*

The Bible, from the beginning to the end, testifies passionately that the triune God is the one and only God (Exod 20:3; Deut 4:35, 39; 6:4; 1 Kgs 8:60; Isa 44:6, 8; John 5:44; 1 Cor 8:4, 6; 1 Tim 2:5; Jas 2:19; see also Jas 4:12). The Greek word for "alone" (μόνος, *monos*) found in John 5:44 means "just, only one, the only entity in the class." It thus asserts that God is the one and only God in heaven above or on the earth beneath (Deut 4:39; Josh 2:11; 1 Kgs 8:23).

The triune God is the only Creator and the only source of life. He is the only guide (Ps 23:1–6), the only Lord of the lords (1 Tim 6:15; see also Ps 95:3), the only King of ages (1 Tim 1:17), the only protector (Ps 121:1–8), the only Father (Matt 23:9), the only answerer of prayers (Luke 18:7), the only lawgiver of the new commandment (John 13:34–35), the only Savior (Rom 3:23–24), the only Redeemer (Rom 6:10–11), the only mediator of the new covenant between God and man (Heb 9:15), the only chief judge (Heb 9:27), the only author of faith (Heb 12:2), and the only God who does great wonders (Ps 136:4).

We, therefore, have only one Father, one Lord, one Spirit, one gospel, one baptism, one faith, and one plan for salvation (Eph 4:3–6).

What does it mean to worship the one and only God?

We must love only God, who is incomparable to any other being. God is almighty and above all other beings (Isa 46:5). People can do nothing secretly without God's knowledge of it (Ps 139:1–4, 7–8, 15–16, 23–24; Jer 23:24; see also 2 Sam 12:12; Job 26:6; Amos 9:2–3). When a man and a woman become one through their love for each other, no one else can come between them. Likewise, God requires exclusive and undivided love from us. If we have two masters in our hearts, our love is not real, for either we will love one and hate the other, or we will devote ourselves to one and despise the other (Matt 6:24; Luke 16:13).

The phrase "before Me" is a proclamation that "the Lord our God is one Lord" (Mark 12:28–30; see also Rom 3:30; 1 Cor 8:4; Jas 2:19), which means that we are to be satisfied with God alone. God is greater than all (John 10:29). A person who believes in the one and only God entrusts all things to His greatness (Ps 95:3; Dan 2:45; Titus 2:13) and does not cherish anything else in his or her heart.

We must believe only in God and serve Him forever. There is no other god besides the one true God. False gods (Deut 32:17; Ps 106:37; 1 Cor 10:19–21) and pagan deities, therefore, are not gods but are worthless, futile, and empty idols (Deut 32:21; Ps 96:5; Isa 41:29; 44:9–20; Jer 2:5, 11; 10:14–15; 16:19–20; 51:17–18; Dan 5:23; Hab 2:18–19, etc.). Worshiping an idol rather than God is a malicious sin (1 Cor 10:20). God alone is the beginning and the end (Rev 1:8, 17; 2:8; 21:6; 22:13); He exists on His own for all eternity and is the sole object of our faith.

> *Thus says the LORD, the King of Israel and his Redeemer, the LORD of hosts: "I am the first and I am the last, and there is no God besides Me. Who is like Me? Let him proclaim and declare it; yes, let him recount it to Me in order, from the time that I established the ancient nation. And let them declare to them the things that are coming and the events that are going to take place. Do not tremble and do not be afraid; have I not long since announced it to you and declared it? And you are My witnesses. Is there any God besides Me, or is there any other Rock? I know of none." Those who fashion a graven image are all of them futile, and their precious things are of no profit; even their own witnesses fail to see or know, so that they will be put to shame. Who has fashioned a god or cast an idol to no profit? Behold, all his companions will be put to shame, for the craftsmen themselves are mere men. Let them all assemble themselves, let them stand up, let them tremble, let them together be put to shame. (Isa 44:6–11)*

God alone has existed from before the foundation of the world and will exist until the end. No one accompanied Him during His work of creation; God alone created all the universe and all creation (Isa 44:24). God has no other being inside Him, nor is He able to divide Himself into different beings. He exists on His own from everlasting to everlasting as one absolute God (Ps 90:1–2). His divine attributes are simple yet unique; God alone is self-existing and unchangeable forever.

Only God is the first to be glorified. If two or more absolute and eternal sovereigns were to exist, neither could be the supreme being or the true God. When we accurately understand and believe in the uniqueness of God, then we will have the conviction that every being has come from Him and will return to Him (Rom 11:36). Then we can live to truly glorify God alone without seeking the glory of men. Thus 1 Corinthians 10:31 states, "Whether, then, you eat or drink or whatever you do, do all to the glory of God."

> *How can you believe, when you receive glory from one another and you do not seek the glory that is from the one and only God? (John 5:44)*

We must believe that there is salvation only through Jesus Christ whom God sent. It is impossible for two one and only Gods to exist. Jesus Christ the incarnate is God the Son; He and God the Father are one (John 10:30; 14:9). No one can come to the Father except through Jesus (John 14:6). Eternal life is knowing the only true God and Jesus Christ, whom God has sent (John 17:3). Hence Peter confessed in the fullness of the Holy Spirit, "There is salvation in no one else; for there is no other name under heaven that has been given among men by which we must be saved" (Acts 4:12).

> *For us there is but one God, the Father, from whom are all things and we exist for Him; and one Lord, Jesus Christ, by whom are all*

things, and we exist through Him. (1 Cor 8:6)

The Jews never thought it was possible for someone to become God or come close to being God. As Jesus healed a paralytic, He said, "Take courage, son; your sins are forgiven," and some of the scribes thought to themselves, "This fellow blasphemes" (Matt 9:2–3).

Jesus asserted His equality with God, saying, "I and the Father are one" (John 10:30). In response, the religious leaders tried to stone Jesus, thinking that it was blasphemous for a man to call himself God (John 10:31–33). The words "blasphemy" (βλασφημία, *blasphēmia*) and "to blaspheme" (βλασφημέω, *blasphēmeō*) in the context of blaspheming the deity occur thirty times in the New Testament.[38] Eight of them are accusations against Jesus (Matt 9:3; 26:65 [2x]; Mark 2:7; 14:64; Luke 5:21; John 10:33, 36). Blasphemy involves profane and irreverent behavior and refers to the unspeakably evil speech or ungodly deeds that hide and dishonor God's glory. The religious leaders saw Jesus as a man who made Himself equal with God and believed His claim to be so blasphemous that they sought to stone Him. They ended up failing to recognize Jesus the incarnate, God the Son, even until the end. There is only one God, the triune God, and salvation comes only through His Son, Jesus Christ (John 14:6; Acts 4:12), the only begotten God (John 1:18).

You might know that the LORD, He is God; there is no other besides Him. (Deut 4:35)

He is God; ... there is no other. (Deut 4:39)

The LORD is our God, the LORD is one! (Deut 6:4)

You are great, ... for there is none like You, and there is no God besides You, according to all that we have heard with our ears. (2 Sam 7:22)

All the peoples of the earth may know that the LORD is God; there is no one else. (1 Kgs 8:60)

You are the God, You alone, of all the kingdoms of the earth. You have made heaven and earth. (2 Kgs 19:15)

You are the God, You alone, of all the kingdoms of the earth. You have made heaven and earth. (Isa 37:16)

I am the first and I am the last, and there is no God besides Me. (Isa 44:6)

Is there any God besides me? ... I know of none. (Isa 44:8)

I am the LORD, and there is no other; besides Me there is no God Men may know from the rising to the setting of the sun that there is no one besides Me. I am the LORD, and there is no other. (Isa 45:5–6)

The LORD will be king over all the earth; in that day the LORD will be the only one, and His name the only one. (Zech 14:9)

Jesus answered, "The foremost [law] is, 'Hear, O Israel! The Lord our God is one Lord.'" (Mark 12:29)

There is only one Lawgiver and Judge, the One who is able to save and to destroy; but who are you who judge your neighbor? (Jas 4:12)

To the only God our Savior, through Jesus Christ our Lord, be glory, majesty, dominion and authority, before all time and now and forever. Amen. (Jude 1:25)

II. Specific Laws Derived from the First Commandment

The first commandment, "Love only the Lord and do not follow other gods," is the greatest of all the Ten Commandments. Exodus 22:18, 20, 29–31; 23:13–19, 24–33 and Deuteronomy 6:14–15; 12:2–13:18; 17:1–7; 18:9–14 teach in detail how God's people must keep the first commandment and serve Him.

Proper Ways to Serve God and Consequential Blessings
(Exod 22:29–31; 23:13–19, 24–33)

Offering to God the firstborn son and the firstborn of the livestock (Exod 22:29-30). God commanded, "The firstborn of your sons you shall give to Me" (Exod 22:29), because offering the firstborn (Exod 23:19; 34:26) was a sign of reverence for the Lord (Deut 26:2, 10; Prov 3:9). God commanded that the firstborn of the calf and the lamb should remain with its mother for seven days, and then "on the eighth day," He said, "you shall give it to Me" (Exod 22:30).

Not eating meat torn by beasts in the field but throwing it to the dogs (Exod 22:31). By forbidding His people from eating any unclean meat, God set them apart so that they could consecrate themselves to Him. Flesh torn by beasts in the field was considered extremely unclean because blood, which is life, was still in the flesh, and God strictly forbade His people to eat it. A dog (כֶּלֶב, *kelev*) was an unclean animal (see Lev 11:27) that represented the wicked, the greedy, and the unclean (2 Sam 9:8; Isa 56:11). Thus Jesus said, "Do not give what is holy to dogs" (Matt 7:6). Likewise, in Exodus God commanded His people to throw what was unholy to the dogs (Exod 22:31). People of God must be holy people who always guard themselves against what is unclean.

Ways to serve God in the promised land (Exod 23:13-19). God commanded, "Do not mention the name of other gods, nor let them be heard from your mouth" (Exod 23:13). God appointed three feasts (the Feast of the Unleavened Bread, the Feast of the Harvest, and the Feast of Ingathering) and commanded all men to come before the Lord these three times a year (Exod 23:14–17). Moreover, in observance of the feasts, no one was to come to God empty-handed (Exod 23:15). The Israelites were to offer the firstfruits to the house of God (Exod 23:19).

The promise regarding the conquest of Canaan and blessings for those who keep the commandment (Exod 23:24–33). Moses' book of the covenant (Exod 20:22–23:33; see also Exod 24:4–7) ends with a stern warning against idolatry: "You shall not worship their gods, nor serve them, nor do according to their deeds; but you shall utterly overthrow them and break their sacred pillars in pieces" (Exod 23:24).

God's blessed reign will touch even the most detailed part of our lives when we obey the first commandment. He will step into our life journeys and bestow blessings of daily bread and water and take away our sicknesses (give us health). He will give us the blessing of childbirth (offspring) and will fulfill the number of our days (with longevity). He will give us the blessing of gradually driving out our enemies (protection and expansion of power) and the blessing of borders in the land that He has chosen (great reward; Exod 23:25–31).

First, if the Israelites would serve the Lord alone, God would bless their bread and water in the land and remove sickness from them. He promised, "There shall be no one miscarrying or barren in your land; I will fulfill the number of your days" (Exod 23:26). The Hebrew verb for "miscarrying" in this verse is שָׁכֹל (*shakhol*), which means "to be bereaved." This verb is used when a child dies either inside the womb or after birth (Gen 43:14; 1 Sam 15:33). God, who is sovereign over life, allows conception and protects babies from miscarriage (Isa 66:9). Furthermore, He would protect the children's lives even after birth. He would also exert power over the limitations of life and give longevity (Exod 23:26). The blessing "I will fulfill the number of your days" (Exod 23:26) means "I will allow you to live a long life." Longevity is a special blessing directly related to godliness (Exod 20:12; Deut

4:40; 5:16; 6:2; 11:9; 12:25, 28; 22:7; 30:20; 1 Kgs 3:14; Pss 21:4; 55:23; 91:16; Prov 3:1–2, 7–8, 16; 4:10, 20–23; 9:11; 16:31; Eccl 7:17; 8:13; Eph 6:1–3).

Second, God said that He would send His "terror" before the Israelites (Exod 23:27). "My terror" (אֵימָתִי, *emathi*) is the combination of the Hebrew word אֵמָה (*emah*), meaning "to fear" or "to dread," and a first-person pronominal suffix; thus the phrase means "my fear" or "my terror." This expression refers to the extreme terror and fear that God would bring upon idol-worshiping gentile nations. They would hear about the wonders and miracles that God had performed on behalf of the Israelites and tremble in immense fear. Such reactions were evident from the testimonies of the people from Moab (Num 22:3) and Jericho (Josh 2:9, 11). This was God's promise that all Israel's enemies would be thrown into confusion so that they would turn and run away.

Third, God promised to send hornets and drive out the Canaanites (Exod 23:28; see also Deut 7:20; Josh 24:12). Hornets are bigger and stronger than regular wasps. They are so strong that one sting could be fatal. This promise to send such terrifying hornets was indeed fulfilled during the conquest of Canaan. In Joshua 24:12, God said, "I sent the hornet before you and it drove out the two kings of the Amorites from before you, but not by your sword or your bow." The hornets were so powerful that they chased and destroyed even those left behind and hiding behind locked doors after Israel's last attack (Deut 7:20). The enemy was thrown into great chaos from fear of the hornets, and eventually everyone was destroyed without exception (Deut 7:20–24). Without the hornets the Israelites would not have been able to drive out the two Amorite kings. The conquest of Canaan was not achieved through swords and bows but through the hornets and the terror sent beforehand by God.

Fourth, God promised to drive out the Canaanites gradually, little by little, not at once (Exod 23:29–30). If the Canaanites had been driven out at once, the land would have become desolate and the wild beasts would have thrived. Hence, God did not drive them out in one year but little by little. This was to protect the people in case the wild beasts thrived in the land while it was yet untilled (Deut 7:22; see also Lev 26:22; Ezek 14:15, 21). God's purpose was to wait for the Israelites to become "fruitful" and take full possession of the land (Exod 23:30). God fulfilled His work of salvation in ways unthinkable to human minds and intervened in the most meticulous ways in order to secure the lives of His chosen people and ensure their prosperity.

Fifth, God promised to set the border "from the Red Sea to the sea of the Philistines, and from the wilderness to the River Euphrates" and to drive out the inhabitants of the land (Exod 23:31). In Exodus 23:31, God said, "I will deliver the inhabitants of the land into your hand, and you will drive them out before you." The statement "you shall drive them out before you" (וְגֵרַשְׁתָּמוֹ מִפָּנֶיךָ, wegerashtamo mippaneykha) literally means "drive them out completely so that you will never see them before your face." God strongly commanded Israel to eradicate the inhabitants so that the Israelites would not become accustomed to seeing and interacting with them and become tempted to follow after their sins (Deut 7:23–26).

After making all these promises, God solemnly warned the people again regarding idolatry. In Exodus 23:32–33, God said, "You shall make no covenant with them or with their gods. They shall not live in your land, because they will make you sin against Me; for if you serve their gods, it will surely be a snare to you." During those days in the regions of Canaan, covenant ratifications usually included a ceremony in which both parties acknowledged each other's gods and worshiped them according to their respective laws of worship (Exod 34:15).

Prohibition of Idol Worship and Regulations on Punishment (Exod 22:18, 20; Deut 6:14–15; 12:2–13:18; 18:9–14)

In the book of Deuteronomy, specific laws derived from the first commandment were treated as national matters and strictly applied.

"You shall not allow a sorceress to live" (Exod 22:18; see Deut 18:9–14). A sorceress refers to a person who served demons, told fortunes, and performed exorcisms. Deuteronomy 18:9–14 lists various types of sorcerers, including those who used divination, practiced witchcraft, interpreted omens, or cast spells or were a medium, a spiritist, or one who called up the dead. Mediums and spiritists were often mentioned together (Lev 19:31; 20:6, 27; 1 Sam 28:3, 9; 2 Kgs 21:6; 23:24; 2 Chr 33:6; Isa 8:19; 19:3). The following chart categorizes the various names for sorcerers, according to the Hebrew text.

Sorcerer מְכַשֵּׁף *mekhashef*	This word is derived from כָּשַׁף (*kashaf*, "sorcery" or "to practice sorcery"). Sorcerers were adept at performing wonders (Exod 7:11), exorcism (Isa 47:9, 12; "many sorceries"), and mystifying people (Mal 3:5; conjury). The word is מְכַשֵּׁפָה (*mekhashefah*) in the feminine form (Exod 22:18; "sorceress").
Diviner קֹסֵם קְסָמִים *qosem qesamim*	This word is derived from קָסַם (*qasam*, "to practice divination"). It includes those who practice belomancy, divination by shaking arrows in a quiver (Ezek 21:21), and necromancy, communicating with the dead and making false prophesies (Ezek 21:29).
One who practices witchcraft מְעוֹנֵן *meonen*	This word is derived from עָנָן (*anan*, "cloud"). It refers to a fortune teller or a magician (Deut 18:10–14) who predicts the future using the shape and movement of clouds.
One who interprets omens מְנַחֵשׁ *menahesh*	This word is derived from נָחַשׁ (*nahash*, "to interpret omens" or "to practice divination"). It refers to an interpreter of omens (Deut 18:10). Interpreters of omens observe a mixture of liquids (water and oil) to practice divination (see Gen 44:5).

One who casts a spell חֹבֵר חָבֶר *hover haver*	The word חֶבֶר (*hever*) means "spell" (Isa 47:9; "your spells"). Psalm 58:5 speaks of a charmer's spell cast upon a venomous serpent.
Medium שֹׁאֵל אוֹב *shoel ov*	A medium communicates with the dead (Deut 18:11; see also Isa 29:4). The Hebrew root word for *shoel* is *shaal* (שָׁאַל, "to ask"). The word *ov* means "medium" or "spirit of the dead." Originally *ov* meant a "hollow of the ground"; the literal meaning of *shoel ov* is "one who asks a hollow of the ground."
Spiritist יִדְּעֹנִי *yiddeoni*	A spiritist is a person who calls out the spirits of the dead or a necromancer (soothsayer). Spiritists "consult the spirits of the dead" (1 Sam 28:9, NLT). In Saul's days a medium at En-dor brought up the spirit of Samuel from the dead (1 Sam 28:7–25).
One who calls up the dead דֹּרֵשׁ אֶל־הַמֵּתִים *doresh el-hammethim*	This phrase means to "call up the dead" or "ask the dead." It refers to one who communicates with the dead in ways different from those used by mediums and spiritists (1 Sam 28:8–14).

The law commands that a man or woman who becomes a medium or spiritist must be stoned to death (Lev 20:27). God's wrath will be poured out upon anyone who follows after a spiritist, and he or she will be cut off from among the Israelites (Lev 20:6). God commanded His people not to believe in a medium or spiritist and not to defile themselves by following after such people (Lev 19:31). In Deuteronomy 18:20, God commanded that any false prophet who "speaks in the name of other gods, that prophet shall die." Revelation 21:8 provides a list of those who will be thrown into the lake that burns with fire and brimstone, which is the second death. The list includes the "abominable" (βδελύσσω, *bdelyssō*, utterly detestable, idolaters), "sorcerers" (φαρμακός, *pharmakos*, those who entice people through magic or divination), and "idolaters" (εἰδωλολάτρης, *eidōlolatrēs*, worshipers of false gods, the greedy).

Spiritism and divination are as popular today as they were in ancient times. Hence, the Bible has a special warning for the saints against this type of idolatry. If a fortune teller wearing a worn-out, dusty straw hat absentmindedly said to you, "You will be rich soon; you will have a very successful future," you might walk past him, thinking that his words were nonsense, yet in your heart you might feel good about what he had said and even want to share the story with someone else. This is the nature of human beings.

It is important to remember, however, that God has strictly forbidden the act of turning to sorcerers and abandoning His Word, as it is idolatry. God reveals His will and purpose in His sovereign way; He works through the Word. The prophets chosen by God preached only the words that they had received from God (Exod 7:2; Deut 18:18; 1 Sam 9:9; Isa 51:16; 59:21; Jer 1:9; 5:14; 27:18; 29:19). There is nothing obscure about God's Word; His answers to us are always certain, and His Word will be fulfilled and will last forever (Pss 19:7–9; 93:5; 111:7–8; Prov 22:21; Isa 55:11; 2 Pet 1:19). All God's saints must examine themselves. When we read God's Word, do we ever view it as less important than a fortune teller's futile false prophesies? We must ask our consciences whether we have broken the first commandment.

"He who sacrifices to any god ... shall be utterly destroyed" *(Exod 22:20)*. Making a sacrifice to another god is equivalent to offering it one's heart, time, and wealth. According to the law, anyone who betrays God in this manner "shall be utterly destroyed" (Exod 22:20). The word "destroyed" is in the Hophal stem (imperfect, passive causative) of the verb חָרַם (*haram*), meaning "to ban." Thus it does not mean merely "to kill" but "to cause to be killed" (see Lev 27:28–29). The word *haram* was also used during Joshua's conquest of the land of Canaan (Josh 6:21; 8:26; 10:28; 11:11). Deuteronomy 7:1–2 states, "When the LORD

your God brings you into the land where you are entering to possess it, and clears away many nations before you, ... seven nations greater and stronger than you, and when the LORD your God delivers them before you and you defeat them, then you shall utterly destroy [*haram*] them. You shall make no covenant with them and show no favor to them" (see also Deut 7:16; 20:16–18).

You shall destroy the places of idolatry, the names and towns of the idols, and the idolaters with their children and animals (Deut 12:2-3; 13:12-18). God commanded the Israelites not to "follow other gods, any of the gods of the peoples" surrounding them once they entered Canaan (Deut 6:14). Moreover, He commanded them to burn and destroy all places and towns of idolatry, all idols and their names, and all idolaters and everything in their towns (Deut 12:2-3; 13:12-18). God also commanded them not to leave anyone alive and to show no mercy to them (Deut 7:2, 16; 20:16-18). In Deuteronomy 7:3-4, God solemnly warned the people against intermarrying with the inhabitants of Canaan and turning away from God to serve other gods lest the anger of the Lord be kindled against them and destroy them (see Exod 34:16).

You shall not inquire about idolatry or mimic it (Deut 12:29-31). Idolatry is hateful and detestable to God, so the Israelites were not to inquire about it or follow after it. In Deuteronomy 12:30, the word "inquire" is דָּרַשׁ (*darash*) in Hebrew, which means "to tread, to frequent, to seek, to worship." Thus God forbade people to seek, follow, inquire about, or serve idols.

You shall stone to death those who entice people to worship an idol (Deut 13:1-11; 17:1-7).

> *If there is found in your midst ... a man or a woman who ... has gone and served other gods and worshiped them, or the sun or the moon or any of the heavenly host, which I have not commanded, and if it is told you and you have heard of it, then you shall inquire thoroughly. Behold, if it is true and the thing certain that this de-*

testable thing has been done in Israel, then you shall bring out that man or that woman who has done this evil deed to your gates, that is, the man or the woman, and you shall stone them to death. (Deut 17:2-5)

When false prophets or dreamers enticed people by performing signs and wonders, God's people were not to follow them but rather to put them to death (Deut 13:1-5). Even if a family member, relative, or friend enticed people to idolatry, they were not to follow or listen to them. They were not to forgive those who attempted to entice people to turn away from God but rather to stone them to death (Deut 13:6-11). The ultimate goal of false prophets or dreamers is to confuse God's children and turn them away from His way so that eventually they will succumb to the powers of the evil spirit, who will enslave them, and live miserable lives. God's saints must follow only after His Word as it is recorded in the Bible and use the Word as the standard for all our decisions. At times people closest to us—a family member, relative, or friend who shares the joys and sorrows of life with us—can become a tempter who lures us into idolatry. In some cases a family member can be the strongest obstacle on our way to God. Thus Jesus said, "A man's enemies will be the members of his household" (Matt 10:36).

Even when we witness the fulfillment of a prophecy or when a dreamer's dream comes true, if it is not biblical, we must not believe in him or her. Even if the words or dreams of false prophets do come true, we must not believe in them. We must believe only in the Word recorded in the Bible. Jesus warned, "See to it that no one misleads you" (Matt 24:4). He went on, "For false Christs and false prophets will arise and will show great signs and wonders, so as to mislead, if possible, even the elect" (Matt 24:24).

You shall observe regulations regarding edible animals and prohibition of blood eating (Deut 12:15-18, 20-28). As long as the animals had not been used for sacrifices, God allowed the Israelites to slaughter and eat meat in their dwelling places (Deut 12:15-16, 20-25). After they entered Canaan, if their homes were far away from the central sanctuary where God had chosen to place His name, they were allowed to slaughter and eat meat as they wished in their own cities. When eating from the herd or flock, they were allowed to eat the animals just as they ate gazelle or deer, without discriminating between the clean and the unclean (Deut 12:21-22). God strictly prohibited them from eating the animals' blood, however; they were to pour the blood out on the ground like water (Deut 12:16, 23-25). God repeatedly prohibited the people, saying, "Only be sure not to eat the blood" (Deut 12:23); "You shall not eat it" (Deut 12:24); and again, "You shall not eat it" (Deut 12:25). The phrase "only be sure" in verse 23 emphasizes resolvedness and unwavering determination with regard to not eating the blood. Furthermore, verse 24, "You shall not eat it; you shall pour it out on the ground like water," includes the command to pour out the life of the animal to the Lord, who alone is the Lord of life.

In the case of sacrificial meats, God commanded His people to eat them in specific designated places according to the regulation (Deut 12:17-18, 26). According to Leviticus 17:3-6, during the wilderness journey the Israelites were to bring all their sacrificial animals to the entrance of the tent of meeting and give them to the priests to sacrifice as peace offerings to the Lord. The animals' blood was sprinkled on the altar of the Lord, while the fat was burnt for a pleasing aroma to the Lord.

When they offered burnt offerings, both flesh and blood were offered on the altar of the Lord. For other types of sacrifices, the blood was poured out on the altar, and the meat was allowed to be eaten by the people (Deut 12:27).

God's regulation stipulated that anyone who violated His Word and ate the blood would arouse His wrath, and God would cut him or her off from among the Israelites (Lev 7:27; 17:10, 14). The regulations regarding blood were applied both to the Israelites and to strangers who sojourned among them (Lev 17:10, 12-13). Abstaining from eating blood was "right in the sight of the Lord," and God blessed anyone who observed this regulation, saying that it would "be well" with them and their sons after them (Deut 12:25). Verse 28 continues, "Be careful to listen to all these words which I command you, so that it may be well with you and your sons after you forever, for you will be doing what is good and right in the sight of the LORD your God."

Why did God strictly forbid His people to eat the blood?

First, the blood is equivalent to the life of the flesh (Lev 17:11). Thus eating an animal's blood was the same as swallowing its life (see Gen 9:4-5).

Second, the life that the blood represents belongs to God the Creator (see Num 27:16; Deut 12:23, 27; 1 Sam 25:29; Pss 42:8; 50:10-12) and lay within the realm of God's sovereignty. Eating blood, therefore, was a violation of God's sovereignty.

Third, drinking the blood of a sacrifice was an extremely evil ritual enjoyed by pagan idolaters. Many gentile nations engaged in rituals involving drinking the blood of sacrificial animals because they believed that they would receive certain spiritual powers or the gods' life through the blood. They even sacrificed human beings and drank their blood. Therefore, by prohibiting the Israelites from drinking the blood of the sacrifice, God distinguished His people completely from cruel and detestable pagan rituals that ignored the value of all life.[39]

Fourth, the blood was the only way to receive atonement (Lev 17:11; Heb 9:22), and it foreshadowed the precious blood of Jesus Christ that would redeem mankind from their sins. The precious blood of Jesus Christ atoned for the sins of humanity once and for all (Heb 9:12, 21-22, 28; 1 Pet 1:18-19; 1 John 1:7; Rev 7:14). Therefore, we have redemption, the forgiveness of our sins, through His blood (Eph 1:7; Col 1:14; Rev 1:5).

Essential Regulations Established During the Council of Jerusalem in AD 49 (Abstaining from Idolatry, Sexual Immorality, Things Strangled, and Blood)

Acts 15 records the essential provisions established during the council of Jerusalem in AD 49. Rather than abolishing all the laws, the council decided on and announced the essential provisions that the church must retain. Here, the phrase "these essentials" (Acts 15:28) is ἐπάναγκες (*epanankes*) in Greek, which refers to things that are "necessary" or "indispensable." Among the regulations that the Israelites kept, some essential regulations were beneficial even for the Gentiles, so the council encouraged everyone to keep them. The requirements included abstaining from "things contaminated by idols and from fornication and from what is strangled and from blood" (Acts 15:20; see Acts 15:29; 21:25). The word "abstain" is ἀπέχεσθαι (*apechesthai*) in Greek. It is the present infinitive verb of ἀπέχω (*apechō*), which means "to keep off" or "to be distant," so the word underscores continued abstinence.

> *We write to them that they abstain from things contaminated by idols and from fornication and from what is strangled and from blood. (Acts 15:20)*

> *Abstain from things sacrificed to idols and from blood and from things strangled and from fornication; if you keep yourselves free from such things, you will do well. (Acts 15:29)*

> *Concerning the Gentiles who have believed, we wrote, having decided that they should abstain from meat sacrificed to idols and from blood and from what is strangled and from fornication. (Acts 21:25)*

Abstinence from the things contaminated by idols (things sacrificed to idols) ***and from sexual immorality.*** The apostle Paul strictly forbade idolatry, saying, "Do not be idolaters, as some of them were" (1 Cor

10:7), and repeated, "My beloved, flee from idolatry" (1 Cor 10:14). In Colossians 3:5, he broadened the boundaries of idolatry, saying, "Consider the members of your earthly body as dead to immorality, impurity, passion, evil desire, and greed, which amounts to idolatry." The apostle Paul was provoked within when he saw the city of Athens full of idols (Acts 17:16). Furthermore, in Ephesus a disturbance occurred because the apostle Paul persuaded people not to worship the silver shrines of Artemis (Acts 19:23-41). The phrase "things contaminated" (Acts 15:20) is ἀλίσγημα (*alisgēma*) in Greek and refers to sacrificial offerings, such as meat, that had been offered to pagan gods. Acts 15:29 and 21:25 clarify that a contaminated offering was meat "sacrificed to idols." Eating what had been sacrificed to idols was forbidden because it created contact with an idol, which could lead to worshiping the idol or inclining one's heart to it (Rev 2:14, 20).

Moreover, the apostle Paul exhorted in Ephesians 5:3, "Immorality or any impurity or greed must not even be named among you, as is proper among saints." The end of sexual immorality is a descent to the chambers of death (Prov 7:25-27). As the second coming of the Lord draws near, we must abstain from sexual immorality and strive to preserve our bodies, souls, and spirits blameless and spotless before the Lord (Eph 5:27; 1 Thess 3:13; 5:23; 2 Pet 3:14).

Abstinence from what has been strangled and from blood. Eating what had been strangled was forbidden because it had blood inside. The Bible strictly forbids the direct consumption of blood (Gen 9:4; Lev 17:10-14; Deut 12:23-25).

The Greek word πνικτός (*pniktos*), translated as "what has been strangled," refers to a strangled animal that has died from suffocation without bleeding. This command warned against eating meat while its blood was still in it. The command to abstain from eating flesh torn by beasts in the field or anything that had died of itself (Exod 22:31; Lev 17:15; 22:8; Deut 14:21) was also because its blood had not been properly removed. In one instance, after a battle with the Philistines, the Israelites were so exhausted that they rushed upon the spoil. They took sheep, oxen, and calves and ate them with the blood, thereby sinning against the Lord (1 Sam 14:31–34).

This law was strictly observed until the New Testament era, so the council of Jerusalem retained these provisions (Acts 15:20, 29; 21:25). Furthermore, the council of Jerusalem confirmed the doctrine of salvation, which states that our salvation comes through faith in Jesus Christ alone. Hence observing the law is not a condition for salvation but rather the rightful code of conduct for Christians who have received grace (Acts 16:31). By the providence of God, the council of Jerusalem firmly established the specific laws that assisted the people in observing the Ten Commandments. These laws became a strong foundation for the church so that the gospel could be preached powerfully throughout the world.

III. Teachings on the Object of Worship

The first commandment clarifies the *object* of worship. God alone is the absolute object of worship. No other god, no parent or child, no person, no creation can become the object of worship. Second Kings 17:35 quotes God's command: "You shall not fear other gods, nor bow down yourselves to them nor serve them nor sacrifice to them" (see also Jer 25:6; 35:15).

The first commandment attests to the one and only God. All gods besides God Himself are false gods.

Memorial Worship Services Are Serious Idolatry

Some churches in Korea encourage their saints to hold memorial worship services in their homes on the anniversary of a person's death. These memorials are unbiblical adaptations of Catholic memorial services combined with Korean ancestral rites for the deceased. The Bible does not mention any such rituals.

The motivation and purpose of memorial worship service are similar to those of Catholic rituals[40] *and ancestral rites traditions.* Catholic tradition encourages people to continue praying for the deceased even after their funerals so that they may live happily before God. Moreover, it allows believers to participate in ancestral rites, asserting that their religion's fundamental spirit lies in performing filial duties to their ancestors. They believe that through ancestral rites people can acknowledge the dignity of life and the origin of their families, live truthful lives according to the will of their deceased ancestors, and achieve harmony within their families and communities.

Some Protestant churches even allow their congregations to bow to their deceased ancestors during these rituals and accept the idea of communicating with the dead. However, these are serious forms of idolatry.[41] During these rituals food is offered to the souls of the deceased as the people pray before the dead or cherish their memories. First Corinthians 10:20 states, "The things which the Gentiles sacrifice, they sacrifice to demons and not to God; and I do not want you to become sharers in demons" (see also 2 Cor 6:15–16).

While the ritual is called memorial worship to God, the people are actually mourning the dead in remembrance of them. During Korean commemorative rituals, people mourn for the dead as they cherish the memory of the deceased. Memorial services are usually held in the home of the eldest son during the mid-autumn festival each year. Also, annual tributes are held to mourn and cherish one's direct ancestors on the anniversaries of those ancestors' deaths (usually for ancestors up to two generations above).

No provision in the Bible, however, teaches the saints to hold such memorial worship services. The Bible teaches us that God is the sole object of worship (Exod 20:3; Deut 5:7). The dead can never become the object of our worship. Worship is only for God. Worshiping the dead or gods other than God Himself is the fearful sin of idolatry.

The Deceased Are Under God's Realm and Authority

The Bible describes death in this way: "The eye of him who sees me will behold me no longer" (Job 7:8) and "I go—and I shall not return—to the land of darkness and deep shadow" (Job 10:21). When David lost his son, he said, "Can I bring him back again? I will go to him, but he will not return to me" (2 Sam 12:23). In the parable of the rich man and Lazarus, Jesus clearly demonstrated that a dead person cannot communicate with this world, telling a story in which Abraham said, "Between us [Abraham and Lazarus] and you [the rich man] there is a great chasm fixed" (Luke 16:26; see Luke 16:19–31). Thus God commanded the people not to allow mediums, spiritists, sorcerers, fortune tellers, and their followers to live but to put them to death (Exod 22:18; Lev 20:6; Deut 18:9–14; Isa 3:1–3; 8:19–22).

The apostle Paul referred to death for believers as being "absent from the body and [being] at home with the Lord" (2 Cor 5:8). Obsession over the dead, therefore, is a great sin before God. No authority under the heavens can manage the dead. Both judgment and reward for the dead are under God's domain. For this reason the apostle Paul said in 1 Thessalonians 4:13, "We do not want you to be uninformed, brethren, about those who are asleep, so that you will not grieve as do the rest who have no hope."

In ancient days, while mourning and praying for the dead, some people cut their own flesh, got tattoos on their bodies, or shaved their foreheads. These were superstitious customs to express that they too belonged to the deceased and were surely idolatrous practices (1 Kgs 18:28; see also Isa 15:2; Jer 16:6; 22:10; 47:5; 48:37). God strictly forbade this by law. In Leviticus 19:28, God said, "You shall not make any cuts in your body for the dead nor make any tattoo marks on yourselves: I am the LORD." In Deuteronomy 14:1, Moses reminded the people, "You are the sons of the LORD your God; you shall not cut yourselves nor shave your forehead for the sake of the dead."

We must refrain, therefore, from thus commemorating the dead or being overly attached to or obsessed with them. Instead, we must believe that the deceased are in God's bosom and entrust them to God (see Deut 26:14; Ps 31:12; Jer 16:5–7; Luke 16:22–23). Regarding having someone in our hearts other than God, Jesus said in Matthew 10:37, "He who loves father or mother more than Me is not worthy of Me; and he who loves son or daughter more than Me is not worthy of Me."

God said that sacrificing to the dead, like those who worshiped the Baal of Peor, is equivalent to the sin of idolatry (Ps 106:28–29). While the Israelites were in Shittim, they indulged in sexual immorality, bowed down to the Baal of Peor, and ate what had been offered to the pagan gods. They kindled God's wrath, and twenty-four thousand people died by a plague (Num 25:1–9). Exodus 22:20 states, "He who sacrifices to any god, other than to the LORD alone, shall be utterly destroyed" (Deut 13:1–18).

We must, therefore, do away with our former manner of life and put aside the old self that follows after the commandments and teachings of men, self-made religion, and futile traditions inherited from our forefathers (Eph 4:22–24; Col 2:20–23; 3:5–10; 1 Pet 1:18).

Catching the First Sunrise of the Year Is Serious Idolatry

Some people spend large sums of money to ensure that they bring in the New Year on a famous mountain or by the seashore in order to catch the year's first sunrise. The following reasons explain why this is serious idolatry.

People make wishes to the sun. People make their wishes as the sun rises on the first day of January, believing that their wishes will come true. Yet we need to remember that the One who fulfills our wishes is God, not the sun. The psalmist reminds us, "Delight yourself in the LORD; and He will give you the desires of your heart" (Ps 37:4; see also Ps 145:19).

People lose their hearts to the sun. People stand in awe as they catch the first glimpse of the rising sun on the first day of the year, and the scene captivates their hearts. However, giving our hearts to anything other than God is an act of betrayal and a wicked sin punishable by God the judge. Regarding this Job 31:26–28 testifies, "If I have looked at the sun when it shone or the moon going in splendor, and my heart became secretly enticed, and my hand threw a kiss from my mouth, that too would have been an iniquity calling for judgment, for I would have denied God above."

People worship the sun. People deify the sun as they celebrate the first sunrise of the year. They delude themselves into thinking that the sun can solve all their problems. The sun, however, is merely one of God's creations. Thus catching the first sunrise of the year violates the Ten Commandments. In Exodus 20:3, God says, "You shall have no other gods before Me."

God prohibited the practice of burning children as a sacrifice to Molech, the god of the sun (Lev 18:21; 20:2–5; Deut 12:31). This abominable act, however, was practiced in the northern kingdom of Israel (2 Kgs 17:17) and even in the southern kingdom of Judah (2 Kgs 16:3; 21:6; Jer 7:31; 32:35). One of the reasons for the fall of the northern kingdom of Israel was their sin of worshiping "all the host of heaven" (2 Kgs 17:16). Manasseh, the fourteenth king of Judah (696–642 BC), worshiped and served all the host of heaven (2 Kgs 21:3, 5; 2 Chr 33:3, 5). The people of Judah and Jerusalem became extremely corrupt, both religiously and ethically, during the fifty-seven-year evil rule of Manasseh and Amon. They became so corrupt that they worshiped the host of heaven on the roofs of their places (Zeph 1:5).

The prophet Zephaniah (active in 640–609 BC) called the priests who worshiped idols, including the host of heaven, *kemarim* (see 2 Kgs 23:5; Hos 10:5; Zeph 1:4). The Hebrew word *kemarim* is derived from *kamar* (כָּמַר), meaning "to desire." When Josiah, the sixteenth king (640–609b BC), initiated a reformation, he deposed those who burned incense to the sun, the moon, the constellations, and all the host of heaven (2 Kgs 23:5, 11; 2 Chr 34:4, 7). The prophet Ezekiel also said that turning one's back to God's temple to worship the sun in the east was an abomination that would provoke God's wrath (Ezek 8:15-18). Korea has traditions in each province by which people either write their wishes on pieces of paper and set them on fire and send them to the moon with the wind or make wishes upon the stars on the first day of the lunar year. These traditions are also idolatrous acts of making wishes upon the moon or the stars (Deut 4:19).

God created the entire universe by Himself (Isa 44:24). The sun is merely God's creation, which He made on the fourth day (Gen 1:14-19; see also Deut 4:19; Pss 19:4; 74:16; 136:7-9). No creation can become the Creator. The sun is not a personal being, and it will pass away in the end. It will lose its light someday. In the book of Revelation, the sun becomes as black as sackcloth when the Lamb breaks the sixth seal (Rev 6:12). When the fourth angel blows his trumpet, a third of the sun, of the moon, and of the stars are struck so that a third of the day, of the night, and the light of the stars will be darkened (Rev 8:12).

Psalm 84:11 states, "The LORD God is a sun." Malachi 4:2 speaks of "the sun of righteousness," and Luke 1:78 refers to Jesus as "the Sunrise." David confessed that God was his "light" (Ps 27:1). The prophet Isaiah prophesied regarding the kingdom of God, "The light of the moon will be as the light of the sun, and the light of the sun will be seven times brighter, like the light of seven days" (Isa 30:26). As a result, he prophesied, "No longer will you have the sun for light by day, nor for brightness will the moon give you light; but you will have the LORD for an everlasting light, and your God for your glory. Your sun will no longer set, nor will your moon wane; for you will have the LORD for an everlasting light, and the days of your mourning will be over" (Isa 60:19-20; see also Rev 21:23).

We must not worship the sun; we must worship only God, who is the Lord and the Creator of the sun (Mal 4:2). The act of worshiping the sun, the moon, and the stars only reveals the spiritual ignorance and foolishness of fallen and corrupt mankind. The prophet Jeremiah declared, "The gods that did not make the heavens and the earth will perish from the earth and from under the heavens" (Jer 10:11). Those who bow down to the host of heaven are to be stoned to death (Deut 17:2–7). Deuteronomy 17:2–5 says, "If ... a man or a woman ... has gone and served other gods and worshiped them, or the sun or the moon or any of the heavenly host, which I have not commanded, ... then you shall bring out that man or that woman who has done this evil deed to your gates, that is, the man or the woman, and you shall stone them to death."

The sun, the moon, and the stars were not created for specific people but for the benefit of all mankind created in God's image. Deuteronomy 4:19 testifies that "the sun and the moon and the stars, all the host of heaven ... [are] those which the LORD your God has allotted to all the peoples under the whole heaven." The New Living Translation renders this verse as, "And when you look up into the sky and see the sun, moon, and stars—all the forces of heaven—don't be seduced into worshiping them. The LORD your God gave them to all the peoples of the earth." The sun, the moon, and the stars cannot dwell in the tent of God; only His saints dwell in His tent (Ps 84:10).

It is serious idolatry when human beings, who are created in God's image, catch the sunrise and serve the sun, which is a mere creation. No matter how immense the sun, the moon, and the stars may be in size, they are merely things created by God, who is "greater than all" (John 10:29; see Ezra 5:8; Neh 4:14; Ps 95:3; Dan 2:45; Titus 2:13). Our God counts the number of the stars and even names each one (Ps 147:4; Isa 40:26). Let us therefore worship only the living God and never worship any of the host of heaven, for worshipers of the host of heaven will surely be cut off (Zeph 1:4–6).

IV. The Fate of Those Who Violated the First Commandment

Stubborn King Saul Who Committed Idolatry

God ordered King Saul through the prophet Samuel, saying, "Go and strike Amalek and utterly destroy all that he has, and do not spare him; but put to death both man and woman, child and infant, ox and sheep, camel and donkey" (1 Sam 15:3). King Saul, however, disobeyed this order and spared the lives of Agag, the king of Amalek, as well as the best of the sheep, oxen, fattened calves, and lambs. He destroyed only the despised and worthless (1 Sam 15:8-9). In response Samuel admonished Saul, saying, "Has the LORD as much delight in burnt offerings and sacrifices as in obeying the voice of the LORD? Behold, to obey is better than sacrifice, and to heed than the fat of rams. For rebellion is as the sin of divination, and insubordination is as iniquity and idolatry. Because you have rejected the word of the LORD, He has also rejected you from being king" (1 Sam 15:22-23).

The Bible makes it clear that bowing to visible idols is not the only form of idolatry; insubordination by disobeying God's Word is also idolatry (1 Sam 15:23). "Insubordination" refers to an obstinately unmoving, stubborn character that does not submit to authority. Hence stubbornness is the evil act of intentional disobedience. It is tantamount to sitting in God's seat and is considered by God to be the great sin of idolatry.

The word "idol" in 1 Samuel 15:23 is תְּרָפִים (*terafim*), which refers to a household god believed to protect the family. People in Mesopotamia brought this household idol with them when they traveled. Rachel stole Laban's *terafim* (Gen 31:19, 34-35), and Michal laid the household idol (תְּרָפִים, *terafim*) on the bed after helping David escape (1 Sam 19:12-16).

The stubborn refuse advice (1 Kgs 12:12-15); they do not like to acknowledge God in their hearts or listen to His Word, nor do they understand His Word (Jer 22:21; Rom 1:28; 2 Cor 3:14-15). They continue practicing unrighteousness until they are abandoned by God (John 12:40; Rev 22:11). Those who are stubborn before God are proud. Pride goes before destruction and a fall; it brings shame and derision (Prov 16:18; 18:12; 29:23).

When Samuel, the father of the nation, died, all Israel lamented him and buried him. At that time Saul removed the mediums and spiritists from the land to win the people's favor (1 Sam 28:3).

In the meantime, however, the Philistines gathered their army and encamped at Shunem (1 Sam 28:4). Saul saw the Philistines' great army but could not muster up the courage he had had in the past (1 Sam 11:6-7). He was afraid, and "his heart trembled greatly" (1 Sam 28:5). This was because God was not with him (1 Sam 15:23; 16:14), and neither was Samuel, who had taught him in the past (1 Sam 15:35; 25:1; 28:3). Extremely anxious, Saul inquired of the Lord, but "the LORD did not answer him, either by dreams or by Urim or by prophets" (1 Sam 28:6). When God did not answer, Saul ordered his servants, "Seek for me a woman who is a medium" (1 Sam 28:7)—one of the same women Saul had removed from the land not long before (1 Sam 28:3). In Dr. Shin-Theke Kang's Hebrew-Korean Old Testament, 1 Samuel 28:7 is translated as, "Seek out a woman who negotiates with the spirits of the dead." God had commanded, "Do not turn to mediums or spiritists; do not seek them out to be defiled by them" (Lev 19:31). According to the law, anyone who followed such people were to be cut off (Lev 20:6). Any man or woman who became a medium or a spiritist was to be stoned to death (Lev 20:27; Deut 18:11-12).

During Saul's days national resources had been unnecessarily depleted because of Saul's chasing after David day after day. The army's morale was low because of Saul's unbelief and extreme fear such that they had essentially lost their battle even before it began. As soon as the Philistines devouringly attacked the Israelite army, the Israelites fled without strength and fell to their deaths on Mount Gilboa. Saul's three sons, Jonathan, Abinadab, and Malchi-shua, also died then (1

Sam 31:1–2). Saul was fatally wounded and greatly distressed, so he fell on his own sword and died a miserable death (1 Sam 31:3–5; 1 Chr 10:1–5). First Samuel 31:6 states, "Saul died with his three sons, his armor bearer, and all his men on that day together" (see 1 Chr 10:6). The Philistines, however, did not stop there. They insulted Saul further by cutting off his head and nailing his headless body to the wall of Beth-shan (1 Sam 31:7–10). Upon hearing this news, the inhabitants of Jabesh-gilead took Saul's body from the wall of Beth-shan, burned it, and took the bones to bury them under a tamarisk tree in Jabesh. Then they fasted seven days (1 Sam 31:11–13; 1 Chr 10:11–12). Indeed, it is difficult to find an account of death more miserable than this in the Bible.

King Saul's tragic end resulted from his stubborn disobedience to God's Word, which was idolatry, and his idolatry by seeking out a medium rather than inquiring of God (1 Chr 10:13–14). Saul actually had an idol (תְּרָפִים, *terafim*) in his house (1 Sam 19:12–16). Even in his final moments, Saul thought it was dishonorable to die at the hand of the uncircumcised Gentile (1 Sam 31:4; 1 Chr 10:4). Yet he himself had not received circumcision of the heart; his heart was full of abominable idolatry, which led to his tragic fate.

King Jeroboam, the Greatest Idolater in the Period of the Monarchy

When God crowned Jeroboam the first king of the northern kingdom of Israel, He promised him, "I will take you, and you shall reign over whatever you desire, and you shall be king over Israel. Then it will be, that if you listen to all that I command you and walk in My ways, and do what is right in My sight by observing My statutes and My commandments, as My servant David did, then I will be with you and build you an enduring house as I built for David, and I will give Israel to you" (1 Kgs 11:37–38). Jeroboam, however, betrayed God by making two golden calves—one to be set in Bethel and one in

Dan—in order to prevent the Israelites from going to Jerusalem to offer sacrifices (1 Kgs 12:26-30). Moreover, he built temples on high places, drove out the Levites, and appointed priests from the people who were not Levites (1 Kgs 12:31; 13:33; 2 Chr 13:9). He also changed the date for the Feast of Booths from the fifteenth day of the seventh month to the fifteenth day of the eighth month as he had devised in his own heart (1 Kgs 12:32-33).

God warned Jeroboam in various ways, but Jeroboam remained hardened in his evil ways and did not abandon his sin of idolatry until the end (1 Kgs 13:1-33). As a result, every living person in the entire house of Jeroboam was destroyed as prophesied in 1 Kings 14:10-11: "I am bringing calamity on the house of Jeroboam, and will cut off from Jeroboam every male person, both bond and free in Israel, and I will make a clean sweep of the house of Jeroboam, as one sweeps away dung until it is all gone. Anyone belonging to Jeroboam who dies in the city the dogs will eat. And he who dies in the field the birds of the heavens will eat; for the LORD has spoken it" (1 Kgs 13:34; 15:29).

When Jeroboam's son became sick, Jeroboam asked his wife to disguise herself and go to Shiloh and inquire of Ahijah the prophet about what would happen to the child (1 Kgs 14:1-3). Ahijah was the prophet who had prophesied that Jeroboam would become king (1 Kgs 11:29-31). This time Ahijah explained plainly that the house of Jeroboam was destroyed because of idolatry. The Lord spoke through Ahijah of Jeroboam, "You also have done more evil than all who were before you, and have gone and made for yourself other gods and molten images to provoke Me to anger, and have cast Me behind your back" (1 Kgs 14:9). From this time on "the way of Jeroboam" became an idiom for people who provoked God's wrath by leading Israel to commit the sin of idolatry (1 Kgs 15:34; 16:2, 19, 26; 22:52; see 1 Kgs 13:33; 15:26; 2 Kgs 3:3; 15:9, 18, 24, 28; 17:22).

V. The Redemptive-Historical Lesson in the First Commandment

Adam violated the first commandment in the garden of Eden. The Lord God had created Adam, but through Eve, Adam accepted the serpent as his new god. He did not believe in God's Word to him, "From the tree of the knowledge of good and evil you shall not eat, for in the day that you eat from it you will surely die" (Gen 2:17). Instead, he listened to and obeyed the serpent, who said, "You surely will not die!" (Gen 3:4). Adam completely forgot the Word of God and listened only to the serpent.

Any thought or idea that we earnestly desire after besides the Word of God is idolatry. Colossians 3:5 broadens the boundaries of idolatry by stating, "Consider the members of your earthly body as dead to immorality, impurity, passion, evil desire, and greed, which amounts to idolatry" (see also Eph 5:5). Worries and anxieties fill the heart once greed enters into it. Judas Iscariot, who was led by his greed, was restless and anxious until he handed Jesus over, only to hang himself in the end. Likewise, a person who is unable to cast away greed is dragged here and there without purpose until his or her ultimate destruction. In 1 John 5:21, John warns, "Little children, guard yourselves from idols [εἰδώλων, *eidōlon* "image, a false god, a vain thing"]."

Idolatry was also rampant during Jesus' days. God the Word became flesh and came to this earth, but the Israelites rejected Jesus, who had come as the Messiah; they thought that He was strange and did not want to believe in Him (John 6:41–42; 7:25–27; 8:56–59). Not believing in Jesus Christ, the true God who came from heaven to this earth, is the most serious form of idolatry. Jesus explicitly pointed out the idolatry of the Jews and told them that God was not their Father but rather that the devil was (John 8:42–44).

Even though Jesus declared several times that He and God the Father were one, the Jews were under the power of the devil and did not want to believe His word.

First, when Jesus healed a man who had been sick for thirty-eight years at Bethesda on the Sabbath (John 5:1–9) and then called God His Father and made Himself equal with God, the Jews not only persecuted Jesus but also tried to kill Him (John 5:10–18). In response Jesus said, "Truly, truly, I say to you, the Son can do nothing of Himself, unless it is something He sees the Father doing; for whatever the Father does, these things the Son also does in like manner" (John 5:19). Jesus went on to say, "All will honor the Son even as they honor the Father. He who does not honor the Son does not honor the Father who sent Him" (John 5:23).

Second, when the Jews pressed Jesus, asking, "Whom do You make Yourself out to be?" (John 8:53), Jesus replied, "If I glorify Myself, My glory is nothing; it is My Father who glorifies Me, of whom you say, 'He is our God'" (John 8:54). Jesus was literally declaring that His Father was the One who glorified Him. Moreover, Jesus proclaimed that only He knew the Father, saying, "You have not come to know Him, but I know Him; and if I say that I do not know Him, I will be a liar like you, but I do know Him and keep His word" (John 8:55). Furthermore, He declared, "Truly, truly, I say to you, before Abraham was born, I am" (John 8:58). Abraham had been born two thousand years before Jesus. Jesus' existence before Abraham reveals His preexistence and divinity. The expression "I am" is ἐγώ εἰμι (*ego eimi*) in Greek, which is expressed in the Old Testament as "I AM WHO I AM" (Exod 3:14). When Jesus revealed that He and the self-existing God were one, the Jews did not understand and tried to stone Him to death (John 8:59).

Third, Jesus declared, "I and the Father are one" (John 10:30). The bloodthirsty Jews again picked up stones to throw at Jesus (John 10:31). They attacked Jesus, saying, "You, being a man, make Yourself out to be God" (John 10:33). Jesus answered, "Do you say of Him, whom the Father sanctified and sent into the world, 'You are blaspheming,' because I said, 'I am the Son of God'? If I do not do the works of My

Father, do not believe Me; but if I do them, though you do not believe Me, believe the works, so that you may know and understand that the Father is in Me, and I in the Father" (John 10:36–38). Here Jesus emphasized that He and the Father were one, saying, "The Father is in Me, and I in the Father" (John 10:38). The Jews did not believe in Jesus' divinity and tried to seize Him, but He eluded their grasp (John 10:39).

Fourth, when Philip, one of Jesus' disciples, asked Jesus, "Lord, show us the Father," Jesus clearly revealed that He was one with the Father, saying, "Have I been so long with you, and yet you have not come to know Me, Philip? He who has seen Me has seen the Father; how can you say, 'Show us the Father'?" (John 14:8–9).

The Word who had been in the beginning (John 1:1) and the One who existed in the form of God had come to this earth in the likeness of men (Phil 2:6–8), but the Jews did not receive Him, let alone honor Him (John 1:11). Jesus was mocked and despised wherever He went. When He preached in a synagogue, the people in the synagogue were furious and brought Him to the edge of the hill on which the town was built to push Him over the cliff (Luke 4:16–30). The Jews, who rejected and disbelieved in Jesus who had come to His own land, were the most frightening idol worshipers of the devil, who was a murderer from the beginning, a liar, and the father of lies (John 8:44).

Today, we must reject all forms of polytheism, syncretism, and materialism, as these serve other gods rather than the true God. Everyone who has been saved by God's grace should have no other gods before Him; we must serve the only true God, the triune God.

CHAPTER

16

THE SECOND COMMANDMENT

You shall not make for yourself an idol, or any likeness of what is in heaven above or on the earth beneath or in the water under the earth. You shall not worship them or serve them.

Exodus 20:4–5; Deuteronomy 5:8–9

The texts in Exodus 20:4–6 and Deuteronomy 5:8–10 are identical. While the first commandment commanded us to serve only the true God, the second commandment teaches us how to worship God properly.

THE SECOND COMMANDMENT

You shall not make for yourself an idol, or any likeness of what is in heaven above or on the earth beneath or in the water under the earth. You shall not worship them or serve them.

לֹא תַעֲשֶׂה־לְךָ פֶסֶל וְכָל־תְּמוּנָה אֲשֶׁר בַּשָּׁמַיִם מִמַּעַל וַאֲשֶׁר בָּאָרֶץ מִתַּחַת וַאֲשֶׁר בַּמַּיִם מִתַּחַת לָאָרֶץ לֹא־תִשְׁתַּחֲוֶה לָהֶם וְלֹא תָעָבְדֵם

Exodus 20:4–5; Deuteronomy 5:8–9

I. Exegesis of the Second Commandment

"An Idol" or "Likeness" (פֶּסֶל, תְּמוּנָה)

Through the second commandment, God forbids worshiping idols or anything of their likenesses. An idol is an image or shape that represents a false god. In Exodus 20:4 and Deuteronomy 5:8, the word "idol" is (פֶּסֶל, *pesel*) in Hebrew and is derived from the word פָּסַל (*pasal*), meaning "to engrave, to carve, to hew into shape." A carved image refers to an idol made by carving or hewing stones, metals, or woods or by fashioning out of clay. The word "likeness" in Exodus 20:4 and Deuteronomy 5:8 is תְּמוּנָה (*temunah*) in Hebrew, which refers to the resemblance of a thing or a copied image of a creature. People turned to idolatry because their intellects, emotions, and volitions had become corrupted entirely after the fall (Isa 44:18–20; Jer 10:14; 51:17; Rom 1:21–23).

E. L. Carlson offers seven reasons for why the Israelites turned to idolatry:

> *(1) It offered them a definite materialistic and tangible object of and for faith. (2) The elaborate ritual and colorful ceremonies and costumes appealed to their aesthetic natures. (3) The idea of the mother goddess, playing on the family idea, e.g. the triad of father, mother, and son, transferred this idea of family to that of gods and the mother goddess who was the mother of gods and man. (4) Sex appeal and extreme immoral orgies appealed to the animalistic nature in the worshipers. (5) The deification of the attributes and functions of the supreme God did away with his transcendence. (6) There was the appeal to the mysterious by use of secret initiations and ceremonies. (7) The stress of need for abundant crops, cattle, sheep, and other necessities made attractive the gods of crops, weather, fertility, and productivity.*[42]

All these thoughts are the product of Israel's corrupt nature.

You shall not make an idol that embodies the invisible Lord. God is Spirit (John 4:24) and does not have any form; He cannot be embodied in any form. Thus only those with pure hearts can see God (Matt 5:8). In Exodus 20:23, God said, "You shall not make other gods besides Me; gods of silver or gods of gold, you shall not make for yourselves" (see Isa 40:18). The reason is revealed in Deuteronomy 4:15: "Watch yourselves carefully, since you did not see any form on the day the LORD spoke to you at Horeb from the midst of the fire."

God was enthroned "between the cherubim" on top of the ark of the covenant. Thus the Scripture refers to Him as "the LORD of hosts who is enthroned above the cherubim" (2 Sam 6:2; see 1 Sam 4:4; Ps 99:1; Isa 37:16) and also "the LORD who is enthroned above the cherubim, where His name is called" (1 Chr 13:6). Furthermore, God spoke from "between the two cherubim" (Exod 25:22; Num 7:89), which was an empty space. It was a special place of God's presence in which nothing was visible. In other words, God testified that He had no visible form in His presence between the two cherubim.[43] While pagan nations made images of their gods and served them, the Israelites were to see God's spiritual image only through faith.[44]

God gave specific commands not to make carved images of Him, whether in human likeness (of a man or a woman); the likenesses of any animal, any winged creature, or anything that creeps on the ground; or the likeness of any fish (Deut 4:16–18). Furthermore, God forbade the worship of the sun, the moon, and the stars (Deut 4:19). All these things were God's creation. Using them to embody God in any physical form was a great sin of minimizing God alongside His creation.

When the Israelites saw that Moses delayed to come down from Mount Sinai, however, they violated the second commandment by asking Aaron, "Make us a god who will go before us" (Exod 32:1). They made a golden calf with Aaron and proclaimed, "This is your god, O Israel, who brought you up from the land of Egypt" (Exod 32:4, 8; see Neh 9:18).

What the Israelites were supposed to keep and cherish in their hearts was not God's physical image but His covenantal Word. This was because the Word of the covenant was a personal bridge between God and Israel. When God manifested His living presence from the midst of the fire, His purpose was not to show the people His image but to make a covenant with them through His Word (voice; Exod 19:16–19; 20:18–20; Deut 4:32–36; 5:22–27).

You shall not make an image of an idol to worship it. Worshiping anything as god is idolatry, whether it is the host of heaven, a cow, a cat, a frog, or human handiwork. People often used stone, wood, or metal to make idols and worship them (Lev 26:1; 2 Chr 33:7; Isa 44:15, 17; Nah 1:14; Hab 2:18; Rev 9:20). Deuteronomy 4:23 reminds us, "Watch yourselves, that you do not forget the covenant of the LORD your God ... and make for yourselves a graven image in the form of anything against which the LORD your God has commanded you." Verse 25 continues, warning God's people not to "act corruptly, and make an idol in the form of anything, and do that which is evil in the sight of the LORD [their] God so as to provoke Him to anger."

All idols, regardless of the type of god from which they are formed, are of no value to human beings. They are worthless and futile as the word "idol" (אֱלִיל, *elil*) in Hebrew means "insufficiency, worthlessness, futility" (Lev 19:4; Ps 97:7). First Chronicles 16:26 states, "All the gods of the peoples are idols," and in 1 Corinthians 8:4, Paul said, "We know that there is no such thing as an idol in the world, and that there is no God but one" (see also Isa 41:21–24).

Idols cannot speak (Hab 2:18–19; 1 Cor 12:2). They cannot see, eat, hear, smell, touch, walk, make a sound with their throats, or breathe (Deut 4:28; Pss 115:4–7; 135:15–17). They cannot even shake the dust off their own bodies. Both the idol maker and the idol worshiper are as foolish as the idol itself (Pss 115:8; 135:18; Isa 44:9–20). Jeremiah 50:2 declares, "Her [Babylon's] idols have been shattered." In this verse the Hebrew word for "idol" is גִּלּוּל (*gillul*) and is derived from the word גָּלַל (*galal*), which means "to roll away, to roll." This implies that idols will eventually roll away. In Ezekiel 30:13, the Lord God says, "I will also destroy the idols." The craftsmen who make the idols will also be put to shame (Isa 44:9–11).

Idol worshipers are as foolish as the people in Jotham's parable of the trees during the period of the judges. The fools threw away all the useful trees (the olive tree, the fig tree, and the vine) and crowned as king the useless bramble that could only be used as firewood (Judg 9:7–16). As foolish as it was for the trees to go to the bramble and ask it to reign over them knowing how useless the bramble was (Judg 9:14), so was the act of making idols, bowing to them, and worshiping them and bringing about one's own ruin.

"You Shall Not Make, Worship, Serve"
(לֹא תַעֲשֶׂה, לֹא־תִשְׁתַּחֲוֶה, לֹא תָעָבְדֵם)

As God gave the second commandment, He commanded, "You shall not make for yourself an idol.... You shall not worship them or serve them" (Exod 20:4–5; Deut 5:8–9). These three verbs progressively emphasize the command not to worship idols.

You shall not make. The verb "make" occurs in the Qal (root) stem of the Hebrew verb עָשָׂה (*asah*). Making an idol requires one's strength, wealth, skill, time, and effort (Pss 115:8; 135:18; Isa 40:19–20; 41:7; 44:12–17; 46:6; Jer 10:3–4, 9). When God gave the Israelites the second set of stone tablets, He urged them, "You shall make for yourself no molten gods" (Exod 34:17), so that His broken covenantal relationship with them could be restored.

You shall not worship (bow down). The verb "worship" occurs in the Hithpael (reflexive) stem of the Hebrew verb שָׁחָה (*shahah*). This word describes the act of showing complete homage by falling prostrate in worship (Exod 34:8; 2 Chr 29:30; Job 1:20). Worshipers voluntarily bow down to an idol as their hearts are completely devoted to the idol.

You shall not serve. The verb "serve" occurs in the Hophal (passive causative) stem of the Hebrew word עָבַד (*avad*) and means "to worship, to revere" (Isa 19:21; Jer 44:3). It refers to the state in which worshipers lose their free wills entirely and become slaves to idols that continuously force them to worship. Idol worship includes religious rites such as expressing respect or burning incense, offering sacrifices, kissing idols, making an offering of materials, and submitting oneself to the idols.

"For I, the Lord Your God, Am a Jealous God"
(כִּי אָנֹכִי יְהוָה אֱלֹהֶיךָ אֵל קַנָּא)

God forbids His people from making carved images or anything in their likeness because He is a jealous God. The word "jealous" in Exodus 20:5 is קַנָּא (*qanna*) in Hebrew and means "full of jealousy" or "burning." Deuteronomy 4:24 states, "The LORD your God is a consuming fire, a jealous God" (see also Exod 34:14; Deut 6:15; 29:20; Josh 24:19). God's jealousy is equivalent to God's love (Isa 9:7; Zech 8:2).

In a positive sense, jealousy is the concentration of love. God loves His people with so much passion that His delight is only in them (Hephzibah; Isa 62:4). God's fiery love does not allow His people to sin, to look away from Him for a moment, or to become distracted from Him at all (Hos 3:1–3). When His people suffer at their enemies' hands, their suffering becomes His, and He avenges their enemies. Isaiah 42:13 describes what God does for His people: "The LORD will go forth like a warrior, He will arouse His zeal like a man of war. He will utter a shout, yes, He will raise a war cry. He will prevail against His enemies" and Zechariah 2:8 states, "He who touches you, touches the apple of His eye" (see also 2 Kgs 19:22; Zeph 3:19).

In a negative sense, jealousy is wrath against the love that has been insulted. The great jealousy of love is aroused when God's people commit adultery or do not properly worship Him. Song of Solomon 8:6 sings, "Put me like a seal over your heart, like a seal on your arm. For love is as strong as death, jealousy is as severe as Sheol; its flashes are flashes of fire, the very flame of the LORD." Just as in the expression "love is as strong as death, jealousy is as severe as Sheol," God's love is so intense that it is described as jealousy.

God's relationship with His people is like that between a married couple (Jer 3:14; 31:32; Hos 2:19–20), which means that being distant from God and worshiping idols is spiritual adultery (Jer 3:8–10). God rises with wrath when His beloved covenant people serve other gods (see Prov 6:34). God's love and concern for His people are more intense than the love of a husband for his beloved wife whom he so cherishes and protects.

"Visiting the Iniquity of the Fathers on the Children to the Third and the Fourth Generation of Those Who Hate Me"
(פֹּקֵד עֲוֹן אָבֹת עַל־בָּנִים עַל־שִׁלֵּשִׁים וְעַל־רִבֵּעִים לְשֹׂנְאָי)

God visits the iniquity of the fathers on the children to the third and the fourth generation of those who hate Him (Exod 20:5). This reveals the seriousness of the sin of idolatry. While God is slow to anger and full of loving-kindness and forgiveness, He does not excuse the guilty. He visits the iniquity of the fathers on the children to the third and the fourth generations (Num 14:18). Since three or four generations normally live contemporaneously, the evil influence of the earlier generation's unbelief typically significantly impacts its descendants. This, however, by no means supports the idea that children of sinful parents should be cursed by predestination (see Deut 24:16; Jer 31:29–30; Ezek 18:1–4).

The phrase "those who hate" in Exodus 20:5 is שָׂנֵא (sane) in Hebrew, which means "to hate, to abhor, to detest." God equates His people's idolatry with hatred toward Him. The word "visit" in "visiting the iniquity" is פָּקַד (paqad) in Hebrew, meaning "to visit," which means that God will seek out idolaters and come to them to judge their sin.

Joshua 24:20 states, "If you forsake the LORD and serve foreign gods, then He will turn and do you harm and consume you after He has done good to you." God's judgment is just; He rewards the righteous but punishes the wicked (Pss 58:11; 75:10). The idolaters whom God hates the most will never prosper (Deut 4:25–26; 27:15; Isa 42:17; 44:9–11).

"But Showing Steadfast Love to Thousands of Those Who Love Me and Keep My Commandments"
(וְעֹשֶׂה חֶסֶד לַאֲלָפִים לְאֹהֲבַי וּלְשֹׁמְרֵי מִצְוֹתָי)

In Exodus 20:6, God says, "[I will show] lovingkindness to thousands, to those who love Me and keep My commandments" (see also Deut 4:40; 5:10; 7:9). The expression "to thousands" is not a mathematical number but a biblical-literary expression for "forever." "Lovingkindness" is חֶסֶד (*hesed*) in Hebrew and refers to God's unchanging covenantal love and endless mercy. God's wrath is temporal, but His love lasts a lifetime (Ps 30:5). God's grace surpasses His wrath (Rom 5:20).

To whom then does God show such loving-kindness? The original Hebrew text refers to "those who love Me" (לְאֹהֲבַי, *leohavay*) and "those who keep My commandments" (לְשֹׁמְרֵי מִצְוֹתָי, *leshomere mitswothay*). Those who love God keep His commandments, and those who keep His commandments love Him (John 14:15). Hence, the two statements are directly related and inseparable. In 1 John 5:3, the Scripture states, "This is the love of God, that we keep His commandments; and His commandments are not burdensome." In John 14:21, Jesus says, "He who has My commandments and keeps them is the one who loves Me; and he who loves Me will be loved by My Father, and I will love him and will disclose Myself to him."

The first and second of the Ten Commandments are interconnected, because those who worship gods other than God construct the god into a visible form. The second commandment states that those who make images or idols, serve them, or bow down before them will be judged. Yet those who love God and keep His commandments will receive His unchanging love and endless mercy (Exod 34:6–7; Deut 7:12–15).

II. Specific Laws Derived from the Second Commandment

Moses solemnly proclaimed the specific laws related to the second commandment so that the Israelites would not violate the commandment after entering the land of Canaan. Since the first and second commandments are often mentioned together, the specific laws previously examined on the first commandment will be omitted here.

Laws Concerning Altars (Exod 20:22–26)

God said, "You shall say to the sons of Israel, 'You yourselves have seen that I have spoken to you from heaven. You shall not make other gods besides Me; gods of silver or gods of gold, you shall not make for yourselves'" (Exod 20:22–23). Then He gave specific regulations regarding the construction of the altar (Exod 20:24–26).

"You shall make an altar of earth for Me" (Exod 20:24). God forbade the making of idols, but He commanded His people to build an altar of earth to offer Him sacrifices. The proper way for a sinner to worship God is not to make and serve a statue of God but to offer God a sacrifice for the atonement of his or her sins and receive His blessing (Exod 20:23–24).

The altar of earth was an altar made of dirt. Unlike altars of stone, altars of earth were easy to build and tear down. This implies that the function of the altar built for God was only to provide assistance and was temporary. It teaches us not to deify any structure made by human hands; only the everlasting God is worthy to be served.

"You shall not build it of cut stones" (Exod 20:25). This ordinance forbade deifying an altar by decorating it. This emphasizes that God is the only object of worship. When Joshua built an altar on Mount Ebal for the Lord God of Israel, the altar was "as it is written in the book of the law of Moses, an altar of uncut stones on which no man had wielded an iron tool" (Josh 8:31). Likewise, the prophet Elijah took twelve

stones according to the number of the twelve tribes of Israel, and "with the stones he built an altar in the name of the LORD" (1 Kgs 18:32).

"You shall not go up by steps to My altar" (Exod 20:26). Priests in Moses' day did not wear separate undergarments. Accordingly, each time a priest would have lifted his leg to climb a high step, his nakedness would have been exposed from the altar where sacrifices were made to the holy God. Thus God commanded Israel not to make any steps to the altar. Josephus wrote that an inclined plane was made to go up to the altar, since God had forbidden the use of steps to the altar (*Ant.* 4.201). Furthermore, priests were to wear linen breeches (underpants) that covered their nakedness from the loins to the thighs (Exod 28:42).

Idols that God Abhors (Deut 6:10–7:26; 16:21–22)

Deuteronomy 16:21–22 states, "You shall not plant for yourself an Asherah of any kind of tree beside the altar of the LORD your God, which you shall make for yourself. You shall not set up for yourself a sacred pillar which the LORD your God hates." Thus God commanded the Israelites to burn any carved images of gods with fire. He forbade the Israelites from bringing an abomination into their homes so that they would not face the same fate as the idols and commanded them to "utterly detest" and "utterly abhor" them because the idols would all be destroyed (Deut 7:26). The objects that the Israelites were to detest and hate were the idols that God abhorred—the carved images and idols of gold and silver that the Canaanites made and served. God continuously warned the Israelites that if they allowed those detestable objects to remain among them, the idols would become snares and traps that would cause them to sin. The idols would become whips on their sides and thorns in their eyes until they perished from the good land of Canaan that God had given them (Exod 23:33; 34:12; Deut 7:16, 25; 20:18; Josh 23:13; Judg 2:3).

III. Teachings on Worship

The second commandment teaches about *how* to worship God. Even when the object of worship is right, if the worshipers do not worship properly, their worship cannot be true worship. Moreover, improper worship can lead to corruption. In Exodus 20:5, God said, "You shall not worship them or serve them" (see also Exod 23:24; Josh 23:7). Here, "worship" (שָׁחָה, *shahah*) means "to lie face down [flat] on the ground" or "to bow down." Thus we must worship only God; we must completely prostrate ourselves before God and seek His compassion, grace, and mercy.

Furthermore, the second commandment emphasizes that God is spirit. Therefore we must worship Him in spirit and in truth. John 4:24 states, "God is spirit, and those who worship Him must worship in spirit and truth." We must worship "in spirit" and "in truth." God's Word is truth (John 17:17). Thus true worship is worship offered in the Holy Spirit and the Word.

IV. The Fate of Those Who Violated the Second Commandment

King Nebuchadnezzar is a good example of a person who violated the second commandment. He built a golden idol and issued a decree for his people to bow down before it.

When Babylon had defeated many nations and gained supremacy in the ancient Near East (Hab 1:10), King Nebuchadnezzar disregarded God and deified his military power and committed all sorts of atrocities. As Habakkuk 1:11 describes, "They will sweep through like the wind and pass on. But they will be held guilty, they whose strength is their god." Filled with extreme arrogance, King Nebuchadnezzar built an enormous golden statue of a god's image and commanded all the people to bow down before it. He mobilized every kind of musical instrument from every nation—the horn, flute, lyre, trigon, psaltery, and bagpipe (Dan 3:5, 7, 10, 15). The great sound that resonated on the plains of Dura overwhelmed the people, and no one, it was believed, would dare to refuse to worship the golden image. In Daniel 3:6, the king said, "Whoever does not fall down and worship shall immediately be cast into the midst of a furnace of blazing fire."

Daniel's three friends (Shadrach, Meshach, and Abednego), however, were brought to King Nebuchadnezzar on the charge that they would not bow down before the golden statue. Without trembling in fear, they boldly said, "O Nebuchadnezzar, we do not need to give you an answer concerning this matter. If it be so, our God whom we serve is able to deliver us from the furnace of blazing fire; and He will deliver us out of your hand, O king" (Dan 3:16–17). They did not bow before the statue to the end but said, "But even if He does not, let it be known to you, O king, that we are not going to serve your gods or worship the golden image that you have set up" (Dan 3:18).

Filled with rage, Nebuchadnezzar bound the three men and threw them into a furnace of blazing fire that had been heated seven times hotter than usual (Dan 3:19–23). Four unbound men, however, were seen walking amid the fire in the furnace, and the fourth man looked like a son of the gods (Dan 3:24–25). Astonished at the scene, King Nebuchadnezzar called the three men to come out, only to find that the fire had not harmed them at all. Not a strand of hair on their heads had been singed, nor were their cloaks damaged; they did not even smell of fire (Dan 3:26–27). In great shock Nebuchadnezzar praised the God of Shadrach, Meshach, and Abednego and confessed that there was no other god who was able to deliver in this manner. He exalted the men who had firmly refused to worship the idol against the king's order (Dan 3:28–30).

Nebuchadnezzar temporarily feared God at this time (Dan 4:1–3), but later he became proud again. While he was relaxing in his home, enjoying his prosperity in the palace, he dreamed about a tree at the center of the land. Daniel interpreted the dream (Dan 4:4–27). He warned the king, saying, "You [will] be driven away from mankind and your dwelling place [will] be with the beasts of the field, and you [will] be given grass to eat like cattle and be drenched with the dew of heaven; and seven periods of time will pass over you, until you recognize that the Most High is ruler over the realm of mankind and bestows it on whomever He wishes" (Dan 4:25).

Nebuchadnezzar, however, was so proud that he ignored Daniel's warning. Twelve months later, while walking on the roof of the palace in Babylon, he boasted of his achievements, saying, "Is this not Babylon the great, which I myself have built as a royal residence by the might of my power and for the glory of my majesty?" (Dan 4:30). While the words were still in his mouth, he was driven from the throne, and he lived like a beast of the field for seven years (Dan 4:31–33). In 539 BC, sixty-six years after Nebuchadnezzar had established Babylon in 605 BC, Babylon fell at the hands of the unified forces of King Darius the Mede and King Cyrus II of Persia. Indeed, this is a clear example of the miserable fate of those who make and worship idols.

V. The Redemptive-Historical Lesson in the Second Commandment

Adam violated the second commandment in the garden of Eden. The woman listened to the serpent's words and looked at the tree of the knowledge of good and evil, and "saw that the tree was good for food, and that it was a delight to the eyes, and that the tree was desirable to make one wise" (Gen 3:6). As a result, the tree of the knowledge of good and evil became a great idol to the woman. After she ate the fruit from the tree first, she gave also to Adam, and he also ate the fruit.

When the Israelites sinned by making a golden calf (Exod 32), God said, "I will not go up in your midst, because you are an obstinate people, and I might destroy you on the way" (Exod 33:3). After hearing this the Israelites mourned and repented, and not one person wore ornaments (Exod 33:4). The Israelites had been carrying their ornaments even after the exodus (Exod 33:5–6). Ornaments were decorative items with which people adorned themselves to look more beautiful (Jer 4:30; Ezek 23:42). Various images of gods were engraved on them, and they essentially became idols for worship. God declared repeatedly that He would destroy the people and commanded, "Put off your ornaments from you" (Exod 33:5). Thus from Mount Horeb onward, the Israelites removed their ornaments (Exod 33:6). Just like the command "Abstain from every form of evil" (1 Thess 5:22), God made them remove everything that might remind them of idols.

When Jacob put an end to his old life and went up to Bethel, he wanted to remove all causes of sin around him. Thus those who were with Jacob buried their ornaments, such as earrings, along with any foreign gods (Gen 35:1–4). Without realizing it, they became more vulnerable to idolatry when they wore ornaments engraved with Egyptian gods. The wearing of such ornaments probably had an indirect influence on the making of the golden calf as well. God foreknew the corrupt nature of the Israelites, so He commanded them to remove all these things.

God is an invisible spirit (John 4:24). He is omnipresent and everlasting (Ps 102:12; Jer 23:24). Therefore, the Scripture clearly states, "No one has seen God at any time" (John 1:18). The only true image of the invisible God for all people to see is Jesus Christ (2 Cor 4:4; Heb 1:2–3). Colossians 1:15 states, "He is the image of the invisible God, the firstborn of all creation." Thus whoever has seen Jesus has seen the Father (John 8:19; 14:9). It is impossible, however, to see God's image in the incarnate Jesus with the eyes of the flesh. It is possible to see God only with a clean heart, eyes of faith without deceit, and bright spiritual eyes (Matt 5:8; Luke 24:31; Eph 1:17–18; 1 Tim 1:5).

We human beings were originally honorable creatures created in God's image (Gen 1:26-27). We tragically fell, however, and lost God's image (Rom 1:23). Then, Jesus Christ, the true image of God (2 Cor 4:4; Col 1:15; Heb 1:3), came as the incarnate One (John 1:14) to restore the lost image and create us anew. We must, therefore, put off the old self and its practices and put on the new self, which "is being renewed to a true knowledge according to the image of the One who created him" (Col 3:10). We must believe in Jesus and focus only on His glory. In 2 Corinthians 3:18, Paul said, "We all, with unveiled face, beholding as in a mirror the glory of the Lord, are being transformed into the same image from glory to glory, just as from the Lord, the Spirit." When Jesus comes a second time, the image of God in us will be restored in Jesus. First John 3:2 states, "Beloved, now we are children of God, and it has not appeared as yet what we will be. We know that when He appears, we will be like Him, because we will see Him just as He is."

Many Christians today are drowning in material greed and filled with the desires of the flesh, the desires of the eyes, and the pride of life. They love the world and serve and bow down before idols. Their lives have nothing to do with God's will (Col 3:5; 1 John 2:15-17). Paul says to these people, "Even though they knew God, they did not honor Him as God or give thanks, but they became futile in their speculations, and their foolish heart was darkened. Professing to be wise, they became fools, and exchanged the glory of the incorruptible God for an image in the form of corruptible man and of birds and four-footed animals and crawling creatures" (Rom 1:21-23). These idolaters will not inherit the kingdom of God (1 Cor 6:9-10; Gal 5:19-21; Eph 5:5). They will remain under the wrath of God (Col 3:5-6) and be thrown into the lake that burns with fire and brimstone (Rev 21:8). They will not be able to enter the holy city but will be abandoned outside the gate (Rev 22:15).

Chapter 17

The Third Commandment

You shall not take the name of the LORD your God in vain.

Exodus 20:7; Deuteronomy 5:11

Exodus 20:7 states, "You shall not take the name of the LORD your God in vain, for the LORD will not leave him unpunished who takes His name in vain." This verse is identical to the Hebrew text in Deuteronomy 5:11.

THE THIRD COMMANDMENT

You shall not take the name of the LORD your God in vain.

לֹא תִשָּׂא אֶת־שֵׁם־יהוה אֱלֹהֶיךָ לַשָּׁוְא

Exodus 20:7; Deuteronomy 5:11

I. Exegesis of the Third Commandment

"Name" (שֵׁם)

A name is proof of the existence of the name holder. Every existence in the past or the present has a name. God's name, likewise, is proof that He lives and exists. Furthermore, all names have meanings that reveal the nature or attributes of the name holder. God's name reflects His divine attributes and eternal self-existence. The psalmist proclaimed in Psalm 102:12, "You, O LORD, abide forever, and Your name to all generations." Similarly, the psalmist sang, "Your name, O LORD, is everlasting, Your remembrance, O LORD, throughout all generations" (Ps 135:13).

At times, people's reputations are either exalted or damaged through their names. Honor or "high esteem" speaks of high respect for something or someone's worth or merit as well as the glory that follows it (Prov 22:1). God's name possesses the highest honor, authority, and nobility. The word that comes from His mouth does not return in vain but accomplishes His desire and succeeds regarding all things about which He has spoken (Isa 55:11). Indeed, this is the greatest honor: "These events will bring great honor to the LORD's name; they will be an everlasting sign of his power and love" (Isa 55:13, NLT).

"The LORD" (יְהוָה)

The name "LORD" (*Yahweh*) means "I AM" or "I AM WHO I AM" (Exod 3:14) and reflects the eternal self-existence of God the Most High (Gen 21:33; Ps 92:8; Isa 33:5; see also Ps 102:26–27; Isa 9:6; 57:15). The name "LORD" (*Yahweh*) was the exclusive name for Israel's God, distinctive from the pagan gods. It is the most frequent reference for God in the Old Testament, with more than 6,823 occurrences.[45] The name "LORD" highlights the following four aspects of God.

The name "LORD" emphasizes that God is the one and only God. God exists on His own, without a creator. He is an independent entity with complete, unlimited freedom. He is an absolute being who does not depend on anything (Deut 6:4). No one in heaven or on earth is like Him, for He alone accomplishes creation, the work of salvation and all other things impossible to mankind (Deut 4:32-35, 39; Josh 2:11; 1 Kgs 8:23, 60; Isa 37:16). In Isaiah 45:5, God said, "I am the LORD, and there is no other; besides Me there is no God" (Isa 42:8; 43:11; 45:6, 18, 21-22; 46:9). No other besides God can say "I AM WHO I AM."

The name "LORD" emphasizes that God self-exists forever. God lives forever—in the past, the present, and the future (Deut 33:27; Ps 90:2; Isa 26:4; 41:4; Jer 10:10; Dan 12:7). Therefore, "I AM" means that "I will always be in the same form without changing." Even during their finite lives on this earth, human beings are unstable and wavering, deviating constantly from their places. The Lord God, however, is a great rock that is unshakable and a secure fortress that is immovable (Deut 32:4; Pss 18:2, 31; 19:14; 31:3-4; 59:9, 16; 62:2, 6-7; 71:3; 73:26; 94:22; 144:1-2).

The name "LORD" emphasizes God's faithfulness to the covenant. The name "LORD" (*Yahweh*) characterizes God as a fulfiller of promises. Abraham, the father of the covenant, called upon the name of the Lord wherever he built an altar (Gen 12:8; 13:4; 21:33). According to His perfect redemptive administration, the Lord remembers His covenant, works within His covenant, and continues to fulfill the covenant (Gen 2:15-17; 3:14-15; 15:18; Exod 24:8; 34:10; Deut 4:31). Deuteronomy 7:9 states, "Know therefore that the LORD your God, He is God, the faithful God, who keeps His covenant and His lovingkindness to a thousandth generation with those who love Him and keep His commandments." God revealed His name as "the LORD" when He appeared to Moses to entrust to him the great mission called the exodus (Exod 3:13-15; 6:2-3, 8). This demonstrates God's strong determination to save His people under the same covenant He had made with their ancestors in the past.

The name "LORD" emphasizes God's mercy and kindness. God is a personal God who draws near to His people. He is a merciful and kind God who intervenes continuously in the flow of history. Thus the Old Testament frequently uses the expression "the LORD your God" or "your God the LORD" (Exod 6:7; 15:26; Lev 19:25; 25:38, 55; 26:13; Num 15:41; Deut 4:4, 34; 5:6). The Lord is a merciful and benevolent God who hears the pain-filled cries of His people and visits them, takes notice of them, and rescues them (Exod 2:23–25; 3:7–10). Thus the name "LORD" (*Yahweh*) is a holy name of hope and comfort that reminded the Israelites of the covenant so that they could hold onto God only. Deuteronomy 4:31 states, "The LORD your God is a compassionate God; He will not fail you nor destroy you nor forget the covenant with your fathers which He swore to them." Anyone who has known, understood, and experienced the Lord rightfully remembers His name and praises His work each day.

> *You shall fear the LORD your God; you shall serve Him and cling to Him, and you shall swear by His name. He is your praise and He is your God, who has done these great and awesome things for you which your eyes have seen. (Deut 10:20–21)*

Hence, insulting the Lord's name or taking it in vain is the great sin of disregarding God's existence and His attributes.

"Your God" (אֱלֹהֶיךָ)

The expression "your God" implies that God had a personal relationship with each person among the Israelites so that He was adequately called their *personal* God. The Hebrew word *Elohim* (אֱלֹהִים) is used in these instances, and it possesses the following meanings.

Elohim *reveals the Almighty God.* The *El* in *Elohim* is derived from אוּל (*ul*), meaning "strong." The name *Elohim* is used when describing the power of the omnipotent God (Gen 1:1; 35:11; Isa 45:8).

Elohim *reveals a God who is to be feared.* Besides "to be strong," *El* also means "to fear" and is derived from the Hebrew word יָרֵא (*yare*). Thus *Elohim* refers to the "God of fear" who should be served with fear and trembling (Gen 22:12; 31:42; 31:53; 42:18; Exod 1:21; 20:20; Lev 19:14, 32; 25:17, 36, 43).

Elohim *represents the one and only triune God.* While the word *Elohim* is plural, the verbs that accompany the word are singular. This shows that God is triune yet one and only (Gen 1:26–27; Deut 4:35; 6:4).

A few compound titles are related to *Elohim*:

אֵל שַׁדַּי (*El Shadday*), "God Almighty" (Gen 17:1; 28:3; 35:11; 43:14)
אֵל עֶלְיוֹן (*El Elyon*), the "Most High God" (Gen 14:18–22; Ps 78:35)
אֵל עוֹלָם (*El Olam*), the "Everlasting God" (Gen 21:33; Isa 40:28)
אֵל רֳאִי (*El Roi*), the "God who sees" (Gen 16:13)

"In Vain" (לַשָּׁוְא)

The phrase "in vain" is לַשָּׁוְא (*lashawe*) in Hebrew and means "useless, vain, false, empty, careless." This a warning not to take God's name carelessly, lightly, and falsely. Thus Exodus 20:7 states, "You shall not misuse the name of the LORD your God, for the LORD will not hold anyone guiltless who misuses his name" (NIV).

The Westminster Larger Catechism, question 113, provides a list of instances that are considered as taking the name of the Lord in vain. They are all precisely from scriptural records, for which we can refer to the following supporting verses.

Not using God's name as is required; praying without believing (see John 14:13–14; 15:6–7).

"If you do not listen, and if you do not take it to heart to give honor to My name," says the LORD of hosts, "then I will send the curse upon you and I will curse your blessings; and indeed, I have cursed them already, because you are not taking it to heart." (Mal 2:2)

Not everyone who says to Me, "Lord, Lord," will enter the kingdom of heaven, but he who does the will of My Father who is in heaven will enter. Many will say to Me on that day, "Lord, Lord, did we not prophesy in Your name, and in Your name cast out demons, and in Your name perform many miracles?" And then I will declare to them, "I never knew you; depart from Me, you who practice lawlessness." Therefore everyone who hears these words of Mine and acts on them, may be compared to a wise man who built his house on the rock. (Matt 7:21–24)

Abusing God's name in an ignorant, vain, irreverent, profane, superstitious, or wicked way, or otherwise using His titles, attributes, ordinances, or works in an insulting or abominable manner.

Do not trust in deceptive words, saying, "This is the temple of the LORD, the temple of the LORD, the temple of the LORD." (Jer 7:4)

I have heard what the prophets have said who prophesy falsely in My name, saying, "I had a dream, I had a dream!" (Jer 23:25)

You will no longer remember the oracle of the LORD, because every man's own word will become the oracle, and you have perverted the words of the living God, the LORD of hosts, our God. (Jer 23:36)

"Where is My respect?" says the LORD of hosts to you, O priests who despise My name. But you say, "How have we despised Your name?" You are presenting defiled food upon My altar. But you say, "How have we defiled You?" In that you say, "The table of the

LORD is to be despised." ... You are profaning it, in that you say, "The table of the LORD is defiled, and as for its fruit, its food is to be despised." (Mal 1:6–12)

Making sinful curses, oaths, and vows.

The son of the Israelite woman blasphemed the Name and cursed. So they brought him to Moses. (Now his mother's name was Shelomith, the daughter of Dibri, of the tribe of Dan). (Lev 24:11)

Now it came about at the end of forty years that Absalom said to the king, "Please let me go and pay my vow which I have vowed to the LORD, in Hebron. For your servant vowed a vow while I was living at Geshur in Aram, saying, 'If the LORD shall indeed bring me back to Jerusalem, then I will serve the LORD.'" ... But Absalom sent spies throughout all the tribes of Israel, saying, "As soon as you hear the sound of the trumpet, then you shall say, 'Absalom is king in Hebron.'" (2 Sam 15:7–10)

"I will make it [a curse] go forth," declares the LORD of hosts, "and it will enter the house of the thief and the house of the one who swears falsely by My name; and it will spend the night within that house and consume it with its timber and stones." (Zech 5:4; see also Isa 48:1–2; Matt 5:33–35)

He [Peter] denied it before them all, saying, "I do not know what you are talking about." ... And again he denied it with an oath, "I do not know the man." ... Then he began to curse and swear, "I do not know the man!" And immediately a rooster crowed. (Matt 26:70–74)

Drawing lots and violating one's own lawful oaths and vows.

My son, if sinners entice you, do not consent. If they say ... "Throw in your lot with us, we shall all have one purse," my son, do not walk in the way with them. Keep your feet from their path. (Prov 1:10–15)

You shall not swear falsely by My name, so as to profane the name of your God; I am the LORD. (Lev 19:12)

When you make a vow to the LORD your God, you shall not delay to pay it, for it would be sin in you, and the LORD your God will surely require it of you. (Deut 23:21; see also Ecc 5:4)

Fulfilling one's own unlawful oaths and vows.

They speak mere words, with worthless oaths they make covenants; and judgment sprouts like poisonous weeds in the furrows of the field. (Hos 10:4)

The king was very sorry, yet because of his oaths and because of his dinner guests, he was unwilling to refuse her. (Mark 6:26)

Do not listen to them, for more than forty of them are lying in wait for him [Paul] who have bound themselves under a curse not to eat or drink until they slay him; and now they are ready and waiting for the promise from you. (Acts 23:21)

Complaining about, being unsatisfied with, doubting, or abusing God's plans and providences *(see also Exod 32:1–6; Num 14:1–4, 26–35).*

Why is the LORD bringing us into this land, to fall by the sword? Our wives and our little ones will become plunder; would it not be better for us to return to Egypt? (Num 14:3)

Because the LORD hates us, He has brought us out of the land of Egypt to deliver us into the hand of the Amorites to destroy us. (Deut 1:27; see also Ps 106:25)

Misinterpreting, misapplying, or perverting the Word of God through making profane jests, posing useless problems, making vain arguments, or asserting false doctrines.

[Paul's letters] the untaught and unstable distort, as they do also the rest of the Scriptures, to their own destruction. (2 Pet 3:16)

There must be no filthiness and silly talk, or coarse jesting, which are not fitting, but rather giving of thanks. (Eph 5:4)

He [anyone who teaches false doctrines] is conceited and understands nothing; but he has a morbid interest in controversial questions and disputes about words, out of which arise envy, strife, abusive language, evil suspicions, and constant friction between men of depraved mind and deprived of the truth, who suppose that godliness is a means of gain. (1 Tim 6:4–5)

Remind them of these things, and solemnly charge them in the presence of God not to wrangle about words, which is useless and leads to the ruin of the hearers. (2 Tim 2:14)

Their talk will spread like gangrene. Among them are Hymenaeus and Philetus. (2 Tim 2:17)

Using creatures or anything under God's name to make amulets or for sinful or lustful acts.

There shall not be found among you anyone who makes his son or his daughter pass through the fire, one who uses divination, one

> who practices witchcraft, or one who interprets omens, or a sorcerer, or one who casts a spell, or a medium, or a spiritist, or one who calls up the dead. (Deut 18:10–11)

> In that day the LORD will take away ... money purses [amulets], hand mirrors, undergarments, turbans and veils. (Isa 3:18–23)

Maligning, scorning, reviling, or opposing God's truth and the ways in which He bestows grace.

> I have come in My Father's name, and you do not receive Me; if another comes in his own name, you will receive him. (John 5:43; see also John 3:18)

> Jesus answered them, "I told you, and you do not believe; the works that I do in My Father's name, these testify of Me. But you do not believe because you are not of My sheep." (John 10:25–26)

> When they had summoned them, they commanded them not to speak or teach at all in the name of Jesus. (Acts 4:18)

> They took his advice; and after calling the apostles in, they flogged them and ordered them not to speak in the name of Jesus, and then released them. (Acts 5:40)

> I thought to myself that I had to do many things hostile to the name of Jesus of Nazareth. (Acts 26:9; see also Acts 9:14)

Making a profession of faith in hypocrisy or for an evil purpose (see also Isa 1:15; 29:13; Matt 23:27–31; Luke 18:9–14).

> When you pray, you are not to be like the hypocrites; for they love to stand and pray in the synagogues and on the street corners so

that they may be seen by men. Truly I say to you, they have their reward in full. (Matt 6:5)

Being ashamed of or bringing shame upon God's name through deeds that sway one away from faith or that are unwise, unfruitful, and offensive, or by betraying His name.

Whoever is ashamed of Me and My words in this adulterous and sinful generation, the Son of Man will also be ashamed of him when He comes in the glory of His Father with the holy angels. (Mark 8:38)

Some of the Jewish exorcists, who went from place to place, attempted to name over those who had the evil spirits the name of the Lord Jesus, saying, "I adjure you by Jesus whom Paul preaches." (Acts 19:13)

You who boast in the Law, through your breaking the Law, do you dishonor God? For "the name of God is blasphemed among the Gentiles because of you," just as it is written. (Rom 2:23–24)

If anyone suffers as a Christian, he is not to be ashamed, but is to glorify God in this name. (1 Pet 4:16)

"You Shall Not Take" (לֹא תִשָּׂא)

The word "take" occurs in the imperfect stem of the Hebrew word נָשָׂא (nasa), which means "to lift, to carry, to take." This refers to the act of continuously making ill-use of God's name by lifting it up for a personal purpose. In the Hebrew-Korean Old Testament, Dr. Shin-Theke Kang highlights this nuance and translates Exodus 20:7 as, "You must not lift up the name of *Yahweh* your God for a vain purpose! It is because, for those who lift His name for a vain purpose, *Yahweh* will not consider them guiltless."

In ancient times people believed that certain names possessed magical powers and used it in sorcery. During the early church era, some Jewish exorcists commanded evil spirits in Jesus' name (Acts 19:13). Today, within the National Council of Churches in Christ in USA, a liberal community of churches corrupted by apostasy and unbelief, some churches refer to God as both "Father" and "Mother" or to Jesus Christ as "God the Child." These acts are also clearly taking God's name in vain.

"Will Not Leave Him Unpunished" (לֹא יְנַקֶּה)

Even in this world, people file charges for defamation in court and require proper compensation if they feel that their names have been dishonored. Would God, the Creator of the whole universe and Redeemer of Israel out of Egypt, allow Himself to be defamed? The statement "will not leave him unpunished" (Exod 20:7) is a proclamation of definite judgment. The word "unpunished" occurs in the Piel (intensive) stem of the Hebrew word נָקָה (*naqah*), which means "without guilt" or "blameless." The word is used with the negation לֹא (*lo*) and the conjunction כִּי (*ki*) in the same sentence so that the phrase "will not leave him unpunished" means "He will not be exempt from punishment and be safe" or "He will surely be punished severely."

II. Specific Laws Derived from the Third Commandment

The specific laws connected to the third commandment, "You shall not take the name of the LORD your God in vain" (Exod 20:7; Deut 5:11), are recorded in Exodus 20:24; 23:20–23 and Deuteronomy

14:1–21. Each of these specific laws explains God's name by expanding its meaning.

God's name is equivalent to God Himself. The psalmist's confession "Your name is near" (Ps 75:1) implies that God is near. God revealed His reason for making the people of Israel captives and then restoring them as "I had concern for My holy name" (Ezek 36:21). Here God affirmed His strong intention to save Israel not because of their righteousness but to vindicate the holiness of His great name, which had been profaned among the nations (Ezek 36:20–23). This is because God's name is equivalent to God Himself and signifies everything about Him.

If the Israelites would not fear God's honored and awesome name, they would face severe consequences: "The LORD will bring extraordinary plagues on you and your descendants, even severe and lasting plagues, and miserable and chronic sicknesses. He will bring back on you all the diseases of Egypt of which you were afraid … until you are destroyed" (Deut 28:58–61).

The Place Where God Put His Name

The holy place where the Lord caused His name to be remembered (Exod 20:24). The tabernacle is the place where God chose to place His name. In Exodus 20:24, He said, "In every place where I cause My name to be remembered, I will come to you and bless you." On numerous occasions Moses commanded the Israelites that they were to gather to worship God "in the place where the LORD [would choose] to establish His name" once they entered Canaan (Deut 16:2; see 12:5–7, 11–14, 21; 14:23–26; 16:6, 11; 26:2). Just like the tabernacle, the temple was for God "a house that [His] name might be there" (1 Kgs 8:16) and a "house for the name of the LORD, the God of Israel" (1 Kgs 8:17–20). God's eyes would be open toward His temple night and day, for He said, "My name shall be there" (1 Kgs 8:29); "I have consecrated this house which you have built by putting My name there forever" (1 Kgs 9:3); and, "I have chosen and consecrated this house that My name may be there forever, and My eyes and My heart will be there perpetually" (2 Chr 7:16; see also 2 Chr 6:5–10, 20; 12:13; 33:4; Ezra 6:12; Neh 1:9; Ps 74:7; Jer 7:10–12, 14). God also described the temple in Jeremiah 7:30 as "the house which is called by My name."

God surely answers our prayers when we honor the temple where He placed His name and pray with hearts that yearn after the temple. Daniel 6:10 states, "When Daniel knew that the document was signed, he entered his house (now in his roof chamber he had windows open toward Jerusalem); and he continued kneeling on his knees three times a day, praying and giving thanks before his God, as he had been doing previously." Because Daniel prayed toward the temple, not only was he saved from the lion's den, but the exiled Israelites were also liberated by God's covenant (see also Dan 9:1–19). Daniel's prayer is comparable to Solomon's prayer during the dedication of Solomon's temple. Solomon prayed in 1 Kings 8:48–49, "If they return to You with all their heart and with all their soul in the land of their enemies who have taken them captive, and pray to You toward their land which You have given to their fathers, the city which You have chosen, and the house which I have built for Your name; then hear their prayer and their supplication in heaven Your dwelling place, and maintain their cause" (see also 2 Chr 6:37–39).

A name is not only an appellation for an object; it represents the entity of the object itself. The placement of the Lord's name in the temple, therefore, confirmed that the Lord Himself would be there and that He was the Lord of the temple.

Hence God commanded His people to "revere" the temple as they would honor their elders. In Leviticus 19:30, He commanded, "You shall keep My sabbaths and revere My sanctuary," and in Leviticus 26:2, He said, "You shall ... reverence My sanctuary; I am the LORD." Here the word "reverence" is יָרֵא (*yare*) in Hebrew, which means "to fear." This is not a command to revere the physical building. The church is a place where God has chosen to establish His name; hence we must respect and treat it with reverence, as we would God—even the physical building with its bricks, rebar, glass, walls, musical instruments, tables, chairs, gardens, etc.—and always keep it clean and well preserved.

Thus defiling the sanctuary (church) in which God's name dwells is no different from the sin of taking God's name in vain. Defiling the sanctuary with words or deeds, speaking evil against it, and furthermore, engaging in inappropriate behavior in the sanctuary are equal to taking God's name in vain. Doing such is a great sin that violates the third commandment.

An angel of the Lord in whom is the name of the Lord (Exod 23:20-23). When God confirmed to Israel that they would indeed possess the land of Canaan, He promised to send His angel before them to protect them on their way and bring them into the place that He had prepared (Exod 23:20) and "destroy" ("cut off") the seven tribes of Canaan (Exod 23:23). The wilderness journey was prone to dramatic climate changes and threats from wild beasts and robbers. Without the guidance of the divinely sent servants, the Israelites would not have been able to enter the land of Canaan. God urged Israel to listen to the angel's voice without rebelling against the angel, because God's name was in him (Exod 23:21). The angel having the "name" (שֵׁם, *shem*) of the Lord meant that the angel had the same authority as God. In his Hebrew-Korean Old Testament, Dr. Shin-Theke Kang translates Exodus 23:21 as follows: "You shall take heed before him and listen to his voice! Do not oppose him! For he will not forgive your violations of the law; for My name is in him." Similarly, 2 Chronicles 20:20 reads, "Put your trust in the LORD your God and you will be established. Put your trust in His prophets and succeed."

God works through His angels in whom He has placed His name in every age according to His providence (Gen 16:7-12; 2 Kgs 19:35; Pss 35:5-6; 91:11-12). The Hebrew word for "angel" is מַלְאָךְ (*malakh*) and means "messenger" when referring to ordinary people. However, when this word is used in context with God, it refers to God's ministers, such as priests and prophets, or to angels. These are people whom God empowers and sends with His authority and wisdom; God commissions them to fulfill His providence (Isa 37:36; Jer 15:16; Hag 1:13; Zech 3:1; Mal 2:7).

The Israelites, however, forgot God's Word and grumbled against Moses and Aaron, God's messengers, throughout the wilderness journey. In doing so they were grumbling against the Lord (Exod 16:7–9). When things did not go their way, the Israelites either immediately turned their backs and grumbled in their tents or raised their voices and cried out, "Let us appoint a leader and return to Egypt" (Num 14:4; see Num 11:4–6, 10; 14:1–4, 27; 16:11, 41; Deut 1:27–28; Ps 106:24–25; 1 Cor 10:10).

In some cases "the angel of the LORD" in the Old Testament referred to Jesus Christ before the incarnation. Jesus appeared in the form of an angel or a man and shared in the people's tribulations, saved them, and accomplished His redemptive work with love and mercy (Josh 5:13–15; Judg 13:21–22; Isa 63:8–9; Dan 3:28). Jesus was God's ambassador and His greatest messenger who came in "the name of *Yahweh*" (Ps 118:26), in the name of the Father (John 5:43; 17:6, 11–12, 26), and in "the name of the Lord" (Matt 21:9; Luke 19:38). His message is the absolute and everlasting message of God, and whoever does not listen to this message will not receive eternal life in the kingdom of heaven.

Today, pastors and ministers of the church are God's messengers who labor as servants for His providence of salvation and will do so until the saints enter heaven, the spiritual Canaan He has prepared (John 14:3). Leaders shepherding God's flock should always be mindful of their callings as God's messengers and be faithful at all times to the work of salvation entrusted to them. Anyone who despises the messengers in whom God has placed His name and disregards the authority of the Word they preach will not go "unpunished" (Exod 20:7), just as those in violation of the third commandment will not (see also Deut 28:58–61).

A Holy People to the Lord Who Were Called by God's Name
(Deut 14:1-21)

After instructing the people not to cut themselves or shave their foreheads for the sake of the dead (Deut 14:1-2), God gave regulations on the consecration of food (Deut 14:3-20). After God gave the regulations, He emphasized again, "You are a holy people to the LORD your God" (Deut 14:21). Children of God and holy people to the Lord are consecrated as holy to devote themselves completely to the one and only true God (Deut 14:2). If the people specially chosen from among the nations to be called by God's name did not discern between clean and unclean foods, as the Gentiles did not, this would be a sin similar to taking God's name in vain.

Israel being called "by the name of the LORD" (Deut 28:10; see 2 Chr 7:14) was a confirmation that God was with them. It was truly an amazing blessing of God's everlasting protection and faithful caring to the end, which He promised based upon His glory, honor, power, authority, and character (see also Isa 4:1).

God's people, therefore, had a duty to ensure that the Lord's name shone in the world. In Deuteronomy 28:10, Moses said to Israel, "All the peoples of the earth will see that you are called by the name of the LORD, and they will be afraid of you." People who use the Lord's name in a deceitful way to dishonor and defame His name will surely receive curses and punishment according to the covenant (Lev 18:21; 19:12; 20:3; 21:6; 24:16; Deut 28:58-68).[46]

The name of the Lord indeed brings great privilege and authority to God's people. At the same time, it is an object of great reverence that cannot be used carelessly. Thus God's name is a "great and awesome name" (Ps 99:3), a "great name" (1 Sam 12:22), and a safe "strong tower" (Prov 18:10).

God is our praise (Deut 10:21; Pss 18:1-3; 109:1). God's name is our reason for praise, as well as our absolute strength and power. Joy and energy will surge in those who lift and praise God's name. Isaiah 25:1

sings, "O LORD, You are my God; I will exalt You, I will give thanks to Your name; for You have worked wonders, plans formed long ago, with perfect faithfulness." Exodus 15:2–3 also sings, "The LORD is my strength and song, and He has become my salvation; this is my God, and I will praise Him; my father's God, and I will extol Him. The LORD is a warrior; the LORD is His name." David lifted up the name of the Lord in praise on the day he was saved from all his enemies and from the hands of Saul. In Psalm 18:1–3, he confessed, "'I love You, O LORD, my strength.' The LORD is my rock and my fortress and my deliverer, my God, my rock, in whom I take refuge; my shield and the horn of my salvation, my stronghold. I call upon the LORD, who is worthy to be praised, and I am saved from my enemies."

God's mighty help and hand of salvation will not cease when we live as honorable and holy people who bear His name. Jeremiah 15:16 reads, "Your words were found and I ate them, and Your words became for me a joy and the delight of my heart; for I have been called by Your name, O LORD God of hosts." Those who have been chosen by God's name and bear His name receive the blessing of eating His Word. The prophet Ezekiel ate the scroll of God's Word in whole and confessed, "It was sweet as honey in my mouth" (Ezek 3:3). The hearts of those who eat the Word are filled with joy and happiness.

Caution Against Swearing Falsely (Lev 19:12)

The command "You shall not take the name of the LORD in vain" (Exod 20:7) means that people were to take extra care in using God's name. Anyone who blasphemed the name of the Lord would surely be put to death (Lev 24:10–16). The Word spoken in the name of the Lord required absolute obedience (Deut 18:19), and any impudent (presumptuous, rude) use of the name of the Lord would result in death (Deut 18:20). Thus swearing by God's name to justify one's lie was a great sin. In Leviticus 19:12, God explicitly commanded, "You shall not swear falsely by My name, so as to profane the name of your God; I am the LORD."

Meaning of "oath." There are two Hebrew words for "oath" in the Bible.

The first Hebrew word for "oath" is שְׁבוּעָה (*shevuah*). *Shevuah* is a passive participial feminine noun derived from the verb שָׁבַע (*shava*) that denotes "to say seven times" or "to swear." Both words originate from the Hebrew word שֶׁבַע (*sheva*), which means "seven." The Jews considered the number "seven" a sacred number that revealed the duration of the creation and a perfect number that could not be added to or subtracted from. Generally, an oath was confirmed through a ceremony related to the number "seven." For example, when entering into a covenant with Abimelech, Abraham set apart seven ewe lambs to confirm the covenant (Gen 21:28–30). A solemn oath was a covenant that was confirmed with a sworn oath (Josh 9:20; Isa 45:23; Ezek 21:23).

The second Hebrew word for "oath" is אָלָה (*alah*). *Alah* is derived from two root verbs that denote "to swear" and "to curse," respectively. Thus this noun by itself may denote an "oath" (Gen 26:28; Deut 29:13; 1 Kgs 8:31; Ezek 17:16–19) or a "curse" (Isa 24:6; Jer 23:10; 29:18; Zech 5:3). Used together with the word *shevuah*, it means an "oath of the curse" (Num 5:21; Neh 10:29; Dan 9:11).

According to the ancient Near Eastern traditions, violating an oath led to a curse, so "oath" also implies a curse. While *shevuah* also connotes a curse (Isa 65:16), the word *alah* possesses a stronger emphasis on the notion of a curse. In Matthew 26:69–75, when a servant girl came up to Peter as he sat in the courtyard of Caiaphas and said to him, "You too were with Jesus the Galilean" (Matt 26:69), Peter at first simply denied it (Matt 26:70). Then the second time he denied it with an oath (Matt 26:72). By the third time he began to curse and swear that he did not know the man (Matt 26:74).

Form of an oath. An oath was sworn by an unchanging truth or authority. Hebrews 6:16 reads, "Men swear by one greater than themselves, and with them an oath given as confirmation is an end of every dispute." During Old Testament times, people would swear by an authority higher than themselves (Gen 31:53; 2 Sam 21:7) by lifting one of their hands to the heavens (Gen 14:22, "sworn" literally means "lifted up one's hand," see KJV, ESV; Deut 32:40; Dan 12:7) or putting one of their hands under another person's thigh (Gen 24:2, 9; 47:29). Sometimes both parties in an agreement would walk between an animal that had been cut (Jer 34:18; see also Gen 15:17).

According to God's regulations, people were to swear by the name of the Lord (Exod 22:11; Deut 6:13). In doing so they acknowledged that God alone was the highest authority over the whole universe. Deuteronomy 10:20 states, "You shall fear the LORD your God; you shall serve Him and cling to Him, and you shall swear by His name."

Hypocritical oath and proper oath. During Jesus' time on Earth, the religious leaders had a wicked habit of using oaths to justify their lies, casually making and then forsaking their oaths and defending their false oaths with sophistry. Every oath was made in God's name and by His authority. Thus Jesus said, "You shall not make false vows … Make no oath at all" (Matt 5:33–36; see also Jas 5:12). Here the Greek phrase μὴ ὀμόσαι ὅλως (*mē omosai holōs*), translated as "make no oath at all," forbids taking all oaths without exception. This prohibition also implied that people should be truthful in their words and deeds so that an oath of any kind would be unnecessary.

Jesus gave a proper interpretation of the law regarding oaths. In Matthew 5:37, He said, "Let your statement be, 'Yes, yes' or 'No, no'; anything beyond these is of evil." In Greek the first half of this verse is ἔστω δὲ ὁ λόγος ὑμῶν ναὶ ναί, οὒ οὔ (*estō de ho logos hymōn nai nai, ou ou*). It instructs people to either say *"nai nai"* (yes, yes) or *"ou ou"* (no, no). The precise double repetitions of the words in the original text emphasize that the answer must be direct, honest, and clear. This verse highlights the importance of truthfulness. Taking an oath to avoid giving a clear answer and disguise a cunning lie as if it were true is falsehood and hypocrisy rooted in evil (Matt 5:37).

Taking a solemn oath in the name of the living God, however, as proof that God's Word is true or as a defense of the sincerity of God's servant is a justified and proper oath (see also Matt 26:63–64; Rom 1:9; 2 Cor 1:23; 11:31; Gal 1:20; Phil 1:8; 1 Thess 2:5, 10).

III. Teachings on Worship

The third commandment teaches us the proper *mindset* of worship. Those who worship must do so with good words, deeds, and attitudes as well as a proper mindset, which begins with glorifying God's name. The temple, or the church where each of us worships, is the place where God has chosen for His name to be honored (Deut 14:23–24; 16:2, 6, 11; 1 Kgs 5:5; 8:20; 1 Chr 22:7; 29:16; 2 Chr 2:4; 6:7–10; see also 1 Kgs 3:2; 8:17–20, 44, 48; 1 Chr 22:8; 2 Chr 2:1; 6:34). God's name is lifted high, therefore, when we listen to His Word, pray, and sing His praises. The psalmist confessed, "I will praise the name of God with song and magnify Him with thanksgiving" (Ps 69:30). We are called to glorify God's name among the Gentiles and not profane it (1 Chr 17:23–24; Rom 2:24; 1 Pet 2:12; 4:11).

King Solomon manifested the fame of God's name. While 2 Chronicles 9:1 simply speaks of "the fame of Solomon," 1 Kings 10:1 speaks of "the fame of Solomon concerning the name of the LORD." The purpose of Solomon's wisdom was to demonstrate God's greatness, excellence, and fame. Solomon's wisdom exceeded that of anyone in Asia and Egypt; it exceeded the wisdom of any king on the whole earth (1 Kgs 4:29–30; 10:23–24). Solomon's wisdom exceeded the wisdom of others who were held in esteem for their wisdom, including Ethan the Ezrahite and the sons of Mahol—Heman, Calcol, and Darda (1 Kgs 4:31; see also). While the queen of Sheba was so overwhelmed by Solomon's wisdom that she felt that there was no spirit left in her, she acknowledged God as the source of that wisdom

(1 Kgs 10:1–10). Whatever we dedicate and use for God's fame will be deemed great and honorable both in this age and in the age to come, remaining forever.

Through the Lord's prayer, Jesus taught the proper object of worship as well as the importance of His name through this petition: "Our Father who is in heaven, hallowed be Your name" (Matt 6:9). I sincerely hope that everything we have is dedicated entirely to glorifying the name of the heavenly Father alone.

IV. The Fate of One Who Violated the Third Commandment

During David's latter years, when three years of famine struck without a known reason, David perceived that it was God's punishment and prayed to Him (2 Sam 21:1). Three consecutive years of famine in the dry Palestinian land certainly was punishment from God (1 Kgs 17:1–7; Neh 5:3). God's answer to David's prayer was that the famine had been caused by Saul and his house who had brutally murdered the Gibeonites (2 Sam 21:1) with whom Israel had entered into a peace covenant (Josh 9:3–27). The covenant had been made so long ago that no one remembered it. While the Gibeonites were members of the Hivites, one of the seven tribes of Canaan (Josh 11:19), they had deceived Joshua by disguising themselves as if from a distant country and had entered into a covenant with Joshua. Joshua had sworn to them by the name of the Lord that he would not kill them (Josh 9:15, 18–21).

Saul's killing of the Gibeonites was clearly an inexcusable sin of murder according to the law (Num 35:31; see also Gen 9:6), but his sin of taking God's name in vain was even greater. He disregarded the covenant with the Gibeonites made in the name of the Lord and killed them for no reason while they were living under God's covenant. This was the sin of taking the Lord's name in vain and bringing reproach to God's glory (Exod 20:7; Deut 5:11).

Using the Lord's name in an oath is a serious matter (Josh 9:9-15). Therefore, any oath, resolution, or vow taken in God's name must be kept (Num 30:2; Deut 23:21; Pss 15:4; 76:11). Ecclesiastes 5:4-5 states, "When you make a vow to God, do not be late in paying it; for He takes no delight in fools. Pay what you vow! It is better that you should not vow than that you should vow and not pay." Jephthah's vow during the battle against the Ammonites is a good example (Judg 11:30-31). Even though the vow involved his one and only daughter, if Jephthah had broken the vow, he would have committed the sin of taking God's name in vain. Thus he confessed, "I have given my word to the LORD, and I cannot take it back" (Judg 11:35).

The Gibeonites' covenant of peace with Joshua appears to have been cunning, but it was an act of faith. Because the Gibeonites had heard of the widespread rumors of Joshua's fame, they acted carefully and wisely to join the ranks of the faithful (Josh 6:27; 9:9-10). Like Rahab (Josh 2:8-11), they chose to stand with God, knowing that their nation would soon perish in His hands (Josh 9:24-25). As a result, although they were intended as targets of destruction (Deut 7:1-5), they survived by entering into a peace treaty (Josh 11:19) and becoming woodcutters and water drawers for the house of God (Josh 9:21, 23, 27).

After dwelling among the Israelites for a long time, the Gibeonites gradually became assimilated with God's people. In God's eyes there was no difference between them and His people. From the time they entered into the peace treaty with Joshua until Israel's return from Babylon, they treasured their tasks in the temple, no matter how menial they were, and carried them out for a long period of time (Ezra 2:43-54, 58). The Gibeonites were called *nethinim* in the Old Testament. As it is written in Joshua 9:27, the Gibeonites' duties included cutting wood and drawing water for the altar of the Lord. The *nethinim* were descendants of prisoners of war who became temple servants. Ezra 8:20 refers to them as "temple servants, whom David and the princes had given for the service of the Levites." The *nethinim* were temple servants who helped the priests and the Levites (Ezra 8:17). After Joshua vowed by God's name that he would not harm the Gibeonites and would allow them to live (Josh 9:15), God treated the Gibeonites as He treated the covenant people of Israel and not as Gentiles (see also Josh 18:25; 21:17). They participated in the faith and history of Israel.

The Gibeonites, however, were afflicted and persecuted because they were not pure Israelites. A key example was their abuse and massacre at the hands of King Saul and his family. Second Samuel 21:2 states, "The king called the Gibeonites and spoke to them (now the Gibeonites were not of the sons of Israel but of the remnant of the Amorites, and the sons of Israel made a covenant with them, but Saul had sought to kill them in his zeal for the sons of Israel and Judah)." This verse states that Saul had killed the Gibeonites out of zeal for the sons of Israel and Judah, but his zeal had gone awry and was for his own ambition and fame (see also Rom 10:2–3).

When David asked the Gibeonites how he could make atonement, they demanded the life of seven sons among Saul's offspring (2 Sam 21:3–6). The seven were the two sons of Rizpah, Saul's mistress (Armoni and Mephibosheth), and the five sons of Merab, Saul's oldest daughter (2 Sam 21:8–9). Just as the decapitated bodies of King Saul and his three sons (Jonathan, Abinadab, and Malchi-shua) had hung on the wall of Beth-shan (1 Sam 31:2, 6–13), so the seven sons of Saul were hung "before the LORD" on a mountain all together (2 Sam 21:9). The Gibeonites chose Gibeah, Saul's hometown (1 Sam 10:26), as the venue for the execution (2 Sam 21:6). Indeed, it was a miserable ending for the family of King Saul.

According to David's command, the people brought the seven bodies, along with Saul and Jonathan's bones, to Zela in the land of Benjamin and buried them in the grave of Kish. After this God listened to the people's entreaty for the land and removed the famine (2 Sam 21:12–14). Likewise, when we today repent of all our sins, including the evil harbored in our hearts, God will send clear answers to our prayers (Ps 66:18; Isa 59:2; 1 John 3:21–22).

V. The Redemptive-Historical Lesson in the Third Commandment

In the garden of Eden, Adam committed the sin of violating the third commandment. The woman conversed with the serpent, and the serpent asked her, "Indeed, has God said, 'You shall not eat from any tree of the garden'?" (Gen 3:1). The woman answered using God's name: "God has said, 'You shall not eat from it or touch it, or you will die'" (Gen 3:3). While she spoke of God's Word, she added to it and thus weakened the meaning of the Word. She called upon "God," but her fear and reverence for God were already gone.

The third commandment is also connected to the first and second commandments. Anyone who believes in God as the absolute sovereign, who exists on His own from everlasting to everlasting, will not take God's name in vain. Without such faith, however, unbelievers can take His name in vain without realizing it. Knowing that the Israelites could take His name in vain because of the Egyptians' polytheistic influence, God prohibited it sternly in the third commandment. Nevertheless, not long after receiving the Ten Commandments, the Israelites took His name in vain by saying, "Why is the LORD bringing us into this land, to fall by the sword?" (Num 14:3) and "the LORD hates us" (Deut 1:27).

The Jewish scribes were so fearful about taking God's name in vain that they pronounced the holy name *Yahweh* as *Adonai* (אֲדֹנָי, "my LORD") each time it appeared in the Scriptures. Yet while they lifted high the name Yahweh with their lips, their hearts drifted far from God. Thus Jesus said, "This people honors Me with their lips, but their heart is far away from Me. But in vain do they worship Me, teaching as doctrines the precepts of men" (Matt 15:7–9; Mark 7:6–8; see also Isa 29:13).

Jesus Christ is God Himself (Phil 2:6). He is the Creator of all things (Col 1:16). His name is above all names. In Philippians 2:9–10,

Paul wrote, "God highly exalted Him, and bestowed on Him the name which is above every name, so that at the name of Jesus every knee will bow, of those who are in heaven and on earth and under the earth" (Eph 1:20–22). The phrase "highly exalted" connotes a superlative degree of exaltation and a grant of the highest sovereignty and authority. The name of Jesus, therefore, possesses the highest authority. We have been saved by the power of Jesus' name (Matt 1:21; Acts 4:12). Even the demons tremble before Jesus' name (Mark 16:17; Luke 10:17; Acts 16:18). We come to faith in Jesus while reading the Bible and by believing we receive eternal life in His name (John 20:31). When we pray in Jesus' name, we receive answers and are filled with joy (John 14:13–14; 16:24). Where two or three gather in Jesus' name, God is in their midst and fulfills every prayer lifted to Him with one heart in the name of Jesus (Matt 18:19–20). Anyone who has left houses, brothers, sisters, parents, children, or lands for His name's sake will receive many times as much and will inherit eternal life (Matt 19:29).

In the end times, the saints will have only the Lord's name to hold onto. In Zechariah 10:12, God declares, "I will strengthen them in the LORD, and in His name they will walk." The New Korean Standard Version of the Bible translates the phrase "in His name they will walk" (וּבִשְׁמוֹ יִתְהַלָּכוּ, *uvishmo yithhallakhu*) as "they will proceed boldly, preceded by my name." Likewise, Micah 4:5 reads, "Though all the peoples walk each in the name of his god, as for us, we will walk in the name of the LORD our God forever and ever."

Those who keep the third commandment will receive great blessings. The Scripture says, "For you who fear My name, the sun of righteousness will rise with healing in its wings; and you will go forth and skip about like calves from the stall" (Mal 4:2). During the remaining years of our lives, therefore, let us all strive to live our lives that we may lift up only God's name.

CHAPTER

18

THE FOURTH COMMANDMENT

Remember the sabbath day, to keep it holy.

Exodus 20:8-11; Deuteronomy 5:12-15

Exodus 20:8 states, "Remember the sabbath day, to keep it holy." Deuteronomy 5:12 also commands, "Observe the sabbath day to keep it holy, as the LORD your God commanded you." Among the Ten Commandments, God spoke at greatest length about the fourth commandment, regarding the Sabbath. By word count, the fourth commandment makes up one third of all the Ten Commandments. The fourth commandment recorded in Deuteronomy (254 characters) has sixty-one more Hebrew characters than the one in Exodus (194 characters). The amount of writing dedicated to the fourth commandment hints at the importance of this commandment compared to all the commandments that the Israelites were to keep when they entered the land of Canaan. The fourth commandment is the fundamental principle of faith that helps God's people keep all the other commandments. Concerning the Ten Commandments at large, the clearest distinction between the records in Exodus and Deuteronomy lies in the fourth commandment (Exod 20:8-11; Deut 5:12-15; see also Deut 15:1-18). Exodus explains the reason for keeping the Sabbath with relation to God's *creation*, while Deuteronomy explains it with relation to the *exodus*.

THE FOURTH COMMAND

Remember the sabbath day, to keep it holy.

זָכוֹר אֶת־יוֹם הַשַּׁבָּת לְקַדְּשׁוֹ

Exodus 20:8–11; Deuteronomy 5:12–15

I. Exegesis of the Fourth Commandment

The commandment of the Sabbath day was not first enacted when God gave Moses the law on Mount Sinai. Genesis 2:3 states, "God blessed the seventh day and sanctified it, because in it He rested from all His work which God had created and made."

The "seventh day" mentioned here is the first record of the Sabbath day in the Bible, indicating that the Sabbath day was already established at the time when God gave the Ten Commandments. We can find many traces of the observance of the seventh day following the creation. After the ark was built, Noah waited for the great flood for seven days (Gen 7:4, 10). Before coming out of the ark, he sent forth a dove once every seven days (Gen 8:10, 12). In his uncle Laban's house in Haran, Jacob served for seven years and received Leah as his wife; after completing seven days with Leah, he received Rachel and served Laban for another seven years for her (Gen 29:27–28). Jacob's funeral procession stopped at the threshing floor of Atad, and the people mourned there for seven days before heading to Canaan

(Gen 50:10). Before receiving the Ten Commandments on Mount Sinai, the Israelites observed the first Feast of Unleavened Bread after the exodus for seven days (Exod 12:15–20; 13:3–10). Before receiving the Ten Commandments, the Israelites began to receive manna in the wilderness of Sin based on a seven-day cycle. They gathered a double portion of manna on the sixth day so that they could observe the Sabbath on the seventh day (Exod 16:4–5, 22–30).

Since the creation of the world, by God's providence, all the calendars of the world have maintained a seven-day cycle as standard for general society; this too is a trace of the ordinance regarding the Sabbath.

"Remember … to Keep It Holy" (זָכוֹר, לְקַדְּשׁוֹ)

According to the Hebrew text, the word "remember" in the command "Remember the sabbath day, to keep it holy" in Exodus 20:8 is זָכוֹר (*zakhor*), the infinitive absolute form of זָכַר (*zakhar*); it occurs in the imperative form. *Zakhar* denotes "to remember, to think of, to keep in mind." The imperative form, *zakhor*, means "surely remember," "keep in mind all the time," or "cherish deep down in the heart." This commandment regarding the Sabbath day must be impressed deeply on the hearts and memories of the saints.

God's command to "remember" the Sabbath day is biblical evidence of the Sabbath day's existence even before Moses' time. The Westminster Larger Catechism, question 121, explains the reason we must "remember" the Sabbath day:

> *[First] because of the great benefit of remembering it, [second] we being thereby helped in our preparation to keep it, and, in keeping it, better to keep all the rest of the commandments [Ezek 20:12, 20], and to continue a thankful remembrance of the two great benefits of creation and redemption [Gen 2:2–3; Heb 4:9–11] …*

[third] because we are very ready to forget it [Num 15:37–40].

After six continuous days spent on worldly matters, the hearts of God's people become lost in the world and cannot think about the glory of rest. Meanwhile, Satan stops at nothing to ensure that people do not remember the Sabbath at all so that they easily fall into lives of disbelief and ungodliness.

The verb "keep" in the phrase "to keep it holy" is written in the Piel (intensive) infinitive construct of קָדַשׁ (*qadash*) denoting "to be holy" or "to consecrate." Used with the preposition "to," the verb means "in order to keep it holy." In this respect the Sabbath day is a consecrated day set apart from other unclean things and is worthy of being offered to God (Gen 2:3). The Sabbath day is set apart from other days for a particular purpose. It is superior to the other days; it is a precious and glorious day. Thus the literal translation would read, "Remember the Sabbath day in order to consecrate it and set it apart from other days." Those who remember the Sabbath day can keep the Sabbath day holy.

In the Hebrew text of Deuteronomy 5:12, a parallel verse of Exodus 20:8, the imperative verb "observe" in the command "Observe the sabbath day to keep it holy" is the infinitive absolute stem of the verb שָׁמַר (*shamar*), which means "to watch," "to build a fence," or "to guard" (Gen 2:15). In the context of the Sabbath, this verb means "to restrain oneself from doing anything on the Sabbath day." Thus Deuteronomy 5:12 means "You shall keep the Sabbath day as His holy day."

"Six Days You Shall Labor and Do All Your Work"
(שֵׁשֶׁת יָמִים תַּעֲבֹד וְעָשִׂיתָ כָּל־מְלַאכְתֶּךָ)

In Exodus 20:9, God said, "Six days you shall labor and do all your work" (Deut 5:13). To observe the seventh day as the Sabbath day, God's people must work hard during the six days. The expression "all" (כֹּל, *kol*) implies that there is "no exception" to the labor, meaning that God's people must work hard no matter what their work may be.

We can carefully note two verbs in the Hebrew text of this verse. The verb "do" (עָשָׂה, *asah*) means "to work" or "to make." The verb "labor" is the imperfect stem of עָבַד (*avad*), which means "to worship," "to cultivate," or "to serve." The word *avad* also describes the act of worshiping God. People must therefore work hard during the six days with hearts of worship toward God. This is the original mission God gave Adam and his descendants (Gen 2:15, "to keep it [the garden]"). The apostle Paul also said that anyone who is unwilling to work does not need to eat (2 Thess 3:10).

Only those who carry out their sacred work and mission from God faithfully during the six days will be able to participate in the blessing of the Sabbath day. Those who are lazy or who waste away the six days cannot keep the Sabbath day holy or participate in its blessing. Before God rested on the seventh day, He focused on His creation work of six days and completed "His work which God had created and made" (Gen 2:3). Likewise, we are to focus on the mission that God has given us during the six days before the Sabbath day (Exod 23:12; 31:15; 34:21; 35:2; Lev 23:3). Only those who carry out their callings can truly observe the Lord's day.

"But the Seventh Day Is a Sabbath of the LORD Your God"
(וְיוֹם הַשְּׁבִיעִי שַׁבָּת לַיהוָה אֱלֹהֶיךָ)

Exodus 20:10 states, "The seventh day is a sabbath of the LORD your God." In the phrase "of the LORD," the preposition לְ (*le*) precedes "the LORD." The meaning of the phrase changes depending on how one interprets the preposition. If *le* is interpreted as a possessive preposition, then the phrase means "the Sabbath day of the LORD." The seventh day belongs entirely to God, and the day is set apart and offered to Him. While the six days are normal days, the seventh is a superior day, a precious day, a glorious day—that is, the head of the days. For this reason it is called "a Sabbath of the LORD." The Bible frequently uses the expression "My sabbaths" (Exod 31:13; Lev 19:3, 30; 26:2; Isa 56:4; Ezek 20:12–13, 16, 20–21, 24; 22:8, 26; 23:38; 44:24).

If, however, the preposition *le* is interpreted as directional, the meaning is "a Sabbath to the LORD." The implication here is that the seventh day is a day to look upon only God. Thus the Sabbath day belongs to God and exists for God alone, so people must look only to God on this day.

"You, or Your Son, or Your Daughter, Your Male Servant, or Your Female Servant, or Your Livestock, or the Sojourner Who Is Within Your Gates"
(אַתָּה וּבִנְךָ־וּבִתֶּךָ עַבְדְּךָ וַאֲמָתְךָ וּבְהֶמְתֶּךָ וְגֵרְךָ אֲשֶׁר בִּשְׁעָרֶיךָ)

Exodus 20:10 states, "The seventh day is a sabbath of the LORD your God; in it you shall not do any work, you or your son or your daughter, your male or your female servant or your cattle or your sojourner who stays with you." Deuteronomy 5:14 also mentions "your ox or your donkey or any of your cattle" and explains, "so that your male servant and your female servant may rest as well as you."

The seven categories of people and animals that must keep the Sabbath include: "you," "your son," "your daughter," "your male servant," "your female servant," "your cattle," and "your sojourner who stays with you." Not only were the parents, children, and servants to observe the Sabbath, but also their livestock and even gentile sojourners staying within the gates of their homes were also to observe the Sabbath day. Exodus 23:12 likewise says, "Six days you are to do your work, but on the seventh day you shall cease from labor so that your ox and your donkey may rest, and the son of your female slave, as well as your stranger, may refresh themselves." Servants, livestock, and even sojourners were also to keep the Sabbath, demonstrating that God has bestowed the Sabbath's blessing upon all creation (Rom 8:19–23).

"You Shall Not Do Any Work" (לֹא־תַעֲשֶׂה כָל־מְלָאכָה)

In the English Old Testament, we see various names for the Sabbath day, such as "sabbath of complete rest" (Exod 31:15; 35:2; Lev 23:3, 32) and "sabbath of solemn rest" (Lev 16:31). In the Hebrew text, however, all these expressions are the same Hebrew word, "rest," which is שַׁבָּת (*shabbath*), repeated twice, that is, שַׁבַּת שַׁבָּתוֹן (*shabbath shabbathon*). This emphatic expression underscores a definite and complete rest, or "sabbath of rest" (KJV), "sabbath rest" (NIV), "sabbath of solemn rest" (RSV), and "sabbath of complete rest" (NASB). This is the inevitable reason that the Israelites were to thoroughly rest on the Sabbath. God commanded that the people should "not do any work" because it was a day of rest (Exod 20:10; Lev 23:3; Deut 5:14). Furthermore, during the wilderness journey God commanded, "Let no man go out of his place on the seventh day" (Exod 16:29).

II. Specific Laws Derived from the Fourth Commandment

The specific laws derived from the fourth commandment are in Exodus 21:1–11, Exodus 23:10–12, and Deuteronomy 15:1–16:17. The specific laws in Exodus expand the ordinance regarding the Sabbath to the Sabbatical Year. Slaves were to be set free in the Sabbatical Year, the final year of the seven-year cycle (Exod 21:1–2; see also Deut 15:12–18), and the land was not to be cultivated so that it could rest (Exod 23:10–11; Lev 25:1–7). The specific laws in Deuteronomy forbid urging debtors to repay their debts quickly. They also include detailed ordinances on setting slaves free in the Sabbatical Year (Deut 15:1–18), the Passover (Deut 16:1–8), the Feast of Weeks (Deut 16:9–12), and the Feast of Booths (Deut 16:13–17).

Ordinances Regarding the Sabbath Day

In the Bible the conditions for the observance of the Sabbath were more particular than those for the other laws.
 No physical work was allowed on the Sabbath (Exod 20:10).
- The Israelites were to keep the Sabbath from evening to evening (Lev 23:32; see also Neh 13:19).
- They were to work hard during the six days (Exod 20:9; Deut 5:13).
- Under no circumstances were they allowed to gather wood on the Sabbath (Num 15:32–36).
- They were not to kindle a fire in any of their dwelling places on the Sabbath (Exod 35:3).
- They were not to engage in trade on the Sabbath (Neh 13:15–21).
- They were not to buy or sell anything on the Sabbath (Neh 10:31; Amos 8:5–6).
- They were not to tread winepresses or move objects on the Sabbath (Neh 13:15; Jer 17:21–22).
- They were to stop working even during plowing and harvesting

seasons on the Sabbath (Exod 34:21).
- They were to turn their feet from doing their pleasure on the Sabbath (Isa 58:13).
- They were not to travel more than the prescribed distance on the Sabbath (Acts 1:12).
- They were to prepare the Sabbath offerings according to God's instructions (Num 28:9–10).

Why were the people to keep the Sabbath day in this manner? God explained the reason in Exodus 20:11: "For in six days the LORD made the heavens and the earth, the sea and all that is in them, and rested on the seventh day; therefore the LORD blessed the sabbath day and made it holy."

This verse begins with the conjunction "for" (כִּי, *ki*). In Hebrew the conjunction (כִּי, *ki*) initiates a motive clause. It was used here specifically to reveal the reason that one should not work on the Sabbath day. The record of God's resting on the seventh day after His creation work for six days does not mean that He was exhausted and tired or that He was in a stationary state. After His creation work, God looked upon creation and saw that "it was very good" (Gen 1:31). Thus God's rest refers to a state of joy and delight-filled satisfaction.

The word "blessed" in Exodus 20:11, "The LORD blessed the sabbath day and made it holy," is written in the Piel (intensive) stem of the Hebrew word בָּרַךְ (*barakh*), which denotes "to kneel, to bless, to praise." Thus the statement "the LORD blessed the sabbath day" means that God blessed the Sabbath with immense blessings. Those who remembered the Sabbath and bowed before God with humble hearts of thanksgiving and praise in keeping the Sabbath would be blessed with prosperity. God would also acknowledge those who kept the Sabbath as people who revered His sanctuary, where He dwelled (Lev 19:30; 26:2).

In Deuteronomy 5:15, Moses reminded the Israelites, "You shall remember that you were a slave in the land of Egypt, and the LORD your God brought you out of there by a mighty hand and by an outstretched arm; therefore the LORD your God commanded you to observe the sabbath day." He emphasized that the Israelites were to remember God, who had redeemed them from Egypt, where they had been enslaved for 430 years, and keep the Sabbath as a celebration of victory (Exod 12:40–42). If the Israelites observed the Sabbath, they would never be enslaved again; they would possess the holy land that God would give them and receive the blessing of becoming the head of the world (Deut 28:1–14).

In some instances work was allowed to be performed on the Sabbath. While the law strictly prohibited labor on the Sabbath, there were some cases in the Old Testament in which work was allowed.

First, traveling on the Sabbath in search of a prophet (a man of God) was allowed. God allowed the Israelites to travel to a prophet to receive God's Word. In 2 Kings 4:8–37, a Shunamite woman's son had died, and before informing her husband of the child's death, she said to him, "Please send me one of the servants and one of the donkeys, that I may run to the man of God and return" (2 Kgs 4:22). He asked her, "Why will you go to him today? It is neither new moon nor sabbath," and she replied, "It will be well" (2 Kgs 4:23). Both the new moon and Sabbath were holy days (holy assemblies) in which the Israelites gathered before God according to His command (Lev 23:2–3; Num 28:11). During those days the people would go and meet the prophet to listen to God's Word. Hence her husband asked her why she wanted to meet the prophet so urgently when it was neither the new moon nor the Sabbath. This implies that the people traveled to meet the prophets on the new moon or the Sabbath.

Second, when the nation faced a crisis, like a war, fighting for the nation and its people was allowed on the Sabbath. The Old Testament mentions often that the Israelites performed their duties even on the Sabbath when the nation was engaged in war with an enemy.

For example, Joshua and the Israelites marched around the city of Jericho with the ark of the covenant at the front of the procession once a day for six days. On the seventh day, at dawn, they marched around seven times.

God commanded Joshua, "See, I have given Jericho into your hand, with its king and the valiant warriors. You shall march around the city, all the men of war circling the city once. You shall do so for six days. Also seven priests shall carry seven trumpets of rams' horns before the ark; then on the seventh day you shall march around the city seven times, and the priests shall blow the trumpets. It shall be that when they make a long blast with the ram's horn, and when you hear the sound of the trumpet, all the people shall shout with a great shout; and the wall of the city will fall down flat, and the people will go up every man straight ahead" (Josh 6:2-5). Thus Joshua and the Israelites marched around the city every day for seven days.

> *Now Joshua rose early in the morning, and the priests took up the ark of the LORD . . . Thus the second day they marched around the city once and returned to the camp; they did so for six days. Then on the seventh day they rose early at the dawning of the day and marched around the city in the same manner seven times; only on that day they marched around the city seven times. (Josh 6:12-15)*

On the seventh and final day, they performed seven times the work they had performed on the normal days according to God's command. Then the city of Jericho fell at once. It was an incredible feat fulfilled according to God's command under His sovereignty. If the first day of their march around the city was on a Sunday, then the last day would have been on the Sabbath. They would have awakened early on the Sabbath to perform seven times the work they had performed on each of the previous six days.

A second example of work being done on the Sabbath during war occurred when Ahab, king of Israel, went up to fight against Ben-hadad, king of Syria, upon hearing the prophecy of God's prophet and the battle lasted for seven days (1 Kgs 20:1-29).

Ben-hadad, king of Syria, led his army to Samaria in the northern kingdom of Israel and threatened it by besieging it (1 Kgs 20:1-12). At that time an anonymous prophet of God prophesied King Ahab's victory, and Ahab won the war in accordance with the prophecy (1 Kgs 20:13-21). Then Ben-hadad retreated and mustered up his army again and went up to Aphek to fight against Israel (1 Kgs 20:22-26). Since his military power was such that "the sons of Israel camped before them like two little flocks of goats, but the Arameans filled the country" (1 Kgs 20:27), Israel was no match for the Syrians. The anonymous prophet of God, however, received the Lord's word and prophesied King Ahab's victory (1 Kgs 20:27-28). The prophecy was accurate. The Syrians and the Israelites faced off for seven days, and on the final day, the Israelites killed one hundred thousand Syrian foot soldiers and achieved a great victory.

They camped one over against the other seven days. And on the seventh day the battle was joined, and the sons of Israel killed of the Arameans 100,000 foot soldiers in one day. (1 Kgs 20:29)

After one hundred thousand soldiers were killed, the surviving Syrian army fled to Aphek and entered the city. The wall of the city, however, fell upon these twenty-seven thousand soldiers (1 Kgs 20:30). Horrified, Ben-hadad hastily fled to the city and went into an inner chamber (1 Kgs 20:30).

Since the Israelites faced off against the Syrian army for seven days, they must have been engaged in battle on the Sabbath. The soldiers in battle could not observe the Sabbath like the other Israelites. Although they were engaged in battle during the Sabbath, God gave them great victory in which they defeated one hundred thousand of their enemies (1 Kgs 20:29-30).

A third example of work being performed during a war was when the allied forces of King Jehoshaphat of Judah, King Jehoram of Israel, and the king of Edom marched through the wilderness of Moab for more than seven days in order to attack the king of Moab.

By the seventh day, the allied forces had no water and were in danger of death (2 Kgs 3:4–9):

> *The king of Israel went with the king of Judah and the king of Edom; and they made a circuit of seven days' journey, and there was no water for the army or for the cattle that followed them. (2 Kgs 3:9)*

The kings went to the prophet Elisha and consulted with him. They brought in a minstrel just as Elisha instructed and allowed him to play. Then God's word came upon Elisha, and he said, "Make this valley full of trenches" (2 Kgs 3:16). The allies dug trenches in the valley as God had instructed Elisha. The next morning water came from the direction of Edom and filled the land. The water strengthened the people, livestock, and animals. When the Moabites rose early in the morning and looked toward the camp of Israel, Judah, and Edom, the water in the land looked like red blood from the sun's reflection on the water. They thought that the allies had fought among themselves and shed blood. Thus the Moabites went to the camp of Israel to plunder it, but the Israelites defeated the Moabites (2 Kgs 3:17–27).

If the soldiers had refrained from work on the Sabbath and their enemies had found out about it, the enemy would have attacked on the seventh day when the allied forces were suffering from thirst, and the allies would have been defeated. From the account in 2 Kings 3:9–27, it is evident that the Israelites fulfilled their military obligation during the war, even on the Sabbath.

A fourth example of work being done on the Sabbath day was when Joash's coronation ceremony was held on the Sabbath because the nation was in a crisis.

After the death of Ahaziah, the king of Judah, his mother, Athaliah, killed all the royal offspring and reigned over the kingdom. In this dark era, Jehoiada the priest risked his life to defend the lamp of the covenant. His wife, Jehosheba (Jehoshabeath), the daughter of King Jehoram as well as Ahaziah's sister, saved Joash from Athaliah's massacre of the royal offspring by hiding him in the temple of the Lord for six years (2 Kgs 11:1–3; 2 Chr 22:10–12). In the seventh year of Athaliah's reign, Jehoiada the priest brought the captains of the hundreds to the temple and made a covenant with them. He put them under oath and showed them the prince and explained to them why the prince must take the throne. Then he gave them instructions on what was to be done on the Sabbath (2 Kgs 11:4–5; 2 Chr 23:1–4). The captains were shocked and filled with joy, as they had believed that all the Davidic seed had been killed. Just as Jehoiada instructed, the captains divided the priests on duty into three groups and placed each of the groups at a vital location to guard the palace. The two divisions of priests who were not on duty and thus went out on the Sabbath were called to guard the king with weapons in their hands. Then Jehoiada placed the crown on Joash the prince, gave him the testimony of the law, and anointed him king (2 Kgs 11:5–12; 2 Chr 23:4–11).

Jehoiada urgently held Joash's enthronement ceremony on the Sabbath day, since it would have been impossible to do it on a weekday (2 Kgs 11:12; 2 Chr 23:11). All the priests in the temple cooperated with crowning Joash king on the Sabbath day.

Offering sacrifices to God and all work related to it (for the priests and Levites) was allowed on the Sabbath. The priests' workload was greater on the Sabbath than on the weekdays. This was because more sacrifices were offered on the Sabbath day, and only priests could administer the work related to the sacrifices.

First Chronicles 23:24–32 records the list of duties that were specifically to be performed by Aaron's sons. Verse 31 states that they were "to offer all burnt offerings to the Lord, on the sabbaths, the new moons and the fixed festivals in the number set by the ordinance concerning them, continually before the LORD." This record implies that certain works were allowed to be performed on the Sabbath. Aaron's sons managed the temple, performed work related to the sacrifices, and served as singers. On every Sabbath the priests brought out the twelve loaves of the bread of the presence from the holy place and replaced them with freshly baked bread (Lev 24:5-9). The bread of the presence was "the continual bread" (Num 4:7). The twenty-four thousand Levites were in charge of preparing the bread of the presence (1 Chr 23:3-4). First Chronicles 23:29 states that their duty was to help the sons of Aaron "with the showbread, and the fine flour for a grain offering, and unleavened wafers, or what is baked in the pan or what is well-mixed, and all measures of volume and size." First Chronicles 9:32 also states, "Some of their relatives of the sons of the Kohathites were over the showbread to prepare it every sabbath."

Jesus said in Matthew 12:5-8, "Have you not read in the Law, that on the Sabbath the priests in the temple break the Sabbath and are innocent? But I say to you that something greater than the temple is here. … For the Son of Man is Lord of the Sabbath." The fundamental law to worship God in the temple is greater than the law to observe the Sabbath. This is why the priests and the Levites carried out more duties on the Sabbaths than on all other days.

Circumcising a male child on the eighth day after his birth was allowed on the Sabbath. In John 7:22-23, Jesus said, "Moses has given you circumcision (not because it is from Moses, but from the fathers), and on the Sabbath you circumcise a man. If a man receives circumcision on the Sabbath so that the Law of Moses will not be broken, are you angry with Me because I made an entire man well on the Sabbath?"

Circumcision symbolized distinction for the Jews from the Gentiles as well as cleansing from sin. It was a "sign of the covenant" between God and the Israelites given by God as an everlasting covenant (Gen 17:10-11). Circumcision was to be performed on the eighth day after birth (Gen 17:12; Lev 12:3), so it was inevitable that some circumcisions were performed on the Sabbath.

Thus while God's command to observe the Sabbath was important and strict, exceptions were made for meeting with a prophet (a man of God); saving the country and the nation from a crisis; working as a priest or Levite for worshiping God; and performing circumcision, the sign of the covenant.

Statutes on the Sabbatical Year

The Sabbatical Year was the seventh year in the seven-year cycle. The Sabbatical Year was an extension of the concept of the Sabbath day. The expansion of the Sabbatical Year was the Year of Jubilee. The Sabbatical Year was called "the seventh year" (Exod 23:11; Neh 10:31), "the end of every seven years" (Deut 15:1; 31:10), and "the year of remission" (Deut 15:9; 31:10; see Deut 15:2).

The land was to rest in the seventh year (Exod 23:10–11; Lev 25:1–7). Leviticus 25:4 states, "During the seventh year the land shall have a sabbath rest, a sabbath to the LORD; you shall not sow your field nor prune your vineyard" (see also Exod 23:10–11). In the Sabbatical Year, the people were not to reap even things that grew naturally. Leviticus 25:5 continues, "Your harvest's aftergrowth you shall not reap, and your grapes of untrimmed vines you shall not gather; the land shall have a sabbatical year." It was natural for the people to wonder what they would eat if they did not sow (Lev 25:20). God, however, promised to give enough crops for three years in the year before the Sabbatical Year relating to the Year of Jubilee (Lev 25:21).

In Leviticus 25:6–7, God says, "All of you shall have the sabbath products of the land for food; yourself, and your male and female slaves, and your hired man and your foreign resident, those who live as aliens with you. Even your cattle and the animals that are in your land shall have all its crops to eat." Here, the expression "sabbath products" may sound odd since no one sowed in the Sabbatical Year. "Sabbath products," however, is וְהָיְתָה שַׁבַּת הָאָרֶץ (*wehaythah shabbath haarets*) and means "the sabbath of the land." Thus it means that the Sabbath of the land (allowing the land to rest) would help the land produce more crops in the future so that the amount of crops would be sufficient not only for the people but also for the animals. The New

Revised Standard Version translates Leviticus 25:6 as, "You may eat what the land yields during its sabbath—you, your male and female slaves, your hired and your bound laborers who live with you."

When the Sabbath was not kept, however, God warned, "The land will enjoy its sabbaths all the days of the desolation, while you are in your enemies' land; then the land will rest and enjoy its sabbaths. All the days of its desolation it will observe the rest which it did not observe on your sabbaths, while you were living on it" (Lev 26:34–35). In fact, because the Israelites did not observe the Sabbatical Year, Jeremiah's prophecy (Jer 25:11–12) was fulfilled. Second Chronicles 36:21 states that Israel was exiled "to fulfill the word of the LORD by the mouth of Jeremiah, until the land had enjoyed its sabbaths. All the days of its desolation it kept sabbath until seventy years were complete."

The repayment of debt was to be deferred in the seventh year. Deuteronomy 15:1–2 states, "At the end of every seven years you shall grant a remission of debts. This is the manner of remission: every creditor shall release what he has loaned to his neighbor; he shall not exact it of his neighbor and his brother, because the LORD's remission has been proclaimed." This statute prohibited creditors from hastening the debtor for payment during the Sabbatical Year; payment was to be deferred one year. Nehemiah 10:31 states, "We will forego the crops the seventh year and the exaction of every debt." Here the word "forego" is נָטַשׁ (*natash*) in Hebrew; it does not mean that the debt would be forgiven but that the payment would be deferred one year. Just as the land rested one year during the Sabbatical Year, so a debtor was given rest from the burden of his debt for one year. If the creditor pressed the debtor for payment, the debtor would not have any true rest even during the Sabbatical Year, as he would either resort to working to pay off the debt or live with stress without rest. By deferring the payment of the people's debts by one year, God allowed them to enjoy the Sabbatical Year. When the year was over, however, the debtor had to return to hard work in order to repay his debt.

Hebrew slaves were to be released in the seventh year (Exod 21:2–6; Deut 15:12–18). Deuteronomy 15:12 states, "If your kinsman, a Hebrew man or woman, is sold to you, then he shall serve you six years, but in the seventh year you shall set him free." When the slaves were returned, they were not to be sent back empty-handed; they were to be sent back with an abundance of goods according to the blessings with which God had blessed their master (Deut 15:13–14). Just as the Israelites had also been liberated by God from slavery, so it was their rightful duty to liberate their own people (Deut 15:15). In some cases, however, a slave loved his master and wanted to remain with him and serve him (Exod 21:5; Deut 15:16). In such cases, the master could take the slave to the door and pierce the slave's ear with an awl, and the servant would then serve his master permanently (Exod 21:6; Deut 15:17).

God promised the blessing of prosperity to those who obey His Word. Deuteronomy 15:18 states, "It shall not seem hard to you when you set him free, for he has given you six years with double the service of a hired man; so the LORD your God will bless you in whatever you do."

Statutes on the Jubilee Year

While the Jubilee Year is not mentioned in the specific laws recorded in Exodus and Deuteronomy, Leviticus contains a detailed record of it. The Sabbatical Year came around every seven years, but the Jubilee Year came around every fifty years, after seven cycles of seven years.

The word "Jubilee" is יוֹבֵל (*yovel*) in Hebrew, which means a "[ram's] horn." This name originated from the practice of blowing a horn in the Year of Jubilee to proclaim the joy of freedom. A Jubilee Year began with a loud horn blown on the Day of Atonement (*Yom Kippur*) on the tenth day of the month of Tishri (the seventh month of the year). Leviticus 25:9–10 states, "You shall then sound a ram's horn abroad on the tenth day of the seventh month; on the day of atonement you shall sound a horn all through your land. You shall thus consecrate the fiftieth year and proclaim a release through the land to all its inhabitants. It shall be a jubilee for you, and each of you shall return to his own property, and each of you shall return to his family."

In the Year of Jubilee, each person was to return to his or her own property and family. Leviticus 25:10 states, "You shall thus consecrate the fiftieth year and proclaim a release through the land to all its inhabitants. It shall be a jubilee for you, and each of you shall return to his own property, and each of you shall return to his family." Just as all the land was returned to its original owners every Jubilee Year, so people living in another person's house were also to return to their own properties and families. Yet, some basic principles applied.

Suppose an Israelite had been forced to sell himself to a fellow Israelite due to poverty. In that case the master was not to treat him as a slave but as a hired worker or a sojourner and was to return him and his family to their home during the next Jubilee Year (Lev 25:39-43, 46).

Gentiles, however, could be taken as slaves (Lev 25:44-45), even permanently (Lev 25:46). God prohibited Israelites from becoming slaves of fellow Israelites because they had been God's own laborers (slaves) whom He had led out of Egypt; they were not slaves of men (Lev 25:42, 55). A man could not take God's laborers as his own slaves. If an Israelite had been sold to a rich foreigner, then any of his brothers, uncles, cousins, or blood relatives could redeem him. Alternatively, he could redeem himself if he later became affluent (Lev 25:47-49). In such a case of redemption, the redeemed person was to pay a redemption price based on the number of years remaining until the next Jubilee Year (Lev 25:50-52). Moreover, the rich foreigner who bought an Israelite was to treat him as a hired worker, not as a slave (Lev 25:53). Even in such cases, the slave and his family were to be sent back during the Jubilee Year (Lev 25:54).

Land was to be returned to its original owner in the Jubilee Year. Certain principles existed in buying and selling land. Above all, land was not to be sold permanently but only temporarily (Lev 25:23). There was to be no deception involved in the buying and selling of land (Lev 25:14, 17). The price had to be calculated "corresponding to the number of years after the jubilee" (Lev 25:15) (the number of years since the last Jubilee). When there were many years left until the next Jubilee Year, the price could be set high; when there were only a few years left, the price would be set lower (Lev 25:15–16). Even after land was sold, it could be redeemed (Lev 25:24). When a person in poverty sold his property, his nearest relative could redeem it (Lev 25:25). Alternatively, the poor man could redeem it himself when he later became affluent (Lev 25:26). The price was calculated based on the number of years left until the next Jubilee (Lev 25:27).

A home was to be returned to its original owner in the Jubilee Year. Basic principles existed in buying and selling a home.

If a house located within the city wall were sold, it could be redeemed within one year after its sale (Lev 25:29). If it could not be redeemed within a year, however, the house became the buyer's permanent property (Lev 25:30). This was because houses within city walls were owned by the wealthy in those days, and the statutes of the Jubilee Year did not give special benefits to the wealthy. Like land, however, a house in a village without walls could be redeemed at any time. It had to be returned to its original owner in the Jubilee Year (Lev 25:31).

As for the cities of the Levites, although they were located within city walls, their homes could be redeemed at any time (Lev 25:32) and had to be returned in the Jubilee Year (Lev 25:33). Since the duties of the Levites involved offering sacrifices, they did not have an inheritance or source of income like those of the other tribes. The pasture fields of their cities, therefore, were never to be sold, as they belonged to the Levites perpetually (Lev 25:34).

The land was to rest in the Jubilee Year. In Leviticus 25:11–12, God said, "You shall have the fiftieth year as a jubilee; you shall not sow, nor reap its aftergrowth, nor gather in from its untrimmed vines. For it is a jubilee; it shall be holy to you. You shall eat its crops out of the field." As in the Sabbatical Year, the land was to rest during the Jubilee Year. The Israelites were not to sow seeds, harvest what grew by itself, or gather grapes from undressed vines.

Since the forty-ninth year is the Sabbatical Year, the land had to rest for two consecutive years, including the Jubilee Year. God gave sufficient produce of the land for three years in the forty-eighth year, before the Sabbatical Year in the forty-ninth year and the Jubilee in the fiftieth year. The people ate this produce in the forty-ninth and fiftieth years, as well as in the fifty-first year until the harvest. In Leviticus 25:21–22, God said, "I will so order My blessing for you in the sixth year that it will bring forth the crop for three years. When you are sowing the eighth year, you can still eat old things from the crop, eating the old until the ninth year when its crop comes in."

There were statutes on interest related to the Jubilee Year. Leviticus 25:35–38 records statutes regarding interest during the Jubilee Year. When a fellow Israelite became very poor and could not support himself, an Israelite was to sustain him so that he could live like a foreigner or a sojourner with him (Lev 25:35). The word "sustain" connotes the act of lending money. The verb is in the Hiphil stem of the Hebrew word חָזַק (*hazaq*), which means "to uphold, to support, to strengthen." The word describes a situation in which a person gave a loan to a fellow Israelite who had lost all financial competency and could not survive without the support; it was similar to a charitable gift in which repayment was not expected. In most cases people in poverty used the borrowed money to purchase seeds to sow for the next harvest, so the financial support was essentially an act of charity.[47] If a person lent money to the poor, he was not to charge interest. In Leviticus 25:36, God commanded, "Do not take usurious interest from him," and He continued in verse 37, "You shall not give him your silver at interest, nor your food for gain." Here the word "interest" (נֶשֶׁךְ, *neshekh*) comes from נָשַׁךְ (*nashakh*), which means "to bite." Thus while the Israelites were allowed to lend money to one another, God forbade charging any type of interest (Exod 22:25; Lev 25:35–37; Deut 23:19–20). The debt itself was a burden on the poor, and the interest would have been an even heavier burden. While charging interest to a fellow Israelite was prohibited (Lev 25:35–37), the Israelites were allowed to charge interest to foreigners (Deut 23:20).

Accumulating unjust wealth like a usurer is a sin before God, and possessions earned with earthly enthusiasm will surely return to the hands of those who are generous to the poor. Thus Proverbs 28:8 states, "He who increases his wealth by interest and usury gathers it for him who is gracious to the poor." Psalm 15 describes those who are worthy to dwell in the Lord's tent and His holy hill: "He does not put out his money at interest, nor does he take a bribe against the innocent. He who does these things will never be shaken" (Ps 15:5).

The statutes regarding interest concluded in Leviticus 25:38 with, "I am the LORD your God, who brought you out of the land of Egypt to give you the land of Canaan and to be your God." The statute forbidding the charging of interest could have completely hindered people from showing compassion to the poor and lending money. Thus God proclaimed that it was only right for the Israelites to show compassion to the poor, just as He had shown them compassion by saving them from slavery (Lev 25:38). Indeed, the essence of the Jubilee is the forgiveness of all debt with both land and houses being returned to their original owners in the Jubilee Year.

III. Teachings on Worship

The first commandment clarified the proper *object* of worship by commanding us to worship only God. The second commandment instructed us on the proper *method* of worship by forbidding the worship of idols or any other image. The third commandment informed us of the proper *mindset* of worship by commanding us not to take the Lord's name in vain but to exalt it in holiness. The fourth commandment instructs us on the proper *time* of worship.

God has designated the Sabbath day as the time for worship. The Sabbath day is an everlasting sign, a sign between God and His people and a sign to be kept perpetually by His people for the generations to come (Exod 31:13, 17). Just as numerous sacrifices were offered on the Sabbath during the Old Testament era (Num 28:9–10; 1 Chr 23:31), so today we must observe the Lord's day by all means as a day to worship God.

The history of worldwide observance of the Sabbath encompasses about two thousand years. This indeed is an inheritance of faith resulting from the dynamic work of the living Word of God. It is a monumental achievement in church history. Many people, of course, have strongly argued for the dismissal of Sunday worship in order to annihilate Christianity. Atheist R. G. Ingersoll argued, "Sunday is a pest. It must be taken out of the way."[48] Similarly, Reverend Sung-ho Han argued, "Sunday worship is not rooted in the Bible and is thus illegal" (June 5 and Sept 26 of *Chosun Ilbo*).

Recently, unmindful church leaders who fear losing their congregations if they emphasize Sunday worship attendance have compromised by suggesting that their congregations may worship on any day of the week, even if it is not specifically Sunday. The Westminster Shorter Catechism, question 59, however, affirms, "From the beginning of the world to the resurrection of Christ, God appointed the seventh day of the week to be the weekly sabbath; and the first day of the week ever since, to continue to the end of the world, which is the Christian sabbath" (Gen 2:2–3; Exod 16:23; Acts 20:7; 1 Cor 16:1–2). The Lord's day cannot be replaced with any other day of the week. This is because Jesus died on the cross on a Friday and rose on the third day, the first day after the Sabbath, which was a Sunday (Matt 28:1; Mark

16:2, 9; Luke 24:1; John 20:1). Jesus appeared before the disciples on the first day after the Sabbath (John 20:19). He appeared to the apostle John also on "the Lord's day" (Rev 1:10). The early church gathered together to break bread and teach God's Word on the first day after the Sabbath (Acts 20:7; 1 Cor 16:2).

We must not step out of the boundaries of the written Word and sin by adding and subtracting to the Word or distorting it according to human preferences (Deut 4:2; 12:32; Prov 30:6; 1 Cor 4:6; Rev 22:18–19).

Keeping the Lord's day is certainly not a heavy burden. It is a holy day set apart for us as a day of blessing, delight, honor, and worship within God's redemptive-historical administration to ultimately bestow upon us true and eternal rest.

> *If because of the sabbath, you turn your foot from doing your own pleasure on My holy day, and call the sabbath a delight, the holy day of the LORD honorable, and honor it, desisting from your own ways, from seeking your own pleasure and speaking your own word, then you will take delight in the LORD, and I will make you ride on the heights of the earth; and I will feed you with the heritage of Jacob your father, for the mouth of the LORD has spoken.* (Isa 58:13–14)

"*I will make you ride on the heights of the earth*" (Isa 58:14). The word "ride" is רָכַב (*rakhav*) in Hebrew, and the verb describes the act of mounting and riding a camel, horse, donkey, wagon, or chariot. The verse literally means, "I will mount you on the high place on this earth." This does not, however, refer to spatial movement. Rather, it connotes a blessing of the conquest of enemies, a victory leading to fame, and a rising to a seat of praise and honor (Deut 32:13; 33:29).

"*I will feed you with the heritage of Jacob*" (Isa 58:14). The word "feed" is the Hiphil (active causative) stem of the Hebrew verb אָכַל (*akhal*). In the Hiphil stem, the word *akhal* ("to eat") means "to feed." The word "heritage" (נַחֲלָה, *nahala*) means "property" or "inheritance."

Thus Isaiah 58:14 is rendered in the New Living Translation, "I will give you great honor and satisfy you with the inheritance I promised to your ancestor Jacob" (see also Deut 14:29; Jer 2:7).

"The heritage of Jacob" refers first to the land of Canaan promised to Jacob (Gen 28:13). Second, it refers to the blessing of Jacob's offspring thriving like the dust of the earth and spreading abroad in every direction (Gen 28:14). They would be blessed so that they would prosper no matter where they went (Gen 13:14–17; 46:3). Third, it refers to the blessing of them becoming a blessing themselves so that all the tribes of the earth would be blessed through Jacob and his offspring (Gen 12:2–3; 28:14).

God acknowledges those who keep the Sabbath as Jacob's offspring, that is, as the covenant people (Ps 105:5–10). He will provide every blessing promised to the people of the covenant and allow them to enjoy it (Gen 28:13–15; 35:9–12; 46:3–4).

God's people must keep the Sabbath with their lives, therefore, and consider it a sign of the covenant throughout their generations (Exod 31:13–17).

God declares in the end, "The mouth of the LORD has spoken" (Isa 58:14). This is like a seal at the end of a document certifying its authenticity. It manifests God's firm resolution to keep His promise of blessing for those who honor and keep the Sabbath.

IV. The Fate of Those Who Violated the Fourth Commandment

God pronounced the gravest punishment upon the violators of the Sabbath: the death penalty. According to Exodus 31:14, anyone who worked on the Sabbath profaned it. The word "profane" occurs in the Piel stem of the Hebrew word חָלַל (halal), which means "to desecrate (something holy and sacred)" or "to defile or profane something divine" (Neh 13:17; Isa 56:2, 6). In this respect anyone who worked on the Sabbath defiled the Sabbath and profaned God's holiness, and Israel was to put such a person to death (Exod 31:14). In fact, during the wilderness journey a certain man was found gathering sticks on the Sabbath day, and the entire congregation stoned him to death according to God's command (Num 15:32-36).

God warned that if His people did not obey His commandment and became so proud that they did not keep the Sabbath holy, He would kindle a fire at the gates of Jerusalem and let its palace burn with unquenchable fire (Jer 17:19-27). Indeed, when the southern kingdom Judah violated the Sabbath, Nebuchadnezzar, the king of Babylon, and Nebuzaradan, the captain of his guards, in fulfillment of God's Word, came to Jerusalem and burned down the temple of the Lord, the palace of the king, "every great house" (2 Kgs 25:9), and all the houses of Jerusalem in 586 BC (2 Kgs 25:8-9; 2 Chr 36:19; Jer 52:12-13). The destruction of the temple and Israel's captivity in Babylon were retribution for their violation of the commandment regarding the Sabbath and the Sabbatical Year (2 Chr 36:21; Neh 13:17-18; see also Lev 26:34-35). God expressed His disdain for those who disobeyed His Word (1 Sam 2:29-30), saying, "If it [the nation] does evil in My sight by not obeying My voice, then I will think better of the good with which I had promised to bless it" (Jer 18:10).

V. The Redemptive-Historical Lesson in the Fourth Commandment

Adam committed a sin equivalent to the violation of the fourth commandment in the garden of Eden. God rested on the seventh day after His creation (Gen 2:1-3), while Adam fled and hid from the face of the resting God, which was a sin of running away from God's rest. After eating from the tree of the knowledge of good and evil, Adam and the woman heard the voice of the Lord God walking in the garden in the cool of the day, but they hid among the trees of the garden away from His face (Gen 3:8). The use of the waw-consecutive in this verse indicates that they hid because they had heard God's voice. In other words, when they ignored God's voice and hid, they left God's rest. God called to Adam who had hidden from Him, saying, "Where are you?" (Gen 3:9). God's rest was broken with the fall of Adam and the woman.

One month after the exodus, God sent the Israelites manna (Exod 16:1-4). At this time God instructed them not to go out and gather the manna on the seventh day, because it was the Sabbath day. On the sixth day, God allowed them to gather a double portion of manna (Exod 16:5, 22-26). Despite God's command, some people went out to gather manna on the next Sabbath day (the seventh day) and returned without any (Exod 16:27). God lamented Israel's disobedience and said, "The LORD has given you the sabbath; therefore He gives you bread for two days on the sixth day" (Exod 16:29). This is God's clear promise that He would not allow His people to experience financial loss because they did not work on the Sabbath. Yet even with this guarantee of blessing, they considered the Sabbath rest a waste of time and did not hesitate to work and have their servants also work on the Sabbath (see also Lev 26:35; 2 Chr 36:21; Neh 13:15-18). During the time of the prophet Amos, the Israelites idolized wealth and were so corrupt that they considered the Sabbath a heavy burden (Amos 8:4-6).

During the time of Jesus, the Jews kept the Sabbath with zeal. The religious leaders, however, had distorted the good law of the Sabbath that had been given to benefit people (Mark 2:27) into an evil law that oppressed and restricted the people. Thus keeping the Sabbath had degenerated into a mere formality. Jesus was grieved and displeased with the Pharisees and scribes because they had forgotten the true meaning and basic principle behind the Sabbath. On the Sabbath Jesus healed a man with a withered hand at the center of the synagogue as they all watched (Matt 12:9-13; Mark 3:1-5; Luke 6:6-10):

> *I say to you that something greater than the temple is here. But if you had known what this means, "I desire compassion, and not a sacrifice," you would not have condemned the innocent. For the Son of Man is Lord of the Sabbath. (Matt 12:6-8)*

The Pharisees heard this and became all the more jealous of Jesus and discussed "how they might destroy Him" (Matt 12:14; see Mark 3:6; Luke 6:11).

What did Jesus mean when He said that "the Son of Man is Lord of the Sabbath"?

First, Jesus meant that He was the lawgiver of the Sabbath. Along with the Father God, Jesus Christ created the heavens and the earth and then rested on the seventh day (Gen 2:1-3; John 1:1-3). Because Jesus was the lawgiver of the Sabbath, He knew best how people were to keep the Sabbath and had the sole authority to articulate how one should observe the Sabbath.[49] The statutes regarding the Sabbath law were not under the religious leaders' jurisdiction; thus they could never become lords of the Sabbath. Jesus alone, as Lord of the Sabbath, can give people eternal rest (Heb 4:1-11).

Second, Jesus meant that all the sovereignty of the Sabbath belonged to Him. Since the Lord of the Sabbath is God, the lawgiver, the Sabbath day is under God's sovereignty (Exod 31:13; Lev 19:3; 26:2; Isa 56:4; 58:13; Ezek 20:12, 20). It is only right, therefore, that we should offer every event we hold on the Sabbath to God for His glory.[50] As such, Jesus must be at the center of every service of worship, fellowship, devotion, ministry, or anything else performed by God's people on the Sabbath.

Whatever we do on the Sabbath, in word or deed, we must do in the name of the Lord Jesus, and we must give thanks to God the Father through Jesus (Col 3:17). Whether we eat or drink, or whatever we do, we must do all things to God's glory (1 Cor 10:31). In every case we must work heartily as for the Lord and not for men (Col 3:23-24). Then God will repay us according to what we have done (Eph 6:8). We who have been called to abide in the Lord are His bondservants as well as His freedmen (1 Cor 7:22). Thus whether we live or die, "we are the Lord's" (Rom 14:7–8).

Third, Jesus meant that true rest came only through Him. There is only one Lord of the Sabbath; there cannot be two. When we meet with Jesus, the Lord of the Sabbath, we can enjoy the freedom, peace, and joy promised to those who keep the Sabbath (John 8:31–32; 14:27; 15:11; 16:24). Those who do not serve Jesus and instead leave Him, however, profane the Sabbath (Ezek 20:13, 16, 21; 22:8, 26) and prevent the Sabbath's blessings from coming. Obedience to Jesus, the Lord of the Sabbath, is the only way to maintain true rest.

Fourth, Jesus meant that everything He did was an observance of the Sabbath. Jesus' years will never come to an end, and He is the same yesterday, today, and forever (Heb 1:12; 13:8). When the Jews persecuted Jesus for working on the Sabbath, He said to them, "My Father is working until now, and I Myself am working" (John 5:16–17). The Jews wanted to kill Jesus all the more after He said this. This was not only because Jesus had violated the Sabbath but because He had made Himself equal with God by calling God His Father (John 5:18). As such, Jesus had risked His life to reveal that He was the Lord of the Sabbath. Those who abide in Jesus by having the Lord of the Sabbath in their hearts always dwell in the blessing of the Sabbath day, the Sabbatical Year, and the Jubilee. Conversely, those who do not accept the Word of Jesus Christ, the true Lord of the Sabbath, are the wicked among the wicked and do not have peace in their hearts (Isa 48:22; 57:19–21).

Jesus healed a woman on the Sabbath day who for eighteen years had suffered with a sickness caused by a spirit (Luke 13:10–13). Having witnessed the healing, the ruler of the synagogue became indignant and said to the crowd, "There are six days in which work should be done; so come during them and get healed, and not on the Sabbath day" (Luke 13:14). The synagogue official was enraged because he felt that Jesus had healed on the Sabbath when the sickness was not urgent. Jesus called the synagogue official and his followers "hypocrites," pointing out that they would rescue their livestock if they fell into a well on a Sabbath (Matt 12:11; Luke 14:5) and would untie and lead their oxen or donkeys to water them on a Sabbath (Luke 13:15). Hence, it was only right to release a person from Satan's hold and heal him or her on the Sabbath (Luke 13:16) and perform good deeds to save lives on the Sabbath (Mark 3:4; Luke 6:9; see also Matt 12:12). In other words, if providing water to animals on the Sabbath was allowed, then it was only right to provide what was necessary for human beings, who are more precious than animals. The Pharisees' hypocrisy toward the Sabbath laws was so serious that they valued animals over human beings. When Jesus said this, His opponents were humiliated, and the crowds rejoiced in all the glorious things He had done (Luke 13:17).

In the Old Testament, the priests baked the bread of the presence in the temple on the Sabbath and then set the loaves on the table. Yet, their work was not in violation of Sabbath law because it was related to making offerings to God (Lev 24:8; Num 28:9-10; Matt 12:5). Jesus was "something greater than the temple" (Matt 12:6) and the Lord of the Sabbath of whom Moses had testified (Matt 12:7; Mark 2:27-28; Luke 6:5). Thus He could do as much work as He wished on the Sabbath. He worked on the Sabbath, saying, "My Father is working until now, and I Myself am working" (John 5:17).

Yet, even as the Jews witnessed Jesus working as the Lord of the Sabbath, they did not realize that He had come as the Sabbath itself. Instead, they only marveled at His work (John 7:21). They judged Him "according to appearance" (John 7:24); they rejected Him and resolved to kill Him (Matt 12:14; Mark 3:6; Luke 6:11; John 5:16, 18).

Ultimately, the Jews persecuted Jesus and crucified Him on a cross, failing to recognize the true purpose of the Sabbath given by God. The apostle Paul pointed out the improper faith of the Jews: "No one is to act as your judge in regard to food or drink or in respect to a festival or a new moon or a Sabbath day—things which are a mere shadow of what is to come; but the substance belongs to

Christ" (Col 2:16-17).

From the New Testament era until today, Christians observe the Lord's day instead of the Sabbath day. By His death on the cross, Jesus offered Himself as a ransom for His chosen people. By His resurrection on the first day after the Sabbath, the Lord's day, He freed us from the power of sin and death (Matt 28:1; Mark 16:2, 9; Luke 24:1; John 20:1; Rev 20:6). "The Lord's day" is the day on which Jesus set us free from sin and death and created us as new people. It is truly the day of new creation and new redemption. While the Old Testament saints observed the Sabbath in order to commemorate God's creation and redemption (Exod 20:11; Deut 5:15), the saints from the New Testament era keep the Lord's day to commemorate the new creation and new redemption through Jesus Christ (2 Cor 5:17; Eph 1:7; 4:22-24; Heb 4:8-9). After Jesus' resurrection and ascension, the saints in the early church designated the Lord's day as the official day of worship (Acts 20:7; 1 Cor 16:2). The apostle John called the first day of the week "the Lord's day" (Rev 1:10).

Just as the Sabbath law foreshadowed Jesus, who came as the Lord of the Sabbath, so the Lord's day reveals that the day of true rest remains for the people of God at Jesus' second coming (Heb 4:4-9). We must strive, therefore, to enter that eternal rest, that is, the kingdom of heaven (Heb 4:11).

Isaiah 56:2 states, "How blessed is the man who does this, and the son of man who takes hold of it; who keeps from profaning the sabbath, and keeps his hand from doing any evil" (Isa 56:2). The phrase "the son of man who takes hold of it" is translated as "the man who keeps the right path until the end" (Korean Common Translation Bible) or "the man who strictly observes righteousness" (New Korean Standard Version). God promised that at the completion of His work of redemption, to "the foreigners who join themselves to the LORD, to minister to Him, and to love the name of the LORD, to be His servants, everyone who keeps from profaning the sabbath and holds fast My covenant" (Isa 56:6), He will give a memorial in His house and an everlasting name (Isa 56:3–6). God prophesied about the nations coming together for the great feast of fellowship every week in the covenant of the Sabbath (Isa 56:7–8; see also Rev 21:24, 26).

May all saints today observe the Lord's day with hearts of thanksgiving for the new creation and new redemption through Jesus Christ's atoning work and, moreover, become true people of God who keep not just the Lord's day but every day as the Lord's day. When we do so, we will ultimately enter God's rest that remains for us (Rom 14:5–6; Heb 4:9–11; see also John 5:17; Heb 4:3).

CHAPTER

19

THE FIFTH COMMANDMENT

Honor your father and your mother.

Exodus 20:12; Deuteronomy 5:16

In Exodus 20:12, God commanded, "Honor your father and your mother, that your days may be prolonged in the land which the LORD your God gives you." Deuteronomy 5:16 reads, "Honor your father and your mother, as the LORD your God has commanded you, that your days may be prolonged and that it may go well with you on the land which the LORD your God gives you." The phrases "as the LORD your God has commanded you" and "that it may go well with you" are added in Deuteronomy.

THE FIFTH COMMAND

Honor your father and your mother.

כַּבֵּד אֶת־אָבִיךָ וְאֶת־אִמֶּךָ

Exodus 20:12; Deuteronomy 5:16

I. Exegesis of the Fifth Commandment

The fifth commandment properly establishes the basic order of society. Violations of the fifth commandment not only destroy order in the family but also have the same dreadful effect on society. The Chinese character for "filial duty" is 孝 (*hyo*, Korean pronunciation, and *xiao*, Chinese pronunciation). The character consists of the character for "son" (子) placed under the word for "aged" (老). This word composition implies that filial duty is defined as children's sincere service and support for their aged parents. Filial duty is the beginning of all orders. When the majority of people in a society do not perform their filial duties, the foundation of ethics and morals begins to shake. This leads to disorder in society and casts a bleak outlook for the family and the nation (Prov 20:20). One of the reasons for the fall of the southern kingdom of Judah was the sin of dishonoring parents (Ezek 22:7).

Even the order of the fifth commandment hints at its importance. Of the Ten Commandments, the fifth through the tenth commandments fall into the category of the commandments associated with relationships among people. The commandment to honor one's parents is the first of the commandments in this category. In Ephesians 6:2, Paul said, "Honor your father and mother (which is the first commandment with a promise)." The word "first" in this verse is πρῶτος (*prōtos*) in Greek, which also connotes "importance" as well as "primary" or "best."

We see first that honoring parents is the primary (most important) commandment among the commandments regarding human relationships.

Second, the sin of dishonoring parents is the origin of all sins committed among people. Those who sincerely honor their parents will not be able to commit murder (the sixth commandment). They will also be unable to commit adultery (the seventh commandment). Those who truly honor their parents cannot steal other people's possessions (the eighth commandment), bear false witness (the ninth commandment), or have covetousness in their hearts (the tenth commandment). In other words, the sin of dishonoring one's parents is greater than murder, adultery, stealing, lying, or covetousness.

"Your Father and Your Mother" (אֶת־אָבִיךָ וְאֶת־אִמֶּךָ)

Everyone's first relationship in life is with their parents—the parent-child relationship. We cannot exist without our parents. The Hebrew phrase אֶת־אָבִיךָ וְאֶת־אִמֶּךָ (*eth-avikha weeth-immekha*) in the fifth commandment (Exod 20:12; Deut 5:16) means "your father and your mother." "Father" in Hebrew is אָב (*av*), and "mother" is אֵם (*em*). In the Old Testament, *av* occurs more than one thousand times and *em* more than two hundred times.

Father (אָב, *av*). The "father" in the Bible is characterized as one who disciplines his children with love (Gen 37:10; 44:20; 50:16–17; Prov 1:8; 6:20; Heb 12:5–8). He blesses his children (Gen 27:10) and is understanding, loving, and concerned about them, even those who are not filial (Gen 26:34–35; 2 Sam 13:37, 39; 19:4; Luke 15:20). A father's heart for his children is only full of endless love.

Jacob is an example of a father with intense love in his heart. He loved each of his many children and suffered heartache at the loss of a child. He had twelve sons (Gen 29:31–35; 30:1–24; 35:16–18, 22–26; 42:13, 32) and daughters (see also Gen 37:35; 46:7). When he heard that his most beloved seventeen-year-old son, Joseph (Gen 37:2), had been torn to death by a fierce animal (Gen 37:31–33), Jacob tore his clothes, put sackcloth on his loins, and mourned deeply for his son for a long time. He refused to be comforted and did not stop weeping, saying, "Surely I will go down to Sheol in mourning for my son" (Gen 37:35). Jacob had devoted love for all twelve of his sons. When Simeon was held hostage in an Egyptian prison (Gen 42:24), and even when Benjamin was about to be taken, Jacob their father lamented to his other sons, "You have bereaved me of my children: Joseph is no more, and Simeon is no more, and you would take Benjamin; all these things are against me" (Gen 42:36).

Later, as his life of vicissitudes was coming to an end at the age of 147 (Gen 47:28), Jacob gathered all twelve of his sons. He leaned on his bed and blessed each one with a blessing appropriate for him (Gen 49:1–28, 33). The blessings revealed "what [would] befall [them] in the days to come" (Gen 49:1), and they were blessings "appropriate to [them]" (Gen 49:28). Jacob had the true love of a father who understood each child's role within God's redemptive-historical administration.

Mother (אֵם, *em*). In the Bible we often see a mother's ultimate sacrifice and burning devotion for her children (1 Kgs 3:16–27; 17:17–23; Matt 15:22–28; see also Prov 1:8; 4:3; 6:20; 10:1). Behind Moses was his mother, Jochebed, a mother of faith who was not afraid of Pharaoh's command (Exod 2:1–3; 6:20). Behind Samuel was his mother, Hannah, who prayed with tears in the temple for a long time (1 Sam 1:26–28). Behind John the Baptist was Elizabeth, who was righteous before God, walking blamelessly in all the commandments and statutes of the Lord (Luke 1:5–6). Behind Jesus was the virgin Mary, who obeyed God at the risk of her life (Luke 1:27–30, 38). Behind Timothy, a man of genuine faith, was his mother, Eunice, and his grandmother Lois (2 Tim 1:3–5). We find numerous accounts of mothers of kings in the books of Kings and Chronicles (1 Kgs 1:11; 2:13, 19–22; 14:21, 31; 15:2, 10, 13; 22:42; 2 Kgs 8:26; 11:1; 12:1; 14:1–2; 15:1–2, 32–33; 18:1–2; 21:1, 19; 22:1; 23:31, 36; 24:8, 12, 15, 18; 2 Chr 12:13; 13:1–2; 15:16; 20:31; 22:2–3, 10; 24:1; 25:1; 26:3; 27:1; 29:1).

"Honor" (כָּבֵד)

The commandment "Honor your father and your mother" is God's law and command for all people. Laws must be kept, and anyone who does not obey them becomes a lawbreaker. Failure to be filial, therefore, is unlawful.

The Hebrew word for "honor" is written in the Piel (intensive) stem of כָּבֵד (kaved), meaning "to be weighty" or "to be respected." It implies respecting the weighty presence of someone and means "to honor" when it is used for God or human beings (especially parents). This word frequently describes the attitude of God's people toward God (Prov 3:9; Isa 43:23). Thus the commandment requires people to show the same devotion for their parents as they would for God (see also Col 3:23). For children, honoring their parents who gave them life is equivalent to honoring God who is the Lord of life. The apostle Paul testified that obeying one's parents is pleasing to God (Col 3:20). Conversely, people who strike or curse their parents must be put to death according to the law (Exod 21:15, 17; Lev 20:9; Deut 21:18–21). Proverb 30:17 reads, "The eye that mocks a father and scorns a mother, the ravens of the valley will pick it out, and the young eagles will eat it."

Let us examine the central ideas of biblical filial duty.

Children must respect their parents (Lev 19:3). Honoring one's parents becomes the fuel to obeying God's Word in its entirety. Children must respect and honor their parents, and be grateful to them and praise them (Prov 31:28). Joseph was separated from his father at the age of seventeen only to meet him again in Egypt twenty-three years later. There was not one day in those twenty-three years, however, in which Joseph forgot about his father. When his brothers came to Egypt seeking food, Joseph repeatedly asked them if his father was alive and well. Without revealing his identity to his brothers, Joseph asked, "Is your father still alive?" (Gen 43:7). When his brothers returned to buy food with Benjamin, his younger brother, he asked again, "Is your old father well, of whom you spoke? Is he still alive?" (Gen 43:27). Then Joseph revealed himself to his brothers and asked them for the third time, "I am Joseph! Is my father still alive?" (Gen 45:3). Joseph's main concern was his father, whether or not he was alive and well (Gen 45:9–13). When his father and brothers came to settle in Egypt, Joseph gave the best of the land for their possession and provided food for his father and his brothers' households (Gen

47:11–12). After Jacob died at the age of 147, Joseph obeyed Jacob's last wishes (Gen 47:28–30; 49:29–32) and buried him in the cave in the field at Machpelah, which Abraham had bought from Ephron the Hittite (Gen 50:12–14).

Children must obey their parents in all things (Col 3:20). In Colossians 3:20, Paul exhorted, "Children, be obedient to your parents in all things, for this is well-pleasing to the Lord." Here the word "obey" (ὑπακούω, *hypakouō*) means "to listen from under" or "to obey completely." This verb describes the act of a doorkeeper hearing a knock at the door, checking to see who is at the door, and then receiving the guest (Acts 12:13). Furthermore, this verb has a stronger connotation than the word ὑποτάσσω (*hypotassō*), which refers to a wife's submission to her husband. The boundaries of children's obedience are "all things." They do not choose what they want to obey; they are to obey unlimitedly and continuously. Children must listen carefully to their parents' words of enlightenment based on their experiences throughout their long lives. Disobeying after answering yes is far more evil than answering no but repenting afterward (Matt 21:28–31).

In most cases parents pass away before they receive all the filial love they deserve. By the time the children realize this and wish to perform their filial duties, many parents pass away before they get the chance to do so. A German proverb says, "A father maintains ten children better than ten children one father." Another old proverb states, "Although a tree wants to stand still, the wind does not cease to blow; a son wants to fulfill his filial duties, but his parents do not wait for him." Children must make their parents happy while they are still alive (Prov 23:25).

Moreover, when parents age, they undergo both physical and mental changes that young people may find difficult to understand. In some cases parents need help changing their bedpans. Children should help without complaining, remembering the countless times their parents did the same for them when they were born, without feeling burdened. We could not exist today without the sacrifice made by our fathers and mothers. We may find new friends or even a new spouse, but if we ever lose our parents, we will never be able to find another set of parents. Rather than being full of regrets after their passing, let us begin showing our filial devotion today.

Children must obey their parents in the Lord (Eph 6:1). Since the commandments regarding our relationship with God come first within the Ten Commandments, we see that true filial piety is God-centered (Matt 8:21–22; 19:29; Luke 9:59–60; 18:29–30). When we show sincere devotion to our heavenly Father, we can also fulfill our filial duties to our earthly parents with sincerity (Matt 12:47–50; Mark 3:31–35; Luke 8:19–21; 11:27–28). True filial piety must be according to the Scriptures. Serving our parents by following idolatrous customs may appear filial, but it is not proper piety. According to old Korean traditions, children pitch a tent by a parent's grave and lament and mourn for three years. This is valued highly as an act of fulfilling one's filial duties, but it is idolatry. The Bible forbids God's people from making any cuts on their bodies for the dead or grieving as those who have no hope (Lev 19:28; Deut 14:1; see also Jer 22:10; Ezek 24:17; 1 Thess 4:13). Moreover, offering food and performing ancestral rites for dead parents is superstition and the great sin of idolatry (see Ps 106:28–29).

Jesus showed an example of the right way to honor parents. Luke 2:51 narrates about Jesus, "He went down with them and came to Nazareth, and He continued in subjection to them; and His mother treasured all these things in her heart." Here the phrase "continued in subjection" is comprised of the present participial form of the word ὑποτάσσω (*hypotassō*; "to submit, to follow") and an imperfect form of the word εἰμί (*eimi*; "exist, appear"). It implies that Jesus was submissive to His parents voluntarily and continuously.

Even as Jesus hung on the cross shedding blood amid horrible, suffocating pain, He looked upon His mother and said, "Woman, behold, your son!" (John 19:26). It was His third of seven sayings on the cross. These were not words of regret for not being filial but proof that He lived on this earth as a true son. These were weighty and loving last words worth more than a thousand pieces of gold. Jesus called Mary "woman" instead of "mother" at this climactic moment on the cross to fulfill the work of redemption. He had moved their mother-son relationship into a relationship of eternal life between a woman and her Redeemer. This was the moment in which Jesus brought His beloved mother to the order of the redeemed (see Acts 1:14). What could be more filial than this? Then He entrusted her to the apostle John, saying, "Behold, your mother!" (John 19:27).

Establishing one's parents in the order of the saved is the most precious and fundamental filial duty. For us, evangelizing our parents and repaying them with eternal life is the greatest fulfillment of filial duty on this earth.

Filial duty among the Gentiles. Filial piety is a universal moral law of family relationships between parents and children or among siblings. Even from long ago in the gentile world, great laws of filial piety were established as inherent virtues and basic ethics. The "Palbanga" (八反歌, "Eight Contrasting Poems") is the twenty-second chapter of *Myungshimbogam* and consists of eight poems that deal with children's improper attitude toward parents. *Myungshimbogam* (明心寶鑑) is a book edited by a civil official, Chujeok (秋適), about seven hundred years ago, during the Goryeo Dynasty ruled by King Chungryeol (the twenty-fifth king of Goryeo, who reigned from 1274 to 1298 and regained power and ruled again from 1299 to 1308). He collected maxims and wise sayings from Chinese classics for the moral cultivation of students of Korean literature (國學). *Myungshim* means "brightening the heart," and *bogam* means a textbook as "a precious mirror." Thus *myungshimbogam* means "a precious book (textbook) that brightens the heart." The book explains heavenly providence and encourages its readers to reflect upon themselves and preserve their innate human consciences in order to develop noble character.

While Palbanga was written about seven hundred years ago, its content is relevant today as if it had been written about current times. Readers find themselves nodding in agreement with its writings about deeds of unfilial children. The saints who have received the commandment to honor their parents from God, the greatest lawgiver, must not fall short of the standard of the Gentiles. We must humbly learn from gentile beliefs of filial duties and repent from the depths of our hearts for our unfilial deeds and sins.

> When your child complains, you take it with delight.
> Yet when your parents become angry, you resist and do not tolerate them.
> How different you are in the treatment of your child and your parents!
> The next time your parents scold you, think about your child, and change your heart.

> 幼兒或詈我 我心覺懽喜
> 父母嗔怒我 我心反不甘
> 一喜懽 一不甘 待兒待父心何懸
> 勸君今日逢親怒 也應將親作兒看

> You enjoy listening to your children even when they speak a thousand words.
> Yet when your parents speak one word, you say they nag much.
> They are not nagging; they are worried about you.
> They speak from many years of experience, so honor the words of the aged, and do not quarrel with them or rebuke them.

> 兒曹出千言 君聽常不厭
> 父母一開口 便道多閑管
> 非閑管親掛牽 皓首白頭 多諳諫
> 勸君敬奉老人言 莫教乳口爭長短

> While you do not detest your children's feces and urine, you hate the saliva of your aged parents.

Did not your six-foot body originate from your parents' spirit and blood?
Your parents spent their youth for you, and now they are old and withered, so serve them well.

幼兒尿糞穢 君心無厭忌
老親涕唾零 反有憎嫌意
六尺軀來何處 父精母血成汝
體勸君敬待老來人 壯時爲爾筋骨敝

A child went to the market early in the morning to buy bread, which appeared to be so filial.
Later the child was full but the parents had not even tasted the bread.
How does a child's heart fall so short of a parent's love!
Buy much bread, and serve your silver-haired parents, for they do not have much time left on this earth.

看君晨入市 買餅又買餻
少聞供父母 多說供兒曹
親未啖兒先飽 子心 不比親心好
勸君 多出買餅錢 供養白頭光陰少

The pharmacy down the street sells medicine to fatten your child, but they do not have medicine to preserve your parents' health.
People are eager to heal their child's illness, but they neglect their parents' illnesses.
Even if you cut the flesh off your leg, it is your parents' flesh, so I urge you to preserve your parents' lives quickly.

市間賣藥肆 惟有肥兒丸
未有壯親者 何故兩般看
兒亦病親亦病 醫兒不比醫親症
割服還是親的肉 勸君極保雙親命

Wealth makes it easier to serve one's parents, but the parents' hearts never find peace.
Poverty makes it difficult to raise children, but the children never go hungry.
This is because the heart toward parents is not as great as the heart toward children.
Mind your parents as much as you mind your children, and do not ever use poverty as an excuse.

富貴養親易 親常有未安
貧賤養兒難 兒不受饑寒
一條心兩條路 爲兒終不如爲父
勸君兩親如養兒 凡事莫推家不富

Having only two parents, the many children shun their responsibilities and quarrel over who will take care of their parents.
Having ten children, you accept the whole responsibility of taking care of them all alone.
Your children are full, yet you ask them if they are hungry; your parents are hungry and cold, yet you do not worry about them.
Serve your parents as best as you can; what you eat and wear all came from them in the first place.

養親只有二人 常與兄弟爭
養兒雖十人 君皆獨自任
兒飽煖親常問 父母饑寒不在心
勸君兩親 須竭力 當初衣食 被君侵

You do not remember being indebted to 100 percent of your parents' love for you.
Yet you make known 10 percent of children's filial piety.
Since you are slow to serve your parents but quick to mind your children, who can fathom the love of parents who raise their children!

I urge you not to trust your son's filial piety in vain; remember you are both a parent to your children and a child to your parents.

親有十分慈 君不念其恩
兒有一分孝 君就揚其名
待親暗待兒明 誰識高堂養子心
勸君漫信兒曹孝 兒曹親子在君身

Because this world is filled with unfilial children, many parents cry in sadness and shed tears of hurt after they have devoted all they had to their children. Regrettably, the number of unfilial children who disobey, oppose, and even kill their parents is dramatically increasing. It is a sign of the end times (Mark 13:12). In 2 Timothy 3:1–2, Paul said, "Realize this, that in the last days difficult times will come. For men will be lovers of self, lovers of money, boastful, arrogant, revilers, disobedient to parents, ungrateful, unholy" (see Isa 3:5; Rom 1:30).

"That Your Days May Be Prolonged and That It May Go Well with You" (לְמַעַן יַאֲרִיכֻן יָמֶיךָ וּלְמַעַן יִיטַב לָךְ)

Among the Ten Commandments, God added promises of blessing only for the second and fifth commandments. In the second commandment, God promised blessing for thousands of generations (Exod 20:6; Deut 5:10). In the fifth commandment, God said, "Honor your father and your mother … that your days may be prolonged and that it may go well with you on the land which the LORD your God gives you" (Deut 5:16; see also Exod 20:12).

What is intriguing about Deuteronomy 5:16 is that in the Hebrew text the word "that" (לְמַעַן, *lemaan*) appears twice. This verse could be translated literally as "Honor your father and your mother so that your days may be prolonged and so that it may go well with you."

This verse emphasizes that those who honor their parents will receive two blessings: longevity and prosperity.

A prolonged or long life means that life has been extended. The Hebrew text uses the Hiphil (causative) imperfect stem of the word אָרַךְ (*arakh*), which means "to cause to prolong continuously" or "to cause to stay long" (see Deut 4:26, 40; 11:9). Exodus 20:12 speaks of "the land which the LORD your God gives you." Primarily, "the land which the LORD your God gives you" refers to the land of Canaan. Although the land of Canaan was not yet Israel's possession, God had promised it to the Israelites in advance. He then added in the fifth commandment that they would enjoy prolonged lives in that covenanted land if they honored their parents (Eph 6:2–3).

The word "well" in the phrase "that it may go well" is used in the imperfect stem of the Hebrew verb יָטַב (*yatav*), which means "to be good, well, glad, and pleasing." In this tense the phrase means "God will allow one to do well continuously." In Ephesians 6:3, Paul said, "Honor your father and mother ... so that it may be well with you, and that you may live long on the earth." The blessing of success and longevity are promised to those who honor their parents. Conversely, those who break their parents' hearts by abusing them or driving them out will not escape shame and reproach (Prov 19:26). Unfilial children who curse their parents will perish, and their lamps will go out in time of darkness (Prov 20:20).

II. Specific Laws Derived from the Fifth Commandment

Our parents are our mothers and fathers who gave birth to us and raised us. The recipients of our filial duty are our parents. Parents in the fifth commandment refer to biological parents but can also refer to anyone who is above us in age or experience. It especially refers to all our superiors in experience and authority by God's ordinance, whether in one's family, church, or country (Westminster Larger Catechism, question 124). The essence of the fifth commandment is that we must honor only those older people who possess wisdom and authority from experience. Furthermore, the authority holders should behave in a manner worthy of the respect they receive and carry out their obligations and responsibilities as leaders.

The specific laws related to the fifth commandment are in the following passages: Exodus 21:15, 17; 22:28 and Deuteronomy 16:18–20; 17:8–18:8, 15–22; 21:18–21. These verses clarify whom God has designated explicitly as subjects to be respected.

Parents, the Highest Authority Figure in the Family

Moses' law ensured that stubborn and rebellious children who did not obey their parents or accept their discipline would be put to death (Deut 21:18–21). God commanded that any unfilial child be put to death. Exodus 21:15 states, "He who strikes his father or his mother shall surely be put to death," and Exodus 21:17 states, "He who curses his father or his mother shall surely be put to death" (see also Lev 20:9). In these cases the parents must bring the child to the elders of the city at the gate of the city and report, "This son of ours is stubborn and rebellious, he will not obey us, he is a glutton and a drunkard" (Deut 21:20), and the people of the city should stone him to death (Deut 21:18–21). God declared, "Cursed is he who dishonors his father or mother," and all the people were to respond with "Amen" (Deut 27:16).

Leaders with Authority in Society (Adults, Kings, Judges, Officers, Priests, and Prophets)

In the ancient society of Israel, many leaders shared social responsibilities and authority through various official positions. First, there were judges and officers (Deut 16:18–20; 17:8–13). Second, there were kings (Deut 17:14–20). Third, there were the Levitical priests (Deut 18:1–8). Fourth, there were prophets like Moses (Deut 18:15–19). Who must we respect today in light of the fifth commandment?

Adults or the elderly (Lev 19:32). Parents include all who are elders, whether in age, moral influence, knowledge, or experience. Students should respect their teachers, young people should respect their elders, and those in lower statuses must respect those above them. Leviticus 19:32 states, "Rise up before the grayheaded and honor the aged, and you shall revere your God. I am the LORD." "Your father" and "your elders" (Deut 32:7) are the wise who remember the past, the history of God's amazing providence, in which God has fulfilled His covenant (see also Job 12:12). Rehoboam ignored the teachings of the elders who had been advisors of his father, Solomon, and consequently the Israelite monarchy fell apart (1 Kgs 12:6–20).

Superiors in the workplace (Eph 6:5–8; Col 3:22–25; 1 Tim 6:1–2; Titus 2:9–10; 1 Pet 2:18). Since creation, human beings were made to work (Gen 3:17, 19; 2 Thess 3:10). There should be a hierarchical order between the work giver (the master) and the work doers (the stewards) in any workplace. A master has a goal and time limit in mind when he assigns work to a steward. If the steward is lazy, he is basically stealing the master's wealth and time, so he will be judged as a wicked servant (Matt 24:48–51; 25:24–30; Mark 13:34–36; Luke 19:20–26). The Bible teaches that we are to serve our earthly masters as we serve our parents, not by way of eye service but with diligence. Whatever we do, we are to do it with sincerity of heart, "as to the Lord, and not to men" (Eph 6:7; see Col 3:22–23). "Sincerity" in Colossians 3:22 refers to quietly and faithfully submitting to the master (Titus 2:9–10), laboring for the master's gain (Gen 24:12), and caring for the master's possessions as if they were one's own.

National rulers (kings and officials; Rom 13:1–7). Romans 13:1–2 states, "Every person is to be in subjection to the governing authorities. For there is no authority except from God, and those which exist are established by God. Therefore whoever resists authority has opposed the ordinance of God; and they who have opposed will receive condemnation upon themselves." Since God granted officials authority and influence to establish order and peace in each nation, we must submit to the authorities (1 Pet 2:13-14, 17). Even Jesus did not neglect His duty toward the government, saying, "Render to Caesar the things that are Caesar's; and to God the things that are God's" (Matt 22:21).

Fellow workers (brethren; Rom 12:10, 15-16). Honor in the fifth commandment applies not only to elders but also to fellow workers. Parents feel hurt and upset when their children fight in front of them. In Romans 12:10, Paul said, "Be devoted to one another in brotherly love; give preference to one another in honor." We must have humble hearts and regard others as better than ourselves (Rom 12:15-16; Phil 2:2-3; see also 2 Cor 13:11; Phil 4:2). Cooperation and respect for others produce good fruit that pleases God. The tragedy of Cain, the firstborn of the first marriage in human history, was caused by jealousy (Gen 4:3-8; 1 John 3:11-12). A tranquil heart gives life to the flesh, but envy causes the bones to rot (Prov 14:30).

When we cover up our brothers' weaknesses with love and understanding (Prov 17:9; 1 Pet 4:8) and do not complain against one another, we ourselves will not be judged by God (Jas 5:9). We will all stand before God's judgment seat (Rom 14:10). Anyone who casts judgment without love will receive the same judgment; those who do not show mercy will receive judgment without mercy (Matt 7:1-2; Mark 4:24; Luke 6:37-38; Jas 2:13).

Church officials (1 Thess 2:6-12; Heb 13:17). In many places in both the Old and New Testaments, those who nurture others' faith are often called "father." When the prophet Elisha suffered from a fatal disease, Joash, king of Israel, visited him and cried, "My father, my father, the chariots of Israel and its horsemen!" (2 Kgs 13:14). Elisha also called his master Elijah "father" (2 Kgs 2:12). While the apostle Paul was not married (see 1 Cor 7:8), he said, "If you were to have countless tutors in Christ, yet you would not have many fathers, for in Christ

Jesus I became your father through the gospel" (1 Cor 4:15). Timothy, Titus, and Onesimus were sons of the apostle Paul whom Paul had begotten by the gospel (1 Tim 1:2, 18; 2 Tim 1:2; 2:1; Titus 1:4; Phlm 1:10). The apostle Peter also called Mark, whom he had begotten in the faith, "my son, Mark" (1 Pet 5:13). Furthermore, Paul experienced labor pains for the church that had been purchased with the Lord's blood (Gal 4:19; 1 Thess 2:7).

In his epistles the apostle John called the saints his "little children" (1 John 2:1, 28; 3:7, 18; 5:21; see also 3 John 1:4). In Galatians 6:6, Paul said, "The one who is taught the word is to share all good things with the one who teaches him." Thus we must honor those who teach and guide us in the faith just as we honor our physical parents (1 Tim 5:17; Heb 13:17).

The absolute authority above all others, however, is God's authority (Acts 5:29). God is above all parents, kings, and presidents. The holder of the highest authority is He who is in heaven (Eph 6:9; Col 4:1). People with authority, therefore, must not threaten or deceive those below them. They must respect them as children of God and fulfill the responsibilities of people with authority (see Gen 31:7).

III. Evangelical Expansion of the Concept of Honoring Parents

Jesus considered the commandment to honor parents as the essential foundation of faith. He saw the Pharisees and scribes following the elders' tradition regarding *korban* and saying, "I cannot serve my parents, since all I had was given to God" (Matt 15:5-6; Mark 7:11-13). Jesus rebuked them, saying, "Why do you yourselves transgress the commandment of God for the sake of your tradition?" (Matt 15:3).

When Jesus came to His land, Israel, legalists tried to satisfy their desires through traditions using God's holy name. One of these traditions was *korban*. *Korban* (κορβᾶν) is the Greek transliteration of the Hebrew word *korban* (קָרְבָּן; Lev 1:2-3; 2:1; 3:1; Num 7:12-17); it refers to "an offering that is set apart for God." Once a property was declared to be *korban*, that is, given to God, it could not be taken for private use. The religious leaders abused this by bringing the portion meant to help their parents and giving it to God and declaring it *korban*. In this manner they avoided their responsibility to support their parents.

The religious leaders unhesitatingly committed detestable sins in the temple, attempting to deceive the eyes and ears of God, their parents, and the people (Matt 15:5). The extremely corrupt priests forsook God's commandment and manipulated the tradition of *korban* in order to give and accept bribes and accumulate wealth. Seared in their consciences as with a branding iron, they felt no shame.

In Matthew 15:4, Jesus rebuked those who had abolished the fifth commandment, saying, "God said, 'Honor your father and mother,' and, 'He who speaks evil of father or mother is to be put to death'" (see Mark 7:9-13). The leaders had disregarded God's authority, which acknowledged their parents' authority, and destroyed the hierarchy that God had created.

Jesus also said to the rich young man who wished to obtain eternal life, "If you wish to enter into life, keep the commandments" (Matt 19:17). When the rich young man asked Him which commandment he should keep, Jesus answered, "You shall not commit murder; you shall not commit adultery; you shall not steal; you shall not bear false witness; honor your father and mother; and you shall love your neighbor as yourself" (Matt 19:18-19). Jesus said that anyone who sought eternal life must honor their parents and keep the commandments regarding human relationships (Mark 10:19; Luke 18:20). Those who did not honor their parents with whom they were divinely joined could not honor the invisible God.

IV. The Fate of Those Who Violated the Fifth Commandment

Absalom, the Perverse and Rebellious Son to His Father, David

David had nineteen sons—six during his seven-and-a-half-year reign in Hebron and thirteen during his thirty-three-year reign in Jerusalem. He also had another son named Jerimoth as well as other children from concubines (2 Sam 3:2-5; 5:13-16; 1 Chr 3:1-9; 2 Chr 11:18). Among his many sons, Absalom was the most unfilial and he drove a nail into David's heart. Absalom killed David's firstborn son, Amnon, who had raped Absalom's sister, Tamar, and then ran away (2 Sam 13:1-37). Then he tried to usurp David's throne (2 Sam 15:1-30). Moreover, he took his father David's concubines, thus committing an unpardonable atrocity against God and men (2 Sam 16:21-23).

Ultimately Absalom, who had been rebellious against his father, died young. His long hair got caught in the branches of an oak tree as he rode his mule. While he was still alive and hanging from the tree, Joab thrust three spears into his heart, and ten young men surrounded and killed Absalom (2 Sam 18:9-15). They threw his body into a great pit in the forest and piled a great heap of stones over it (2 Sam 18:17).

Joab sent a Cushite messenger to inform David that Absalom, the world's worst unfilial son, had died. When David heard this, he fell into great sorrow and went to the chamber over the gate. He wept and cried aloud. "O my son Absalom, my son, my son Absalom! Would I had died instead of you, O Absalom, my son, my son!" (2 Sam 18:33). Although Absalom was a traitor and a heartless son who faced the death he deserved, the heart of his father sought to spare his son's life even at the cost of his own. This was a display of a father's love that remained unchanged even for a lifetime.

Hophni and Phinehas, the Worthless Sons Who Derided Their Father, Eli

Eli's two sons, Hophni and Phinehas, committed one of the vilest sins ever committed in God's temple when they seduced the women who served at the entrance of the tent of meeting (1 Sam 2:22). As they shamelessly and openly repeated their misdeeds, rumors about their deeds eventually reached Eli's ears (1 Sam 2:23). Eli admonished them, saying, "No, my sons; for the report is not good which I hear the LORD's people circulating" (1 Sam 2:24). Hophni and Phinehas, however, did not listen to their old father (1 Sam 2:25).

Finally, as a man of God had prophesied (1 Sam 2:34), Hophni and Phinehas died on the same day and time during a battle against the Philistines (1 Sam 4:11, 17). Even though they were the sons of the high priest, the supreme leader of Israel, they were in fact worthless men[51] who did not know God and derided their parents (1 Sam 2:12). Their end came about after Israel lost a battle against the Philistines and so brought out the ark of the covenant for the next battle. Israel ended up losing the ark to the Philistines, however, bringing great shame and sorrow upon the nation (1 Sam 4:2-11). When Phinehas' pregnant wife heard that the ark had been captured and that her husband and father-in-law were dead (1 Sam 4:18), the shock brought the pain of childbirth upon her. As she too died, giving birth, she named the child "Ichabod," saying, "The glory has departed from Israel" (1 Sam 4:21).

The Redemptive-Historical Lesson in the Fifth Commandment

Adam violated the fifth commandment in the garden of Eden. God had taught Adam His Word just as a father and mother teach a child. God had entered into the covenant of works with Adam (Gen 2:15-17), and Adam had shared this covenant with the woman. Adam and Eve, however, did not respect God or obey His Word. As a result, they could not live long in Eden and were expelled from the land that God had given them (Gen 3:23–24).

After the exodus, the Israelites opposed Moses, the mediator of God's covenant. Despite their miraculous crossing of the Red Sea, they reproached Moses as soon as worries about water and food arose (Exod 15:22–24; 16:1–3; 17:1–3). Blaming Moses was equivalent to blaming God. Exodus 16:8 states, "Your grumblings are not against us but against the LORD."

The Bible frequently compares God's love to a parent's love and the relationship between God and His people to the relationship between a father and son. To the Israelites in a covenantal relationship with God, God was their "Father" (Deut 32:6; Ps 68:5; Isa 9:6; Jer 3:4, 19; Mal 2:10). Psalm 89:26 reads, "You are my Father," and Isaiah 63:16 states, "You, O LORD, are our Father" (see Isa 64:8). God also calls His covenant people "son" (Exod 4:22–23; Deut 8:5; Ps 82:6; Isa 43:6; 45:11; 49:15; Hos 11:1; Mal 3:17).

As parents love their children, God loves us today as His precious children and protects us as the apple of His eye (Deut 1:31; Isa 49:15; Matt 23:37; Heb 12:5–9).

Jesus, the Son of God, fulfilled the greatest filial piety to God the Father. When Jesus was on this earth, He always called God "Father" (177 times).[52] As the Son, He endured innumerable sufferings in obedience to the Father (Heb 5:8). Jesus obeyed, believing that the Father's command was eternal life (John 12:50). Even as He prayed so earnestly at Gethsemane that His sweat became like drops of blood, He did not pray according to His own thoughts but according to the Father's will and offered up supplication with loud cries and tears (Matt 26:36–42; Mark 14:32–39; Luke 22:39–46; Heb 5:7). From the beginning until the last moment on the cross, where He gave up His body according to God's will, Jesus obeyed completely (Phil 2:6–8).

Jesus taught that the God whom He obeyed was our "Father who is in heaven" (Matt 5:16, 45; 6:1; 7:11; 18:14; 23:9; Mark 11:25; see Matt 5:48). Through the blood of Jesus Christ on the cross, we have become children of God so that we too may call Him "Father" (John 1:12). In Romans 8:14–15, Paul said, "All who are being led by the Spirit of God, these are sons of God. ... You have received a spirit of adoption as sons by which we cry out, 'Abba! Father!'" Similarly, in Galatians 4:6, he said, "Because you are sons, God has sent forth the Spirit of His Son into our hearts, crying, 'Abba! Father!'" People who have been most blessed are those who have God as their Father. Those who have God, who is greater than all (John 10:29), as their Father indeed possess the greatest authority and the most abundant wealth (1 Kgs 3:13; 1 Chr 29:11–12; 2 Chr 1:12; 20:6; Rom 11:36; 1 Tim 1:17; Rev 5:13).

Jesus also forgave and loved His disciples to the end. Jesus was a good teacher and a good father who taught and nurtured Israel's multitudes and His beloved disciples with God's Word (John 10:30; 14:7–11). Indeed, the disciples who followed Jesus' teaching transcended physical bloodlines and joined a heavenly family whose members hoped to live out the Father's will (Matt 12:50; Mark 3:35; Luke 8:21; see also Jer 31:1). During the Last Supper with His disciples, Jesus broke bread and poured wine and said, "This is My blood of the covenant, which is poured out for many for forgiveness of sins" (Matt 26:28; see Matt 26:26–29; Mark 14:22–25; Luke 22:14–20; 1 Cor 11:23–25). Once Jesus was arrested, however, the disciples left Him and ran away (Matt 26:56; Mark 14:50). They were unfilial to Jesus and did not show an inkling of respect. Yet after the resurrection, Jesus warmly embraced the undeserving runaways (John 20:19–29; 21:1). While they deserved to be abandoned, Jesus loved them to the end with *agape* love (John 13:1).

We must be true filial children today to our physical parents, to our spiritual leaders who nurture our faith here on Earth, and to our true Father, God, above.

CHAPTER 20

THE SIXTH COMMANDMENT

You shall not murder.

Exodus 20:13; Deuteronomy 5:17

Exodus 20:13 states, "You shall not murder." This verse in Hebrew is identical to the text in Deuteronomy 5:17. The latter half of the Ten Commandments—the sixth to the tenth commandments—is much shorter than the first half. These five deal heavily with relationships among neighbors. It is noteworthy that the command "You shall not murder" comes first among the latter five.

THE SIXTH COMMAND

You shall not murder.

לֹא תִּרְצָח

Exodus 20:13; Deuteronomy 5:17

I. Exegesis of the Sixth Commandment

The fundamental idea of the sixth commandment, "You shall not murder," is that we must respect all life. The Ten Commandments prioritize the dignity of life above all else. Today, people devalue life and reports of gruesome murder and suicide are unceasing. The command "You shall not murder" highlights the importance of the Ten Commandments in the world in which we live today. We can solemnly obey the command "You shall not murder" when we understand the meaning and value of life.

"Life" (נֶפֶשׁ, חַי)

Life is innate to all living things and the power that sustains them. Every life comes from God (Gen 1:20–31). Thus the Bible describes God as "the fountain of life" (Ps 36:9), "the God of my life" (Ps 42:8), and "God, who gives life to all things" (1 Tim 6:13). Not one sparrow will fall to the ground without permission from God, the sovereign over life (Matt 10:29).

Two Hebrew nouns (*hay* and *nefesh*) and three Greek nouns (*zoeh*, *bios*, and *psyche*) are typically used in the Bible in reference to life.

Hay (חַי) means "living, alive, life." *Hay* is derived from *hayah* (הָיָה, "to live") and occurs about five hundred times in the Old Testament. Generally, it refers to physical life (Deut 28:66). It can also denote the duration of life, lifetime, or livelihood (Gen 27:46; 1 Kgs 4:21). Deuteronomy 30:19–20 states, "I have set before you life [חַי, *hay*] and death, the blessing and the curse. So choose life in order that you may live, you and your descendants, by loving the LORD your God, by obeying His voice, and by holding fast to Him; for this is your life [חַי, *hay*] and the length of your days."

Nefesh (נֶפֶשׁ) means "breathing being, soul, life." The noun *nefesh* is from its cognate verb *nafash* (נָפַשׁ), which means "to take a breath" or "to refresh oneself." Thus the noun means "a creature that breathes, soul, or life." It occurs about 750 times in the Old Testament. *Nefesh* can be used alone to denote "life" (Gen 9:4–5; 19:17; 37:21; Lev 17:11, 14). When written together with *hay* as *nefesh hayah*, however, the phrase means "a living being" (Gen 2:7; see 1:24, 30; 2:19; Lev 11:10, 46; Ezek 47:9).

Zoeh (ζωή) means "life." Zoeh occurs about 135 times in the New Testament and indicates life as the opposite of death, that is, the state of being alive (Luke 16:25; Acts 17:25; Rom 8:38; 1 Cor 3:22; Phil 1:20; Jas 4:14). It refers mainly to the blessed life that created people enjoy as they communicate with God, their Creator. It is new life in Christ (John 1:4), life attained by faith (Rom 6:4; 2 Cor 2:16; Eph 4:18; 1 John 5:12), and eternal life that overcomes death (2 Cor 5:4; 2 Tim 1:10).

Bios (βίος) means "the present life, daily life." Bios generally means "life, lifetime, or the process of life." It can also mean "livelihood, occupation, or property." *Bios* occurs ten times in the New Testament, and each occurrence refers mainly to our present life on the earth (Luke 8:14; 1 Tim 2:2; 2 Tim 2:4; 1 John 2:16).

Psyche (ψυχή) means "life, soul, inner self." Psyche is derived from *psycho* (ψύχω, "to breathe, to blow"), which occurs many times in the Septuagint mainly as a translation of *nefesh*. *Psyche* refers to individual human life (John 12:25; Mark 10:45; Acts 20:10) or to a person's soul, which holds inner life and emotions (Matt 16:26; Luke 1:46; 2:35; 12:20; John 12:27; Heb 10:39; 1 Pet 1:9).

If we divide the created world into three categories—animal kingdom, plant kingdom, and mineral kingdom—we see that human beings clearly possess superior value above all other creatures. This is because God created human beings after His own image (Gen 1:26–27). Genesis 2:7 states, "The LORD God formed man of dust from the ground, and breathed into his nostrils the breath of life; and man became a living being." Only human beings have received God's breath of life and can communicate with Him (Ps 25:14; Prov 20:27). The life activity of humans is made possible by the breath of life that God has breathed into them (Gen 2:7; see also Job 27:3; 33:4; John 20:22).

Originally, our life activity involved more than just physical life, for our souls had fellowship with God and were designed to be eternal (John 5:24; 1 John 5:11).

In Matthew 16:26, Jesus elevated the value of human life over the whole universe by saying, "What will it profit a man if he gains the whole world and forfeits his soul? Or what will a man give in exchange for his soul?" (see Mark 8:36–37). Life is more valuable than the whole world; it is unique and eternal. It bears God's image. It is an eternal life of dwelling with the Lord in the heavenly kingdom forever (1 John 2:25).

"You Shall Not Murder" (לֹא תִרְצָח)

The commandment "You shall not murder" prohibits the killing of precious life. The verb "murder" is רָצַח (*ratsah*) in Hebrew, which originally means "to break in pieces." Murder is so horrific that in the specific laws God even prohibited the eating of an ox that had gored a man or woman to death (Exod 21:28). Since the power to give or take life belongs to God alone (Deut 32:39; 1 Sam 2:6; Matt 10:28; Rom 4:17; Heb 11:19), taking a person's precious life is a blasphemous challenge against God's sovereignty over life. God will surely judge such bloodshed (Ps 9:12) and will not forgive it (2 Kgs 24:4).

The sin of murder includes not only premeditated murder (Exod 21:12, 14) but also the accidental taking of someone's life (Exod 21:13; Deut 19:5; 22:8) as well as the taking of one's own life.

Murder within a community of faith is strictly prohibited, as it destroys peace and order within the community. Defensive killing during war or capital punishment imposed through a legal process, however, does not fall within the category of the sin of murder.

Do not take another person's life. There are various ways to harm a person's life.

First, murder with hands. Joab, the chief commander of David's army, killed Abner, the commander of Saul's army, and Amasa, the commander of Absalom's army (2 Sam 3:27; 20:10), by stabbing them in the stomach. Joab also killed Absalom by taking three spears in his hand and thrusting them through Absalom's heart (2 Sam 18:14).

Second, murder with hatred. Anyone who hates his or her brother, or harbors ferocious hatred toward them, is already a murderer. First John 3:15 states, "Everyone who hates his brother is a murderer; and you know that no murderer has eternal life abiding in him."

Third, murder with the tongue. The Jews killed Jesus with their tongues, that is, by bearing false witness (Matt 26:59–62; Mark 14:55–60; John 18:29–30). The tongue is sharper than the sword (Ps 57:4). James 3:8 testifies, "No one can tame the tongue; it is a restless evil and full of deadly poison."

Fourth, murder with a pen. David wrote a letter to Joab ordering him to kill David's loyal servant Uriah the Hittite. Accordingly, Joab assigned Uriah to the front line on the battlefield so that he could not survive the battle (2 Sam 11:14–17).

Fifth, murder through conspiracy. Saul plotted to kill David at the hands of the Philistines, saying, "My hand shall not be against him, but let the hand of the Philistines be against him" (1 Sam 18:17). Jezebel, Ahab's wife, devised a wicked plan to take Naboth's vineyard away. She hired two worthless men to falsely accuse Naboth so that he would be dragged outside the town and stoned to death (1 Kgs 21:1–16). King Herod called the wise men privately to ascertain what time the star had appeared before them. He sent them away, saying, "When you have found Him, report to me, so that I too may come and worship Him" (Matt 2:8). He pretended that he wanted to worship Jesus, but he was planning a murder in his heart (Matt 2:16).

Sixth, murder by consenting to murder. As Stephen's blood was being shed at his martyrdom, Saul was on the side of those who were killing Stephen and took care of their garments (Acts 7:54–60; 8:1; 22:20).

Seventh, murder with authority. While Pilate was in the seat of authority, he knew that Jesus was innocent (Matt 27:17–18; Luke 23:4, 14–15; John 18:38; 19:4, 6), and he reconfirmed Jesus' righteousness through his wife's dream (Matt 27:19). Nevertheless, he delivered Jesus to the place of death (Luke 23:22–25; John 18:31; 19:10–16).

Eighth, murder through heartlessness. In Jesus' parable a priest and a Levite, having seen a man who had been robbed and was about to die, passed by on the other side of the road. They had already committed murder (Luke 10:30–32; see also Rom 1:31).

Ninth, murder through abortion. Today in the name of "planned parenthood," abortion, that is, removal of God-given life in the womb, has become widespread. Abortion is clearly murder, and assisting it is also a form of murder (see also Job 3:16; Eccl 6:3–4). A baby in the womb is a precious life created by God (Isa 44:2; Jer 1:5; see also Gen 25:23; Luke 1:41, 44). According to the law, anyone who caused a miscarriage by hitting a pregnant woman was guilty of sin and must pay the penalty (Exod 21:22–25).

No one regards his or her own life as trivial (Matt 16:26). We must therefore regard our neighbors' lives as precious as our own and show concern and offer assistance to those in difficult situations. Heartlessness is far from God's will (Prov 21:13; 2 Tim 3:3).

Do not take your own life. The command "You shall not murder" includes taking one's own life. Suicide includes killing oneself both directly and indirectly.

First, killing oneself indirectly. Being entangled with worldly grief and worry kills us indirectly. In 2 Corinthians 7:10, Paul said, "Sorrow of the world produces death." In the parable of the sower, Jesus likened a person weighed down with the worries of the world to a field with thorns (Matt 13:22; Mark 4:18–19; see also Ezek 28:24).

Worries are like thorns that prick and kill. Anxiety for the wrong reasons causes all sorts of diseases. For this reason the apostle Peter encouraged the saints to cast all their anxieties on the Lord (1 Pet 5:7). Worrying is distrusting the Lord who gives life (Matt 6:25). Jesus reminded us that life is more valuable than food and the body more than clothing. God feeds and clothes even the birds of the air and the lilies of the field. Will the heavenly Father not take care of our lives, which are far more valuable than everything in the whole universe (Matt 6:26–30)? The only worries the saints should entertain are about the members of the body of Christ (1 Cor 12:12–27), the church (2 Cor 7:10–11; 11:28–29), and God's will (2 Cor 7:10).

Jealousy also kills us indirectly. Jealousy leads to hatred and is a horrific poison that kills us by rotting the bones (Job 5:2; Prov 14:30; Jas 3:14). Cyprian, the bishop of Carthage, once called jealousy "a secret wound."[53] While anger is expressed outwardly, jealousy settles deep inside the heart, making the blood dry up and the bones rot (Prov 14:30).

When a person's heart becomes full of jealousy, it can lead to ghastly murder (Matt 27:18; Mark 15:10; Acts 5:17–18; 7:9; 13:45; Rom 1:29). It was jealousy that led the religious leaders to crucify Jesus. Matthew 27:18 reads, "He [Pilate] knew that because of envy they had handed Him over."

Jealousy is a devilish, worldly passion that is against God's will (Gen 26:14; 37:11; Num 11:29; 1 Cor 3:3; 2 Cor 12:20; Jas 3:14–15; 1 Pet 2:1). Where jealousy exists, there is only disorder and evil of every kind (Jas 3:16). There can never be prosperity where jealousy is.

> *You lust and do not have; so you commit murder. You are envious and cannot obtain; so you fight and quarrel. You do not have because you do not ask. (Jas 4:2)*

While human jealousy brings murder and conflict, the Holy Spirit's jealousy over us brings life and peace. James 4:5 states, "Do you think that the Scripture speaks to no purpose: 'He jealously desires the Spirit which He has made to dwell in us'?" We must do away with human jealousy and embrace the Holy Spirit's jealousy, which is a yearning to redeem dying souls and a passion for good deeds.

Second, killing oneself directly. Today, many people become pessimistic about their lives and commit suicide. South Korea in particular earned the dishonorable nickname "Republic of Suicide," as it ranked top among all OECD-member countries for its suicide rate for much of the first decade of the 21st century.[54] In 2010, 15,566 people committed suicide in South Korea. That is an average of forty-three people a day, or one person every thirty-four minutes. Suicide is the leading cause of death in South Korea among teenagers and people in their twenties and thirties. The suicide rate for highly educated people also increases every year, and that of the elderly is much higher (2.6 times) than in other countries. Reasons for suicide in this country include mental issues (29.5 percent), disease (23.3 percent), financial problems (15.7 percent), and relationship issues (15 percent) (according to statistics from the Korean National Police Agency). Cases of suicide with unknown reasons are rapidly increasing as well.[55]

Biblical figures also committed suicide. During the battle against the Philistines, Saul, the first king of Israel, refused to die at the Philistines' hands and committed suicide by falling on his own sword (1 Sam 31:1-4). Ahithophel, David's counselor (2 Sam 15:12), conspired with Absalom, but when Absalom did not follow his plan, Ahithophel went home and hanged himself (2 Sam 17:23). Zimri, king of northern Israel, committed suicide by setting fire to the king's palace (1 Kgs 16:18). Judas Iscariot, having sold Jesus, his teacher, for thirty pieces of silver, hanged himself. Falling headlong from the tree on which he hung, his body burst open, and his bowels gushed out (Matt 26:15-16; 27:5; Acts 1:18). What these people share in common is that their lives had nothing to do with God's will.

Today suicide is widely accepted as a global issue. The commandment "You shall not murder" has become more important than at any other time. Our society can eliminate suicide if we can establish a biblical perspective on the value of life and work together to protect and save lives.

We must establish a proper view of life based on the Bible. First, people are noble beings because they are created in God's image. Second, sovereignty over life belongs to God, so no human being has the right to commit suicide. Committing suicide, therefore, is rebellion against God's sovereignty. Third, the human body is the sanctuary in which God's Holy Spirit dwells. We must keep it holy so we can enjoy the inheritance of eternal life (1 Cor 3:16–17; 6:19–20).

II. Specific Laws Derived from the Sixth Commandment

The specific laws derived from the sixth commandment, "You shall not murder" (Exod 20:13; Deut 5:17), are in Exodus 21:12–14, 18–36; 23:4–5 and Deuteronomy 19:1–22:8. It is noteworthy that there are many more specific laws derived from the sixth commandment than from the other commandments (ninety-six verses). Unlike the other laws, this commandment is directly related to life and is thus very important. God established many merciful laws to prevent even a root of murder from sprouting. The sixth commandment is easily overlooked, as people say to themselves, "I would never kill anyone." We must think deeply, however, about how we can be murdered in various unexpected ways and also how we can commit sinful murders in our daily lives.

Premeditated and Unpremeditated Homicides (Exod 21:12–14, 18–36)

Premeditated murder was punishable by death (Exod 21:12, 14). For manslaughter, however, an exception to the provision allowed the murderer to escape to a place designated by God (Exod 21:13).

The laws addressed cases of harm to a neighbor's body (Exod 21:18–32) and damage to another person's property differently (Exod 21:33–36).

Deliverance from Involuntary Manslaughter and the Command to Love One's Neighbors (Exod 23:4–5; Deut 19:1–22:8)

Protect innocent life by designating cities of refuge (Deut 19:1–13). God designated cities of refuge to protect innocent lives. Cities of refuge protected people who had killed unintentionally from those seeking revenge (Deut 19:1–13). This law prevented the shedding of guiltless blood from the evil cycle of revenge and taught people to cherish life.

In the case of premeditated murder, however, God commanded the people to remove the guilt of shedding innocent blood from Israel by handing the murderer over to the avenger of blood without mercy (Deut 19:11–13, 18–21).

Do not move a neighbor's boundary mark (Deut 19:14). The law included the clause, "Cursed is he who moves his neighbor's boundary mark" (Deut 27:17). A boundary mark was a stone pillar placed to mark the boundaries of an individual's property, a region, or the line between countries. Moving this stone was the great crime of stealing another person's property (Job 24:2; Prov 22:28; 23:10; Hos 5:10; see also Isa 5:8). This regulation prohibited the theft of property that a person needed to sustain life.

Remove any dangers from your neighbor's way (Deut 22:8). In consideration of people's neighbors, God's commanded, "When you build a new house, you shall make a parapet for your roof, so that you will not bring bloodguilt on your house if anyone falls from it" (Deut 22:8). This warning was so that they would "not bring bloodguilt on [their] house if anyone [fell] from it" (Deut 22:8). This law of love encouraged people to cherish their neighbors' lives in meticulous consideration.

Actively perform good deeds for your neighbors (Exod 23:4–5; Deut 22:1–4). God commanded the people to return a neighbor's ox or sheep to its owner if they saw that it had gone astray; they must not act as if they had not seen it (Deut 22:1). This commanded people to actively share the responsibility of looking for a neighbor's lost possession until it was found. God also gave detailed instructions for different cases, including even when the owner was unknown.

- The finder was to bring home the animal that had gone astray or the lost property (Deut 22:2).
- The finder was to keep it safe until the owner sought it (Deut 22:2).
- The finder was to take it back to the owner (Exod 23:4; Deut 22:1–2).
- This law applied to *everything* that a neighbor had lost, including an ox, sheep, donkey, or garment (Exod 23:4–5; Deut 22:3–4).
- This law applied not only to the property of neighbors with which one was acquainted but also to the property of strangers, and not only to that of close neighbors but also to that of distant neighbors (Deut 22:2), even to that of enemies and those with whom one was in a hostile relationship (Exod 23:4–5).

These instructions did not take into account the finder's opinion or situation. They only explained in detail the particular situations and conditions of the neighbors who had lost their properties. This law could not be understood or practiced without one putting oneself in the neighbor's place. Indeed, no other law better expresses the essence of the command to love one's neighbor as oneself. This law is entirely different from other laws that distinguish ownership boundaries between a person and his neighbor (e.g., "You shall not covet" or "You shall not steal"). This law is unparalleled in mercy and goodness; God commands the people to voluntarily protect their neighbors and their neighbors' property as if it were their own and to share responsibility for it.

Moreover, this law is recorded not as a simple warning but as a solemn command. God demands His people to practice perfect love, even toward their enemies and those who hate them. Thus the command "You are not allowed to neglect them" appears three times (Deut 22:3; see Deut 22:1, 4). The laws of this world dictate that a person is guiltless as long as he does not harm anyone else. Today it is commonplace for people to pretend not to see when someone has lost money or a belonging. The essence of God's laws, however, is love for our neighbors, and failure to actively practice love (goodness) is considered a sin (Jas 4:17). We must remember Jesus' parable in which the people on His left were sent into eternal fire not because they did evil against other people but because they did not practice the good that they should rightfully have done to the least of them (Matt 25:31–46).

In our society today, people are facing hardships everywhere. Our world is full of lawlessness, and love has grown cold (Matt 24:12). If we neglect our neighbors' troubles or losses, or fail to carry out love toward them, we will be judged in righteousness, since such behavior is also an act of murder (see also Deut 32:4; Pss 89:14; 111:7; 140:12; 146:7).

Do not harm nature (Deut 20:19–20). Murder includes not only the taking of human life but also the destruction of nature. Destruction of nature is considered indirect murder, because it creates an unlivable environment for people. Deuteronomy 20:19–20 states, "When you besiege a city a long time, to make war against it in order to capture it, you shall not destroy its trees by swinging an axe against them; for you may eat from them, and you shall not cut them down. For is the tree of the field a man, that it should be besieged by you? Only the trees which you know are not fruit trees you shall destroy and cut down, that you may construct siegeworks against the city that is making war with you until it falls." The forest is directly related to human life, as people survive on fruit trees and many other benefits that the forest provides. Since forests are essential to human survival, they must not be cut down in haste. Even in dire situations such as war, God sternly commanded the people not to cut down the forest, especially its fruit trees. Even if the enemy was hiding in the forest, the trees must not be cut down, and the land must not be devastated in order to capture the enemy.

Concerning the conquest of Canaan, God said, "I will drive them out before you little by little, until you become fruitful and take possession of the land" (Exod 23:30; see Deut 7:22). God did not chase out the Canaanites all at once, for He did not want the land to "become desolate and the beasts of the field become too numerous" for the Israelites who would dwell in the land (Exod 23:29; see Deut 7:22).

III. Evangelical Expansion of the Concept of Murder

Types of Murder According to Jesus' Teaching

> *You have heard that the ancients were told, "You shall not commit murder" and "Whoever commits murder shall be liable to the court." But I say to you that everyone who is angry with his brother shall be guilty before the court; and whoever says to his brother, "You good-for-nothing," shall be guilty before the supreme court; and whoever says, "You fool," shall be guilty enough to go into the fiery hell. (Matt 5:21–22)*

Being angry toward a brother. The word "angry" is ὀργίζω (*orgizō*) in Greek; it means "to become furious" or "to become enraged." It refers to continuous wrath with malice and intent to harm others. Hating others and causing them to feel aggrieved is the same sin as shedding those peoples' blood (1 John 3:15). Although no actual blood is shed, causing a neighbor to shed tears is equivalent to murder. As the saying "Anger is the mother of murder" states, there is a high possibility that hatred and anger will lead to murder. Joseph's brothers hated him because their father loved him (Gen 37:4). They hated him all the more when Joseph spoke of his dreams (Gen 37:5, 8). When Joseph told them about his second dream, they became envious (Gen 37:11) and ultimately conspired to kill him (Gen 37:18). The brothers stripped Joseph of his colorful robe and threw him into a pit (Gen 37:23–24). While Joseph begged them for his life (Gen 42:21), they sat idly and ate their meals (Gen 37:25). They then sold Joseph to the Ishmaelites for twenty shekels of silver and deceived their father by telling him that Joseph was dead (Gen 37:27–28, 31–32).

Hatred itself is the sin of murder. First John 3:15 states, "Everyone who hates his brother is a murderer; and you know that no murderer has eternal life abiding in him." The work of life cannot occur in a heart full of hatred. Proverbs 27:4 reads, "Wrath is fierce and anger is a flood, but who can stand before jealousy?" Thus we must not let the sun go down while we are still angry (Eph 4:26).

Defaming a person's character. The word ῥακά (*rhaka*), which means "stupid" or "moron," was often used in ancient times to insult someone. Jesus designated the usage of such words as murder.

Insulting someone is the act of killing with words. In Romans 3:13, Paul said, "Their throat is an open grave." People lie with their tongues, and venom drips from their lips (Rom 3:13). Their mouths are filled with cursing and bitterness (Rom 3:14). Furthermore, their feet rush to shed the blood of the innocent (Rom 3:15; Isa 59:7). "The tongue of the wise" brings healing (Prov 12:18), joy, and pleasure (Prov 15:23; 23:16; 27:9), but the evil tongue is a killing sword and poisonous (Pss 59:7; 64:3; Jas 3:8). It is a scorching fire that can destroy a person's entire life (Prov 16:27; Jas 3:6). This is why life and death depend on the tongue (Prov 18:21). God's solemn judgment, like a warrior's sharp arrow, will come upon "deceptive tongues" (Ps 120:2–4). Jesus said, "I tell you that every careless word that people speak, they shall give an accounting for it in the day of judgment" (Matt 12:36–37). Thus whoever desires life and loves to see good days must keep his tongue from evil (Ps 34:12–13; 1 Pet 3:10). Those who are careful with their mouths and tongues will preserve their lives and even rescue themselves in times of trouble (Prov 12:13; 13:3; 21:23).

Sitting in God's seat to condemn others. The word "fool" (μωρός, *mōros*) means "faithless" or "unbelieving." The term was used in ancient times to refer to people who denied God. People who use this word place themselves in God's seat and thoughtlessly condemn other people as "those who are to be judged" (see also 2 Tim 2:23). Jesus declared that people who sit in God's seat to condemn others are murderers. Thus judging other people's faith is not within human jurisdiction but God's. Condemning others from God's seat, therefore, could be considered the sin of murder.

Ways to Prevent Murder

Seek the good of others. The command "You shall not murder" includes the command to do one's best to preserve other people's lives as well as one's own. If we can apply this in our everyday lives, all sins of murder will disappear from us.

Preserving other people's lives means that we seek the good of others over our own. In 1 Corinthians 10:24, the apostle Paul encouraged his readers, saying, "Let no one seek his own good, but that of his neighbor." First Corinthians 10:33 states, "I also please all men in all things, not seeking my own profit but the profit of the many, so that they may be saved" (see 1 Cor 13:5). Those who are strong must be considerate of the weak rather than thinking only about themselves (Rom 15:1–2). This is the essence of seeking the good of others.

Be slow to anger. Anger disrupts a person's focus and peace of mind. It causes a person to lose control and become like an unreasoning beast and fail to make proper judgments. In Genesis 49:6, Jacob said of Simeon and Levi, "In their anger they slew men, and in their self-will they lamed oxen." Those who are quick to anger without waiting for God's rich administration of grace to unfold will bring evil upon themselves and fail to achieve His righteousness.

James 1:19–20 states, "Everyone must be quick to hear, slow to speak and slow to anger; for the anger of man does not achieve the righteousness of God." Similarly, Proverbs 16:32 reads, "He who is slow to anger is better than the mighty, and he who rules his spirit, than he who captures a city."

Anger gives the devil a great opportunity to sneak in (Gen 4:5–7). Even Moses, who was meeker than anyone in the world (Num 12:3), could not enter the land of Canaan because he had become angered by the Israelites' grumblings and struck the rock twice (Num 20:10–12; Deut 1:37; 3:23–27; 34:1–8; Ps 106:32–33).

When David returned after defeating Goliath the Philistine commander, King Saul was enraged at the women who sang, "Saul has slain his thousands, and David his ten thousands" (1 Sam 18:7). He began to fear losing the throne to David (1 Sam 18:8). As resentment captivated his heart, an evil spirit came upon him (1 Sam 18:10) that led him to throw a spear at David in an attempt to kill him (1 Sam 18:11).

Make peace with your brother, and quickly reconcile. Jesus taught, "If you are presenting your offering at the altar, and there remember that your brother has something against you, leave your offering there before the altar and go; first be reconciled to your brother, and then come and present your offering" (Matt 5:23–24). He continued, "Make friends quickly with your opponent at law while you are with him on the way, so that your opponent may not hand you over to the judge, and the judge to the officer, and you be thrown into prison" (Matt 5:25).

Not once did Jesus become angry with Judas Iscariot. Instead, He urged him many times to repent. Jesus' love is indeed deeper than the sea and wider than the sky and unfathomable to the human mind. Jesus prayed continuously for the forgiveness of those who were crucifying Him (Luke 23:34). As the mediator of peace between God and the world (Eph 2:11–18), He sacrificed Himself as a propitiation for our sins (Rom 3:25; 1 John 2:2). Furthermore, He gave us the ministry of reconciliation (2 Cor 5:18) and entrusted us with the message of reconciliation (2 Cor 5:19). Indeed, it is impossible to prevent murder by human effort alone; we absolutely need the help of God's grace.

IV. The Fate of Those Who Violated the Sixth Commandment

We find many brutal and horrific murder cases in the Old and New Testaments. Cain, who killed his brother, Abel, was the very first murderer (Gen 4:8). Lamech, Cain's descendant, killed a young man because of a small wound inflicted upon him (Gen 4:23-24). At the time of Moses' birth, the Egyptian Pharaoh killed the Israelite boys (Exod 1:15-16, 22). During the period of the judges, Abimelech, one of Gideon's sons, killed sixty-nine of his seventy brothers, except for Jotham, the youngest one, in order to rule over Shechem (Judg 8:30-31; 9:5). Upon King Saul's command, Doeg killed all in the land of Nob—eighty-five priests as well as men, women, and even babies—based on the false accusation that they had helped David escape (1 Sam 22:18-19). Joab killed Abner, who had killed his brother Asahel (2 Sam 3:27), and Amasa, who had joined Absalom's rebellion (2 Sam 20:10). Having lain with Bathsheba, Uriah's wife, David sent Uriah to the forefront of the battlefield, where he would die so David could hide his sin (2 Sam 11:1-17, 26-27). Absalom commanded his servants to kill his half-brother Amnon, who had violated his sister, Tamar (2 Sam 13:28). Ahab and his wife, Jezebel, hired false witnesses against Naboth so that Naboth would be stoned to death and they could seize his vineyard (1 Kgs 21:7-15). Hazael, a servant of Ben-hadad, king of Aram, killed Ben-hadad and became king in his place (2 Kgs 8:15).

Athaliah, the wife of Jehoram, king of Judah, was the daughter of Ahab and Jezebel. When her son King Ahaziah went to see the wounded King Joram of Israel, he was killed by Jehu. Athaliah then killed all David's royal offspring except for Joash, who was hidden by Jehosheba, and made herself queen (2 Kgs 11:1-3; 2 Chr 22:10-12).

Herod the Great ordered a large-scale massacre of all boys under the age of two at the time of Jesus' birth in order to kill the Messiah (Matt 2:16). Herod Antipas beheaded John the Baptist, who had rebuked him for his immoral marriage to Herodias, the wife of his brother Phillip (Matt 14:6-11; Mark 6:16-28). The religious leaders and chief priests in the New Testament era, as well as the inhabitants of Jerusalem, killed Jesus, who had come to His own land as the Messiah (Matt 26:59-68; 27:15-26; John 19:14-16; Acts 13:27-28). They also stoned Stephen to death (Acts 7:57-60). Herod Agrippa I murdered James, the brother of the apostle John (Acts 12:1-2).

Of these cases we will take a closer look at the first murderer, Cain, Adam's firstborn, and the murder committed by Ahab and Jezebel during the age of the divided kingdom.

The Murderer Cain, Who Killed Righteous Abel

Cain became angry when God received Abel and his offering but rejected Cain and his offering (Gen 4:3-6). Dr. Shin-Theke Kang translates Genesis 4:6 as, "And Yahweh told Cain, 'Why is anger in you? And why are your countenances fallen (to the ground)?'" God sought Cain and earnestly warned him to control the embers of sin in his heart, that is, the desire of sin (Gen 4:7). Cain, however, deliberately led his brother, Abel, to the field and secretly stuck him to death (Gen 4:8).

When God asked Cain, "Where is Abel your brother?" Cain lied to Him, saying, "I do not know. Am I my brother's keeper?" (Gen 4:9). However, the voice of Abel's blood appealed to God from the ground, which had opened its mouth to receive his blood (Gen 4:10-11). Thus God punished Cain, saying, "When you cultivate the ground, it will no longer yield its strength to you; you will be a vagrant and a wanderer on the earth" (Gen 4:12).

Cain shamelessly complained that his punishment was too harsh and that he could not bear it (Gen 4:13-14). God showed His mercy even to Cain by giving him a mark so that he would not be killed by anyone he met (Gen 4:15). Eventually, however, Cain turned his back on God and left to settle in the land of Nod, east of Eden (Gen 4:16).

The Murderers Ahab and Jezebel, Who Killed Righteous Naboth

Ahab, the king of the northern kingdom of Israel, and Jezebel, his wife, wickedly killed Naboth and moved a boundary mark using their power (see also Job 24:2; Prov 22:28; 23:10; Isa 5:8; Hos 5:10). When Ahab could not buy Naboth's vineyard, he returned to his palace and lay on his bed, vexed and sullen, and refused to eat (1 Kgs 21:1-4). Jezebel, seeing her husband vexed, devised an abominable plot to kill Naboth using false witnesses. The false witnesses accused innocent Naboth of cursing God and the king to cause him to be stoned to death outside the city. Upon Naboth's death, Ahab seized his vineyard (1 Kgs 21:5-16).

God then sent the prophet Elijah to meet Ahab to prophesy about how miserably Ahab and his descendants would die (1 Kgs 21:17-29): "In the place where the dogs licked up the blood of Naboth the dogs will lick up your blood, even yours" (1 Kgs 21:19). This prophecy was fulfilled during the battle of Ramoth-gilead when Ahab took an arrow and died. The dogs indeed licked up Ahab's blood from his chariot when it was being washed by the pool of Samaria (1 Kgs 22:34-38). The prophecy against Ahab's descendants (1 Kgs 21:21) was fulfilled later, during Jehu's rebellion, when Jehu destroyed the whole family of Ahab, including Joram, Ahab's son, and Jezebel, Ahab's wife (2 Kgs 9:24-26, 30-37; 10:1-11, 15-17).

It is what comes out of the mouth that defiles a person. In Matthew 15:18-19, Jesus said, "The things that proceed out of the mouth come from the heart, and those defile the man. For out of the heart come evil thoughts, murders, adulteries, fornications, thefts, false witness, slanders." Here Jesus said that murder is one of the sins that defile a person. Also, in the book of Revelation, murder is one of the sins for which the survivors of the plague of the sixth trumpet did not repent (Rev 9:20–21). According to Revelation 21:8, murderers will enter into "the lake that burns with fire and brimstone," and Revelation 22:15 testifies that they will be outside the New Jerusalem.

V. The Redemptive-Historical Lesson in the Sixth Commandment

Adam committed a sin similar to violating the sixth commandment in the garden of Eden. The woman not only ate the fruit from the tree of the knowledge of good and evil, but she also gave it to her husband so that he ate it and also died (Gen 3:6). Because Adam, who represented all mankind, violated the covenant of the works, death came and spread to all humanity (Rom 5:14; 6:23). Romans 5:12 states, "Just as through one man sin entered into the world, and death through sin, … so death spread to all men, because all sinned."

During Jesus' time the religious leaders did not understand the Lord's teachings. In John 8:37, Jesus pointed out, "I know that you are Abraham's descendants; yet you seek to kill Me, because My word has no place in you." Not understanding the Word and not receiving Jesus is equivalent to killing Jesus (John 7:19). Before His crucifixion Jesus said to the religious leaders, "You are of your father the devil, and you want to do the desires of your father. He was a murderer from the beginning" (John 8:44). It came about just as Jesus had spoken: the religious leaders, who were controlled by the devil, the murderer, killed Jesus.

Yet, while Jesus was on the cross, He prayed for these murderers, saying, "Father, forgive them; for they do not know what they are doing" (Luke 23:34). Even the most heinous murderer will be forgiven if he believes in Jesus and repents (Acts 2:38; see also Matt 12:31; Mark 3:28).

Today, we commit the sin of murder when we hate anyone or carelessly pass judgment upon anyone within our faith communities (1 John 3:15). We must be careful what we say to others, as the words we speak can kill or give others life (Prov 18:20–21; Jas 3:8). It is a grave sin to judge others, condemn them, and spread vicious rumors about them without knowing the real facts. Jesus said, "I tell you that every careless word that people speak, they shall give an accounting for it in the day of judgment. For by your words you will be justified, and by your words you will be condemned" (Matt 12:36–37; see Rom 2:1). Those who desire life and love to see good days must control their tongues and stop speaking evil and deceitful words (1 Pet 3:10).

CHAPTER

21

The Seventh Commandment

You shall not commit adultery.

Exodus 20:14; Deuteronomy 5:18

Exodus 20:14 states, "You shall not commit adultery." Its Hebrew text is the same as in Deuteronomy 5:18.

THE SEVENTH COMMAND

You shall not commit adultery.

לֹא תִּנְאָף

Exodus 20:14; Deuteronomy 5:18

I. Exegesis of the Seventh Commandment

The seventh commandment, "You shall not commit adultery," is an important commandment that preserves the sanctity of the family created by God. Adultery is the sin of breaking a sound marriage by engaging in an extramarital relationship. It is a fatal sin that destroys families established by God and stands in the way of God's redemptive history. The gravity of the sin of adultery is evident in Joseph's speech: "How then could I do this great evil and sin against God?" (Gen 39:9). Job also said of adultery, "That would be a lustful crime; moreover, it would be an iniquity punishable by judges. For it would be fire that consumes to Abaddon, and would uproot all my increase" (Job 31:11-12).

The Original Husband and Wife (the Primordial Couple) (תְּמוֹל אִשָּׁהוְאִישׁ)

God established the family as the building block of God's kingdom, and the seventh commandment teaches us the dignity of the family. Because the family is the basic unit of the covenant community, the family must be holy before a society or a nation can be holy. The consecration of the family depends on the sanctity of the couple in marriage. Adultery, therefore, is a potent poison that instantly destroys the family that God has established. Just as we understood the gravity of the sin of murder by defining the dignity of life, so we can realize the gravity and fearfulness of adultery by understanding the dignity of the family (a married couple).

A husband and wife share an unbreakable relationship in flesh and blood. All nations and individuals living today are descendants of the divinely consecrated couple (Adam and Eve). Genesis 2:24 reads, "A man shall leave his father and his mother, and be joined to his wife; and they shall become one flesh." The word "joined" (דָּבַק, *davaq*) means "to cling" or "to keep close." According to God's principle of creation, the marital relationship is closer and stronger than even the parent-child relationship. Concerning its degree of kinship, one's spouse is one's closest relative. Adam said in Genesis 2:23, "This is now bone of my bones, and flesh of my flesh; she shall be called Woman, because she was taken out of Man." Thus a couple has the most compactly united relationship of any other on the earth (Matt 19:6; Mark 10:9).

A husband and his wife are not two but one. In a marriage a man and a woman are united and "become one flesh" (Gen 2:24). Matthew 19:6 states, "They are no longer two, but one flesh. What therefore God has joined together, let no man separate." Henceforth, a real "one person" can neither be just one woman or just one man in the biblical sense. When a man and a woman become one flesh, they become "one person" in God's eyes. The apostle Paul also speaks about this in 1 Corinthians 6:16, saying, "The two shall become one flesh," and he repeats it in Ephesians 5:31, saying, "A man … shall be joined to his wife, and the two shall become one flesh." When a man treasures his wife and loves her, he loves himself. Ephesians 5:28 states, "He who loves his own wife loves himself," and 1 Peter 3:7 states, "You husbands, in the same way, live with your wives in an understanding way, as with someone weaker, since she is a woman; and show her honor as a fellow heir of the grace of life."

The husband and his wife were both naked but were not ashamed. Genesis 2:25 attests, "The man and his wife were both naked and were not ashamed." "Shame" is an unnatural and unstable mental state caused when someone loses holiness by forgetting God's Word and sinning (see Ezra 9:5; Jer 17:13). As long as Adam and Eve held onto God's Word to them as the center of their lives, they never felt shame and were always filled with joy. They were clothed with the fullness of God's glory (see Rom 10:11; 13:14). Yet although the first couple and the first family were noble, shame came upon them after the fall because of their sins. Realizing their nakedness, they made loin coverings with fig leaves (Gen 3:7). When they heard the voice of the Lord, they hid themselves from Him among the trees of the garden (Gen 3:8).

A harmonious family is a loving nest, a resting place, and the foundation of happiness. An individual's happiness, the church's growth, and a nation's prosperity and peace stem from a harmonious family. Our God is the God of the family (Jer 31:1). God's administration of redemptive history will be fulfilled through sanctified families (Mal 2:15). A couple paired by God must love one another; the sin of not loving one another becomes the origin of ten thousand sins. We must be contrite and repent deeply if we have not managed our families properly (1 Tim 3:2, 5, 12; 5:8; Titus 1:6).

Committing "Adultery" (נָאַף)

Adultery refers to an extramarital affair, a sexual relationship with a person besides one's spouse, or being unfaithful to one's spouse. The definition itself is unpleasant and something people want to avoid discussing. Adultery severs a body that has become one, destroys the family, and topples the foundation of God's kingdom. Adultery is a grave sin, as it destroys the covenant made with God, who established the family (see Gen 39:9; 2 Sam 12:7-14). Thus faithfulness and purity in a marriage are far more critical than anything. Faithfulness is more valuable than life, as broken faith destroys life and desecrates the holiness of the family. A family with broken faith can neither give birth to good children nor adequately train their children.

God is a pure and holy spirit, so He casts out all impurity. The Hebrew word for "adultery" in both Exodus 20:14 and Deuteronomy 5:18 is נָאַף (*naaf*). This word is different from זָנָה (*zanah*), which refers to every type of improper sexual relations. The Bible uses the word *naaf* with two connotations.

Sexual relations outside marriage (Lev 20:10; Jer 29:23; Hos 4:13–14). God strictly prohibited adultery in order to preserve the sanctity of the family, which is the fundamental unit of the covenant community (Prov 6:29). Leviticus 20:10 states, "If there is a man who commits adultery with another man's wife, one who commits adultery with his friend's wife, the adulterer and the adulteress shall surely be put to death." Proverbs 6:32 also states, "The one who commits adultery with a woman is lacking sense; he who would destroy himself does it."

Adultery as the idolatry of the covenant people of Israel (Jer 3:6–9; 5:7–9; Ezek 23:36–37; Hos 4:12–14). When Moses received the two stone tablets on Mount Sinai, Aaron, along with the Israelites, made a golden calf and worshiped it and offered sacrifices. Exodus 32:6 narrates, "The next day they rose early and offered burnt offerings, and brought peace offerings; and the people sat down to eat and to drink, and rose up to play." Here, the expression "play" is a translation of the Hebrew word צָחַק (*tsahaq*), which implies "sexual behavior" when it occurs in its Piel (intensive) stem (Gen 39:14, 17). Thus the Israelites committed adultery as they worshiped the golden calf.

The Bible defines idolatry as a wife abandoning her husband and engaging in an unfaithful and adulterous act. The Bible likens the relationship between God and Israel to that of husband and wife. This is because the covenantal relationship is intimate, noble, sacred, and personal, just like a marriage. The prophet Ezekiel also likened the relationship between God and His covenant people of Israel to the relationship between a husband and his wife (Ezek 16, 23). In Isaiah 54:1–8, God said of Himself, "Your husband is your Maker" (Isa 54:5). Thus if Israel worshiped an idol, it was an act of adultery against God, her husband. Expressions such as "play the harlot with their gods" appear quite often in the Bible (Exod 34:15–16; Lev 17:7; 20:5; Deut 31:16; Judg 2:17; Jer 3:9; Ezek 6:9). The prophet Isaiah called idolatrous Israel the "offspring of an adulterer and a prostitute" (Isa 57:3). Worshiping other gods, therefore, is like a prostitute abandoning her husband to commit adultery. It is a double violation of both the first and seventh commandments.

II. Specific Laws Derived from the Seventh Commandment

The meaning of the seventh commandment, "You shall not commit adultery" (Exod 20:14; Deut 5:18), is expanded and explicated in Exodus 22:16-17, 19 and Deuteronomy 22:9-23:18. God gave various specific laws against adultery to preserve the sanctity of the family and the marriage.

Prohibition of Incestuous Marriage (Lev 18:6-18; 20:11-14, 17, 19-21; Deut 22:30; 27:20, 22-23)

According to the law, if a man took both a woman and her mother, all three must be burned to death (Lev 20:14). Furthermore, the law strongly prohibited having sexual relations with one's mother (Lev 18:7), stepmother (Lev 18:8; 20:11; Deut 22:30; 27:20), sister or half-sister (Lev 18:9; 20:17; Deut 27:22), granddaughter (Lev 18:10), stepsister (Lev 18:11), aunt (Lev 18:12-13; 20:19), uncle's wife (Lev 18:14; 20:20), daughter-in-law (Lev 18:15), brother's wife (Lev 18:16; 20:21), or mother-in-law (Deut 27:23). It also prohibited sexual relations with both a woman and her daughter or granddaughter (Lev 18:17).

Moreover, the law cursed anyone who had sexual relations with an animal (Exod 22:19; Lev 18:23; 20:15-16; Deut 27:21). Also, if a man had sexual relations with another man as with a woman, both men must be put to death (Lev 18:22; 20:13; see also Gen 19:5; Rom 1:27). If a man had sexual relations with a woman during her menstrual period, both the man and the woman were to be cut off from among the people (Lev 18:19; 20:18).

These improper sexual acts were abominable practices that had spread throughout the land of Canaan at the time. It was a reflection of how corruption had peaked among the inhabitants of Canaan. Thus God commanded the Israelites to possess a conscious awareness of their sanctity and preserve it by not intermarrying with Canaan's inhabitants. He solemnly warned them that if the Israelites engaged in unclean and abominable sexual acts in the land of Canaan, the land would spew them out as it had spewed out the nations that had dwelt in the land before them (Lev 18:24–30).

Preservation of the Purity of Marriage and of Chastity (Deut 22:13–21)

Certain specific laws protected a woman from a man who took her as his wife, lay with her, and then falsely accused her of not being a virgin in order to cast her away. The law allowed a man to abandon a woman, a new bride, who was not found a virgin. If a man married a virgin and had relations with her and then falsely charged her with shameful deeds because he hated her, the woman's parents had to show evidence of her virginity (a garment that one spread on the bed on the first night of marriage to prove virginity; Deut 22:17) to the elders of the city. If the woman was proven to be a virgin, the elders were to chastise the man who had falsely charged his wife with shameful deeds and fine him a hundred shekels of silver, which were to be given to the wife's father. The man could not divorce her all his days (Deut 22:13–19). If the newlywed bride could not show evidence of her virginity, however, the elders were to bring the woman to her father's house, and the men of the city were to stone her to death. This was because by playing the harlot in her father's house, she had committed evil within Israel (Deut 22:20–21). God preserved purity and faith within the marriage in order to establish proper order within the family, society, and the entire people of Israel.

Prevention of Sexual Crimes (Deut 22:22–29)

First, if a man committed adultery with a married woman, both the man and the woman were put to death (Deut 22:22).

Second, if a man met a betrothed virgin in the city and had sexual intercourse with her, both the man and the woman were brought out to the gate of the city and stoned to death (Deut 22:23–24).

Third, if a man raped a betrothed woman in the field (an unpopulated area), only the man would be put to death (Deut 22:25–27).

Fourth, if a man was found in the act of lying with a non-betrothed virgin, the man had to give the woman's father fifty shekels of silver and take the woman as his wife. He could not divorce her for the rest of his life (Deut 22:28–29; see also Exod 22:16–17).

For God, the purity of the body for a married couple is as important as their lives. In any period in history, when chastity in marriage was lost, society became corrupt and sick. By encouraging mutual trust and transparency concerning chastity in married couples, God maintained the holiness of the entire people of Israel, whom He had consecrated among the nations (Lev 20:23–24, 26).

The Law of Jealousy (Num 5:11–31)

The "law of jealousy" (Num 5:29) was a way to remove a husband's doubt about his wife's chastity. When a wife had committed adultery but there was no evidence of it (Num 5:13), or when a husband doubted his wife even though she was innocent (Num 5:14, 30), the husband had to bring his wife to the priest so that he could perform the rite to prove her innocence or guilt. Unlike the law that punished those caught at the scene of adultery, this law reflects God's understanding of human weaknesses (inclination to doubt and become jealous; Num 5:14) and limitations (limited knowledge of hidden facts; Num 5:13) as He sought to preserve consecrated families. Through this law God prevented husbands from doubting without evidence and allowed wives to live without their chastity in question. The purity of a family could not be preserved without the law of jealousy, which put doubt to rest.

A husband's doubt about his wife's adultery could have triggered harsh feelings and even abnormal aggression, which could have led him to force his innocent wife to make a false confession. On the contrary, without this law, an adulterous wife might have cunningly asserted her innocence.

The law of jealousy began with offering a "grain offering of jealousy" to remind the people of their iniquity (Num 5:15). A priest entrusted with God's authority performed this grain offering, and the procedure was solemn and intricate. This reflected the importance of this offering, as it was a matter of life and death for each family and for Israel.

The procedure to prove a wife's innocence or guilt was as follows (Num 5:11–31):

- The priest drew the woman near to stand before the Lord (Num 5:16).
- The priest took holy water in a vessel (Num 5:17).
- The priest took some dust from the tabernacle floor and put it into the water (Num 5:17). The dust was a reminder of sorrow and death (Exod 8:16–17; Josh 7:6; Job 2:12–13; 30:19).
- The priest allowed the woman to untie her hair and then placed in her hands the grain offering of memorial, which was the grain offering of jealousy (Num 5:18). The offering contained a tenth of an ephah of barley flour (about 2.34 liters) without oil or frankincense in it (Num 5:15). Untying one's hair was an expression of unworthiness, extreme sorrow, and despair (Lev 10:6; 13:45; 21:10).
- The priest held in his hand the water of bitterness that brought the curse (Num 5:18). "The water of bitterness" (מֵי הַמָּרִים, *me hammarim*) did not speak merely of its bitter taste but of the bitter effect of the curse and judgment that would be upon sinners. This water was the "water that [brought] a curse" (5:22, 24, 27) or the "water of bitterness that [brought] a curse" (Num 5:18, 24).
- The priest made her take an oath (Num 5:19–22).

- The priest wrote the curses in a scroll and washed them off in the water of bitterness (Num 5:23).
- The priest took the grain offering of jealousy from the woman's hand, waved it before the Lord, and brought it to the altar (Num 5:25). The priest took a handful from the grain offering as its memorial portion and burned it on the altar (Num 5:26).
- The priest made the woman drink the water of bitterness that brought the curse (Num 5:24, 26).
- They waited for the result of drinking the bitter water of the curse. If the woman was innocent, she would be free from the curse and would conceive children (Num 5:28). If she was guilty, however, her womb would swell and her thigh would waste away (Num 5:27), and she would be a curse among the people (Num 5:27). The womb swelling referred to a miscarriage with the accumulation of fluid in the abdomen or severe edema of the body. The word "thigh" is a euphemism for the female reproductive organ (see Gen 24:2, 9). Thus the expression "thigh will waste away" implied sexual dysfunction or the curse of infertility.

If the wife's chastity was proven, the curse did not return to her husband who had doubted her. Numbers 5:31 states, "The man will be free from guilt." This is because the husband had entrusted all his problems to God's law, ultimately to pursue purity and peace in the family.

God demonstrated several things by establishing the law of jealousy: First, God preserved the family's purity by preventing obscure doubts that could destroy the family. Second, unlike the judges of this world, God can expose sin even when there is no evidence of it and render His judgment upon it (Num 5:13, 27). Hidden iniquities were brought to light, as nothing can escape the sight of the righteous God. Third, God strictly dealt with adultery so that His dwelling place maintained absolute purity.

Prohibition of Male or Female Cult Prostitutes (Deut 23:17–18)

God commanded, "None of the daughters of Israel shall be a cult prostitute [קְדֵשָׁה, *qedeshah*], nor shall any of the sons of Israel be a cult prostitute [קָדֵשׁ, *qadesh*]" (Deut 23:17). God strongly prohibited cult prostitutes among the men and women of Israel. The religions of the nations surrounding Israel used male and female prostitutes in sexual rituals to meet with their gods (see Gen 34:31; 38:21–22). Claiming that they were making offerings while in a sexually ecstatic state, they attracted people passing by with their lustful dances and words and led them to perform obscene sexual acts. These prostitutes were often called temple prostitutes, both male and female. The people of Judah actually built a house for male cult prostitutes in the temple of God for their enjoyment (2 Kgs 23:7). Such practices were prevalent under the reign of Rehoboam, Solomon's son (1 Kgs 14:24), as well as under Abijam and Asa (1 Kgs 15:12; 22:46). They disappeared temporarily during Josiah's time through his reformation (2 Kgs 23:7). The prophet Hosea accused the people in his days, who were engrossed with committing adulterous acts without a sense of guilt, and prophesied God's fierce judgment upon them (Hos 4:11–19).

Furthermore, God said, "You shall not bring the hire of a harlot or the wages of a dog into the house of the LORD your God for any votive offering, for both of these are an abomination to the LORD your God" (Deut 23:18). God delights in clean offerings from wages properly earned through sweat and labor.

Historically, male and female prostitution has undermined the sexual morality of the family, the fundamental building block of society. It has also corrupted God's temple and shaken the root of innocent people's faith. Indeed, it is a great warning for the church today. Just as it had been in the past, many church pastors and congregations put on a pretense of faith. Yet in reality they seek after sensual pleasure and thirstily pursue filthy thoughts and deeds like animals. Hence, Revelation 2:22–23 warns, "Behold, I will throw her on a bed of sickness, and those who commit adultery with her into great tribulation, unless they repent of her deeds. And I will kill her children with pestilence, and all the churches will know that I am He who searches the minds and hearts; and I will give to each one of you according to your deeds."

Prohibition of Harlots (Lev 19:29)

Leviticus 19:29 commands, "Do not profane your daughter by making her a harlot, so that the land will not fall to harlotry and the land become full of lewdness." Here, the word "harlot" (זָנָה, *zanah*) referred to people who engaged in sexual activity for payment. This was God's way of preserving the sexual purity of Israel's women. The act of making one's daughter a prostitute reflected the parents' evil intentions. Such an obscene and vile custom could spread so fast and so powerfully that it could engulf the whole country and bring about its eventual collapse. Rumors like "She is having an affair!" or "He is having an affair!" are sounds that can shatter the sacred family and bring about the nation's destruction. This is why God strictly forbade everything related to prostitution (see Prov 7:1–27).

Prohibition of Inappropriate Clothing (Deut 22:5)

God clarified gender identity by forbidding a woman to wear a man's clothing and a man from wearing a woman's clothing. Not wearing clothing according to one's gender was an abomination before God.

> *A woman shall not wear man's clothing, nor shall a man put on a woman's clothing; for whoever does these things is an abomination to the LORD your God. (Deut 22:5)*

Cloak (שִׂמְלָה)

① **A casual outer garment made from one piece of square cloth**
Exod 22:26-27; see also Matt 21:7-8

② **Made of wool**
"You shall not wear a material mixed of wool and linen together" (Deut 22:11).

③ **Used as a blanket at night**
"You shall surely return the pledge to him, that he may sleep in his cloak" (Deut 24:13).

④ **Used as a wrap to carry things**
Exod 12:34; Judg 8:25

A round opening at its top
Exod 28:32; 39:23

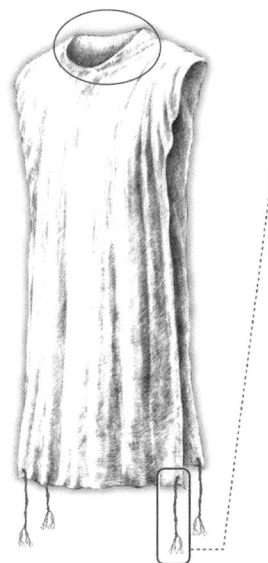

Places for tassels: tassels added on the four corners of the cloak
"You shall make yourself tassels on the four corners of your garment with which you cover yourself" (Deut 22:12).

Tassels

① ***Gadil*** (גְּדִל) — "You shall make yourself tassels on the four corners of your garment with which you cover yourself" (Deut 22:12).

② ***Chiychit*** (צִיצִת) — "Tell them that they shall make for themselves tassels on the corners of their garments" (Num 15:38).

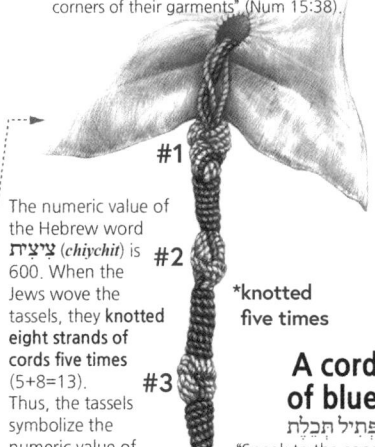

#1
#2
*knotted five times
#3

A cord of blue
פְּתִיל תְּכֵלֶת
"Speak to the sons of Israel, and tell them that they shall make for themselves tassels on the corners of their garments throughout their generations, and that they shall put on the tassel of each corner a cord of blue" (Num 15:38).

#4
#5

The numeric value of the Hebrew word צִיצִת (*chiychit*) is 600. When the Jews wove the tassels, they **knotted eight strands of cords five times** (5+8=13). Thus, the tassels symbolize the numeric value of **613**, which corresponds to the six hundred thirteen articles of the law.

"It shall be a tassel for you to look at and remember all the commandments of the Lord, so as to do them and not follow after your own heart and your own eyes, after which you played the harlot,[40] so that you may remember to do all My commandments and be holy to your God" (Num 15:39-40).

*eight strands of cord (including one blue cord)

God established clear boundaries regarding appropriate clothing for men and women so as to remove detestable sins from both society and the family. In doing so, He preserved sexual purity and prevented prevented the people from committing adultery.

Commandment to Hang Tassels on the Four Corners of One's Garments (Num 15:37–40; Deut 22:12)

Through the law God gave instructions on the shape and form of the garments to be worn by the consecrated people of Israel, especially for outer garments worn outside the house rather than those worn in the home. The purpose was not simply for external appearance. It was a reminder to the covenant people of their sacred identity and mission whenever they wore their cloaks or looked upon each other's cloaks. Their ordinary cloaks (שִׂמְלָה, *simlah*) were usually square-shaped outer coverings woven out of wool in one piece without seams (Exod 22:26–27). It was fashionably worn as a cloak or shawl during the day and served as a blanket at night. It had an opening on the top for the head (see Exod 28:32; 39:23). Moreover, it was thick enough so that people could use it as a wrap to carry things (Exod 12:34; Judg 8:25; Matt 21:7–8).

Through the specific laws, God forbade His people from wearing garments woven of two kinds of materials, wool and linen, mixed together (Lev 19:19; Deut 22:11). He also instructed them to make tassels on the four corners of their cloaks. Deuteronomy 22:12 specifies, "You shall make yourself tassels on the four corners of your garment with which you cover yourself." The "tassel" in Hebrew is גָּדִל (*gadil*). The word is derived from גָּדַל (*gadal*), meaning "to twist," because the tassels were made of twisted threads (1 Kgs 7:17).

The word "tassel" in Numbers 15:37–40 is צִיצִת (*tsitsith*) in Hebrew. Like *gadil*, tassels were flower-shaped ornaments on the corners of the cloaks, which symbolized that the law was the flower of life.

God gave special instructions in Numbers 15:38, saying, "Speak to the sons of Israel, and tell them that they shall make for themselves tassels on the corners of their garments throughout their generations, and that they shall put on the tassel of each corner a cord of blue." The high priests wore blue robes under their ephods (Exod 28:31; 39:22). The cord of blue, therefore, one of the threads for the tassel, probably reminded the Israelites of their identity as a kingdom of priests (see Exod 19:6).

The numeric value of the Hebrew word *tsitsith* is 600. Eight additional strands of cord were tied with five knots so that the total numerical value of the tassels was 613 (600 + 8 + 5). The value 613 was equivalent to the total number of articles of the law, so it was a reminder of the Word of God and a motivation to obey all the laws. In Numbers 15:39–40, God said, "It shall be a tassel for you to look at and remember all the commandments of the LORD, so as to do them and not follow after your own heart and your own eyes, after which you played the harlot, so that you may remember to do all My commandments and be holy to your God." Here in the phrase "your own heart and your own eyes, after which you played the harlot," the word "harlot" (זָנָה, *zanah*) describes the sinful inclination of the eyes and the heart. Whenever people looked upon the tassels, they would think about the laws of God and were less inclined to commit adultery. Human beings are forgetful; they hear the Word of God but easily forget it. They are weak; they know the Word but lack the strength to obey it. God knew these weaknesses and gave His people the tassel as a reminder of His Word. In Jesus' day the religious leaders enlarged their tassels for display and distorted the tassles' intended purpose. Jesus pointed out their hypocrisy and cursed them seven times and sternly rebuked them and judged them (Matt 23:5–7, 13–36).

Even today the importance of our outer garments is obvious. The law gave the Israelites tassels to remind them of God's Word and of their identity as His people. Likewise, our outer clothing today should exude the fragrance of God's Word, our faith, and grace (2 Cor 2:15–16).

More important, however, is the invisible garment of the inner self, which is the garment of those entrusted with God's Word. If their cloak is stripped off, they will be no different from criminals and fugitives, much like Adam and Eve when they realized that they were naked and became terrified (Gen 3:7–10; see also Isa 20:4; Amos 2:16; Mark 14:51–52). They will also find themselves in a state similar to pitiful debtors (Job 22:6; 24:9–10; Prov 20:16; Ezek 18:7, 16; Amos 2:8).

People with a mission always wore their garments (1 Sam 2:18–19; 18:4). The blue-colored robe that the high priests wore under their ephods was called "the robe of the ephod" (Exod 28:31; 29:5; 39:22). Moses clothed Eleazar with Aaron's robe to signify that the high priesthood was being passed down (Num 20:25–28). In obedience to God's command to make Elisha the prophet in his place, the prophet Elijah cast his cloak upon Elisha (1 Kgs 19:16, 19). When Elijah was taken to heaven, Elisha took Elijah's cloak and performed miracles (2 Kgs 2:8–14). During King Hezekiah's time, the tunic of Shebna the treasurer was put on Eliakim as a symbol of the impending transition of power from Shebna to Eliakim (Isa 22:15, 20–21).

We who have been baptized into Christ must be clothed with Jesus Christ (Gal 3:27). Our salvation is nearer to us than when we first believed, so we must cast off our garments of darkness and the garments of the flesh that desires after lust and put on the garments of light (Rom 13:11–14).

III. Evangelical Expansion of the Concept of Adultery

Lust in the Heart

Expanding the definition of adultery, Jesus clarified that harboring lustful thoughts was also adultery, not just the physical act itself. In Matthew 5:27–28, He said, "You have heard that it was said, 'You shall not commit adultery'; but I say to you that everyone who looks at a woman with lust for her has already committed adultery with her in his heart." Here the verb "looks" is a translation of a present active participial form of the Greek word βλέπω (blepō), which connotes not merely "to see" but "to observe closely." Thus even without physical relations, anyone who observes a woman intently with lust in his heart has committed adultery. This means that it is the heart that motivates adultery. Jesus explained that the eyes that stimulate the heart and even the fingertips that arouse sensory nerves are subject to God's judgment. He resolutely commanded, "If your right eye makes you stumble, tear it out and throw it from you ... If your right hand makes you stumble, cut it off and throw it from you" (Matt 5:29–30). He precisely pointed out that unless the motive of adultery is uprooted from the heart, it will be difficult for anyone to avoid committing adultery.

Proverb 6:29 states of "the one who goes in to his neighbor's wife" that "whoever touches her will not go unpunished." Thus the apostle Paul said in Ephesians 5:3, "Immorality or any impurity or greed must not even be named among you, as is proper among saints." Sexual immorality is the path to the chambers of death (Prov 7:24–27).

In our world today, we are bombarded with stories of sexual molestation of children and sexual assault unimaginable as human beings. The Bible offers the best advice to avoid committing adultery: we are to flee from sexual temptation (1 Cor 6:18; 2 Tim 2:22). When Potiphar's wife attempted to seduce Joseph day after day, his response was to *flee* from the situation (Gen 39:7–12). The fact that the Bible instructs us to flee from such situations rather than overcome them hints at how difficult it is for human beings to actually overcome the temptation to commit adultery. As the second coming of the Lord draws near, we must keep away from temptations and the sins of sexual immorality. We must strive to keep our bodies, souls, and spirits pure, without spot or blemish, before the Lord (Eph 5:27; 1 Thess 3:13; 5:23; 2 Pet 3:14).

Improper Divorce (Destruction of the Family)

Jesus declared that wrongful divorce is also adultery. In Matthew 5:31–32, He said, "It was said, 'Whoever sends his wife away, let him give her a certificate of divorce'; but I say to you that everyone who divorces his wife, except for the reason of unchastity, makes her commit adultery; and whoever marries a divorced woman commits adultery." In light of Jesus' teaching, divorcing a wife when she has not committed adultery is the grave sin of making both the divorced woman and any man who marries her commit adultery.

Jesus declared, "What therefore God has joined together, let no man separate" (Matt 19:6). The Pharisees argued, "Why then did Moses command to give her a certificate of divorce and send her away?" (Matt 19:7). Jesus answered, "Because of your hardness of heart Moses permitted you to divorce your wives; but from the beginning it has not been this way" (Matt 19:8). Here the phrase "from the beginning" comes from the Greek words ἀπ' ἀρχῆς (*ap archēs*), which denote "from the first" or "originally." Jesus used the fundamental principle of creation to declare that adultery not only involves engaging in sexual activities to fulfill one's sexual lust but also includes abandoning one's wife to marry another woman (Matt 19:9).

Originally, sex was God's blessing upon married couples so that they can share their love and preserve the human race through the family so that they may subdue the earth. However, when people misuse sex only for fleshly pleasure, they commit the grave sin of destroying the order of God's creation and opposing His redemptive administration. Thus Hebrews 13:4 states, "Marriage is to be held in honor among all, and the marriage bed is to be undefiled; for fornicators and adulterers God will judge." The sin of adultery not only defiles one's body, but it is also closely related to spiritual corruption. "Every other sin that a man commits is outside the body, but the immoral man sins against his own body" (1 Cor 6:18). Hosea 5:4 states, "A spirit of harlotry is within them." Our bodies do not belong to us (1 Cor 6:19); they were bought with a price, so we must glorify God with our bodies (1 Cor 6:20) and serve the church, the body of Christ, with all our hearts. Our bodies are instruments of righteousness (Rom 6:13). First Corinthians 6:13 says, "The body is not for immorality, but for the Lord, and the Lord is for the body."

IV. The Fate of Those Who Violated the Seventh Commandment

The history of the Old and the New Testaments shows that adulterers were strictly judged (2 Pet 2:10). God will judge the adulterers and the sexually immoral (Heb 13:4). Adultery was one of the reasons for the fall of Sodom, Gomorrah, and their surrounding cities (Jude 1:7). Revelation 2:22 states, "I will throw her on a bed of sickness, and those who commit adultery with her into great tribulation, unless they repent of her deeds." Those who do not repent for their sin of adultery will certainly be subject to God's judgment (Rev 21:8; 22:15).

Among the sins in the Bible that are punished by death, many of them pertain to the specific laws associated with the seventh commandment regarding the sin of adultery (Exod 22:19; Lev 20:10–16; Deut 22:22–25; see also Lev 18). Furthermore, history shows that a countless number of people have been killed because of adultery. Proverbs

7:25–26 states, "Do not let your heart turn aside to her ways, do not stray into her paths. For many are the victims she has cast down, and numerous are all her slain."

Adultery with the Moabite Women in Shittim of Moab

The temptation to commit adultery was the last temptation Israel underwent just before entry into Canaan. Numbers 25 contains the record of the events at the end of the forty-year wilderness journey while the people were in Shittim awaiting entry into the promised land (1407 BC). The Moabite women seduced the Israelites into eating sacrifices offered to the Moabite gods. The Israelites bowed down to these gods, thereby yoking themselves to Baal of Peor (Num 25:1–3). While God commanded Moses to kill all the chiefs of Israel, Moses killed only those who had yoked themselves to Baal of Peor (Num 25:4–5). To make matters worse, Zimri, the chief of the Simeonites, shamelessly brought a Midianite woman named Cozbi into his tent in the sight of Moses and the whole congregation (Num 25:6). Phinehas, the son of Eleazar the son of Aaron, saw that Zimri had brought Cozbi into his tent. Phinehas stood up among the congregation, took a spear in his hand (Num 25:7), and went after Zimri into the tent (Num 25:8). He publicly killed both Zimri the Israelite and Cozbi the Midianite woman (Num 25:14-15) by piercing their bellies with a spear (Num 25:8). At this time a plague, which had killed twenty-four thousand people, was stopped (Num 25:9; see also twenty-three thousand people in 1 Cor 10:8).

Phinehas was jealous with God's jealousy (Num 25:11) and killed the two adulterous people and made atonement for Israel (Num 25:13). Through his righteous act, he received God's covenant of peace that bestowed perpetual priesthood upon his descendants (Num 25:12-13). The Bible testifies that a Phinehas' act was righteous and deserved to be acclaimed throughout the generations (Ps 106:28–31). Phinehas had the zeal of God (see 2 Cor 11:2). He regarded God's enemy as his own enemy. We are often too generous when we deal with sin. The Bible tells us, however, to fight against sin to the point of shedding blood (Heb 12:4). If we tolerate sin, become indifferent to it, or consent to it, sin will eventually swallow us (2 Pet 2:19).

Israel's sin of sexual immorality with the Moabite women at Shittim was so grave that both the Old and New Testaments make frequent reference to the event (Num 31:16; Deut 4:3–4; 23:3–6; Ps 106:28–31; Hos 9:10; 1 Cor 10:8).

The Moabite women seduced Israel's men to eat food offered to their idols and have sexual relations with them. This led the Israelites to turn away from God and sin against Him by worshiping Baal. The Gentiles lusted after (played harlot with) the Moabites' gods for fertility and prosperity (Exod 34:15–16; Lev 17:7; 20:5; Deut 31:16; Judg 2:17; 1 Chr 5:25; Jer 3:9; 23:10; Ezek 6:9; Hos 4:12). The Israelites' tragic deaths with the promised land of Canaan in sight was the result of their idolatry and adultery. They had been seduced by the Moabite women, first to eat, then to bow down to their gods (Num 25:2), and ultimately to play the harlot with the women (Num 25:1). As a result, twenty-four thousand Israelites died of the plague. The consumption of food sacrificed to Moabite gods and the act of bowing down to these gods demonstrate the depth of Israel's proactive participation in the sacrificial rites (see Ps 106:28; Rev 2:14). The apostle Paul warned that eating sacrifices offered to idols is no different from idolatry itself (1 Cor 10:14, 18–21).

David, Who Saw Uriah's Wife (Bathsheba) and Lay with Her

David coveted Bathsheba, the wife of Uriah the Hittite, one of his commanders. Israel was in the middle of a war against Ammon (2 Sam 11:1). While Uriah the Hittite kept the law regarding abstinence during the battle (2 Sam 11:11; see Deut 23:9–11), David violated it. One late afternoon David came out from his bed and walked on the roof of his palace. From the roof he saw a beautiful woman bathing and brought her to himself and lay with her (2 Sam 11:2–4). When he heard that she was pregnant (2 Sam 11:5), David caused her husband Uriah's death by deploying Uriah to the frontlines so that David's sin would not be exposed (2 Sam 11:6–25). God, however, exposed David's sin through the prophet Nathan. Nathan said to David, "Why have you despised the word of the LORD by doing evil in His sight? You have struck down Uriah the Hittite with the sword, have taken his wife to be your wife, and have killed him with the sword of the sons of Ammon" (2 Sam 12:9). In response to David's sexual immorality and his sin of taking a neighbor's wife, God declared that the sword would never leave David's house. Through a great misfortune in his house, David's wives would be given to another and raped in broad daylight (2 Sam 12:10–11).

Just as God had spoken, He made David pay retribution for his sin of sexual immorality (2 Sam 15:13–33). Just as the prophet Nathan had prophesied—"The child also that is born to you shall surely die"—so the Lord struck the baby born to David through Uriah's wife so that it became severely sick and died (2 Sam 12:14–23). After receiving Nathan's rebuke regarding his shameful adulterous sin of coveting Uriah's wife (2 Sam 12:1–4), David repented with a broken spirit and drenched his bed and blanket with his tears (Pss 6:6; 51). Throughout his life David did what was right before the Lord except in the matter of Uriah the Hittite (1 Kgs 15:5).

The Miserable End of Those Who Committed Incest

In the Old and the New Testaments, those who committed incest were cursed or faced miserable deaths. Reuben lay with his father Jacob's concubine Bilhah (Gen 35:22) and was cursed with the loss of his birthright (Gen 49:3–4; 1 Chr 5:1).

Absalom lay with his father David's concubines in a tent pitched on the roof of the palace (2 Sam 16:21-22). Later, when his long hair was entangled in the oak tree and his body was hanging in the air, Joab stabbed his heart, and ten other young men surrounded him and struck him to death (2 Sam 18:9-15).

Adonijah asked King Solomon for the young and beautiful concubine Abishag the Shunammite (1 Kgs 1:1-4), whom their father David had taken in his old age. For this he was killed at the hands of Benaiah, who had been sent by Solomon (1 Kgs 2:13-25).

The apostle Paul greatly rebuked the church of Corinth when he heard that someone had lain with his father's wife and committed incest, which was prohibited even among the Gentiles (1 Cor 5:1-3). The church rebuked the sinner greatly to the point that they said of him, "Deliver such a one to Satan" (1 Cor 5:5). The apostle Paul called those who practiced sexual immorality "the unrighteous" (1 Cor 6:9) and emphasized that they would not inherit the kingdom of God (1 Cor 6:9-10; Gal 5:19-21; Eph 5:5). First Corinthians 5:9 and 11 command the people not to engage in fellowship with such people or eat with them.

Moreover, besides the sin of not keeping the Sabbath, the sins of idolatry and sexual immorality were rampant in Israel. These sins were the reasons for the destruction of the southern kingdom of Judah and its deportation to Babylon in 586 BC (Ezek 16:23-43). The people's sexual immorality exceeded that of Sodom and Samaria (Ezek 16:47-52). It provoked God's wrath (Ezek 16:26) until Judah finally met with the complete destruction of its kingdom.

The Bible tells us how potent the poison of adultery is. First, it is a sin committed against one's own body (1 Cor 6:18). Second, it destroys one's soul and brings one dishonor, disgrace, and unwashable shame (Prov 6:32-33). Third, an adulterer cannot inherit the kingdom of God (1 Cor 6:9-10; Gal 5:19-21). Fourth, an adulterer becomes one with the body of a prostitute and cannot be a dwelling place for the Spirit of God (1 Cor 3:16-17; 6:15-19). Fifth, adultery leads to poverty and the loss of precious life at the hands of the adulteress (Prov 6:26; Luke 15:13). Sixth, the final destination of adultery is the chamber of death (Prov 5:3–6; 7:27). Seventh, the adulterer will have his or her place in the lake that burns with fire and brimstone (Rev 21:8) and will be outside the city in shame (Rev 22:15).

V. The Redemptive-Historical Lesson in the Seventh Commandment

Adam's sin in the garden of Eden was equivalent to the violation of the seventh commandment. Adam and Eve lost their hearts to the fruit of the tree of the knowledge of good and evil when they ate it. All the trees in the garden were pleasing to the sight and good for food (Gen 2:9, 16), and the tree of life was the tree that made one wise (Gen 3:22; Prov 3:18). Yet the tree of the knowledge of good and evil seemed to them also a source of wisdom, implying that their hearts had fallen for the tree after the serpent had seduced them. People who spiritually or mentally give their hearts to anything other than God are committing adultery. James 4:4 reads, "You adulteresses, do you not know that friendship with the world is hostility toward God? Therefore whoever wishes to be a friend of the world makes himself an enemy of God." Spiritual adultery is being closer to the world than to God.

In the account of the wedding feast at Cana, the apostle John introduced Jesus as the true bridegroom (John 2:1–11). John the Baptist introduced himself as a friend of the bridegroom while making clear that the one who takes the bride as his wife is the bridegroom (Jesus; John 3:28–29). Similarly, the apostle Paul introduced himself as a matchmaker between Christ and believers when he said, "I betrothed you to one husband, so that to Christ I might present you as a pure virgin" (2 Cor 11:2). Jesus also testified of Himself that He was the bridegroom, saying, "The attendants of the bridegroom cannot mourn as long as the bridegroom is with them, can they? But the days will come when the bridegroom is taken away from them, and then they will fast" (Matt 9:15; see Mark 2:19–20; Luke 5:34–35). Furthermore, in Matthew 25:1–13, in His parable Jesus likened the saints preparing for His second coming to ten virgins who went to meet the bridegroom. Revelation 19:7–8 says, "The marriage of the Lamb has come and His bride has made herself ready. It was given to her to clothe herself in fine linen, bright and clean; for the fine linen is the righteous acts of the saints." Blessed are those who are invited to the wedding feast of the Lamb (Rev 19:9). The one hundred forty-four thousand who will stand on Mount Zion with the Lamb (Rev 14:1) will not have "been defiled with women" (Rev 14:4). They will not have worshiped the beast and will have kept the commandment of God and their faith in Jesus to the end (Rev 14:12). Those who do not accept Jesus the bridegroom are all committing spiritual adultery (see Eph 5:31–33).

Chapter 22

The Eighth Commandment

You shall not steal.

Exodus 20:15; Deuteronomy 5:19

Exodus 20:15 reads, "You shall not steal." Its Hebrew text is identical to Deuteronomy 5:19.

THE EIGHTH COMMAND

You shall not steal.

לֹא תִּגְנֹב

Exodus 20:15; Deuteronomy 5:19

I. Exegesis of the Eighth Commandment

"Steal" (גָּנַב)

The eighth commandment, "You shall not steal," prohibits the violation of a neighbor's property rights. Stealing applies not only to visible properties but also to invisible ones, including a neighbor's life and wellbeing. Everyone, once born into this world, begins to have his or her own possessions. This commandment teaches us to cherish our neighbors' possessions in the same way we cherish our own. The sixth commandment teaches about the dignity of a neighbor's life, the seventh about the dignity of a neighbor's family, and the eighth about the dignity of a neighbor's possessions.

While thieves have existed in every era, no one is born a thief. Thieves, however, make up an overwhelming percentage of prisoners compared to other criminals. Yet from the perspective of God's commandment, there are more thieves outside prison than inside. That is to say, many people have had their consciences seared (1 Tim 4:2) and do not feel guilty even after stealing other people's property.

The word "steal"(גָּנַב, *ganav*) means "to sweep off, take away by stealth, deceive." There are two types of stealing.

Cruelly seizing or forcefully taking a neighbor's possessions. Stealing is taking another person's possessions (anything under someone else's ownership) without the owner's permission. It is the act of seeking personal benefit, even if it violates someone else's rights. A neighbor's possessions include property such as money, male and female servants, clothing, livestock, grains, and jewelry (Exod 22:1-15). Borrowing money and not paying it back is stealing. Psalm 37:21 states, "The wicked borrows and does not pay back, but the righteous is gracious and gives."

Deceiving a neighbor's eyes and doing something in stealth. Doing something in stealth to deceive others is also considered stealing (Gen 31:7, 27). Stealing can be defined as cunningly luring someone into a trap for one's own benefit or acting stealthily. Deceiving someone is stealing, even if the act does not cause financial loss. Peeking at someone's property is also stealing. Furthermore, not working hard to perform one's duties during the time appointed for work, being lazy, and doing irrelevant things are stealing. God has equally distributed the wealth of time to all people; it is His gift. Anyone who uses time positively and works hard will obtain great wealth on this earth and enjoy an eternal inheritance. Anyone who is lazy or uses time for evil will fall into poverty. Wasting the short time God has entrusted to us in our finite lives on this earth is also a sin (Ps 90:4–5, 12; Eph 5:15–17); this is robbing from oneself. Proverbs 6:10–11 reminds us, "'A little sleep, a little slumber, a little folding of the hands to rest'—your poverty will come in like a vagabond and your need like an armed man" (see also Prov 24:33–34).

II. Specific Laws Derived from the Eighth Commandment

The eighth commandment, "You shall not steal" (Exod 20:15; Deut 5:19), is expanded and explained in Exodus 21:16 and 22:1–15 as well as in Deuteronomy 23:19–24:7.

Compensation Laws for the Loss of or Damage to a Neighbor's Property (Exod 21:16; 22:1–15)

The specific laws derived from the eighth commandment included detailed instructions on compensation for the various cases involving property theft. The Hebrew word for "to make good" (שָׁלֵם, *shalem*) means "to finish, to complete, to fulfill, to restore" (Lev 24:18; 1 Kgs 9:25). This means that a debtor was to pay back the debt and restore the property of the creditor. Only after payments and compensations were fully made could all things be restored to their original condition, achieving the beautiful peace (שָׁלוֹם, *shalom*) that is most pleasing to God.

In this respect Jesus taught, "If you are presenting your offering at the altar, and there remember that your brother has something against you, leave your offering there before the altar and go; first be reconciled to your brother, and then come and present your offering" (Matt 5:23–24). When harmony with one's neighbor has been broken through theft or deception, God will not receive the person's worship, because he or she is in an imperfect, broken state. Once the worshiper makes compensation and reconciles with the neighbor, however, God will receive the offering as a pleasing sacrifice.

There are compensation laws for stolen property and the damage caused by stealing.

Kidnapping and abduction (Exod 21:16). Exodus 21:16 states, "He who kidnaps a man, whether he sells him or he is found in his possession, shall surely be put to death" (see Deut 24:7). The phrase "kidnaps a man" refers to human trafficking, especially kidnapping with the intent to enslave a person. In this case the kidnapper was to make compensation with his or her own life.

Theft of a neighbor's property (Exod 22:1-4). When an ox or sheep was stolen and killed or sold, the thief was to repay five times the value of the ox and four times the value of the sheep (Exod 22:1). An ox is bigger and wilder than the smaller, tamer sheep, so stealing an ox would have required meticulous planning and boldness. Consequently, the crime was considered more heinous, and compensation for an ox was higher. If the stolen animal was found alive, however, the thief only repaid double the animal's value (Exod 22:4). If the thief could not afford to make the payment, he was to raise the money to make restitution, even if he needed to sell himself (Exod 22:3). Compared to the restitution law's standard (Exod 21:22-27), this compensation law for theft was severe and harsh. Nevertheless, such harsh punishment for theft taught the Israelites to protect their neighbor's property and to earn their own wealth through hard labor. These laws ultimately played a crucial role in preventing theft within Israel's society.

If a thief broke into a home in the night and was killed, it was not considered murder. If the thief was killed during the day, however, the house owner was guilty of murder (Exod 22:2-3). This is because struggling with a thief at night could easily lead to murder, as it was difficult to recognize the enemy or defend oneself during the night. Although both cases involved killing and death, punishment was applied differently depending on whether the killing had occurred during the day or the night. This is a reflection of God's great love and desire to protect even the life of a criminal.

Damage to a neighbor's property due to improper management of livestock or due to fire (Exod 22:5-6). Except for cases in which an animal accidentally grazed in another person's field, if the owner of livestock intentionally brought the livestock to someone else's field to feed them, the law states, "He shall make restitution from the best of his own field and the best of his own vineyard" (Exod 22:5). The word "best" (מֵיטָב, *mytav*) originates from יָטַב (*yatav*), which means "to be good, to be excellent, to be pleasing" (Judg 19:6), and it refers to the most excellent or best part of something (Gen 47:6; 1 Sam 15:9, 15).

Furthermore, Exodus 22:6 states, "If a fire breaks out and spreads to thorn bushes, so that stacked grain or the standing grain or the field itself is consumed, he who started the fire shall surely make restitution." Here "thorn bushes" are not referring to naturally grown thorns but those that a landowner had planted to mark his field's boundaries. The law commanded proper restitution if a person started a fire and burned up a neighbor's field and fruit trees that were ripe for harvest, causing significant financial loss to his neighbor.

Damage to an entrusted property (Exod 22:7-9). In ancient times people customarily entrusted their valuables to their neighbors before going on long trips. This law was for cases in which these entrusted valuables were stolen. If the thief was caught, the thief had to repay the original owner double the item's value (Exod 22:4). The person who had been entrusted with the valuables was not held responsible (Exod 22:7). If the thief was not caught, however, the person to whom the valuables were entrusted was suspected of taking the items. He had to stand before a judge and undergo an investigation to determine whether he had taken the items (Exod 22:8). Regardless of what the items were, if the original owner pointed to certain items and said, "This is mine that I lost," and there was a dispute over ownership of those items, the judge would investigate both sides, and the person whom he condemned had to repay the other person double the value of the property. If the judge condemned the one entrusted with the property, he had to pay the original owner double the property's value. Conversely, if the judge condemned the owner, he also had to compensate double the property's value to the other person (Exod 22:9). This law embodies God's attentive and thoughtful heart that considers the heartache of one who is unfairly accused.

Accidental damage to an entrusted property (Exod 22:10–13). In some cases a property that had been entrusted to someone was lost accidentally, not due to the caretaker's negligence or evil intention (Exod 22:10). In such cases the person to whom the property had been entrusted had to take an "oath before the LORD … that he [had] not laid hands on his neighbor's property" (Exod 22:11). An oath taken in God's name and by His authority was the most solemn oath a person could take. Thus a person showed his sincerity by taking an oath in God's name. Then the owner had to "accept it, and he [could] not make restitution" (Exod 22:11). Despite any suspicions the owner might have had, an oath taken in God's name was final (Heb 6:16) and must be accepted. Even if it turned out to be a lie, the punishment must be entrusted to God. Through this law God taught faith in His absolute sovereignty. He also prevented the prolonging or worsening of conflict and discord between neighbors.

If it was certain that an entrusted animal had been stolen because of negligence, the caretaker must make restitution to the owner (Exod 22:12). If a beast had killed an entrusted animal, however, the caretaker could be relieved of his responsibility by providing evidence to the owner (Exod 22:13).

Damage to borrowed property (Exod 22:14–15). If a man in need of an animal borrowed it, and the animal became injured or died when the owner was not present, the borrower must make full restitution (Exod 22:14). If the borrowed animal had been injured or had died in the owner's presence, however, the borrower did not have to make restitution (Exod 22:15).

Mandatory Clauses for the Liberty and Happiness of One's Neighbors (Deut 23:19– 24:7)

Several clauses defined a neighbor's property as tangible wealth and property as well as intangible rights to liberty, happiness, and even life, and these must not be taken away.

Do not charge interest on money or food borrowed by neighbors (Deut 23:19-20). The noun "interest" in Deuteronomy 23:19 is נֶשֶׁךְ (*neshekh*) and is derived from the verb נָשַׁךְ (*nashakh*), which means "to bite"; it is always used in connection with a bite as from a snake (Gen 49:17; Num 21:6; Prov 23:32; 10:11). It implies that charging heavy interest on a loan is no different from a snake or a viper biting a man to death.

God commanded His people to lend money without interest to fellow countrymen (Exod 22:25; Deut 23:19). He prevented His people from receiving unearned income. In Exodus 22:25, God referred to Israel's countrymen as "[His] people, … the poor among [them]." If anyone who was poor came to a fellow countryman to borrow money to cover living expenses, it had to be lent without interest. Leviticus 25:36–37 clarifies the reason: "Do not take usurious interest from him, but revere your God, that your countryman may live with you. You shall not give him your silver at interest, nor your food for gain." God guaranteed His people basic living conditions so that everyone could live together in the community and fear Him. They could charge interest, however, if the borrower was a foreigner (Deut 23:20). To all those who obeyed this law, God promised that He would bless them in all that they undertook (Deut 23:20). Similarly, Psalm 15:5 states, "He does not put out his money at interest. ... He who does these things will never be shaken."

In the days of Nehemiah, the Jews who had returned from Babylon faced hardship as they rebuilt the city walls. To make matters worse, they suffered from a bad harvest due to a famine in the land and from hefty taxes imposed upon them. Moreover, high-interest lenders were forcing the people to sell their children as slaves (Neh 5:1–13).

"He who increases his wealth by interest and usury gathers it for him who is gracious to the poor" (Prov 28:8; see also Prov 13:22). Ultimately, nothing will be theirs.

Fulfill your vow to God (Deut 23:21–23). A vow is a solemn promise made to God in which a person voluntarily commits to performing an unrequested act or service. First, it is an extraordinary resolution and determination in one's heart for God. Second, it is a confession of one's devotion to God. Third, it is a pledge of one's resolute heart for God.

A vow that was made could not be broken (Deut 23:21–23). Leviticus 19:12 states, "You shall not swear falsely by My name, so as to profane the name of your God; I am the LORD." Similarly, Numbers 30:2 states, "If a man makes a vow to the LORD, or takes an oath to bind himself with a binding obligation, he shall not violate his word" (Ps 15:4). No one was to delay fulfilling what had been vowed; it was better not to have vowed than to have made a vow and not fulfilled it (Deut 23:21; Eccl 5:4–5). Not fulfilling one's vow is deceiving oneself and God. Ultimately, it is a sin of seeking one's own benefit and stealing from God.

Show mercy and compassion to neighbors who are starving (Deut 23:24–25). This law of mercy guaranteed the poor the basic right to life by allowing them to enter into a neighbor's vineyard and eat until they were fully satisfied (Deut 23:24). They were not to put any in a basket, however, or use a sickle in the vineyard (Deut 23:24–25). If anyone abused the law and caused damage to someone else's property, it was considered theft.

A newly wed man was given a year deferment from his military duties (Deut 24:5). A newly wed man was released from his military duties for one year so that he could enjoy happiness with his wife. This law not only gave a reminder of the sanctity of marriage but also guaranteed the right to happiness for newlyweds, as the family (spouse) is precious and should not be taken away from others.

Taking a neighbor's millstone as a pledge was forbidden, as it was as precious as a neighbor's life (Deut 24:6). When a debtor could not pay his debt and offered his millstone as a pledge, either the whole millstone or the top part of it, the creditor was not to accept it. A millstone was a basic necessity of daily life, as it was used to grind grain into powder. This law guaranteed the protection of the basics of life for the poor, as taking the whole millstone or an upper millstone as a pledge was no different from taking one's life as a pledge (Deut 24:6). Here the phrase "take in pledge" (חָבַל, *haval*) means "to hold in pledge" or "to keep as collateral." This law prevented creditors from threatening a neighbor's life with debt.

Forbidding the abduction of a fellow Israelite (Deut 24:7). Deuteronomy 24:7 states, "If a man is caught kidnapping any of his countrymen of the sons of Israel, and he deals with him violently or sells him, then that thief shall die; so you shall purge the evil from among you." Here the verb "to kidnap" originates from the word גָּנַב (*ganav*), which is also the root word for "theft" and refers to abduction. Furthermore, the word "any" (נֶפֶשׁ, *nephesh*) means "soul" or "life." Abduction can lead to a brutal result, as it threatens a person's life or soul. It was therefore punished with the death penalty (Exod 21:16).

III. Evangelical Expansion of the Concept of Stealing

The Bible forbids the stealing of both tangible and intangible property.

Prohibition of Stealing the Word of God

In Jeremiah 23:30, God warned, "'Behold, I am against the prophets,' declares the LORD, 'who steal My words from each other.'" The verb "to steal" is written in the Piel (intensive) participial stem of גָּנַב (ganav) in Hebrew. During the days of the prophet Jeremiah, many false prophets deceived the people. They either took the words of the true prophets and deceptively spoke as if they themselves had received them, or they proclaimed something as God's Word when God had never spoken it. Jeremiah 23:31 states, "'Behold, I am against the prophets,' declares the LORD, 'who use their tongues and declare, "The Lord declares."'" This verse means that God would not tolerate prophets who used their tongues freely to speak what they said was from God. God would not tolerate those who stole His words and would surely judge them (Jer 23:32).

Prohibition of Stealing People's Hearts

Second Samuel 15:6 states, "In this manner Absalom dealt with all Israel who came to the king for judgment; so Absalom stole away the hearts of the men of Israel."

Here the word "stole" is written in the intensive stem of גָּנַב (ganav) and refers to how thoroughly Absalom deceived the people and captured their hearts. Absalom woke up early in the mornings and stood by the city's gate to meet people who were on their way to the king to ask him to make judgments on their difficult cases. After listening to their cases first, Absalom told them that it was unfortunate that the king had not designated anyone to hear their cases, which were good and right. Then he won over their hearts by saying, "Oh that one would appoint me judge in the land, then every man who has any suit or cause could come to me and I would give him justice" (2 Sam 15:4). He steered the people's hearts away from King David to himself; this was the sin of stealing people's hearts (2 Sam 15:5–6).

Prohibition of Stealing Time

Time comes from God. Hence wasting time is the sin of stealing time. In Ephesians 5:16, Paul told the believers to make the most of their time, because the days were evil.

Anyone who steals time and uses it for the desires of the flesh, the desires of the eyes, and the pride of life might fail to be ready for the Lord when He returns at a time when no one expects it (see 1 John 2:16). In Matthew 24:42–44, Jesus said, "Be on the alert, for you do not know which day your Lord is coming. But be sure of this, that if the head of the house had known at what time of the night the thief was coming, he would have been on the alert and would not have allowed his house to be broken into. For this reason you also must be ready; for the Son of Man is coming at an hour when you do not think He will" (see Luke 21:34–36).

People who make the best use of time and stay awake to do God's will are children of light and children of the day, but those who steal time and indulge themselves in the world belong to the darkness (1 Thess 5:1–8). We must manage our time that God has given us and discern God's time well so that we can become the "the faithful and sensible slave whom his master put in charge of his household to give them their food at the proper time" (Matt 24:45).

Prohibition of Stealing Offerings and Tithes

Malachi 3:8 states, "Will a man rob God? Yet you are robbing Me! But you say, 'How have we robbed You?' In tithes and offerings." The word "rob" (קָבַע, *qava*) means "to extort, to plunder, to rip off," which possesses a stronger connotation than גָּנַב (*ganav*; Prov 22:23). This shows that stealing from God the offerings and the tithes is a more heinous sin than any other theft; denying the sin makes it even more heinous.

No one was to steal offerings. The prophet Malachi plainly exposed the robber's mind deeply hidden in the human heart (Mal 3:8). Everything under heaven belongs to God. Nevertheless, people think that everything belongs to them and are stingy about offering thanksgiving with their wealth. Such a mind is displeasing to God and equivalent to the sin of robbery. The Bible commands several times, "Give thanks to the LORD" (1 Chr 16:41; Pss 106:1; 107:1; 118:1, 29; 136:1-26 [alluded twenty-six times]), "Be thankful … , giving thanks through Him to God the Father" (Col 3:15–17), and "In everything give thanks; for this is God's will for you in Christ Jesus" (1 Thess 5:18). "In everything give thanks" is a command to be thankful to God in all circumstances with a good heart and an upright attitude. Thanksgiving must be expressed through material offerings as well (Matt 6:21).

No one was to steal the tithes. Malachi 3:10 reads, "'Bring the whole tithe into the storehouse, so that there may be food in My house, and test Me now in this,' says the LORD of hosts, 'if I will not open for you the windows of heaven and pour out for you a blessing until it overflows.'" People paid tithes at the time, but not many gave the whole tithes. God pointed out the whole tithe, indicating that His people were no longer God-centered. They gathered for themselves, their faith had deteriorated to human-centered faith, and they were unfaithful to God. Offering tithes that were not whole was a sinful act of stealing from God.

Haggai 2:8 states, "'The silver is Mine and the gold is Mine,' declares the LORD of hosts," and Deuteronomy 8:18 states, "You shall remember the LORD your God, for it is He who is giving you power to make wealth." The offering of tithes, which is one-tenth of all income, is a confession of faith that all wealth belongs to God. The number "ten" symbolizes fullness. The offering of tithes is an offering of one-tenth, but it is also a confession that even the remaining nine-tenths belong to God. Furthermore, since the nine-tenths also belong to God, we must not use them to fulfill our desires.

Anyone who steals from God will face great judgment. Malachi 3:9 states, "You are cursed with a curse, for you are robbing Me, the whole nation of you!" No one should put his or her hand upon God's property; all must be offered to God in full. Even if it is late, if a person calculates everything and makes the offering, God will open the gates of heaven and pour out blessings until there is no place to store them. God commands His people to test Him to see whether or not He will pour His blessings (Mal 3:10). This is God's firm promise that He will pour down more than enough blessings (see Gen 41:49).

IV. The Fate of Those Who Violated the Eighth Commandment

Achan, Who Stole the Things Under the Ban (that Were Dedicated to God)

Achan was the son of Carmi, the son of Zabdi, the son of Zerah of the tribe of Judah (Josh 7:1). He participated in the battle of Jericho, stole some of the spoils, and deceived his countrymen by putting what he had stolen in his house (Josh 7:11). The word "deceived" means "to cause harm with deception." Joshua had firmly instructed in advance, "As for you, only keep yourselves from the things under the ban, so that you do not covet them and take some of the things under the ban, and make the camp of Israel accursed and bring trouble on it" (Josh 6:18). Achan, however, caused God's anger to burn against Israel by taking things offered to God (things under the ban) and putting them in his house (Josh 7:1). He had stolen "a beautiful mantle from Shinar and two hundred shekels of silver and a bar of gold fifty shekels in weight" (Josh 7:21). He had coveted these items, taken them, and hidden them inside his tent under the ground, with the silver at the bottom.

This event caused Israel's defeat in the city of Ai (Josh 7:1–5). God said, "The sons of Israel cannot stand before their enemies; they turn their backs before their enemies, for they have become accursed. I will not be with you anymore unless you destroy the things under the ban from your midst" (Josh 7:12). The phrase "they have become accursed" is a fearful statement that Israel was accursed because the nation had stolen things offered to God. The word "accursed" (חֵרֶם, *herem*) refers to devoted things or things devoted to the ban (Lev 27:28–29; Num 18:14). First, what was devoted to God must be offered to Him. Second, anyone who stole what had been offered to God opposed God and must be destroyed.

God instructed Israel in three ways in which they could win the battle in this situation: First, "[Remove] the things under the ban from your midst" (Josh 7:13). Second, "Consecrate yourselves" (Josh 7:13). Third, "The one who is taken with the things under the ban shall be burned with fire, he and all that belongs to him, because he has transgressed the covenant of the LORD, and because he has committed a disgraceful thing in Israel" (Josh 7:15).

When Achan's sin was exposed at last, Joshua brought him, his sons and daughters, and all that he had—the silver, the cloak, and the bar of gold; his oxen, donkeys, and sheep; and his tent—up to the Valley of Achor (Josh 7:23–24). Joshua declared, "Why have you troubled us? The LORD will trouble you this day" (Josh 7:25). Immediately the entire people of Israel stoned and burned Achan, his family, and all his property and raised over them a great heap of stones (Josh 7:25–

26). Then the Lord's burning anger ceased, and the place was called "the valley of Achor" (valley of Trouble; Josh 7:26).

Later Phinehas the priest, along with the chiefs of the ten tribes, recalled Achan's sin (Josh 22:20). Achan's sin is recorded in the genealogy of the tribe of Judah in 1 Chronicles 2:6–7. Verse 7 states, "The son of Carmi was Achar, the troubler of Israel, who violated the ban." Achar in this verse is the same person as Achan, as "Achar" also means "troubler." His story teaches us that stealing what has been offered to God brings great harm to both the individual, the person's family, and his or her nation.

Judas Iscariot, the Thief Who Was in Charge of the Moneybag and Often Stole from It

There was a thief among Jesus' twelve beloved disciples. John 12:6 states, "He [Judas] said this, not because he was concerned about the poor, but because he was a thief, and as he had the money box, he used to pilfer what was put into it." Among the twelve disciples, Judas Iscariot was in charge of the money bag, and he would secretly take money from it.

When Jesus was dining in the house of Simon the leper at Bethany, Mary came to Him with costly perfume worth three hundred denarii that she had prepared for His burial. She broke the vial of perfume and poured it all over Jesus' feet and wiped His feet with her hair (Mark 14:3–5; John 12:3–5). She was offering her whole body and soul to Jesus as He was on His way to the crucifixion (Mark 14:6–9; John 12:7–8). Because of what she did, the whole house was filled with the fragrance. Judas Iscariot, with his treacherous heart and materialistic greed, provoked the other disciples' unbelief. He incited the others, saying, "Why was this perfume not sold for three hundred denarii and given to poor people?" (John 12:4–5). The other disciples then became indignant and rebuked the woman who had shown her tearful devotion, saying, "Why this waste?" (Matt 26:8; see Mark 14:4). These words that they spoke before Jesus, who was facing imminent death, cut through Him like the cold and heartless winter wind.

Knowing Judas Iscariot's wicked intention, Jesus responded, "Let her alone, so that she may keep it for the day of My burial. For you always have the poor with you, but you do not always have Me" (John 12:7–8).

Realizing that there was no more source of income, Judas Iscariot went to the chief priests and asked, "What are you willing to give me to betray Him to you?" (Matt 26:15). When they weighed for him thirty pieces of silver, from then on Judas began to look for an opportunity to hand Jesus over to them when no one was around (Matt 26:14–16; Mark 14:10–11; Luke 22:3–6). Judas Iscariot plotted a detailed, step-by-step arrest plan. He agreed on a sign to indicate to them who Jesus was and told them to "seize" Jesus (Matt 26:48; Mark 14:44). Judas and the religious leaders knew that their efforts could be in vain because of Jesus' supernatural powers, so they prepared swords and clubs as if they were seizing a criminal (Mark 14:48). Judas Iscariot's betrayal was truly detestable and cowardly.

Judas Iscariot was a thief within the household; he delivered Jesus over to the religious leaders for thirty pieces of silver, knowing that Jesus was innocent. Later Judas confessed, "I have sinned by betraying innocent blood" (Matt 27:4). He threw the pieces of silver into the temple sanctuary (ναός, *naos*) and hanged himself (Matt 27:5). Knowing that Jesus—his teacher whom he had betrayed—would be crucified, he committed suicide before his teacher's crucifixion, after Pilate sentenced Jesus to death on Friday at dawn. After Judas hanged himself, he fell headlong, and his middle burst open, and all his intestines spilled out (Acts 1:18). He ultimately went where he belonged (Acts 1:25). Just as prophesied in the Old Testament (Ps 69:25; Zech 11:12–13), the chief priests bought the potter's field with the unrighteous wage, the thirty pieces of silver that Judas had thrown down in the temple. They turned the field into a burial place for strangers and called it

Hakeldama ("Field of Blood"; Matt 27:6; Acts 1:19–20). Judas Iscariot was deceived by his own greed, by the power of the religious leaders, and by the public opinion of the masses that he thought he knew based on what he had seen.

Thieves are included in the list of people who cannot inherit the kingdom of God. First Corinthians 6:10 states, "Neither … thieves, nor the covetous, nor drunkards, nor revilers, nor swindlers, will inherit the kingdom of God." Furthermore, in the book of Revelation, those people who were not killed by the plague of the sixth trumpet did not repent of the works of their hands, including "their thefts" (Rev 9:20–21).

V. The Redemptive-Historical Lesson in the Eighth Commandment

Adam committed a sin that was equivalent to the violation of the eighth commandment in the garden of Eden. The fruit of the tree of the knowledge of good and evil was forbidden from the beginning (Gen 2:17). Adam never had ownership of the tree. Adam and Eve, however, stole what belonged to God by secretly taking and eating the forbidden fruit from the tree of knowledge. Their stealing ended up driving all human beings to death and thus became the greatest act of theft as it stole the lives of all mankind.

After the exodus, the Israelites received the Ten Commandments and the teachings of the law, but they still challenged Moses' leadership. Korah, Dathan, Abiram, and On, along with 250 chiefs of the congregation, assembled themselves against Moses and Aaron (Num 16:1–3). They tried to steal Moses' leadership. The earth, however, opened its mouth and swallowed up the men, their families, everyone who belonged to Korah, and their belongings (Num 16:32–33). Also, fourteen thousand seven hundred people died from a plague, aside from those who had died because of Korah's rebellion (Num 16:49), for complaining about the deaths of Korah and his associates. This incident plainly demonstrates the gravity of the sin of stealing leadership that has been established by God.

During Jesus' days the religious leaders stole the people's hearts and instigated them to kill Jesus. They had a tradition in which one prisoner was released during the feast according to the people's request. Pilate wanted to release Jesus because he knew that the chief priests wanted to kill Jesus out of jealousy (Mark 15:6–10). The chief priests, however, stirred up the crowd so that the people would request the release of Barabbas, a criminal, instead (Mark 15:11). Ultimately Pilate delivered Jesus to be crucified on the cross in order to please the crowd (Mark 15:15). In this way the chief priests stole the people's hearts and drove Jesus to the cross. Even today many false pastors steal the hearts of the saints, drive them to do things opposite to the will of God, and shut the gates of heaven before people. They are like the scribes and Pharisees, who neither entered nor allowed anyone else to enter the kingdom (Matt 23:13).

CHAPTER
23

The Ninth Commandment

You shall not bear false witness against your neighbor.

Exodus 20:16; Deuteronomy 5:20

Exodus 20:16 states, "You shall not bear false witness against your neighbor." In this verse the word "false" is שֶׁקֶר (*sheqer*) in Hebrew, and in Deuteronomy 5:20, it is שָׁוְא (*shawe*). The word *sheqer* means "false oath, deception, falsehood, or fraud" (Exod 5:9; Lev 19:12; Jer 5:31; 20:6; 29:9). On the other hand, *shawe* means "emptiness, vanity, worthlessness, or lie" (Job 15:31; Pss 31:6; 41:6; Isa 1:13; Mal 3:14).

THE NINTH COMMAND

You shall not bear false witness against your neighbor.

לֹא־תַעֲנֶה בְרֵעֲךָ עֵד שָׁקֶר

Exodus 20:16; Deuteronomy 5:20

I. Exegesis of the Ninth Commandment

Bearing false witness destroys the true covenant community. The ninth commandment condemns falsehood and teaches the dignity of the truth. It demonstrates that frightening evil comes upon neighbors when a person bears false witness. This commandment of utmost love not to bear false witness protects the weakest people in society (the poor, sojourners, widows, and orphans) from being condemned by false witnesses.

Language and the Tongue (דָּבָר, לָשׁוֹן)

God created mankind to offer up to Him their praise, the fruit of their lips. God said in Isaiah 43:21, "The people whom I formed for Myself will declare My praise." "The fruit of lips" refers to the sacrifice of praise to God (Heb 13:15). The psalmist confessed that he praised God seven times a day (Ps 119:164). Praising God is a joyful sacrifice in His sanctuary (Ps 27:6). God dwells amid praises (Ps 22:3). Through true thanksgiving and praise, one can sincerely repent and return to God (Hos 14:2). Praise is a living sacrifice offered through our bodies, which is better than sacrificing a bull (Ps 69:30–31; Rom 12:1).

On the other hand, the Old and New Testaments warn of the gravity of sins committed through the human tongue. While God created all mankind upright, human beings have sought out many devices (Eccl 7:29). Misuse of the tongue corrupts the whole body, and the tongue becomes as the fire of hell and burns the entire course of one's life (Jas 3:6). Anyone who does not stumble in his speech is a perfect person (Jas 3:2). Speech is like wine; the longer it ages before it comes out, the better it is. Words spoken hastily can scar a neighbor's heart or trigger conflict within the church. The saints' lips must be like clear springs that yield only sweet water, such as springs of praise, springs of thanksgiving, and springs of truth without falsehood (Eph

4:25; 5:4; Jas 3:10–12). Lips that sing praise must not curse or criticize others (Ps 15:3; Jas 3:10). Ephesians 4:29 states, "Let no unwholesome word proceed from your mouth, but only such a word as is good for edification according to the need of the moment, so that it will give grace to those who hear." Here "word" is λόγος (*logos*) in Greek; it is also translated as "communication" (KJV). God's Word breaks down walls to facilitate communication, but lies are devastating evil that block all communication.

"False Witness" (עֵד שָׁקֶר)

The word "neighbor" in Exodus 20:16 is a translation of the Hebrew word רֵעַ (*rea*) for "friend" or "companion," which is derived from *raah* (רָעָה), meaning "to associate with, to be a friend." Here "neighbor" refers to a close relationship as in a friendship. The word "false" in the phrase "false witness" generally refers to "a statement different from the truth or fabricating as if it were the truth." It includes deliberate actions or speech intended to deceive others. The opposite of a lie is a fact, something that actually happened, or truth, something that is real.

The Hebrew word for "witness" is עֵד (*ed*), which means "eyewitness, witness, or evidence." These are legal terms associated with testimonies made in court.

The term "false witness," therefore, refers to a false statement that conceals sin and testifies of innocence in a public place like a court (Isa 5:23). It also refers to a false statement deliberately made to accuse an innocent person of sin (Prov 25:18). Indeed, telling lies is a serious sin that causes severe damage to an innocent neighbor's reputation and leaves scars in his or her heart and life. Thus the Bible completely condemns all forms of lies and bearing false witness.

Types of bearing false witness that God forbids. Based on the Westminster Larger Catechism Q145, God forbids the following cases of bearing false witness in the Scriptures:

- Fabricating lies to abet the bearing of false witness (Prov 6:19; 19:5)
- Hiring false witnesses (Mark 14:55–59; Acts 6:13)
- Stubbornly opposing the truth and deliberately defending what is evil (Jer 9:3–5; Acts 24:2–5)
- Delivering an unjust sentence (Ps 82:2; Isa 10:2; 59:4)
- Calling an evil person good and a good person evil (1 Kgs 21:9–14; Prov 17:15; Isa 5:23)
- Forgery (1 Kgs 21:8; Jer 8:8)
- Concealing the truth and keeping silence out of cowardice (Lev 5:1; Matt 27:23–24; Acts 5:3–4, 8–9; Eph 4:25)
- Keeping silent and not rebuking a person who criticizes or complains about another person from an evil heart (Lev 19:17)
- Speaking with malicious intent (1 Sam 22:9–10; Ps 52:1–5)
- Speaking the truth in a malicious way, or perverting the truth, or expressing the truth in a vague way (Gen 3:1, 3–5; Isa 59:13)
- Doing an injustice to the righteous or provoking them with useless matters (Isa 29:20–21)
- Leaking someone else's secrets unnecessarily or spreading false rumors (Exod 23:1; Prov 25:9)
- Closing one's ears against a just defense (Acts 7:57)
- Envying or complaining about someone else's deserved credit or honor or trying to sabotage it (Dan 6:3–8; Matt 21:15)
- Disrespectful contempt and vainglorious boasting (Ps 12:3–4; Matt 28:28–29; Rom 1:30; 1 Cor 3:21; 2 Pet 2:18; Jude 1:16)
- Whispering about others, mocking, and sarcasm (Gen 21:9; Isa 28:22; Rom 1:29; 2 Cor 12:20)
- Using flattery to seek someone's favor (Ps 12:3–4; Prov 26:28; Acts 24:3–4; Rom 16:18; 2 Cor 12:20)
- Breaking up a good relationship by speaking ill of one person or the other (Prov 6:19; 16:28)

- Adding to or subtracting from God's revelation (Deut 4:2; 12:32; Prov 30:6; Rev 22:18–19)
- Bearing false and heretical testimony in order to lead people astray (Matt 24:4–5)

The father of all lies, the slanderous devil. All the lies above can be categorized into one word: "slander." Slander refers to the act of damaging someone's reputation or honor with groundless or harmful statements. Slander is the work of the devil. The "devil" is διάβολος (*diabolos*) in Greek, which refers to the sharp tongued who like to "accuse, criticize, slander, or bring charges with evil intent" (see Job 1:9–11; 2:4–5; Rev 12:10). Jesus also said that the devil is the father of all lies (John 8:44).

Slandering is murdering with the tongue. It includes speaking ill about people behind their backs or damaging a person's reputation with words when the person is not present. Psalm 101:5 states, "Whoever secretly slanders his neighbor, him I will destroy; no one who has a haughty look and an arrogant heart will I endure." Many people of God and prophets were slandered by the wicked. Moses (Exod 16:2–3; Num 12:1–2; 14:1–4; 16:12–14; 21:5), the apostle Paul (Rom 3:8; 1 Cor 4:11–13), and even Jesus Christ (Matt 9:11; 11:19; Mark 2:18; Luke 5:30; 7:34; John 7:12) suffered from their enemies' slander.

The tongue is so powerful that Augustine once said, "A lying, deceitful tongue cuts more deeply than the sword." While a man can tame a beast, no man can tame the tongue, which is an uncontrollable evil filled with deadly poison (Jas 3:7–8). Ecclesiastes 5:6 states, "Do not let your speech cause you to sin," and Psalm 5:6 states, "You destroy those who speak falsehood." Psalm 101:7 further states, "He who practices deceit shall not dwell within my house; he who speaks falsehood shall not maintain his position before me." Proverbs 19:9 states, "A false witness will not go unpunished, and he who tells lies will perish," and Proverbs 21:28 says, "A false witness will perish."

The key to spurning false witnesses. Truth and honesty create the power that defeats all lies. Honesty lies at the center of all ethics; it is the basic element of all morals. Proverbs 11:3 states, "The integrity of the upright will guide them, but the crookedness of the treacherous will destroy them." Proverbs 12:19 also states, "Truthful lips will be established forever, but a lying tongue is only for a moment."

All human beings are liars; God alone is true (Ps 116:11; Rom 3:4). People are so foolish that they lie and deceive themselves with their own lies (Prov 26:27–28). One who speaks lies fills himself with his own schemes; he is a fool who harms himself (Prov 1:31). Regarding liars the prophet Isaiah said, "They hatch adders' eggs and weave the spider's web; he who eats of their eggs dies, and from that which is crushed a snake breaks forth" (Isa 59:5). While "bread obtained by falsehood is sweet to a man," he will later feel uneasy about his lies, as if there were gravel in his mouth (Prov 20:17).

God is upright and does not tell lies (1 Sam 15:29; Ps 25:8; Titus 1:2; Heb 6:18). God's Word (His wisdom), therefore, is flawless, blameless, pure, clean, and perfect (Pss 12:6; 18:30; 19:7; 111:7). God's Word is always upright (Pss 19:8–9; 33:4; Hos 14:9). In Proverbs 8:6–7, the sage confessed, "Listen, for I will speak noble things; and the opening of my lips will reveal right things. For my mouth will utter truth; and wickedness is an abomination to my lips."

God hates liars the most, as the serpent destroyed Adam in the garden of Eden with his lie: "You surely will not die!" (Gen 3:4; see also Prov 6:16–19; John 8:44). Lying is in no way a minor sin. Liars will be thrown into the lake that burns with fire and brimstone at the end of the world when Satan, the father of lies, is thrown in (Rev 21:8, 27).

II. Specific Laws Derived from the Ninth Commandment

The ninth commandment, "You shall not bear false witness against your neighbor" (Exod 20:16; Deut 5:20), is expanded and expounded in Exodus 22:21–27; 23:1–3, 6–9 and Deuteronomy 24:8–25:4.

Prohibition of Bearing False Witness (Exod 22:21–27; 23:1–3, 6–9)

Concern for sojourners, widows, orphans, and the poor commanded (Exod 22:21–27; 23:3, 9). The ninth commandment forbids bearing false witness to ensure that those who might easily be neglected in society possess legal rights. This matter will be discussed further when the specific laws written in Deuteronomy are expounded.

Bearing false witnesses is prohibited (Exod 23:1–3; see also Lev 19:16). A false witness in a murder case can have a detrimental impact on a person's life or death. Thus the law prevents sentencing a person to death on the testimony of a single witness (Deut 17:6–7). When malicious lies alienate a person from the people around him or her, we must remember that this can lead to unfair trials for that person and even result in his or her death.

> *You shall not go about as a slanderer among your people, and you are not to act against the life of your neighbor; I am the LORD. (Lev 19:16)*

In this passage the Hebrew word for "slanderer" is רָכִיל (*rakhil*) and refers to a person who goes about as a talebearer (Prov 11:13; Jer 6:28), one who goes about slandering others (Prov 20:19), and a person who slanders to shed blood (Ezek 22:9). The passage is a warning against people who go about aimlessly slandering others and alienating people. God solemnly warns against pushing people to the point of death through such hostile acts (Lev 19:16). God is truly never indifferent to

His people whom He created when they cry out because of injustice.

"You shall not bear a false report" (Exod 23:1). The Hebrew phrase for "a false report" is שֵׁמַע שָׁוְא (*shemah shawe*), which also can be translated as "a false rumor" or "a groundless rumor." Seeking to form public opinion by spreading false reports rather than the truth and causing damage to other people's reputations, property, and lives are wicked deeds.

"Do not join your hand with a wicked man" (Exod 23:1). The New Living Translation renders this verse as, "You must not cooperate with evil people," and the New International Version, "Do not help a guilty person."

"You shall not ... be a malicious witness" (Exod 23:1). A malicious witness fabricates lies and turns them into believable stories to frame someone and cause that person trouble and hardship.

"You shall not follow the masses in doing evil" (Exod 23:2). This is a stern warning against following the masses. Rather than following the crowd in doing evil, we must follow those individuals who are in proper relationship with God and do what is good.

"You shall not ... testify in a dispute so as to turn aside after a multitude in order to pervert justice" (Exod 23:2). This command sternly warns against bearing false witness out of a herd mentality. Naboth was ensnared by the false witnesses commissioned by Jezebel and died cruelly because of a herd mentality (1 Kgs 21:1–16).

"You shall not ... be partial to a poor man in his dispute" (Exod 23:2–3; see Exod 23:6). The court must carry out justice without showing partiality to the rich or poor. Being partial means there is an unfair bias in favor of one side; it favors and protects one party over the other. A judge must not reach a favorable or unfavorable verdict simply because one party is weak and poor.

"You shall take not take a bribe" (Exod 23:8). "A bribe blinds the clear-sighted and subverts the cause of the just" (Exod 23:8). God does not show partiality, nor is He swayed by bribes (Deut 10:17; 2 Chr 19:7; see also Job 34:19; Acts 10:34; Rom 2:11; Gal 2:6; Eph 6:9).

Regulation Regarding the Protection of the Weak (Deut 24:8–25:4)

Four specific commands regarding leprosy (Deut 24:8-9). Specific laws concerning lies begin with the law regarding leprosy. Leprosy is discussed in length in the book of Leviticus (Lev 13–14, total 116 verses). In Deuteronomy, on the other hand, only two verses explain four specific commands regarding leprosy (Deut 24:8–9).

The first command is "Be careful against an infection of leprosy" (Deut 24:8). The second command follows: "Diligently observe and do according to all that the Levitical priests teach you" (Deut 24:8). The third command is "As I have commanded them, so you shall be careful to do" (Deut 24:8). The fourth and last command is "Remember what the LORD your God did to Miriam on the way as you came out of Egypt" (Deut 24:9; see also Num 12:1–16). Since leprosy was a critical matter, God commanded the Israelites to remember why Miriam had broken out with leprosy to ensure that the people would follow His instructions. This passage thus reminded the people about Miriam's leprosy, which had been caused by her speech against Moses the servant of God (Num 12:1–2, 8).

The term "speak against" in Numbers 12:8 refers to speaking against someone out of jealousy and greed in order to bring that person down. The content of Miriam's criticism was an exaggerated lie or untrue to the facts (Deut 22:14–17; Luke 5:30; Acts 13:45; 1 Pet 2:12). Simply put, Miriam's leprosy was a warning against slandering someone with lies. It especially taught that evil criticism against leaders established by God was a challenge against God's sovereignty. This was a solemn command to respect the authority of the priests and Levites established by God and to obey their instructions so that order in the temple would be maintained.

God listens to the pleas of the poor (Deut 24:10-15). The law states that people can become righteous and receive God's blessings depending on how well they love their neighbors who are poor and could easily become outcasts. If God's people did not help the poor, they would be branded as unrighteous and receive the curse. This law embodies God's great compassion and love even for the poor, for God created them also (Prov 22:2). Anyone who oppresses the poor commits the sin of despising God (Prov 14:31), whereas showing compassion to the poor is lending to the Lord (Prov 19:17; see also Matt 25:40, 45). God does not despise the pleas and prayers of the poor (Ps 102:17).

This law spoke, first, of those who received blessings through the pleas of the poor. The law prohibited a creditor from recklessly entering his debtor's house and taking things as collateral (Deut 24:10–11). When a debtor was poor, the creditor could take his cloak as a pledge during the daytime but had to return it before sunset (Deut 24:12–13). In those days people used their cloaks at night as blankets, so they were necessities. Thus the Bible states, "You shall surely return the pledge to him, that he may sleep in his cloak and bless you; and it will be righteousness for you before the LORD your God" (Deut 24:13).

To the extent that you did it to one of these brothers of Mine, even the least of them, you did it to Me. (Matt 25:40)

This law also spoke of those who were cursed through the pleas of the poor. The law required an employer to pay poor and needy laborers their wages before sunset (Deut 24:14–15). If a laborer cried out to God because of delayed wages, the sin would be upon the employer who had not paid the wages (Deut 24:15; see also Deut 15:9).

The law to protect sojourners, orphans, and widows (Deut 24:17–22). A sojourner is a person who is traveling away from home or temporarily in a different place. Sojourners did not have land allocated in their names. Since they had no houses and no legal rights, they could easily be looked down upon and neglected. Orphans and widows had lost their fathers or husbands and did not have their livelihoods guaranteed. To prevent them from being oppressed, God said in Exodus 22:21, "You shall not wrong a stranger or oppress him, for you were strangers in the land of Egypt." Here God urged the Israelites to remember that they had been redeemed from miserable lives as slaves in Egypt, where they had been bound to die (Deut 24:18, 22). Furthermore, God pronounced a curse upon those who oppressed sojourners, orphans, or widows (Deut 27:19). If these people were oppressed and cried out to God, He would express His great fury by making the oppressors' wives widows and their children orphans (Exod 22:22–24).

God showed unconditional love for sojourners, orphans, and widows. He commanded the Israelites to leave some grain, olives, and grapes in their fields for these people during the harvest seasons (Deut 24:19–21). God would bless those who obeyed by blessing all the work of their hands (Deut 24:19). Indeed, God is the protector of sojourners, the father of orphans, and the judge of widows (Pss 68:5; 146:9).

As the old saying goes, poverty is incurable. Across all ages and countries of the world, the poor have always existed in great numbers (Deut 15:11). Jesus also said, "You always have the poor with you" (Matt 26:11).

As we remember the gift of eternal life and the debt of grace that we have received, we must help those groaning in poverty with hearts of love. We must not be hesitant to share some of what we have and return to our needy neighbors what is rightfully their portion (2 Cor 9:8–9; Heb 13:16; 1 John 3:17–18). Jesus also encouraged us to give without expecting anything in return (Matt 5:42; see also Acts 20:35). In the Bible the proclamation of the good news to the poor (Isa 61:1; Matt 11:5; Luke 4:18) is a sign of the coming of the Messiah.

III. Evangelical Expansion of the Concept of False Witness

Everything that comes forth from the corrupted heart of human beings defiles them. Jesus said in Matthew 15:18–19, "The things that proceed out of the mouth come from the heart, and those defile the man. For out of the heart come evil thoughts, murders, adulteries, fornications, thefts, false witness, slanders." Here Jesus listed "false witness" as one of the things that defile a person.

The New Testament expands the concept of "false witness." First John 2:4 defines a liar: "The one who says, 'I have come to know Him,' and does not keep His commandments, is a liar, and the truth is not in him." Again, in 1 John 4:20, a liar is one who says, "'I love God,' and hates his brother."

The devil is a liar and the father of lies (John 8:44). Those who bear false witness, therefore, will ultimately stand on the devil's side. Jesus warned the elect not to be tempted by lies in the end times. Matthew 24:23–24 states, "If anyone says to you, 'Behold, here is the Christ,' or 'There He is,' do not believe him. For false Christs and false prophets will arise and will show great signs and wonders, so as to mislead, if possible, even the elect." False christs will lead people astray with false wonders and with all the deception of wickedness (2 Thess 2:9–10). Then "God will send upon them a deluding influence so that they will believe what is false, in order that they all may be judged who did not believe the truth, but took pleasure in wickedness" (2 Thess 2:11–12). The antichrist will seduce people to follow a different gospel (a false gospel) rather than the true gospel. Those who do not believe in the truth but instead love unrighteousness will follow after him and receive judgment, and the preachers of this different gospel will be cursed (2 Cor 11:4; Gal 1:6–9).

The worst lie among all false witnesses is seducing people to follow a false Christ through a different gospel. The saints must therefore follow Jesus Christ alone through the Word of truth. Ultimately, the ninth commandment rejects lies and false witness as part of our daily lives. Furthermore, it rejects all lies that oppose the Word of God, the true gospel.

IV. The Fate of Those Who Violated the Ninth Commandment

Gehazi, the Servant of Elisha

Gehazi (גֵּיחֲזִי) means "valley of vision" or "gorge of illusion." When Elisha healed the leprosy of Naaman, the captain of the Aramean army, Naaman returned to Elisha with gifts. Elisha refused, however, and vowed that he would never accept any gifts (2 Kgs 5:15-16). Yet not long after Naaman then left for his country, Elisha's servant, Gehazi said to himself, "Behold, my master has spared this Naaman the Aramean, by not receiving from his hands what he brought. As the LORD lives, I will run after him and take something from him" (2 Kgs 5:20). Then he pursued Naaman and lied to him, saying, "My master has sent me, saying, 'Behold, just now two young men of the sons of the prophets have come to me from the hill country of Ephraim. Please give them a talent of silver and two changes of clothes'" (2 Kgs 5:22). Thus Naaman gave him a talent of silver and two changes of clothing, and Gehazi returned to Elisha after hiding them in his house (2 Kgs 5:23-24). When Elisha asked him, "Where have you been, Gehazi?" Gehazi answered, "Your servant went nowhere" (2 Kgs 5:25). Then Elisha said to him, "Did not my heart go with you, when the man turned from his chariot to meet you? Is it a time to receive money and to receive clothes and olive groves and vineyards and sheep and oxen and male and female servants?" (2 Kgs 5:26). The question "Did not my heart go with you, when the man turned from his chariot to meet you?" meant "Did you not know that I was there in spirit?" Elisha rebuked Gehazi, saying, "The leprosy of Naaman shall cling to you and to your descendants forever" (2 Kgs 5:27). When Gehazi left Elisha's presence, he was a leper as white as snow.

Lying is a fearful sin that can instantly destroy the liar and his family. This is why the Bible says, "It is better to be a poor man than a liar" (Prov 19:22). People devise and fall into their own traps. People may deceive other people, but they cannot deceive God, whose eyes are like a flame of fire (Rev 1:14; 2:18; 19:12). God stores up sound wisdom for the upright (Prov 2:7), and light arises from darkness for the upright (Ps 112:4). God gives wealth without sorrow (Prov 10:22) and withholds no good things from the upright (Ps 84:11). Gathering wealth by deceiving others, however, is like the snare of death and a fleeting vapor (Prov 21:6). Such wealth only adds sorrow and brings disaster to one's house.

Ananias and Sapphira, Who Lied to God

The name "Ananias" (Ἀνανίας) means "the Lord is gracious." His wife's name "Sapphira" (Σάπφιρα) means "beautiful" and "joyful" (Acts 5:1–11). Barnabas sold his field and brought the money he made before the apostles (Acts 4:36–37). Ananias and Sapphira saw this and decided to sell their property too and give the proceeds as an offering (Acts 5:1). Yet when it came time to make the offering, they were reluctant to offer everything and decided to give only a part of the proceeds (Acts 5:2). When Ananias brought some of the money before the apostles, Peter rebuked him, "Ananias, why has Satan filled your heart to lie to the Holy Spirit and to keep back some of the price of the land?" (Acts 5:3). Peter reminded him, "You have not lied to men but to God" (Acts 5:4). When Ananias heard these words, he fell to the ground and died, and all who heard of this incident were frightened (Acts 5:5). Then the young men covered up Ananias, carried him out, and buried him (Acts 5:6).

Three hours after the burial of Ananias, Sapphira came before Peter, unaware of her husband's death. Peter asked her, "Tell me whether you sold the land for such and such a price" (Acts 5:8). She answered, "Yes, that was the price" (Acts 5:8). Peter responded, "Why is it that you have agreed together to put the Spirit of the Lord to the test? Behold, the feet of those who have buried your husband are at the door, and they will carry you out as well" (Acts 5:9). Then Sapphira fell before Peter's feet and died (Acts 5:10). Just as Peter had spoken, the young men came back from Ananias's burial and carried Sapphira out to bury her next to her husband (Acts 5:10). Thus great fear came upon the whole church and all who heard about the incident (Acts 5:11).

Ananias and Sapphira's offering was not from the depths of their hearts; it came from a hypocritic desire to boast in front of others. They committed the great sin of lying before God and tried to deceive to the end until they were suddenly struck to death.

Although the dishonest ways of the wicked may appear glorious for a moment, they ultimately lead to death (Ps 1:6; Prov 4:19). The Bible says of these people, "Even in laughter the heart may be in pain, and the end of joy may be grief" (Prov 14:13). The dishonest laughter of the wicked is full of the shadow of grief, sorrow, and anxiety. In Luke 6:25, Jesus also says, "Woe to you who laugh now, for you shall mourn and weep."

V. The Redemptive-Historical Lesson in the Ninth Commandment

Adam's sin in the garden of Eden was equivalent to the violation of the ninth commandment. Eve lied to the serpent, saying, "God has said, 'You shall not eat from it or touch it, or you will die'" (Gen 3:3; see also Gen 2:16–17). The serpent also lied to her, saying, "You surely will not die!" (Gen 3:4). Second Corinthians 11:3 testifies that "the serpent deceived Eve by his craftiness." Here the word "craftiness" (πανουργία, *panourgia*) means "cunning" or "treachery."

When God asked Adam, "Have you eaten from the tree of which I commanded you not to eat?" (Gen 3:11), Adam answered, "The woman whom You gave to be with me, she gave me from the tree, and I ate" (Gen 3:12). With this answer Adam put the responsibility for his sin primarily on God and secondarily on Eve. This was a lie. The primary responsibility was on Adam himself, who had received God's Word directly but had not taught Eve properly. Thus all the lies in the garden of Eden led all mankind to the path of death.

God gave the ninth commandment to the Israelites and then the specific laws to denounce all forms of lies (Lev 6:2–7). In Exodus 23:7, God said, "Keep far from a false charge, and do not kill the innocent or the righteous, for I will not acquit the guilty." In Leviticus 19:11, He said, "You shall not steal, nor deal falsely, nor lie to one another."

Yet when Moses returned from his sixth ascent of Mount Sinai after receiving the two stone tablets of the Ten Commandments, Aaron, who had made the golden calf, lied to Moses. Moses asked him, "What did this people do to you, that you have brought such great sin upon them?" (Exod 32:21). Aaron answered, "I said to them, 'Whoever has any gold, let them tear it off.' So they gave it to me, and I threw it into the fire, and out came this calf" (Exod 32:24). It was surely Aaron who had molded the gold gathered from the people into the shape of a calf (Exod 32:3–4). Yet he lied and spoke as if the golden calf had formed by itself. A leader filled with lies cannot lead the people to the way of truth.

During Jesus' days the religious leaders searched frantically for a way to kill Jesus. They brought many false witnesses in order to find a pretext to kill Him. While many made false testimonies against Jesus, they contradicted one another (Mark 14:56–59). Surely their testimonies could not agree with one another because they were all false. The religious leaders were blinded by their ultimate goal of killing Jesus and employed deceptive methods.

Liars meet a tragic end. "All liars" are included in the list of people who will enter the lake of fire and brimstone, as found in Revelation 21:8. According to Revelation 21:27, "nothing unclean, and no one who practices abomination and lying" will enter the new Jerusalem. Furthermore, Revelation 22:15 includes "everyone who loves and practices lying" in the list of the people outside the new Jerusalem.

Godly saints must never bear false witness and always stay true. Revelation 17:14 states, "These will wage war against the Lamb, and the Lamb will overcome them, because He is Lord of lords and King of kings, and those who are with Him are the called and chosen and faithful." In the end times, the one hundred forty-four thousand standing on Mount Zion when the Lord returns will be "blameless," and "no lie" will be found in their mouths (Rev 14:1, 5). Falsehood will fail, and the truth will prevail. God's Word is the truth (truthfulness and true; John 17:17; see also Rev 19:11, 13). Therefore, God's saints who cling to His Word and hold onto the truth until the end will surely be victorious.

CHAPTER

24

The Tenth Commandment

You shall not covet your neighbor's house.

Exodus 20:17; Deuteronomy 5:21

Exodus 20:17 states, "You shall not covet your neighbor's house; you shall not covet your neighbor's wife or his male servant or his female servant or his ox or his donkey or anything that belongs to your neighbor." The same commandment is written in Deuteronomy 5:21 as, "You shall not covet your neighbor's wife, and you shall not desire your neighbor's house, his field or his male servant or his female servant, his ox or his donkey or anything that belongs to your neighbor." In Deuteronomy the order of the commands regarding one's "neighbor's house" and one's "neighbor's wife" is switched, and the words "his field" are added.

THE TENTH COMMAND

You shall not covet your neighbor's house.

לֹא תַחְמֹד בֵּית רֵעֶךָ

Exodus 20:17; Deuteronomy 5:21

I. Exegesis of the Tenth Commandment

The tenth commandment is the conclusion of the Ten Commandments as well as the last commandment regarding love for our neighbors. Through this last commandment, God forbids covetousness. Covetousness is a greedy desire in the heart to possess more than what one currently has. Despite already having an appreciable amount of possessions, a covetous person is not satisfied and wants more (Prov 30:15). A good example is a child whose mouth and hands are filled with cookies who yet reaches out to take a friend's cookie.

It is certainly not easy to protect our hearts from the temptations of covetousness. Proverbs 4:23 states, "Watch over your heart with all diligence, for from it flow the springs of life." We must banish covetousness from our hearts as soon as it enters, before it is too late. We must become warriors of faith who guard our hearts against unwanted guests so that we do not have the springs of life taken away from us (Prov 16:32; 25:28). It is foolish to trust our own hearts (Prov 28:26).

The God of love showed humanity the path to the springs of life, which is the commandment to rule over our hearts. Through the commandment "You shall not covet your neighbor's house," we come to understand the dignity of self-sufficiency and contentment.

"You Shall Not Covet" (לֹא תַחְמֹד)

External and internal covetousness. The word "covet" in Exodus 20:17 is חָמַד (*hamad*) in Hebrew and means "to desire" or "to take pleasure in." This word primarily refers to greedy behavior driven by an emotional impulse after having seen an external object.

Another Hebrew word for "covet" in Deuteronomy 5:21, however, is אָוָה (*awah*), which means "to incline, to long for, to desire." *Awah* refers primarily to greed driven by an existing internal desire of the heart. While *hamad* is external greed caused by an object's inherent value, *awah* is internal greed rising from within a person's heart.

These two different words for covetousness show that God prohibited both external and internal covetousness. Furthermore, both חָמַד (*hamad*) in Exodus 20:17 and אָוָה (*awah*) in Deuteronomy 5:21 are written in the imperfect stem. This implies that God continuously prohibited both external and internal covetousness. A strong desire for a neighbor's possession can be very dangerous because it can lead one to take action to possess it if one cannot restrain oneself. This is why it is necessary to have a commandment to control such desires (Jas 1:14–15).

The pretext for covetousness. Since covetousness is commonly found in everyone, regardless of age or gender, many people mistake it as an instinctual psychological phenomenon. Even the saints often do not regard covetousness in their hearts as sin, so they do not think to repent of it. Covetousness rising from the heart, however, is clearly sinful. Proverbs 23:7 states, "As he thinks within himself, so he is. He says to you, 'Eat and drink!' But his heart is not with you." This verse explains that what a person thinks in his heart before his thoughts are revealed through actions defines his character. Just as Adam and Eve experienced in the garden of Eden through the cunning serpent, covetousness disguises itself so well that anyone can easily be deceived by it. The apostle Paul described this disguise as "a pretext for greed" in 1 Thessalonians 2:5. Here the Greek word for "pretext" is πρόφασις (*prophasis*), meaning "a disguise" or "to pretend to feel a certain way." Every deed, whether small or great, of a person who wears a mask is fake. The Pharisees in Jesus' day were "lovers of money" (Luke 16:14). The scribes were also avaricious and lawless tricksters who devoured widows' houses (Mark 12:39–40; Luke 20:46–47). To hide their true intentions, however, they disguised their outer appearances with beauty and cleanliness like white-washed tombstones (Matt 23:25–28). The people saw their external piety and strict observance of the law and followed after them, believing that they were righteous and upright (see Matt 23:2–7; Mark 12:38–40; Luke 18:9–12; 20:46–47).

Conclusion of all other commandments. With the command "Beware, and be on your guard against every form of greed" (Luke 12:15), Jesus affirmed that covetousness was an enemy against which all the saints must fight. The apostle Paul even considered covetousness as a violation of the first commandment, that is, idolatry (Eph 5:5; Col 3:5). Covetousness is indeed a violation of the first and second commandments, and if it is not curbed, it will lead to the violation of the remaining commandments. Thus covetousness is the root of all sins (see 1 Tim 6:10). Even if one kept all the commandments from the first to the ninth, it is not easy to keep the tenth. The rich young man who knelt before Jesus seeking eternal life confidently confessed, "All these things I have kept" (Matt 19:20). Yet he went away grieving because of the one thing he lacked, which was a willingness to lay down his greed for wealth (Matt 19:16–22; Mark 10:17–22; Luke 18:18–23). We must do well in obeying the final commandment to ensure that we keep all the commandments.

In the parable of the sower, Jesus likened the human heart to a field and explained that the thorns are temptations to wealth, or covetousness (Matt 13:22; Mark 4:18–19; Luke 8:14). As long as covetousness is in one's heart, God's Word cannot bear any fruit, since the thorns of covetousness choke the Word. God's Word, even when a person has read, heard, and understood it, cannot bear fruit when covetousness hinders the seed from growing.

"Neighbor's House" (בֵּית רֵעֶךָ)

In Exodus 20:17, God said, "You shall not covet your neighbor's house." Human beings are not content with their own possessions; instead they covet what is beyond their neighbors' fences because of their fallen natures. The Hebrew word for "house" (בַּיִת, *bayith*) refers not only to a physical building but also to a family (Gen 7:1; 12:17; 35:2; 42:19) or property (Esth 8:1). Thus the phrase "your neighbor's house" refers to one's neighbor's possessions overall. In this respect the latter part of Exodus 20:17 commands, "You shall not covet … anything that belongs to your neighbor."

"Neighbor's Wife" (אֵשֶׁת רֵעֶךָ)

Deuteronomy 5:21 commands, "You shall not covet your neighbor's wife." Unlike in Exodus 20:17, "wife" is mentioned first, before "house." Why? It is because a person's wife is his most precious possession. In the last chapter of Proverbs, the sage sang that an excellent wife is far more precious than jewels (Prov 31:10–31). A righteous wife is her husband's crown and joy (Prov 12:4). For this reason Proverbs 18:22 sings, "He who finds a wife finds a good thing and obtains favor from the LORD." Proverbs 19:14 also says, "House and wealth are an inheritance from fathers, but a prudent wife is from the LORD" (Prov 5:18–19). Coveting a neighbor's wife, therefore, is equivalent to coveting a neighbor's most precious possession or coveting everything the neighbor has.

God also added "field" among the things not to covet in Deuteronomy 5:21, which was spoken when the Israelites were preparing to conquer Canaan. God commanded this to prevent the tribes from committing the sin of covetousness as they distributed the land among them (Deut 19:14; 27:17; see also Prov 22:28; 23:10; Hos 5:10).

"His Male Servant or His Female Servant" (וְעַבְדּוֹ וַאֲמָתוֹ)

A faithful servant manages and oversees all that the master owns (Gen 39:4–6). Eliezer, Abraham's oldest servant, "had charge of all that he [Abraham] owned" (Gen 24:2). A faithful servant is more valuable than any of the master's assets. Everything on this earth is maintained by the work of many such servants. Thus the sin of coveting a neighbor's servant cannot be lighter than the sin of stealing his most prized possession.

"His Ox or His Donkey or Anything that Is Your Neighbor's"
(וְשׁוֹרוֹ וַחֲמֹרוֹ וְכֹל אֲשֶׁר לְרֵעֶךָ)

The latter part of Exodus 20:17 commands one not to covet a neighbor's ox or his donkey or anything that belongs to a neighbor.

The tenth commandment forbids again what is already forbidden in the seventh commandment, "You shall not commit adultery," and the eighth commandment, "You shall not steal." It completely forbids our eyes and hearts to desire a neighbor's wife or his possessions. Even when a person does not yet have the intention to steal, once covetousness enters his or her heart, the person could subconsciously act out evil intentions and thoughts. Through the tenth commandment, God demands that our hearts and thoughts be filled fully with love for Him and His Word so that we may press on to maturity.

II. Specific Laws Derived from the Tenth Commandment

The tenth commandment, "You shall not covet your neighbor's house; you shall not covet your neighbor's wife or his male servant or his female servant or his ox or his donkey or anything that belongs to your neighbor" (Exod 20:17; see Deut 5:21), is expanded and explained in Deuteronomy 25:5–26:15.

Prohibition of Coveting a Neighbor's Wife (Deut 25:5-12)

Performing the duty of a husband's brother (Deut 25:5-10). Deuteronomy 25:5-10 states that if brothers lived together and one of them died without a son, then his widow cannot marry anyone outside the family. She must marry the brother of her deceased husband (Deut 25:5). The firstborn son of the widow must become the heir of the deceased brother so that the deceased brother's name would not be cut off from Israel (Deut 25:6). This was "the duty of a husband's brother" (Deut 25:5, 7) and was known as a levirate marriage or a widow's inheritance. This law has significant implications.

First, the law helped prevent possible halts within redemptive history. Levirate marriages appeared for the first time in Genesis 38. Upon the death of his oldest son, Er, Judah told his second son, Onan, to carry on Er's family name by performing the brotherly duty and marrying Tamar, Er's wife. Judah said to Onan, "Raise up offspring for your brother" (Gen 38:8). Onan knew that any son Tamar bore would not be his son, so when he lay with her, he cunningly "wasted his seed on the ground in order not to give offspring to his brother" (Gen 38:9). God killed Onan as He had killed Er, because what Onan did was "evil in the sight of the LORD" (Gen 38:7; see Gen 38:10; 1 Chr 2:3). Judah was worried that his third son, Shelah, would be killed like his brothers so he did not give Shelah to Tamar (Gen 38:11). Then Tamar disguised herself as a prostitute, lay with Judah, and conceived (Gen 38:14-18). The levirate marriage was a precious tradition to God, as it ensured that the covenant family would continue to exist until the Messiah's coming.

In cases where there was no brother, the closest relative, called a "kinsman" or "redeemer" (a close relative; Lev 25:24-34; Ruth 2:20), was to take on the duty. The Hebrew term for "redeem" is *gaal* (גָּאַל, "to deliver" or "to ransom"), and the tradition of taking on such a duty is called goel. In the book of Ruth, Boaz acted as a kinsman redeemer who carried on the name of Ruth's husband (Ruth 2:1, 20; 3:12-13; 4:4).

Ruth 4:10 states that he did this "so that the name of the deceased [would] not be cut off from his brothers or from the court of his birth place" (see Ruth 4:5).

The genealogy of Jesus Christ records both the levirate marriage (Deut 25:5-10) through which Judah became the father of Perez and Zerah by Tamar (Matt 1:3; see also 1 Chr 2:4) and the goel tradition (Lev 25:24-34) through which Boaz became the father of Obed by Ruth (Matt 1:5; see also Ruth 4:21). Indeed, the tenth commandment and the specific laws derived from it contributed to the continuation of redemptive history. They ensured the presence of heirs to carry on the family line each time there was a threat of cutting off the path of Jesus Christ's coming.

Second, this law showed God's special concern for the widow. Above all else, the levirate marriage law was God's protection for widows who had lost their husbands and were also childless, as they had no one to rely on. It guaranteed ultimate protection and the right to a livelihood for any widow who was without both husband and child. If the husband's brother refused to fulfill his duty, the widow could bring a charge to the elders standing at the gate and say, "My husband's brother refuses to establish a name for his brother in Israel; he is not willing to perform the duty of a husband's brother to me" (Deut 25:7). The elders of the city would try to persuade him, but if he still refused to marry her, the widow was to pull his sandal off and spit in his face. She was to declare, "Thus it is done to the man who does not build up his brother's house" (Deut 25:9). Then the man's house was to be called "the house of him whose sandal is removed" (Deut 25:10).

Had God not established this law, widows would have been alone and helpless as they struggled to settle into society in Israel. This might have led them to marry gentile men and become acclimated to their pagan culture and lose their pure faith in the Lord (Exod 34:16; Deut 7:3-4; Josh 23:12-13). Hence the levirate marriage law and goel were specific laws that naturally prevented the violation of the tenth commandment, "You shall not covet your neighbor's wife."

Cutting off the hand of a woman who seizes a man's genitals (Deut 25:11-12). A woman was prohibited from seizing a man's testicles when she found her husband fighting with another man. The word "seize" (הֶחֱזִיקָה, *heheziqah*) means "to take tight hold of"; it is the Hiphil (causative) stem of the verb חָזַק (*hazaq*), meaning "to tie fast." An act of seizing the testicles implied the harmful intention to maim a man's sexual organs. Through this law God prohibited acts that threatened a man's ability to reproduce and have children (Deut 25:11). The people were to cut off the hand of a woman who seized a man's testicles, and the law stressed, "You shall not show pity" (Deut 25:12).

Prohibition of Coveting a Neighbor's Property (Deut 25:13–26:15)

Fair business practice (Deut 25:13-16). God forbade the use of "differing weights" and "differing measures" (Deut 25:13-14) in order to ensure fair business practices among the people. If people had full and just weights and full and just measures, God would prolong their days in the land that He had given them (Deut 25:13-15). Unfair scales, however, were an abomination to the Lord (Deut 25:16). Proverbs 20:23 states, "Differing weights are an abomination to the LORD, and a false scale is not good" (see also Lev 19:35-36; Prov 11:1; 20:10, 23; Mic 6:11).

The command to wipe out Amalek (Deut 25:17-19). God warned the Israelites not to forget to blot out the name of Amalek from under heaven after He had given them rest in the land of Canaan, their inheritance. God commanded, "You shall blot out the memory of Amalek from under heaven; you must not forget" (Deut 25:19; see also Exod 17:8-16; 1 Sam 15:2-3). The Amalekites did not fear God; they had attacked Israel as Israel came out of Egypt, especially the faint and weary stragglers at the rear (Deut 25:17-18). They had attacked the weak who had not had the power to protect themselves, which tied in with violating the tenth commandment, "Do not covet."

Firstfruits and Tithes After Settlement in the Land of Canaan (Deut 26:1–15)

God commanded Israel to offer the firstfruits (the firstborn) of all things and the whole tithe when they entered Canaan, the land of their inheritance (Exod 23:19; 34:26; Deut 14:22). This command made them acknowledge that all things inherently belong to God and that they were merely stewards who protected and managed God's property. It was God's way of preventing evil hearts of covetousness from sprouting.

God is the One who institutionalized all these laws in detail so that the people could keep them. Without discussing it with Moses, God established these laws and then commanded Moses to proclaim them to the people. All these laws reflect God's profound love for and desire to save the sinners of this world and His thoughtful consideration even of their weaknesses and vulnerability to sin. All the specific laws derived from the first to the tenth commandments exude the fragrance of God's *agape* love and His enduring patience, mercy, and compassion toward sinful mankind.

III. Evangelical Expansion of the Concept of Covetousness

Covetousness comes from distrust and resentment in those who do not believe in the grace and providential care that God gives each and every saint throughout his or her life. When we understand the providence of the living God, nothing stands as a stumbling block; we are filled with smiles of thanksgiving and greatly exalt God's glory (Pss 8:4; 136:1; 144:3). The wicked, however, are insensitive to God's providence. In their pride they are devoid of thanksgiving, peace does not abide in them even briefly, and, consequently, they are filled with worry and anxiety about everything (Pss 10:3–4; 32:10; Isa 48:22; 57:21;

Col 3:15). The psalmist gave thanks to God for His providence and confessed, "The LORD is the portion of my inheritance and my cup; You support my lot" (Ps 16:5). The Good News Translation translates this verse as, "You, LORD, are all I have, and you give me all I need; my future is in your hands." Jesus also said, "Seek first His kingdom and His righteousness, and all these things will be added to you. So do not worry about tomorrow; for tomorrow will care for itself. Each day has enough trouble of its own" (Matt 6:33–34; see also Luke 12:31).

Let us now examine the fundamental key to overcoming covetousness based on both Jesus' words and the apostle Paul's confessions.

Being on Guard Against Every Form of Greed

A person from out of the multitude spoke to Jesus about the issue of inheritance: "Teacher, tell my brother to divide the family inheritance with me" (Luke 12:13). But Jesus rebuked him and said, "Man, who appointed Me a judge or arbitrator over you?" (Luke 12:14), and said to the crowd, "Beware, and be on your guard against every form of greed; for not even when one has an abundance does his life consist of his possessions" (Luke 12:15). The Greek word for "greed" is πλεονεξία (pleonexia), which refers to the desire to have more or to the greed of seeking more than what is appropriate. Here Jesus added the word "every" (πᾶς, pas) before "greed" to emphasize our need to be on guard against every form of greed that would make us want to possess more than what God has allowed. The Greek word for the phrase "be on your guard" is a present middle voice of φυλάσσω (phylassō), which means "to observe, to watch, to guard." Jesus wanted the people to guard themselves against all types of excessive greed.

Here Jesus pointed out the covetousness in the man's heart; the man's greed for wealth outweighed his concern for harmony between him and his brother. To make matters worse, the man intended to use Jesus' authority and reputation to obtain what he wanted. Covetousness leads to bold and shameless attempts to obtain what one desires even by using God and one's faith.

To the greedy man Jesus told the parable of the rich fool who was never content. After the harvest a rich man realized that he had harvested in abundance. He was now even wealthier than he had been. He thought to himself, "What shall I do, since I have no place to store my crops? ... This is what I will do: I will tear down my barns and build larger ones, and there I will store all my grain and my goods" (Luke 12:17-18). Then he spoke to his soul, "Soul, you have many goods laid up for many years to come; take your ease, eat, drink and be merry" (Luke 12:19). God asked, however, "You fool! This very night your soul is required of you; and now who will own what you have prepared?" (Luke 12:20).

God can summon a rich man's soul on the very night that he has made plans for years of pleasure to come. On that day all that he has prepared, along with his soul, will be taken. Indeed, he cannot take anything with him when he dies (Ps 49:17). We all come to this earth empty-handed and will leave empty-handed (Job 1:21; 1 Tim 6:7). A sinful man's wealth is stored up for righteous people (Prov 13:22). We can spend our short lives on this earth entangled with futile matters and struggling to store up wealth, but we do not know who will gather it eventually (Ps 39:4-6). In the end our wealth will sprout wings like an eagle and fly away (Prov 23:5). This is the Bible's consistent warning to those who covet material wealth (Job 27:16-19; Ps 49:10; Prov 28:8; 2:18-21; Jer 17:11; 1 Tim 6:9-10, 17; Jas 4:13-14).

Luke 12:15 states, "Not even when one has an abundance does his life consist of his possessions." The rich fool was so greedy that he did not share any of his wealth, even when he had an abundance of it. He was a swindler and a thief, for he did not remember where his sudden blessing had come from and did not give thanks to God (see Deut 8:17-18). When his possessions grew indefinitely, his heart was filled only with himself. He wasted his life pursuing only his own enjoyment until the night when the invader called "death" came and dragged him away. He may have felt that he owned the whole world, but he essentially lost his existence. Because he was not rich toward God, his life proved to be vanity, as he was left with nothing on the settlement day of his life.

We must therefore make good use of "today" (2 Cor 6:2, NLT), the opportunity given by God, and strive to be rich toward God (1 Tim 6:18–19). May every day become our "today"—the day to meet God, the day to be blessed, the day to believe, the day to pray, the day to evangelize, the day to serve and dedicate our lives to God, the day to forgive, the day to repent, the day to be steadfast, and the day to make our vows to God (2 Cor 6:1–2).

Self-Sufficiency and Contentment

All covetousness begins with dissatisfaction about one's life and the possessions that have been bestowed on one by God. In 1 Timothy 6:6–8, Paul said, "Godliness actually is a means of great gain when accompanied by contentment. For we have brought nothing into the world, so we cannot take anything out of it either. If we have food and covering, with these we shall be content." Here "contentment" (αὐταρκείας, *autarkeias*) is derived from the word "content" (αὐτάρκης, *autarkēs*; "satisfied with what one has") found in Philippians 4:11. This compound word consists of the pronoun for "oneself" (αὐτός, *autos*) and "enough, sufficient" (ἀρκέω, *arkeō*). Together the two words connote a state of self-satisfaction.

I have received everything in full and have an abundance. The apostle Paul confessed, "I have learned to be content in whatever circumstances I am" (Phil 4:11). He then explained, "I know how to get along with humble means, and I also know how to live in prosperity; in any and every circumstance I have learned the secret of being filled and going hungry, both of having abundance and suffering need" (Phil 4:12). The verb "have learned" in Philippians 4:11 is μανθάνω (*manthanō*) in Greek and means "to learn through practice or experience." Paul declared in Philippians 4:12, "I have learned the secret of being filled" ("I have learned the secret of living in every situation") (NLT). This confession surpassed the highest intellectual enlightenment of man and the heights of all philosophical realms. Hence Paul confessed, even though he had nothing, "I have received everything in full and have an abundance" (Phil 4:18).

Even when Jacob met his brother, Esau, after twenty long years of hard labor in his uncle Laban's house, he confessed that he was content with his possessions (Gen 33:1-11). Genesis 33:11 records, "'Please take my gift which has been brought to you, because God has dealt graciously with me and because I have plenty.' Thus he urged him and he took it." The statement "I have plenty" (וְכִי יֶשׁ־לִי־כֹל, *wekhi yesh-li-khol*) can be translated as "I have everything." While Jacob did not possess everything, he was able to make this great confession because he realized that those who have God never lack anything (Ps 23:1). No matter how much people try, they will never possess everything. Even if God gave them everything, they would not be able to handle it. True happiness comes from being thankful and content with everything that God has provided.

Momentary, light affliction. Paul's secret of being content in any and every situation was none other than living in God's grace. Self-sufficiency is not simply feeling satisfied with oneself; it is a state of genuine satisfaction with God's grace. Paul experienced this not when things were peaceful and he had plenty but when severe affliction threatened his life. He learned this while he was in poverty, not when he was rich; when he was laboring day and night, not when he had leisure time; and when he was physically worn out, not when he was healthy.

Afflictions were endless throughout Paul's life. It would be hard to find anyone who experienced more hardships than Paul did. Second Corinthians 11:23–27 provides vivid details of his afflictions:

Are they servants of Christ?—I speak as if insane—I more so; in far more labors, in far more imprisonments, beaten times without number, often in danger of death. Five times I received from the Jews thirty-nine lashes. Three times I was beaten with rods, once I was stoned, three times I was shipwrecked, a night and a day I have spent in the deep. I have been on frequent journeys, in dangers from rivers, dangers from robbers, dangers from my countrymen, dangers from the Gentiles, dangers in the city, dangers in the wilderness, dangers on the sea, dangers among false brethren; I have been in labor and hardship, through many sleepless nights, in hunger and thirst, often without food, in cold and exposure.

Paul also said in 2 Corinthians 1:8–9, "We do not want you to be unaware, brethren, of our affliction which came to us in Asia, that we were burdened excessively, beyond our strength, so that we despaired even of life; indeed, we had the sentence of death within ourselves so that we would not trust in ourselves, but in God who raises the dead." Paul lived a life full of hardships, from the time he received his calling as an apostle at a young age until the day he was beheaded (1 Cor 4:9–13; 2 Cor 6:4–5; 11:23–33). Yet he referred to his troubles as "momentary, light affliction" (2 Cor 4:17). Only those with such an extraordinary view of faith can live lives of contentment and thanksgiving in the midst of affliction.

Having nothing yet possessing everything. The apostle Paul labored more than any other apostle (1 Cor 15:10). Yet he confessed that he did everything not by his own strength but only by God's grace (1 Cor 15:10). When Paul prayed for the healing of his eye disease, which was to him a thorn (see Gal 4:15), God responded, "My grace is sufficient for you, for power is perfected in weakness" (2 Cor 12:7–9). From the human perspective, a thorn in the flesh could be seen as a hindrance to evangelism. Nevertheless, the secret to Paul's contentment was his belief that the thorn in his flesh was actually a blessing that bound God's grace to him (2 Cor 12:10).

Paul worked day and night as he preached the gospel to ensure that there were no obstacles in spreading the gospel and to avoid becoming a burden to anyone (Acts 18:3; 1 Cor 4:12; 1 Thess 2:9; 2 Thess 3:8). Paul worked as a tent mender (Acts 18:3). He was not supported by the churches for his living expenses (1 Cor 9:7, 12, 15, 18). Not wanting to burden the believers, he refused support from the church at Corinth (2 Cor 12:13-14). Instead he supported the Corinthian church with wages he had received from other churches (2 Cor 11:8). Even if it meant that he had to live poorly, Paul was careful not to burden others and was determined to continue this effort (2 Cor 11:9). He never coveted what belonged to others or cheated anyone or took advantage of others (Acts 20:33; 2 Cor 7:2; 12:17-18). He always worked for his living and taught others to work with their hands (Eph 4:28; 1 Thess 4:11; Titus 3:14). He practiced with joy what Jesus had taught: "Freely you received, freely give" (Matt 10:8; see also Acts 20:35).

The apostle Paul was "as sorrowful yet always rejoicing, as poor yet making many rich, as having nothing yet possessing all things" (2 Cor 6:10). This was because he attained all the treasures of wisdom and knowledge hidden in Jesus Christ (Col 2:2-3). Indeed, this was the unhesitant confession of faith from a person who enjoyed Jesus' feast of abundance in his life (Phil 4:18). As a result, Paul was able to do all things through Him who gave him the power to be self-sufficient and content (Phil 4:13).

IV. The Fate of Those Who Violated the Tenth Commandment

While covetousness may start with mere feelings of greed in the heart, these emotions eventually make a person act them out and sin, ultimately leading to the devastating outcome: death (Jas 1:15). Proverbs 1:19 states, "So are the ways of everyone who gains by violence;

it takes away the life of its possessors."

Unending Covetousness (Sexual Depravity) that Brought About the Great Flood

Regarding the depravity of the people during Noah's days, Genesis 6:2 describes, "The sons of God saw that the daughters of men were beautiful; and they took wives for themselves, whomever they chose." The sons of God saw the daughters of men and were sexually attracted to them. Each man was to have only one wife, but these men took many wives. Thus Noah's days brought about an age of extreme sexual depravity, a corrupt era in which people were fascinated by concealed, secretive sins (Prov 9:17; Eph 5:12).

What were the outcomes of the people's endless covetousness?

First, it grieved (עָצַב, *atsav*; "to hurt" or "to cause pain") God's heart (Gen 6:6).

Second, it corrupted the whole earth (Gen 6:11–12). The word "corrupt" means "to break and collapse"; it refers to a tragic state of hopelessness in which restoration is impossible.

Third, "the earth was filled with violence" (Gen 6:11, 13). "Violence" refers to stubbornness, heinousness, ferociousness, or fierceness. Hence this expression describes a state of anarchy in which the societal order had collapsed as everyone wielded cruel violence and reckless murder, robbery, use of brute force, and theft.

Fourth, the people's covetousness brought irreversible judgment. God pronounced His judgment: "The end of all flesh has come before Me; … behold, I am about to destroy them with the earth" (Gen 6:13). The apostle Peter recounted, "[God] did not spare the ancient world … when He brought a flood upon the world of the ungodly" (2 Pet 2:5). Nevertheless, the covetous people of Noah's time did not understand that their actions would result in judgment until the flood came and took them all away (Matt 24:38–39).

Ahab, Who Coveted Naboth's Vineyard

Ahab, the wicked king of the northern kingdom of Israel, coveted Naboth's vineyard, which Naboth had inherited from his forefathers. Ahab eventually framed Naboth, stoned him to death, and took his vineyard (1 Kgs 21:1-16). At that time the Word of the Lord came upon Elijah the Tishbite (1 Kgs 21:17). God told him to go to Ahab and say, "In the place where the dogs licked up the blood of Naboth the dogs will lick up your blood, even yours" (1 Kgs 21:19). Nevertheless, Ahab's covetousness continued, and he sought to wage war against Aram to take over Ramoth-gilead (1 Kgs 22:3-4). Through the prophet Micaiah, God proclaimed that Ahab would die if he went to the battle (1 Kgs 22:19-23). Ahab, however, placed the prophet in jail and went into battle in disguise (1 Kgs 22:26-27, 30). Ahab was indeed struck by a random arrow and died from excessive bleeding, and the dogs licked his blood, just as Elijah had prophesied (1 Kgs 22:34-38).

Achan, Who Coveted and Stole What Had Been Offered to God

After defeating the city of Jericho during the conquest of Canaan, Achan saw and covetously took a mantle, two hundred shekels of silver, and a bar of gold weighing fifty shekels (Josh 7:21). As a result, three thousand men of Israel were defeated in the battle against the city of Ai, which was smaller than Jericho (Josh 7:2-5). When Israel cast lots to learn why they had been defeated, "Achan, son of Carmi, son of Zabdi, son of Zerah, from the tribe of Judah, was taken" (Josh 7:18). As the price for coveting what had been offered to God, Achan and his sons and daughters were stoned to death at the valley of Achor. His tent, along with all his possessions, was also stoned and burned (Josh 7:24-26).

Judas Iscariot, Who Became a Slave to Money and Sold Jesus Out

Judas Iscariot was so trusted among the twelve disciples that he was put in charge of the moneybag. His covetousness for money grew, however, and he became a thief who often stole money from the bag (John 12:6). A few days before Jesus' crucifixion, Mary devoted herself to Jesus by breaking an expensive bottle of perfume worth three hundred denarii on Jesus' feet (John 12:1-3, 5). Then Judas Iscariot, under the pretext that Mary had wasted money that could have been used to help the poor, scolded her and instigated the other disciples to complain (Matt 26:7-9; John 12:4-5). Jesus had already been aware of Judas's wicked intentions, so He said to him, "Let her alone, so that she may keep it for the day of My burial. For you always have the poor with you, but you do not always have Me" (John 12:7-8). Later Judas Iscariot bargained with the chief priests over Jesus, received thirty pieces of silver, and delivered Jesus to them (Matt 26:14-16; Mark 14:10-11; Luke 22:3-6). In the end, however, he hanged himself to death; the rope he hung from broke so that he fell headlong, bursting open in his middle, and all his intestines gushed out (Matt 27:3-10; Acts 1:16-18).

As seen above, the sin of covetousness always leads to fearful judgment and tragic death (Isa 57:17; Rom 6:23; Jas 1:14-15). Satan first lures us with sweet temptations and sows covetousness in our hearts. He then drags us everywhere to sin, only to desert us in the end to a horrifying desolation and nakedness, and to devour our flesh and burn us up with fire (Rev 17:16). The greatest tragedy for mankind is the inability to control the heart and overcome covetousness. Indeed, covetousness is not an inconsequential sin. It is a serious and terrifying sin that, without exception, brings about the fatal consequence of death for all who fall for it.

V. The Redemptive-Historical Lesson in the Tenth Commandment

Adam committed a sin equivalent to the violation of the tenth commandment in the garden of Eden. When the woman saw the fruit of the tree of the knowledge of good and evil after listening to the serpent, it appeared to her that the tree was "good for food, and that it was a delight to the eyes, and that the tree was desirable to make one wise" (Gen 3:6). The woman ate the fruit first and then gave some to Adam, and he also ate it. The expression "delight to the eyes" is לְעֵינַיִם תַאֲוָה־הוּא (thaawah-hu laenayim) in Hebrew. The word תַּאֲוָה (taawah) means "desire, lust, wish" and is derived from the word אָוָה (awah), which means "to long for" (internal covetousness in Deut 5:21; see also Prov 19:22; Isa 26:8).

The phrase "to be desired" (חָמַד, hamad; external covetousness in Exod 20:17) means "to covet, to desire, to take pleasure in" and refers to people wanting to possess something and keep it in their homes (Prov 21:20). The expressions "a delight to the eyes" and "desirable" show how strongly Eve coveted—out of both internal and external greed—to have the fruit of the knowledge of good and evil. Losing all her ability to make a sound judgment, she stretched out her hand and ate its fruit first. Then she gave some to her husband to eat (Gen 3:6).

Adam and Eve's covetousness made them disobey God and destroyed the entire order of God's creation. Their covetousness led to their banishment from the garden of Eden (Gen 3:22–24). The Ten Commandments plainly expose the nature of the original sin that completely captivated Eve's heart after she saw the fruit of the tree of the knowledge of good and evil. By exposing covetousness as the root of the original sin that corrupted Adam and Eve, the Bible shows that the key to overcoming this sin lies in keeping the Ten Commandments, or the "ten words," of God. Indeed, the Ten Commandments are the path to life for believers (Lev 18:5; Deut 4:4–6; 32:46–47).

Even today the covetousness that corrupted Adam and Eve tenaciously clings to people, seeking every chance to entrap and incite us. Each time this occurs, we must master sin's desires, just as God warned Cain. Genesis 4:7 reads, "Its desire is for you, but you must master it." These were truly precious words by which God admonished Cain out of love to strengthen him so that he would overcome sin. Nevertheless, Cain could not overcome his sin and ultimately killed Abel.

Covetousness was the root cause of the Israelites' sins after the exodus. Even after receiving the commandment "You shall not covet" in the Ten Commandments (Exod 20:17), it was not long before they began to covet. The rabble who lived among the Israelites had greedy desires that led the Israelites to weep and grumble, saying, "Who will give us meat to eat?" (Num 11:4). God sent quail for the people, but He killed those who had greedy desires while the meat was still between the people's teeth. Thus the place was named Kibroth-hattaavah (קִבְרוֹת הַתַּאֲוָה, "graves of gluttony"; Num 11:33–34). The psalmist retold the story in Psalm 106:14 and said that the people "craved intensely in the wilderness, and tempted God in the desert" (see also Ps 78:18). We must remember that death is the only destination for the greedy (Ps 78:30–31; Jas 1:15).

In the days of Jesus, the religious leaders (the Pharisees and scribes) were lovers of money. Luke 16:14 testifies that the Pharisees were "lovers of money" and that they devoured widows' houses (Mark 12:40; Luke 20:47). While the high priesthood was supposed to be assigned to only one person, there were two high priests, Annas and Caiaphas, during that time. Both father-in-law and son-in-law served as high priests, reflecting the corruption prevalent in the religious circle of that day (Luke 3:1-2). For this Jesus said in Matthew 23:25, "Woe to you, scribes and Pharisees, hypocrites! For you clean the outside of the cup and of the dish, but inside they are full of robbery and self-indulgence." These extremely corrupted priests and high priests brought charges against the innocent Jesus out of envy (Matt 26:57–68;

27:12, 18; Mark 14:53–65; 15:3, 10; Luke 22:66–71; 23:10; John 18:19–24). The Greek word for "envy" is φθόνος (*phthonos*), meaning "jealousy." The high priests even incited the crowd to shout aloud and demand that Jesus be crucified. As a result, Barabbas, who had been rightfully imprisoned for revolt and murder, was released, and Jesus was delivered to be crucified (Matt 27:15–26; Mark 15:6–15; Luke 23:13–25; John 18:35, 38–40; 19:6, 15–16). The religious leaders were thieves who coveted even the properties of the poor and of widows (Matt 21:13; Mark 11:17; Luke 19:46; John 10:1, 8). They were as greedy as dogs, for they had the greatest privileges but were still unsatisfied (Isa 56:11; see also Phil 3:2). They were murderers whose excessive greed drove them to envy Jesus and crucify Him as a condemned criminal.

Many people on this earth are enslaved by money (materialism) and sex. These lovers of money (1 Tim 6:10) see riches as their ultimate purpose in life. They pursue only money and completely engross themselves in it. For this reason the Bible describes them as "those who want to get rich" (1 Tim 6:9) and not as actually rich. The Greek word for "want" is written in the present participial form of βούλομαι (*boulomai*), meaning "to desire" or "to will," and describes the state of constantly striving to fulfill one's endless greed to be rich. Proverbs 28:20 uses the expression "he who makes haste to be rich."

Lovers of money will ultimately be enticed to leave the right path of truth. They will wander away from the faith they first possessed and go down the way of corruption. They will suffer many griefs, and in the end, the money that they love so much will pierce them to death (1 Tim 6:10).

Let us not set our hope on the uncertainty of riches (1 Tim 6:17; see also Prov 23:4). We must place our hope in God, who gives us everything freely and allows us to enjoy it all. We must be zealous for His good works (Eph 2:10; Titus 2:14) and strive to share what we have with the needy. When we are able, we must not withhold good from those who deserve it (Prov 3:27; 22:9). "There is one who scatters, and yet increases all the more, and there is one who withholds what is justly due, and yet it results only in want" (Prov 11:24). In 1 Timothy 6:18–19, Paul said, "Instruct them to do good, to be rich in good works, to be generous and ready to share, storing up for themselves the treasure of a good foundation for the future, so that they may take hold of that which is life indeed."

There is no limit to the lust in those who are enslaved by sex. They would remain unsatisfied even if they conquered the world and had all the men or women in it. Second Peter 2:14 speaks of such people, who have "eyes full of adultery that never cease from sin, enticing unstable souls, having a heart trained in greed, accursed children." Some sin ceaselessly out of lust. To some their excessive covetousness feels only natural because it has been part of them for so long. The Bible warns that such people are "children of wrath," men of "lawlessness," sons of "destruction," and "accursed children" (Eph 2:3; 2 Thess 2:3; 2 Pet 2:14). Lust is as expansive as Sheol; like death, it is never satisfied (Hab 2:5). Those who fall into the snares of an adulteress will lose all honor; their flesh will be consumed until only their skin remains, and their lives will be left in ruins (Prov 5:1–23). The practice of every kind of impurity begins with greediness (Eph 4:19). This greed is "the lust of the flesh and the lust of the eyes and the boastful pride of life" (1 John 2:16).

So many hypocritical believers today act as if they have purged themselves of all greed, even though the depths of their hearts are filled with "degrading passions" (Rom 1:26). We must examine ourselves at all times to ensure that this is not the case with us (see Gal 6:1).

All greed is from the devil (John 8:44); it is the source of sin and the beginning of death (Jas 1:14–15). Joy and peace will disappear from the hearts of those who have covetousness in their hearts. Their hearts will be conquered by anxiety, nervousness, hatred, despair, and discouragement. Those who covet a neighbor's wife or a neighbor's belongings will shorten their lives and ultimately lose them. Proverbs 21:6 states, "The acquisition of treasures by a lying tongue is a fleeting vapor, the pursuit of death." Proverbs 1:19 reads, "So are the ways of everyone who gains by violence; it takes away the life of its possessors."

Those who hate covetousness, however, will prolong their days (Prov 28:16). The apostle Paul strongly exhorted, "Immorality or any impurity or greed must not even be named among you, as is proper among saints" (Eph 5:3). When our hearts lean toward greediness, we must quickly divert them back to the Word of God. Devoting our hearts and giving our ears to the Word leads us to the path of wisdom that leads to life (Ps 119:36; Prov 23:12; Eccl 7:12). It is my earnest prayer that we will enjoy eternal life by engraving the following teaching in our hearts: "Watch out! Be on your guard against all kinds of greed; life does not consist in an abundance of possessions" (Luke 12:15, NIV).

CONCLUSION

THE GREAT COMMANDMENTS OF THE TEN COMMANDMENTS

On Tuesday of the passion week, as Jesus' crucifixion was imminent, a lawyer tested Jesus, saying, "Teacher, which is the great commandment in the Law?" (Matt 22:36). At the time the religious leaders had classified the laws into 613 provisions and further grouped them into 248 more important laws and 365 less important laws. Yet which laws were more or less important was always fiercely debated. Under these circumstances, one lawyer questioned Jesus on which commandment was the greatest.

Jesus answered, "'You shall love the Lord your God with all your heart, and with all your soul, and with all your mind.'" This is the great and foremost commandment. The second is like it, 'You shall love your neighbor as yourself.' On these two commandments depend the whole Law and the Prophets" (Matt 22:37–40). The word "depend" is κρεμάννυμι (*kremannymi*) in Greek and means "to hang on, be dependent on," which is further expanded to imply "core principle." Hence this expression often refers to the epitome or compendium that sums up the creed, doctrine, policies, codes, or criteria of certain jobs or organizations (Ps 119:160). The rabbis at the time sought to condense the numerous laws on ethnics into a few principles. These condensed principles were called *kremannymi*. The expression "the whole Law and the Prophets" referred to the entire Old Testament, not just the books of laws and the prophets (see Luke 24:27, 44). Thus the Ten Commandments are the epitome of the Old Testament, and the Ten Commandments are summed up in two great commandments: first, to love God, which encompasses the first through the fourth commandments, and second, to love one's neighbors, which encompasses the fifth through the tenth commandments.

I. Love the Lord Your God

God is to be the only object of our love. Jesus' first commandment is "You shall love the Lord your God with all your heart, and with all your soul, and with all your mind" (Matt 22:37). Jesus was quoting the law in Deuteronomy 6:5, which states, "You shall love the LORD your God with all your heart and with all your soul and with all your might" (see also Deut 10:12; 2 Kgs 23:25). Only those who love God can keep the Ten Commandments (Deut 11:1; John 14:15, 21, 23, 24; 15:10; 1 John 5:2-3). Furthermore, anyone who has received God's love, believed in it, and understood it must love in return. The love that we receive from God is so great and infinite that we must also love Him with all that we have. Deuteronomy 6:5 repeats the word "all" (בְּכָל, *bekhal*) three times; it means "with all that one can do." In other words, we are to love God with our utmost—all our hearts, souls, and strength.

"With All Your Heart"

The word "heart" in Deuteronomy 6:5 is לֵבָב (*levav*) in Hebrew and generally refers to the physical heart, but it also refers to the place where a person's thoughts, will, and emotions are stored. The word "heart" in Matthew 22:37 is καρδία (*kardia*) in Greek and refers to the center of the physical and psychological life. The heart not only makes plans but also deeply contemplates matters of wisdom and discernment (Ps 49:3). Unlike the brain, the heart is the center of the senses and emotions, especially love. From the heart come the strength and senses that enable our natural life activities. From it springs forth the power of life that inspires and touches the deep inner world within each person that is not visible to the eyes (Prov 4:23).

Thus we must devote our whole hearts to keeping God's commandments (Prov 3:5). God is pleased with wholehearted thanksgiving (Ps 138:1) and fervent prayers from the heart (Jer 29:13). Faith is not about knowledge and words from the lips but about the complete inclination of the heart toward God. Many people draw near to God with their lips, but their hearts are far away from Him (Matt 15:8). They honor God by imitating traditions that they have learned but often without true faith in their hearts (Matt 15:8–9; Mark 7:6–7). True faith involves complete devotion of the heart (Prov 23:26). Isaiah 29:13 states, "This people draw near with their words and honor Me with their lip service, but they remove their hearts far from Me, and their reverence for Me consists of tradition learned by rote."

"With All Your Soul"

The word "soul" in Deuteronomy 6:5 is נֶפֶשׁ (*nefesh*) in Hebrew and means "breath, life, soul"; it also refers to a person's character or temperament. Its parallel verse in Matthew 22:37 uses the Greek word ψυχή (*psychē*) for "soul," which has the same meaning. Loving with all our souls signifies giving all that we have been given since birth—in other words, our very lives. When Jesus asked "What will a man give in exchange for his soul?" (Matt 16:26; Mark 8:37), He was referring to a person's living self, which is so precious that it cannot be exchanged for anything else in this world. Hence Jesus proclaimed that only God is worthy to receive what is most precious in the whole world—our living selves—and mandates us to offer ourselves to Him. First John 3:18 states, "Little children, let us not love with word or with tongue, but in deed and truth." Love and service to God, therefore, involve our holistic beings, including the whole heart, intellect, emotion, will, and even life itself.

"With All Your Might"

The word "might" in Deuteronomy 6:5 is מְאֹד (*meod*) in Hebrew and means "force, abundance, exceeding." Loving with "all our might" refers to offering our best, the best that we can possibly offer, including all our energy and labor. The apostle Paul confessed that he suffered exceedingly to spread the gospel (2 Cor 1:8). Loving God with all our might, however, is possible only "by the strength which God supplies" (1 Pet 4:11; see Phil 4:13; Col 1:29). God receives glory when we labor by the strength He supplies us (see 1 Cor 15:10; 1 Pet 4:11).

The parallel verse in Matthew 22:37 uses the expression "with all your mind." The word "mind" is διάνοια (*dianoia*) in Greek and means "ability to perceive" or "understanding." Thus loving with all our might also implies thinking deeply about the overflowing blessings with which God has filled our lives and utilizing them all to love Him in return.

It is impossible to serve God with only part of ourselves. "With all your heart," "with all your soul," and "with all your might" are inseparable and consist of the whole. Since loving God involves our whole beings, lives, and possessions, this essentially means that nothing is reserved for ourselves in loving God (see Job 1:21), and we must have no ulterior motives. Just as the apostle Paul confessed when he was in prison, such love brings our entire beings to exalt Christ alone, whether by life or by death (Phil 1:20–21).

Everything we do in our lives to satisfy ourselves and our families apart from the will of God will bring only regret without reward. Yet love for God and obedience to His Word will bring us everlasting gratification and happiness.

God is to be the only object of our love. Only God is our earnest hope and expectation. Psalm 16:2 states, "I said to the LORD, 'You are my Lord; I have no good besides You.'" God shows His loving-kindness to thousands of generations of those who love Him and keep His commandments (Exod 20:6; Deut 5:10).

II. Love Your Neighbor

Love with the Same Love You Have for God

Jesus' second commandment is "You shall love your neighbor as yourself" (Matt 22:39). Here the word "like" ("as") is ὅμοιος (*homoios*) in Greek and is used to compare two similar things. Thus the commandment to love our neighbor is as important as the commandment to love God. Loving our neighbors as we love ourselves expresses our love for God and measures how great that love is (see Mark 9:37). Therefore, love for God and love for our neighbors are inseparable. First John 4:20–21 states, "If someone says, 'I love God,' and hates his brother, he is a liar; for the one who does not love his brother whom he has seen, cannot love God whom he has not seen. And this commandment we have from Him, that the one who loves God should love his brother also."

The word "love" in "You shall love your neighbor as yourself" in Matthew 22:39 is the same word in Greek, ἀγαπάω (*agapaō*), that is used in the commandment to love God in Matthew 22:37. This signifies that we must love our neighbors with the same love that we have for God. Those who love God and serve Him well will be given the strength to love their neighbors (1 John 4:21).

Thus we must love our neighbors with all our hearts, as serving the Lord rather than men (Col 3:23). We must serve our neighbors not by way of eyeservice or as men pleasers but heartily, as to the Lord (Eph 6:6–7).

Moreover, whatever we do, whether in word or deed, we must do it in the name of Jesus and give thanks to God through Jesus (Col 3:17). Love for our neighbors returns to us according to the mysterious principle that we will be loved in the same way in which we love others (1 Tim 6:18–19). God promises that anyone who takes pity on the poor and serves them lends to God and that He Himself will repay them (Prov 19:17; see Prov 11:24–25). God promises that anyone who considers the helpless will be delivered from trouble (Ps 41:1). Jesus also said that anything we do for "even the least of them" we do for Him (Matt 25:40). Conversely, anyone who oppresses the poor taunts God (Prov 14:31; 17:5). Anyone who closes his ears to the cries of the poor will not be heard when he cries out (Prov 21:13). When a wealthy person sees a brother struggling and does not have the heart to help him, he does not have God's love in him (1 John 3:17).

Love Your Neighbor as Yourself

Jesus said in Matthew 22:39, "You shall love your neighbor as yourself" (see Mark 12:31, 33; Luke 10:27–28). Here the expression "as yourself" is ὡς σεαυτοῦ (*hōs seautou*) in Greek. There is no greater love for others (for our neighbors) than to love them as we love ourselves. This is the "royal law" (Jas 2:8). Although there are other commandments, this commandment sums up all the laws (Rom 13:9). Galatians 5:14–15 states, "The whole Law is fulfilled in one word, in the statement, 'You shall love your neighbor as yourself.' But if you bite and devour one another, take care that you are not consumed by one another."

We invest unsparingly in ourselves. Loving someone as we love ourselves means that we love expecting nothing in return. We must give generously even if the other person cannot give us anything in return. Luke 6:34 states, "If you lend to those from whom you expect to receive, what credit is that to you? Even sinners lend to sinners in order to receive back the same amount."

Indeed, the great commandment to love others as we love ourselves is truly difficult to practice. A lawyer came to Jesus to test Him and asked how he could receive eternal life (Luke 10:25). Jesus, however, asked him in reply, "What is written in the Law? How does it read to you?" (Luke 10:26). The lawyer gave the correct answer by quoting Deuteronomy 6:5 and Leviticus 19:18 (Luke 10:27). Jesus said to the lawyer, "You have answered correctly; do this and you will live" (Luke

10:28). But the lawyer did not stop here. Wanting to justify himself, he asked, "And who is my neighbor?" (Luke 10:29). Through the parable of the good Samaritan, Jesus taught clearly who was the good neighbor (Luke 10:30–36) and advised the lawyer, saying, "Go and do the same" (Luke 10:37).

The lawyer probably realized that it was not easy for him to keep the command to love his neighbors, one of the greatest commandments among the laws that he often recited. The good deeds of the Samaritan were nearly impossible for people to replicate. The Samaritan was on his way from Jerusalem to Jericho when he met a man who was near death because he had met a robber. Yet the Samaritan did not pretend he did not see and go on his way. He took pity on the man who had been robbed and poured oil and wine on his wounds and bandaged him up. He placed the man on his own beast and took him to an inn and took care of him (Luke 10:33–34). The next day he paid the innkeeper two denarii unsparingly and took responsibility for the man, saying, "Take care of him; and whatever more you spend, when I return I will repay you" (Luke 10:35). The Samaritan devoted his time, resources, and heart to the man with the hope that he would recover. This good Samaritan truly loved God with all his heart, life, and might; he also loved his neighbor as he loved himself (Luke 10:27). No one is good except God alone (Matt 19:17; Mark 10:18; Luke 18:19). Jesus is the true good Samaritan who practices love for His neighbors as written in the law; He is the true neighbor and the One who gives eternal life (see Luke 10:29–37).

Jesus died for us while we were still sinners. He fulfilled and perfected the two greatest commands, to love God and to love His neighbors, on the cross. Blood poured out from the thick thorns that pierced His head and thickened in His eyes so that He could not open them. The nails that pierced both His hands and His feet tore His flesh and ruptured His cells and tendons. The resulting pain that rushed through His body was excruciating and unbearable, even for a moment. Nevertheless, the first word Jesus spoke when He was in extreme pain was the greatest expression of love one could express to one's neighbors—forgiveness of one's enemies. Jesus offered up His entreaty to God, saying, "Father, forgive them; for they do not know what they are doing" (Luke 23:34; see also Matt 5:44, 46; 18:21–22, 35). Indeed, God demonstrated His love for us on the cross while we were yet His enemies (Rom 5:8).

It is impossible to keep all God's commandments by human strength or will. However, when we truly understand the atoning love of Jesus, who fulfilled all the commandments on the cross, we too can practice the greatest love for our neighbors by laying down our lives for them (John 15:13; 1 John 3:16). Then, by God's sovereignty, we will also be acknowledged as having kept all the Ten Commandments (Gal 5:14; see Rom 10:4). This is because when we love one another, we know that we are born of God, that we know God, and that we are of the truth (1 John 3:19; 4:7). When we love one another, we abide in the Lord and He in us, and we know He abides in us by the Holy Spirit whom He has given us (1 John 3:23–24; 4:13). We will also pass from death to life (1 John 3:14). Also, God's love will be perfected in us (1 John 4:12) so that we will receive the amazing blessing of courage without fear on the day of judgment (1 John 4:17–18). Romans 13:8 also states, "Owe nothing to anyone except to love one another; for he who loves his neighbor has fulfilled the law." The cross of Jesus Christ, therefore, which demonstrated the greatest perfection of love, is truly the epitome, fulfillment, and perfection of the Ten Commandments.

Jesus came not to abolish the law but to fulfill it. Matthew 5:17–18 states, "Do not think that I came to abolish the Law or the Prophets; I did not come to abolish but to fulfill. For truly I say to you, until heaven and earth pass away, not the smallest letter or stroke shall pass from the Law until all is accomplished" (see Matt 24:35; Mark 13:31; Luke 21:33). Romans 10:4 states, "Christ is the end of the law for righteousness to everyone who believes." Thus by believing in Jesus Christ, who is the fulfiller and end of the Ten Commandments and all laws, we are acknowledged as righteous (Gal 3:24) and firmly establish the law. Romans 3:31 states, "Do we then nullify the Law through faith? May it never be! On the contrary, we establish the Law."

Furthermore, obeying the Ten Commandments is a heartfelt expression of thanksgiving to God for the grace and love He has bestowed upon us. God gave the Israelites the Ten Commandments after He saved them from hard labor and toil in Egypt. The Israelites were mere slaves (עֶבֶד, *eved*; "servants") in Egypt. From their lowly states they rose to become God's firstborn, His own possession, a kingdom of priests, and His holy nation (Exod 4:22; 19:5-6).

The wages of sin is death (Rom 6:23). God took hopeless human beings who were enticed by sin and destined for death, and He "so loved" them that He sent His only Son, Jesus Christ, and gave us the gift of eternal life (John 3:16). God "first loved us" while we were enemies with Him (1 John 4:19; see 1 John 4:10). When we were far away from God, He brought us near through His *agape* love by the precious blood of Christ (Eph 2:13).

Thus keeping the Ten Commandments is our response to the joy surging from the depths of our hearts as we are captivated by God's unfathomable grace and boundless love. Every law in the Ten Commandments and all the specific laws expanding upon them overflow with God's zealous love, which has more than enough power to save all mankind (Isa 9:7; Ezek 39:25; see 2 Cor 11:2). When we abide, therefore, in Jesus Christ and His atoning love on the cross and obey God's commandments with faith and joy, we will encounter God's holiness and eternal life and experience transfiguration every day of our lives.

Notes

1. "Abimelech" (אֲבִימֶלֶךְ) means "my father is king" and refers to the Philistine king of Gerar (Gen 26:1–33). This Abimelech was not the same person who lived during Abraham's time. He was a different Abimelech who lived about a century later and had dealings with Isaac. "Abimelech" was not the name of a king but an appellation for a king. It was similar to the appellation "pharaoh" used in Egypt.
2. Darrell L. Bock, *Luke*, vol. 1, Baker Commentary on the New Testament (Grand Rapids, MI: Baker, 1994), 182.
3. Gerhard Kittel and Gerhard Friedrich, eds., *Theological Dictionary of the New Testament*, vol. 4, electronic ed. (Grand Rapids, MI: Eerdmans, 1964), 620.
4. See also Gen 22:16–18; 24:7; 26:3; 50:24; Exod 6:8; 13:5, 11; 17:16; 32:13; 33:1; Num 11:12; 14:16, 21–23; 32:10–11; Deut 1:8, 35; 4:21, 31; 6:10–13, 18–19, 23; 7:8, 12–13; 8:1, 18; 9:5; 10:11; 11:9, 21; 13:17; 19:8; 26:3, 15; 28:9, 11; 29:12–13; 30:20; 31:7, 20–21, 23; 34:4; Josh 1:6; 5:6; 21:43–44; Judg 2:1; 1 Chr 16:16; Neh 9:15; Pss 89:3, 35, 49; 105:9; 110:4; Jer 11:5; 16:15; 32:22; 44:26; Ezek 16:8, 59; 17:18–19; 20:5–6, 28, 42; 47:14; Mic 7:20; Luke 1:73; Heb 6:13–17.
5. It took about 45 days to reach the wilderness of Sinai after the exodus since the Israelites journeyed from Rameses on the fifteenth day of the first month (Num 33:3) and arrived in the wilderness of Sinai on the *first day* of the third month (Exod 19:1). Exodus 19:1 states, "In the third month after the sons of Israel had gone out of the land of Egypt, on that very day they came into the wilderness of Sinai." Here, "in the third month" (בַּחֹדֶשׁ הַשְּׁלִישִׁי, *bahodesh hashelishi*) refers to the first day of the third month. It is because the word "month" (חֹדֶשׁ, *hodesh*) means "new moon" (the first day of the month) when it occurs with a definite article at the beginning of a sentence (Ps 81:3; Amos 8:5). In addition, "on that very day" (19:1b) points emphatically to the day of the new moon, not the month itself, which further supports the view that the Israelites arrived on the *first day* of the new lunar month (third month).
6. Exod 6:4; 13:5, 11; 32:13; 33:1; Lev 14:34; 20:24; 26:42; Num 11:12; 14:23; 32:11; Deut 1:8, 35; 3:18; 4:31; 5:31; 6:10, 23; 7:8, 12–13; 8:1, 18; 9:5; 10:11; 11:9, 21; 12:10; 19:2, 8, 14; 20:16; 24:4; 25:19; 26:1, 3, 15; 28:11; 29:13; 30:20; 31:7, 20; Josh 1:6; 5:6; 18:3; 21:43; Judg 2:1; 1 Kgs 8:34, 36, 40, 48; 14:15; 2 Kgs 13:23; 21:8; Acts 7:5; 26:6; Gal 3:17; Heb 11:9.
7. Rashi, *The Torah: With Rashi's Commentary Translated, Annotated, and Elucidated*, vol. 2 (Brooklyn, NY: Mesorah, 1995).
8. John I. Durham, *Exodus*, Word Biblical Commentary 3 (Dallas: Word, 1998), 263.
9. Carl Friedrich Keil and Franz Delitzsch, *Commentary on the Old Testament*, vol. 1 on Exodus 19:5 (Peabody, MA: Hendrickson, 1996).
10. Robert Jamieson, A. R. Fausset, and David Brown, *Commentary Critical and Explanatory on the Whole Bible* on Exodus 19:16 (Oak Harbor, WA: Logos, 1997).
11. Durham, *Exodus*, 270–71.
12. Colin Brown, ed., *New International Dictionary of New Testament Theology*,

vol. 3 (Grand Rapids, MI: Zondervan, 1986), s.v. "trumpet."
13. H. D. M. Spences-Jones, ed., *Exodus*, vol. 2, The Pulpit Commentary (London, England: Funk and Wagnalls, 1909), 224.
14. Douglas K. Stuart, *Exodus*, The New American Commentary 2 (Nashville, TN: Broadman & Holman, 2006), 555.
15. Noel D. Osborn and Howard A. Hatton, *A Handbook on Exodus*, UBS Handbook Series (New York, NY: United Bible Society, 1999), 750.
16. Willem VanGemeren, ed., *New International Dictionary of Old Testament Theology and Exegesis*, vol. 4 (Grand Rapids, MI: Zondervan, 1997), 38.
17. Yong-guk Won, *Commentary on the Book of Deuteronomy* (Seoul: Word of Life Books, 1993), 190.
18. Samuel A. Berman, ed., *Midrash Tanhuma-Yelammedenu* (Hoboken, NJ: KTAV, 1996), 615–16.
19. Ludwig Koehler, Walter Baumgartner, M. E. J. Richardson, and Johann Jakob Stamm, *The Hebrew and Aramaic Lexicon of the Old Testament* (Leiden, Netherlands: E. J. Brill, 1999), electronic ed., 1710.
20. Wilhelm Gesenius and Samuel Prideaux Tregelles, *Gesenius' Hebrew and Chaldee Lexicon to the Old Testament Scriptures* (Bellingham, WA: Logos, 2003), 608.
21. VanGemeren, *Old Testament Theology and Exegesis*, vol. 2, 1142–43.
22. The word חֻקָּה (*huqqah*) in Psalm 119:16 is the feminine form of חֹק (*hoq*). Both *huqqah* and *hoq* are rooted in the word חָקַק (*haqaq*), which denotes "to engrave [on a rock], to cut in, to draw, to prescribe." In the Old Testament, *huqqah* occurs 104 times in 100 verses (twice in each of the following verses: Num 9:14; 15:15; Ezek 5:6; 43:11), and *hoq* occurs 130 times in 127 verses (twice in each of the following verses: Gen 47:22; Lev 10:13, 14). In Psalm 119, *huqqah* occurs once, and *hoq* occurs 21 times.
23. R. Laird Harris, Gleason L. Archer Jr., and Bruce K. Waltke, eds., *Theological Wordbook of the Old Testament* (Chicago, IL: Moody, 1999), 731.
24. VanGemeren, *Old Testament Theology and Exegesis*, vol. 2, 1070.
25. Derek Kidner, *Psalms 73–150: An Introduction and Commentary*, Tyndale Old Testament Commentaries 16 (Downers Grove, IL: InterVarsity Press, 1975), 454.
26. Matt 5:18, 26; 6:2, 5, 16; 8:10; 10:15, 23, 42; 11:11; 13:17; 16:28; 17:20; 18:3, 13, 18, 19; 19:23, 28; 21:21, 31; 23:36; 24:2, 34, 47; 26:13, 21, 34; Mark 3:28; 8:12; 9:1, 41; 10:15, 29; 11:23; 12:43; 13:30; 14:9, 18, 25, 30; Luke 4:24; 12:37; 18:17, 29; 21:32; 23:43.
27. John 1:51; 3:3, 5, 11; 5:19, 24, 25; 6:26, 32, 47, 53; 8:34, 51, 58; 10:1, 7; 12:24; 13:16, 20, 21, 38; 14:12; 16:20, 23; 21:18.
28. Spence-Jones, *Exodus*, vol. 2., 140–42.
29. Ibid., 130.
30. VanGemeren, *Old Testament Theology and Exegesis*, vol. 3, 552–53.
31. Stuart, *Exodus,* 442.
32. Joe M. Sprinkle, *The Book of the Covenant: A Literary Approach* (Sheffield, England: Sheffield Academic Press, 1994), 25–26.
33. Norbert Lohfink, S. J., "The Great Commandment" in *The Christian*

Meaning of the Old Testament, trans. R. A. Wilson (London, England: Burns & Oates, 1969), 87–102.
34. Dennis T. Olson, *Deuteronomy and the Death of Moses: A Theological Reading* (Minneapolis, MN: Fortress, 1994), 40–48.
35. Edward Fisher, *The Marrow of Modern Divinity* (Philadelphia, PA: Presbyterian Board of Publication, 1788), 35–36.
36. Stuart, *Exodus*, 280.
37. Young-yup Cho, *Doctrine of God*, fifth ed. (Seoul, Korea: CLC, 2012), 36.
38. The words "blasphemy" (βλασφημία, *blasphēmia*) and "to blaspheme" (βλασφημέω, *blasphēmeō*) in the context of blaspheming the deity occur thirty times in the New Testament: *blasphēmia* (11x) - Matt 12:31; 26:65; Mark 3:28; 14:64; Luke 5:21; John 10:33; Rev 2:9; 13:1, 5, 6; 17:3.
blasphēmeō (19x) - Matt 9:3; 26:65; Mark 2:7; 3:28, 29; Luke 12:10; 22:65; John 10:36; 13:45; 18:6; 19:37; 26:11; Rom 2:24; 1 Tim 1:20; Jas 2:7; Rev 13:6; 16:9, 11, 21.
39. James M. Freeman and Harold J. Chadwick, *Manners and Customs of the Bible* (North Brunswick, NJ: Bridge-Logos, 1998), 172. Also, John E. Hartley, *Leviticus*, Word Biblical Commentary 4 (Dallas, TX: Word, 1998), 278.
40. Cho, *An Analysis and a Critique of the Catechism of the Catholic Church* (Seoul, Korea: CLC, 2010), 102.
41. Ibid.
42. Everett F. Harrison, ed., *Baker's Dictionary of Theology* (Grand Rapids, MI: Baker, 1960), 252.
43. U. Cassuto, *A Commentary on the Book of Exodus* (Jerusalem, Israel: Magnes, 1997), 334.
44. Waldemar Janzen, *Exodus*, Believers Church Bible Commentary (Waterloo, ON: Herald, 2000), 340–41.
45. Cho, *Doctrine of God*, 42.
46. Seock-Tae Sohn, *Exposition of Exodus* (Seoul: ESP, 2005), 155.
47. Jung-jin Chun, *How to Read Leviticus* (Seoul, Korea: Scripture Union, 2004), 265.
48. P. B. Fitzwater, *Christian Theology: A Systematic Presentation* (Grand Rapids, MI: Eerdmans, 1948), 373.
49. Leon Morris, *The Gospel According to Matthew*, Pillar New Testament Commentary (Grand Rapids, MI: Eerdmans, 1992), 304.
50. Matthew Henry, *Matthew Henry's Commentary on the Whole Bible: Complete and Unbridged in One Volume* (Peabody, MA: Hendrickson, 1994), 1671.
51. The translation "worthless men" comes from *veliyyaal* (בְּלִיַּעַל), which refers to "the quality of being useless" or "worthlessness." This word is a composite noun that consists of *bely* (בְּלִי, "not, without") and *yaal* (יַעַל; "worth"). In the New Testament, the cognate term Belial is used to refer either to a lawless man, Satan, or the anti-Christ (2 Cor 6:15; 2 Thess 2:3).
52. **Matt** 5:16, 45, 48; 6:1, 4, 6(2x), 8, 9, 14, 15, 18(2x), 26, 32; 7:11, 21; 10:20, 29, 32–33; 11:25–27(3x); 12:50; 13:43; 15:13; 16:17, 27; 18:10, 14, 19, 35; 20:23; 23:9; 24:36; 25:34; 26:29, 39, 42, 53, 28:19 (forty-four times in Matthew); **Mark** 11:25, 26; 13:32; 14:36 (four times in Mark); **Luke** 2:49; 6:36; 9:26; 10:21(2x)–22(3x); 11:2; 13; 12:30, 32;

22:29, 42; 23:34, 46; 24:49 (seventeen times in Luke); ***John*** 2:16; 4:21, 23(2x); 5:17, 19, 20-23(2x), 26, 36(2x)-37, 43, 45; 6:27, 32, 37, 40, 44-46(2x), 57(2x), 65; 8:16, 18-19(2x), 28, 38, 42, 49, 54; 10:15(2x), 17-18, 25, 29(2x), 30, 32, 36-38(2x); 11:41; 12:26-28, 49-50; 14:2, 6, 7, 9(2x), 10(3x), 11(2x), 12, 13, 16, 20-21, 23-24, 26, 28(2x), 31(2x); 15:1, 8-10, 15-16, 23-24, 26(2x); 16:3, 10, 15, 17, 23, 25-28(2x), 32; 17:1, 5, 11, 21, 24-25; 18:11; 20:17(3x), 21 (one-hundred-ten times in John); ***Acts*** 1:4, 7 (two times in Acts).

53. Cyprian of Carthage, "On Jealousy and Envy," trans. Robert Ernest Wallis in *The Ante-Nicene Fathers: Fathers of the Third Century: Hippolytus, Cyprian, Caius, Novatian, Appendix*, vol. 5, ed. Alexander Roberts, James Donaldson, and A. Cleveland Coex (Buffalo, NY: Christian Literature Company, 1886), 493.
54. Gil-Seong Mun and Jeong-Yong Ahn, "Exploring the Features of Suicide Mortality in Korea: A Descriptive Study," *Journal of the Korean Official Statistics* 25, no. 4 (2020): 84.
55. Ibid., 87.

Bibliography

Berman, Samuel A., ed. *Midrash Tanhuma-Yelammedenu*. Hoboken, NJ: KTAV, 1996.

Bock, Darrell L. *Luke*. Vol. 1., Baker Commentary on the New Testament. Grand Rapids, MI: Baker, 1994.

Brown, Colin, ed. *New International Dictionary of New Testament Theology*. Vol. 3. Grand Rapids, MI: Zondervan, 1986.

Cassuto, U. *A Commentary on the Book of Exodus*. Jerusalem, Israel: Magnes, 1997.

Cho, Young-yup. *An Analysis and a Critique of the Catechism of the Catholic Church*. Seoul, Korea: CLC, 2010.

Cho, Young-yup. *Doctrine of God*. Fifth ed. Seoul, Korea: CLC, 2012.

Chun, Jung-jin. *How to Read Leviticus*. Seoul, Korea: Scripture Union, 2004.

Durham, John I. *Exodus*. Word Biblical Commentary 3. Dallas: Word, 1998.

Fisher, Edward. *The Marrow of Modern Divinity*. Philadelphia, PA: Presbyterian Board of Publication, 1788.

Fitzwater, P. B. *Christian Theology: A Systematic Presentation*. Grand Rapids, MI: Eerdmans, 1948.

Freeman, James M. and Harold J. Chadwick. *Manners and Customs of the Bible*. North Brunswick, NJ: Bridge-Logos, 1998.

Gesenius, Wilhelm, and Samuel Prideaux Tregelles. *Gesenius' Hebrew and Chaldee Lexicon to the Old Testament Scriptures*. Bellingham, WA: Logos Bible Software, 2003.

Harris, R. Laird, Gleason L. Archer Jr., and Bruce K. Waltke, eds. *Theological Wordbook of the Old Testament*. Chicago, IL: Moody, 1999.

Harrison, Everett F., ed. *Baker's Dictionary of Theology*. Grand Rapids, MI: Baker, 1960.

Hartley, John E. *Leviticus*. Word Biblical Commentary 4. Dallas, TX: Word, 1998.

Henry, Matthew. *Matthew Henry's Commentary on the Whole Bible: Complete and Unbridged in One Volume*. Peabody, MA: Hendrickson, 1994.

Jamieson, Robert, A. R. Fausset, and David Brown. *Commentary Critical and Explanatory on the Whole Bible*. Oak Harbor, WA: Logos, 1997.

Janzen, Waldemar. *Exodus*. Believers Church Bible Commentary. Waterloo, ON: Herald, 2000.

Josephus, Flavius and William Whiston. *The Works of Josephus: Complete and Unabridged*. Peabody: Hendrickson, 1987.

Keil, Carl Friedrich and Franz Delitzsch. *Commentary on the Old Testament*. Vol. 1. Peabody, MA: Hendrickson, 1996.

Kidner, Derek. *Psalms 73–150: An Introduction and Commentary*. Tyndale Old Testament Commentaries 16. Downers Grove, Il.: InterVarsity Press, 1975.

Kittel, Gerhard and Gerhard Friedrich, eds. *Theological Dictionary of the New Testament*. Vol. 4, electronic ed. Grand Rapids, MI: Eerdmans, 1964.

Koehler, Ludwig, Walter Baumgartner, M. E. J. Richardson, and Johann Jakob Stamm. *The Hebrew and Aramaic Lexicon of the Old Testament*. Leiden, Netherlands: E. J. Brill, 1999.

Lohfink, S. J., Norbert. *The Christian Meaning of the Old Testament*. Trans. R. A. Wilson. London, England: Burns & Oates, 1969.

Morris, Leon. *The Gospel According to Matthew*. Pillar New Testament Commentary. Grand Rapids, MI: Eerdmans, 1992.

Mun, Gil-Seong and Jeong-Yong Ahn. *Journal of the Korean Official Statistics* 25. No. 4, 2020.

Olson, Dennis T. *Deuteronomy and the Death of Moses: A Theological Reading*. Minneapolis, MN: Fortress, 1994.

Osborn, Noel D. and Howard A. Hatton. *A Handbook on Exodus*. UBS Handbook Series. New York, NY: United Bible Society, 1999.

Rashi, *The Torah: With Rashi's Commentary Translated, Annotated, and Elucidated*. Vol. 2. Brooklyn, NY: Mesorah, 1995.

Roberts, Alexander, James Donaldson, and A. Cleveland Coex, eds. *The Ante-Nicene Fathers: Fathers of the Third Century: Hippolytus, Cyprian, Caius, Novatian, Appendix*. Vol. 5. Buffalo, NY: Christian Literature Company, 1886.

Sohn, Seock-Tae. *Exposition of Exodus*, Seoul: ESP, 2005.

Spences-Jones, H. D. M., ed. *Exodus*. Vol. 2. The Pulpit Commentary. London, England: Funk and Wagnalls, 1909.

Sprinkle, Joe M. *The Book of the Covenant: A Literary Approach*. Sheffield, England: Sheffield Academic Press, 1994.

Stuart, Douglas K. *Exodus*. The New American Commentary 2. Nashville, TN: Broadman & Holman, 2006.

VanGemeren, Willem, ed. *New International Dictionary of Old Testament Theology and Exegesis*. Vol. 4. Grand Rapids, MI: Zondervan, 1997.

Won, Yong-guk. *Commentary on the Book of Deuteronomy*, Seoul: Word of Life Books, 1993.

Index

acrostic poem, 152
arguments, 305
atonement, ministry of, 27, 49, 58, 93, 113, 137, 187, 263, 289, 320, 341, 418
Abednego, 292
Abel, 393, 394, 481
abhor, 69, 221, 287, 290
Abihu, 90, 126, 128
Abimelech, 31, 32, 315, 393, 500
Abinadab, 274, 320
Abiram, 441
Abishag, 421
Abner, 381, 393
Abraham, 31, 32, 39, 44, 46, 47, 50, 62, 63, 77, 79, 112, 140, 157, 178, 185, 268, 278, 299, 315, 360, 396, 465, 500
Absalom, 303, 373, 381, 384, 393, 421, 434, 435
Achan, 227, 437-39, 478
Achar, 439
Achor, Valley of, 227, 438-39, 478
adulteress, 224, 403, 422, 483
adultery, 233, 396, 406
Ahab, 333-34, 381, 393-95, 478
Ahaziah, 335, 393
altar, 43, 57, 89, 121-23, 223, 290, 299, 302, 408, 428; of earth, 289-90; of the Lord, 262, 319
Amalek, 273, 469
Amasa, 381, 393
Ammon, 419, 420
Amnon, 373, 393
Amorites, 54, 255, 305, 320
anarchy, 477
ancestors, 41, 231, 267, 299
ancestral rites, 267, 361
angel of the Lord, 101, 311
anger, 135, 218, 389, 439
animal kingdom, 379
animal's blood, 263
Annas, 481

Apis, 132
apostasy, 308
ark of Noah, 171, 324
ark of the covenant, 109, 144, 199, 203, 283, 332, 374
Artemis, shrines of, 265
Asahel, 393
Athaliah, 335-36, 393
atheist, 345
Athens, 265
atonement, 263, 320, 341, 418
author: God, 203, 207, 248; of Hebrews, 114; of Psalms, 152, 153, 164, 168, 175, 179, 181, 186

branded, 452
bribes, 122, 372, 450
begotten God, the only, 251
Baal, 269, 418-19
Baal of Peor, 269, 418
Babylon, 284, 291, 293, 319, 348, 421, 432
Barabbas, 442, 482
barley flour, 407
battle, 265, 334, 374, 384, 395
bed, 273, 358, 395, 420
belomancy, 257
Benaiah, 421
Ben-hadad, 30, 333-34, 393
Benjamin, 320, 357, 359
bestiality, 224
Bethel, 275, 294
Bethesda, 278
Beth-shan, 275, 320
Bilhah, 420
bitter water, 408
blanket, 412, 420
blaspheme, 221, 251, 303, 307, 314
blood: of atonement, 58; of Christ, 59, 67, 107, 125, 232, 263, 496; of the covenant,

Index 511

43, 57, 59, 90, 123-24, 127, 376; of Naboth, 395, 478; of the sacrfice, 43, 57, 59, 263
blue cord, 179
Boaz, 467, 468
book of the covenant, 43, 49, 57, 89, 120, 123-24, 164, 254
book of the law, 144, 289
bottomless pit, 112
boundary mark, 386, 395, 429. *See also* mark(s)
bows, 54, 255
breath, 378-79, 490
breath of life, 379
bribe(s), 122, 344, 372, 450
burned with fire, 224, 438

cliff, 279
careless word, 390, 397
Carlson, 282
carved image, 282
certificate of divorce, 233, 416
chamber of death, 422
chariot, 346, 395, 455
chariots of Israel, 370
charmer's spell, 258
chastise, 223, 405
chastity, 406, 408
children of wrath, 483
church officials, 370
cities of refuge, 386
commandment(s): concerning our relationships with God and others, 213-14, 234; for all generations, 204; of love, 444
compassion, 120, 141, 204, 291, 344, 350, 432, 452, 470
complaint, 132
conceive, 408

consecrate, 87, 105, 106, 253, 313, 326, 400, 406
conspiracy, 381
consuming fire, 112, 129, 286
contentment, 214, 462, 473, 475
controversial questions, 305
costly perfume, 439
Council of Jerusalem, 264
covenant for all generations, 42, 63, 208, 236
covenant made with blood, 57, 59
covenant meal, 90, 127, 129
covenant of peace, 319, 418
covenant on the plains of Moab, 44, 60, 62, 70-71, 144, 216, 334, 418
covenant ratification, 44, 72, 90, 98, 99, 126
covetousness, 218, 227, 236, 356, 462
craftiness, 457
Creator, 102, 246, 248, 263, 271, 308, 321, 379
creditor(s), 339, 427, 433, 452. *See also* lenders
cross, the blood of, 205, 375
cross, the Word of, 183
curse, 315, 408
Cyprian, 383, 503

Dathan, 441
Doeg, 393
damage, 82, 122, 386, 428, 430, 433, 445, 450
Daniel, 38, 202, 293, 310
Dan, tribe of, 303
darkness, 38, 42, 82, 101, 109, 113, 119, 158, 367, 456
dawn, 186, 333, 440
day of the LORD, 111, 328, 346
day to repent, 473

death penalty, 121, 228, 347, 433
debtor(s), 330, 339, 414, 427, 433, 452
deer, 262
deifying an altar, 289
designated places, 262
desire of sin, 394
desires of the eyes, 295, 435
desires of the flesh, 295, 435
desolate, 255, 389
despise, 81, 133, 175, 247, 273, 279, 302, 312, 420, 452
destruction, 135, 176, 305
Dibri, the daughter of, 303
dignity, 103, 214, 267, 378, 400, 426
dignity of life, 214, 267, 378, 400
dignity of self-sufficiency, 214, 462
dignity of truth, 214, 444
discernment, 153, 161, 489
discipline, 228, 357, 368
disputes, 305
divination, 257, 259, 273, 305
divine attributes, 38, 250, 298
diviner, 257
divorce, 232-33, 405-06, 416-17
double violation, 403
doubt, 406, 407
dove, 324
dowry, 225
drawing lots, 304
drinking the blood, 263
drunkard, 368
dry land, 101, 114, 204
Dura, the plains of, 292

eagle, 70, 100, 472
extorted, 225, 226
early church, 187, 231, 246, 308, 346, 353
earthquake, 109, 113
eating the blood, 262

Ebal, 289
edible animals, 261
elderly, 369, 384
eldest, the home of, 82, 267
Eleazar, 414, 418
Eliakim, 414
Elijah, 289, 370, 395, 414, 478
Elim, 204
Elisha, 335, 370, 414, 455
Elizabeth, 358
ephah, 407
Ephron the Hittite, 360
essential regulations, 264
Etham, 204
Eunice, 358
Eve, 229, 400, 458, 480
everlasting binding power, 169-70
everlasting sign, 298, 345
evil cycle, 386
evil spirit(s), 307, 308
ewe lambs, 315
extramarital affair, 402
eye disease, 475
eye of a needle, 234
eyes of the flesh, 294

filthiness, 305
Flood, Great, 477
fugitives, 414
faithful God, 55, 299
faithfulness, 39, 47, 55, 63, 99, 156, 188-89, 299, 314, 402
fall, 27, 163, 229, 271, 349, 401, 464
fame, 104, 317, 319, 320, 346
famine, 318, 320, 432
fatal sin, 400
father, 369-71, 373-76
Feast of Booths, 276, 330
Feast of Ingathering, 254

Feast of the Harvest, 254
Feast of the Unleavened Bread, 254
feast(s): in the covenant meal, 127, 128; of Jesus, 476; to the Lord, 83-84, 132; of Passover, 164; wedding, 180, 422-23
fiery law, 113, 206
fig tree, 285
filial duty (piety), 356, 359, 361-67, 375
final confirmation, 126
final judgment, 107
finger of God, 48, 66, 91, 92, 94, 130, 144, 194, 199, 206, 209
firstborn, 69, 80, 100, 102, 122, 204, 253, 294, 470, 496
first covenant, 48
first murderer, 393
flower of life, 412
forehead, 268
foreigner, 341, 343, 353, 432
fortune teller, 257, 259, 268
four Gospels, 187
fruit of our lips, 166
fullness, the number of, 42, 65, 202, 236, 250, 401, 437
funeral, 324
furnace, 45, 88, 108, 112, 206, 292

gazelle, 262
gift, 27, 156, 212, 343, 427, 453, 474, 496
giver of the law, 203
glorious day, 326, 328
glory of God, 67, 112, 119, 129, 134, 144, 250, 295, 319, 350, 401, 470
glory of the Lord, 91, 129, 295
God of the living, 62
God of truth, 191
God's army, 47
God's children, 37, 261, 295, 371, 375
God's commandments, 179-80, 194, 229, 489, 495-96

God's domain, 268
God's faithfulness, 47, 55, 188-89, 299
God's grace, 46, 49, 177, 203, 279, 288, 393, 474-75
God's judgment, 64, 109, 111, 163-67, 228, 288, 370, 390, 409, 415, 417
God's law, 158, 189, 358, 408
God's love, 41, 180, 286, 375, 489, 493, 495
God's ordinances, 163
gods, other, 118, 214, 215, 217, 222, 243, 283, 287, 289, 403
God's precepts, 174
God's presence, 53, 61, 112, 120, 123, 283
God's promise, 184
God's scale, 219
God's statutes, 167
God's (strong) determination, 299
God's temple, 38, 271, 374, 409
God's testimonies, 160-61, 194
God's voice, 47, 89, 109, 111, 113-14, 119, 129, 206, 349, 402
God's ways, 181
God's Word, 151, 170, 172, 184, 188-90, 314
golden calf, 48, 92, 93, 131, 132, 138, 283, 294, 403, 458
good fruit, 370
good Samaritan, 494
good shepherd, 176-77
gospel of the grace, 177
great heap of stones, 227, 373, 438
great nation, 46
greed, 227, 247, 253, 259, 265, 415, 451, 471-72, 480, 483
grumbling(s), 61, 132, 312, 375, 392
guarantee, 40-41, 164, 349
guard, 326, 471
guilt offering, 225-26

high priest, 374

high step of the altar, 290
hail, 82, 100
Hakeldama, 441
Haran, 324
harlotry, 225, 410, 417
hatred, 213, 218, 287, 381, 383, 389, 390, 483
Hazael, 393
head of the days, 328
head of the house, 435
heartlessness, 382
heaven and earth, 160, 207, 221, 229, 252, 495
Hebron, 303
heir, 236, 467
hell, 182, 230, 389, 444
Hephzibah, 286
heritage of Jacob, 346, 347
Herod, 381
Herod Agrippa I, 394
Herod Antipas, 394
Herodias, 394
Hezekiah, 49, 414
high place, 346
Hivites, 54, 318
homage, 285
homosexuality, 224
honeycomb, 241
honor, 136, 247, 298
honoring parents, 215, 217
Hophni and Phinehas, 374
Horeb, 61, 71, 97, 134-35, 283, 294
hornet, 54, 255
human-centered faith, 436
human ethics, 194
human trafficking, 121, 428
Hur, 90, 128, 131

Ichabod, 374

idolatry, 53, 228, 276, 282, 284, 287, 289, 294, 361, 403, 421, 464; abstaining from, 264; catching the first sunrise, 269-72; in Egypt, 204, 245; of divination, 259; of golden calf, 94, 134; of memorial worship, 266-69; with the Moabite women, 419; prohibition of, 121, 254; of stubbornness, 273-75
image: graven/carved, 221, 249, 276; of a calf, 132; of an idol, 214, 277, 282-85, 290, 345; of King Nebuchadnezzar, 291-92; on the ornaments, 294
image of an ox, 134
image of God, 144, 272, 283-84, 294-95, 379-80, 385
incense, 270, 286
infant, 273
Ingersoll, 345
inheritance from God: Canaan, 51, 469; faith, 345; eternal life, 322, 385, 427; heritage of Jacob, 346; the Lord, 471; one's wife, 465;
innocent life, 386
inquire (*darash*), 260
inscribe, 49, 167-68, 179, 211
inspired by God, 209
insubordination, 273
intercessory prayer, 49, 93, 98, 138, 140
interest, 31, 122, 305, 343, 344, 431, 432
in vain: take the name of the Lord, 118, 214, 297-301, 311, 313, 314, 318-19, 321; worship God, 232, 321
Isaac, 31, 32, 44, 46, 63, 140, 178, 500

Jabesh, 275
jealousy, 287, 383, 406
Jebel Musa, 97
Jehoram, 334-35, 393
Jehu, 393, 395

Jephthah's vow, 319
Jericho, 199, 255, 332-33, 437, 478, 494
Jeroboam, 275, 276
Jethro, 157
Jezebel, 381, 393-94, 395, 450
Joab, 373, 381, 393, 421
Joash, 335-36, 370, 393
Job, 105, 270, 400
Jochebed, 358
John, the apostle, 59, 174, 187, 191, 346, 353, 362, 371, 394, 422
Jonathan, 30, 274, 320
Joram, 393, 395
Joseph, 31, 45, 357, 359, 360, 389, 390, 400, 415
Jotham, 285, 393
Jubilee, 111, 338, 340, 351
judge(s), the: God, 112, 270, 453; Jesus, 166-67, 248, 252, 471; of this world, 122, 226, 246, 368, 392, 400, 430, 435, 450; the period of the judges, 285, 393
judge, to: as *mishpat*, 163; as *paqad*, 287; others, 391, 397
judgment(s): of God, 135, 153, 163, 408, 417, 434; human, 164, 166; of Jesus, 166-67, 248, 413

kemarim (host of heaven), 270
kingdom of God, 27, 70, 73, 230, 234, 271, 295, 421, 441
kingdom of heaven, 229, 234, 302, 312, 353, 380
kingdom of priests, 86, 101, 102, 103, 413, 496
kneel, 233, 310, 331

Laban, 29, 32, 273, 324, 474
lake that burns with fire and brimstone, 258, 295, 396, 422, 448
lament, 361
lamp, 153, 185, 335
laqah (לָקַח, "to take"), 141
Last Supper, the, 59, 376
last trumpet, the, 111
lawgiver, 248, 252, 350, 363
lawlessness, 302, 388, 483
law of jealousy, 406
law of love, 386
law of the LORD, 160
lawyer, 235, 488, 493-94
Leah, 324
least, the, 156, 229, 388, 452, 493
lend, 492
lenders, 432. *See also* creditor(s)
leprosy, 451, 455
Levites, 93, 136, 175, 221, 276, 319-20, 336-37, 342, 451
liberation, 66, 205, 310
life of the flesh, 263
lightning, 87, 109, 119, 206
lilies, 383
lips, 166, 321, 390, 444, 448, 490
livestock, 79, 82, 100, 253, 329, 335, 352, 426, 429
living being, 379
living waters, 204, 212
Lois, 358
Lord of the temple, 310
Lord's prayer, 318
loving-kindness, 116, 287, 288, 491
lust in the Heart, 415

miscarriage, 254, 382, 408
money: idolize, 247, 269, 306, 366; lending, 343-44, 431-32; lovers of, 219, 455, 463, 479, 481-82; neighbor's possession, 388, 426; for restitution, 225, 428

moral laws, 230
magician, 257
Malchi-shua, 274, 320
malicious witness, 226, 450
Mandatory Clauses, 431
manna, 101, 204, 325, 349
Marah, 101, 164, 168
mark(s), 395. *See also* boundary mark
Mark, son of the aposle Peter, 371
marriage, 404, 405, 417
married couple, 287, 400, 406
Martin Luther, 193
Mary, 180, 358, 362, 439, 479
materialism, 279, 482
maxims, 362
mediator, 40, 57, 59, 392
mediator of the new covenant, 59, 248
meditation, 158, 186
medium, 257, 258, 274, 275, 306
memorial worship, 266
mercy, 300, 312, 370, 386-87, 395, 432, 470
Meshach, 292
Mesopotamia, 50, 273
Messiah, 36, 277, 394, 453, 467
Micaiah, the prophet, 478
Michal, 273
Midianite woman, 418
midwives, 45-46
mind set on the flesh, 67
ministers, 312
Miriam, 451
mislead, 261, 454
misuse, 301, 417
Moab, the plains of, 117, 144, 334
Molech, 270
Monday, 85, 99, 104, 143
money box, 439
moral cultivation, 362
most holy place, 199, 203
mountain of God, 43, 91, 97, 101, 119, 129
multiply, 52, 178

murderer(s), 121, 391, 396, 397, 482
murder: the sin of, 380, 388, 390-91, 397, 400
Myungshimbogam, 362

Nebuchadnezzar, 291, 348
Nebuzaradan, 348
Nehemiah, 160, 339, 432
nakedness, 290
name of the Lord, 174, 297, 350
narrow gate, 183
nature, 388
necromancer, 258
necromancy, 257
new covenant, 27, 59, 73, 144
new creation, 353, 354
New Jerusalem, 396
new moon, 111, 332, 352, 500
Noah, 44, 63, 171, 178, 324, 477
nobles of the sons of Israel, 90, 126

oak tree, 373, 421
oath, 39, 72, 111, 303, 315, 319, 430
Obed, 111, 468
obedience, 72, 156, 164, 168, 180, 314, 360, 375, 414, 491
obey, 87, 106, 116, 178
obstinate people, 138, 294
offering, 372, 436
omen, 257
Onan, 467
Onesimus, 371
oppressor, 228, 453
original form, 216, 229
ornaments, 93, 140, 165, 294, 412
other party in the covenant, 38, 44, 61, 208

polytheism, 279
polytheistic, 321
Paddan-aram, 99
pagan culture, 468
Palbanga, 362
parents' authority, 372
partial(ity), 450
passions, 483
Passover, 83, 164, 330
peace, 39, 182, 351, 428, 470, 483
peace offering, 57, 90, 123, 132, 262, 403
peace treaties, 30
Pentateuch, 163, 212, 216
Perez, 468
perfect number, 315
perfect righteousness, 230
period of the monarchy, 275
permanent statute, 245
persecute, 158, 231
pest, 345
Peter, the apostle, 103, 232, 250, 303, 315, 371, 383, 401, 456-57, 477, 483
Pharaoh, 31, 41, 47, 70, 79, 101, 181, 204, 393
Philetus, 305
Philistines, 256, 265, 274, 374, 381, 384
Phinehas, 374, 418, 439
Pilate, 382-83, 440, 442
pillar of fire, 204
place of the covenant, 61, 63
plague(s), 54, 138, 170, 309; in Korah's rebellion, 442; plague of flies, 81; plague of locusts, 81, 100; in Shittim of Moab, 269, 418-19; of the sixth trumpet, 396, 441; the ten, 81-82, 100-01, 202, 204, 246
pleasant land, 51
plunder, 304, 335, 436
poison, 381, 383, 400, 421, 447
Potiphar's wife, 415

power: in the exodus, 79, 86, 100-01, 204, 313; of God's covenant, 32, 62; of God's name, 298, 301, 313, 322; to keep the law, 214, 476; of life, 378, 380, 489; presence of God, 112-13; of salvation, 37, 496; of the tongue, 447; of the Word, 113, 169-70, 172-73, 183, 207
praise, 63, 166, 189, 292, 300, 313, 317, 331, 444
preachers, 193, 454
precept, 155, 174-75
presentness of the covenant, 61
preserve, 265, 390
pride of life, 295, 435, 483
primordial couple, 400-01
principle of creation, 401, 416
principle of love, 214
profane, 251, 302, 304, 305, 315, 317, 347, 351, 410, 432
promised land, 50, 53, 133, 253, 418
promised seed, 65
prostrate, 141, 285, 291
punishment, 318
purity, 172, 214, 402, 405, 408, 410, 412
purity of the body, 406

quail, 101, 481
quake, 88, 108, 113, 206
queen of Sheba, 317

retributive justice, 226
rabbi, 187
rabble, 227, 481
Rachel, 273, 324
Rahab, 319
ram without defect, 226
ransom, 353, 467
rea, 445

reaffirmation, 60, 62, 73
reconciliation, 32, 60, 126, 153, 392
Red Sea, 72, 101, 204, 256, 375
reformation, 270, 409
Rehoboam, King, 175, 369, 409
repayment, 339, 343
Rephidim, 101, 204
restitution, 122, 225-26, 428-431
resurrection, 111, 345, 353, 376
Reuben, 420
revenge, 386
reward, 229, 254, 268, 307, 491
rhaka (ῥακά, "stupid"), 390
rich young man, 233, 247, 372, 464
righteous judge, 167
righteousness, 158, 163, 164, 189, 309, 353, 382, 388, 452; the anger does not achieve, 391-92; of God, 135, 167, 174, 471; of Jesus who fulfilled the law, 66, 159, 230, 495; instruments of, 417; the sun of, 271, 322
righteous, the, 158, 165, 288, 418, 426, 446, 458
right hand, 206, 415
right to happiness, 433
river, 204, 256, 475
robbery, 225, 481
robe of the ephod, 414
rock, 101, 141, 204, 299, 302, 314, 392, 501
rulers, 122, 143, 369
Ruth, the book of, 467-68

sabbath of complete rest, 222, 329
Sabbath, work on the, 327, 330-38, 349
Sabbatical Year, 51, 123, 330, 338, 343, 348, 351
sacred number, 315
sacrifice, 67, 80, 133, 156, 262, 266, 273, 276, 286, 336, 342, 345, 350, 428

sacrificed to idols, 264-65
sacrifice of praise, 166, 444
sacrificial blood, 124
sacrificial meats, 262
sacrificial rites, 419
Samaritan, 235, 494
Samuel, 258, 273, 274-75, 320, 358, 434, 501
sanctity, 400, 402, 404, 433
satisfaction, 331, 473, 474
Saul, the king, 273, 275, 320, 392, 393
scribes, 66, 187, 230, 231, 251, 321, 349, 371, 442, 463, 481
sea, 101, 114, 172, 256, 331, 392, 475
seal, 271, 286, 347
seared, 372, 426
second coming, 109, 111, 149, 174, 265, 353, 416, 423
self-indulgence, 481
self-sufficiency, 473
sensuality, 219, 232, 409
sermon on the Mount, 66, 151, 230
serpent, 258, 277, 293, 321, 422, 448, 457, 463, 480
servant teacher, 187
sexual relations, 106, 402, 404, 419
Shadrach, 292
shame, 116, 131, 161, 249, 274, 285, 307, 367, 372, 374, 401, 421, 422
Shelomith, 303
Shittim, adultery in, 269, 418, 419
Shunamite, 332
signs, 45, 261, 454
Sihon, king of the Amorites, 54
silver, 227, 265, 283, 290, 384, 455, 478, 479
Simeon, the tribe of, 357, 391
Sinai, ascents of, 85-96
Sinai, Mount, 43, 57, 70, 79, 85, 97, 205, 283, 324, 403, 458
Sinai, the wilderness of, 43, 60, 85, 97
Sinaitic covenant, 43, 57, 70, 77, 85, 98,

120, 199, 228
sin of adultery, 400, 417
sin of divination, 273
slander, 138, 219, 232, 396, 454; as false witness, 447, 449, 451
slave(ry): in Egypt, 69, 208, 330-31, 453, 496; freedom from the house of, 203-05, 208, 244; to idols, 261, 286; to the law, 65-66; to money, 479, 482; redeemed out of, 41, 45; ordinances for, 121, 224, 330, 338-40; of sin and death, 37
snake, 431, 448
societal order, 477
solemn oath, 124, 315, 317, 430
Solomon's temple, 109, 202, 310
Solomon's wisdom, 317
Son of Man, 307, 337, 350, 435
sons of God, 376, 477
sorcerer, 306
sorcery, 257, 308
sovereign grace, 100
sovereignty over life, 380, 385
sovereign work, 53
spear, 392, 418
spell, 152, 258, 306
spies, 53-54, 303
spiritist, 257, 258, 274, 306
spirit of the dead, 258
spiritual adultery, 287, 423
spiritual wisdom, 241
spotless, 232, 265
spouse, 106, 361, 401, 402, 433
sprinkling of the blood, 58, 107, 124, 131
statue, 289, 291, 292
status, 46, 103, 214
statute(s), 48, 72, 110, 153, 157, 160, 167, 174, 182, 189, 194; as the definition of *hoq*, 163-64, 167-70; of Jubilee Year, 342-44; of Sabbatical Year, 338-340; regarding the sabbath, 350
steal (stole), 225, 425-42, 437, 466, 478

Stephen, 133, 382, 394
stone pillar, 32, 386
stone tablets: in the ark of the covenant, 178, 199, 206; the first set of, 114, 130, 139; the second set of, 49, 142-43, 208, 210, 285; shattered, 130, 135, 403, 458; written by the finger of God, 48, 209
stubborn, 223, 368
submission, 360
suicide, 378, 384-85, 440
suicide rate, 384
sum: of Lord's word, 151, 188-89; of the Ten commandments, 231
summarize(s), 149, 211
Sunday, 85, 129, 333, 345
sunrise, 186
sword, 48, 54, 92, 136, 220, 255, 275, 304, 381, 390, 420, 447
synagogue, 187, 279, 306, 349, 351

Tamar: with Absalom, 384; with Judah, 467
thunder, 87, 109, 113, 119, 206
trap, 66, 427
tabernacle, 53, 77, 85, 130, 175, 178, 309, 407
tabernacle, pattern of the, 91, 129
tablets: of our hearts, 211; to inscribe on, 168
tamarisk tree, 275
tattoo, 268
teacher, 187, 376, 384, 440
temple servants, 319
temporary tent of meeting, 93, 140
tent of meeting, 262, 374
terafim, 273, 275
testimony(ies), 155, 160, 210
testimony of the LORD, 161
thief, 303, 429
thigh (in making oath), 32, 316

thousand generations, 35, 63, 149, 178, 366, 491
throne, 45, 100, 109, 126-27, 293, 336, 373, 392
Timothy, 60, 219, 358, 366, 371, 473, 483
Tishbite, 478
Titus, 40, 191, 249, 272, 369, 371, 402, 448, 476, 482
top of the mountain, 85, 91, 108, 130, 206
trade, 30, 330
tradition, 231, 267, 371, 442, 467, 490
tribulation, 163, 169, 180, 202, 312, 410, 417
true freedom, 66, 205
truth, 67, 110, 151, 156, 188, 291, 306, 317, 459, 495
tutor, 65

unbelief, 36, 232, 274, 287, 308, 439
unchanging truth, 151, 183, 315
unclean, 65, 106, 253, 262, 313, 326, 405, 458
unpremeditated homicides, 385
unrighteousness, 112, 274, 454
unrighteous wage, 440
unsatisfied, 304, 482
Uriah the Hittite, 381, 393, 419
Urim, 274

veil, 95, 143
violence, 228, 476, 484
virginity, 405
visit, 138, 174, 287
vow, 303-04, 319, 432

watchman, 186

water drawers, 319
way of Jeroboam, 276
wealth, 79, 182, 235, 247, 259, 285, 344, 349, 369, 372, 376, 427, 429, 431-32, 436-37, 456, 464, 465, 471, 472
Wednesday, 93-94, 140
widow, 122, 467-68
wind, 101, 110, 271, 291, 360, 440
winepresses, 330
wisdom, 104, 161, 168, 202, 241, 312, 317, 368, 422, 448, 456, 476, 484, 489
Word from the beginning, 172, 186, 236
work of life, 390
worthless, 374
wrath, 112, 135, 141, 228, 262, 269, 271, 276, 286, 288, 295, 421

Yahweh Nissi, 101

Zabdi, the son of, 437, 478
zeal of God, 419
Zela, in the land of Benjamin, 320
Zephaniah, the prophet, 270
Zerah, the son of, 437, 468, 478
Zimri, 384, 418